THE GEORGE GUND FOUNDATION
IMPRINT IN AFRICAN AMERICAN STUDIES

The George Gund Foundation has endowed
this imprint to advance understanding of
the history, culture, and current issues
of African Americans.

EMANCIPATION BETRAYED

AMERICAN CROSSROADS

*Edited by Earl Lewis, George Lipsitz, Peggy Pascoe,
George Sánchez, and Dana Takagi*

EMANCIPATION BETRAYED

The Hidden History of Black Organizing and
White Violence in Florida from Reconstruction
to the Bloody Election of 1920

PAUL ORTIZ

UNIVERSITY OF CALIFORNIA PRESS
BERKELEY LOS ANGELES LONDON

University of California Press
Berkeley and Los Angeles, California

University of California Press, Ltd.
London, England

©2005 by the Regents of the University of California

Library of Congress Cataloging-in-Publication Data

Ortiz, Paul, 1964–
    Emancipation betrayed : the hidden history of Black
organizing and white violence in Florida from
Reconstruction to the bloody election of 1920 / Paul
Ortiz.
        p.   cm.—(American Crossroads; 16)
    "George Gund Foundation imprint in African
American studies."
    Includes bibliographical references and index.
    ISBN 0–520-23946-6 (alk. paper)
    1. African Americans—Florida—politics and
government—19th century. 2. African Americans—
Florida—Politics and government—20th century.
3. African Americans—Civil rights—Florida—History.
4. African Americans—Florida—Social conditions.
5. Racism—Florida—History—19th century.
6. Racism—Florida—History—20th century.
7. Violence—Florida—History—19th century.
8. Violence—Florida—History—20th century.
9. Florida—Race relations. 10. Florida—Politics and
government—1865–1950. I. Title.
E185.93.F5078   2005
305.896'0730759'09034—dc22   2004015439

Manufactured in the United States of America
13   12   11   10   09   08   07   06   05
10   9   8   7   6   5   4   3   2   1

In memory of the African Americans in Florida
who were martyred in the election campaign of 1920

and for A. I., Sam, and Laura Dixie,
who carried the struggle on

Let all true believers in democracy and equality today strengthen ourselves by studying what they did and how they did it.

C.L.R. JAMES,
Every Cook Can Govern

CONTENTS

ILLUSTRATIONS

Illustrations follow page 100

FIGURES

MAPS

TABLES

◀| Preface |▶

ELECTION DAY IN FLORIDA

I can live, maybe not in full yet, but I'm proud of the distance that black people have come because I can't explain it all but it was, if you allow me, it was hell back then.[1]

MALACHIA ANDREWS
Tallahassee, 1994

THE PRESIDENTIAL ELECTION IN FLORIDA has revealed the state of democracy in America on at least three occasions. Contested Florida ballots played a key role in the election of 1876 that ultimately spelled the end of Reconstruction. More recently, the 2000 Bush-Gore debacle cast a troubling shadow over the nation. People from all walks of life debated the bewildering chain of events that culminated with the Supreme Court's dramatic intervention in the contested election. The U.S. Commission on Civil Rights noted, "The state of Florida's electoral process took center stage as the world paused to observe the unfolding drama of identifying the next President of the United States."[2] Most accounts of the crisis missed the decisive factor in the election's outcome: the disfranchisement of many African American, Latino, and Haitian voters under dubious pretenses.[3] After sifting through one hundred thousand pages of documents and listening to the testimony of more than one hundred people, the Commission on Civil Rights concluded: "Voting is the language of our democracy. As the Supreme Court observed, 'no right is more precious in a free country than that of having a voice in the election of those who make the laws under which, as good citizens, we must live.' It is clear that many people in Florida were denied this precious right."[4]

The 1920 presidential election in Florida is less noted, but it held the key to the fate of legal segregation in America. On January 1, 1919 (Emancipation Day), African Americans in Jacksonville began planning a voter registration drive. Soon activists across the state began gathering to conduct secret voter education workshops in lodges, churches, and union meetings. African American women marched in groups to county court-houses demanding the right to register to vote within hours of the Nine-teenth Amendment's passage. Black workers—male and female—infused politics with demands for economic justice and launched strikes for better wages and working conditions. African Americans throughout Florida mobilized to defeat white supremacy, economic oppression, and one-party rule.

The Florida voter registration movement faced staggering obstacles. Florida boasted the highest per capita lynching rate in the country. The state's governor openly extolled racial violence. Florida had been "redeemed" by white supremacy in 1876, and since that time conservative Democrats had used every available weapon including terror, murder, fraud, and statute to disfranchise African Americans. In this climate the act of registering to vote took extraordinary courage.

African Americans found that courage within the vibrant interior life of the Florida movement. Black Floridians who participated in the move-ment gave themselves permission to think of each other as integral citizens of a state that had damned their existence for decades. Black women demanded—even before they themselves were enfranchised—that men register to vote. Eighty-year-old Civil War veterans urged newly returned World War I soldiers to claim their rights; voter education workshops instructed thousands in the mechanics of voting. Some of the leading political activists of the day, including Mary McLeod Bethune, James Weldon Johnson, and Walter White, poured everything they had into the campaign. The National Association for the Advancement of Colored People (NAACP) used the Florida movement as the tip of its spear for piercing one-party rule in the South.

The Florida voter registration movement expanded as organizers spread the gospel of voting from Pensacola through the Panhandle and down the peninsula to Dade County. Charles Thompson of Jacksonville fired off a letter to Republican presidential candidate Warren G. Harding expressing his joy at being able to vote for the first time in his life: "Kind and most loving sir: i am nothing but a poor colored house painter. But i am forced to drop you a few lines to let you no that you stands on the top rung of the longest ladder in Florida with my race."[5] By October, African American organizers had spread the voter registration movement to more than half of the counties in the state. Black Floridians had accomplished this by building a movement that had room for young and old, middling and poor, highbrow and plain-spoken. The goals of the campaign emerged from conversations and debates that involved ever-widening groups of African Americans in churches, lodge halls, women's clubs, labor unions, and other organizations. The participants of these discussions created a movement to confront the gravest problems of their time: lynching, economic oppression, disfranchisement, and the loss of dignity that they suffered under white domination. Organizers recruited thousands of new voters to the struggle because they took their cues from the people and not the other way around.

On November 2, 1920, African Americans prepared to storm the walls of segregation. In the stillness of first light on Tuesday morning some black Floridians undoubtedly whispered the lyrics of native son James Weldon Johnson: "Have not our weary feet come to the place for which our fathers sighed?" as they prepared to cast their ballots. African Americans in Florida had created the first statewide civil rights movement in U.S. history.

The origins of the Florida movement can be found only by carefully examining black history, culture, and politics between the end of slavery and World War I. The major fact that emerges from this inquiry is that the period after the fall of Reconstruction was not characterized primarily by black acquiescence to Jim Crow or legal segregation, but rather by open struggles to fight racial oppression. Understanding the linkages between these earlier battles against white supremacy and the emergence of the Florida movement is the goal of this work. This book contains lessons for scholars and activists interested in the question of what it takes to create a social movement in the modern world.

What black Floridians did—and how they did it—should be placed in the context of a nationally resurgent African American freedom struggle after World War I. Black southerners reorganized and launched local and even regional battles against legal segregation or Jim Crow in places such as Elaine, Arkansas; Norfolk, Virginia; Birmingham, Alabama; Atlanta, Georgia; North Carolina; and East Texas.[6] African Americans in Florida used many of the same tactics employed by their counterparts throughout the South. Black Floridians organized new branches of the NAACP, unionized, and engaged in acts of armed self-defense against white supremacist violence. What was distinctive about the struggle in Florida was the fact that black Floridians were able to build a statewide social movement that linked rural folk with urban residents. Putting a spotlight on African American insurgency in Florida deepens what we already know about the black freedom struggle in other parts of the nation even as it suggests new places, sources, and methods to look for as-yet-unknown social movements.

The genesis of this book lies in my work with the oral history project called Behind the Veil: Documenting African American Life in the Jim Crow South, based at the Center for Documentary Studies at Duke University.[7] After two weeks of interviewing African American elders in Tallahassee in the summer of 1994, I called the office of the American Federation of State, County, and Municipal Employees (AFSCME), hoping to meet retirees who would agree to be interviewed. The union staffer who answered the phone told me: "You need to talk with Mrs. Laura Dixie. She is a retired hospital worker, one of the founders of our union—she can take you *way back*." Bursting with excitement, I phoned Mrs. Dixie, who quickly agreed to an interview.

The following day I arrived with my tape recorder and a stack of blank tapes to interview Laura Dixie and her husband Samuel, a retired custodian. What followed was a series of interviews that completely changed my understanding of American history and social change. The Dixies began their narrative where they assumed I wanted them to begin: the civil rights movement in Tallahassee in the 1950s. They led me through their participation in the historic Tallahassee Bus Boycott, which had closely followed the heels of the Montgomery, Alabama, struggle. But Mrs. and Mr. Dixie used this familiar narrative to teach me a more profound truth: the modern civil rights movement in Florida was based on a lineage of struggle that reached back several generations. In Laura Dixie's mind, the female elders in her family who raised her during the Great Depression, especially her mother, gave her the courage to become a labor and civil rights activist. Samuel Dixie reminded me—then and over the next several years—that there were always "some brave black men" who fought against white supremacy.

It turned out that one of those men was Mr. Dixie's older brother, A. I., an eighty-one-year-old former sharecropper and retired minister living in nearby Quincy. Sam Dixie drove me out to speak with his big brother who he said possessed a wealth of stories about African American life during the "crucial times" in rural Gadsden County. The younger brother did not exaggerate. Rev. Dixie guided me through the underground formation of the NAACP in Gadsden in the 1940s, the turbulent 1960s civil rights battles in the county, and the story of how he and his wife had hosted young Congress of Racial Equality (CORE) workers involved in voter registration activities. Rev. Dixie's own daughter and son were in the forefront of that campaign.

Again, however, the story of the modern movement in Quincy was just the latest installment of a decades-long freedom struggle. By way of example, Rev. Dixie told me of a sacred oath taken by the members of an African American secret society in Gadsden County after World War I. The members of this lodge, the Colored Knights of Pythias, took a pledge to stand together against racial oppression. At some point, local whites heard of the oath, and a major gun battle ensued between whites and blacks on the outskirts of Quincy.

I spent a year searching the archives for evidence of this pledge. I was on the verge of quitting when one day I found a reference to the oath in a totally unexpected source. Further research proved that the pledge—to pay poll taxes and register to vote—had been uttered by thousands of members of the Knights of Pythias in Florida. Only then did I begin to grasp the meaning behind the awesome metaphor that Rev. A. I. Dixie used to describe the Pythians, who, as he put it, "covered Florida like water covered the sea." In ways that I began to understand only as my research progressed, the historic oath that the Pythians took helped to propel one of the most remarkable social movements in American history.

This is a study about how people resist oppression and create new social movements. The Florida movement shows what an organized group of individuals can accomplish in the face of violence, discrimination, and economic misery. Lynching, starvation wages, and disfranchisement placed formidable barriers in the way of creating a social movement in Jim Crow Florida.[8] In a larger context, voter registration activists in 1920 operated in a country that legally prevented African Americans, first-generation immigrants, and much of the nation's working population from exercising full citizenship.[9] Black Floridians adopted tactics to fight oppression that were grounded in a specific time and place. However, the methods that African Americans used to gain what they called "universal freedom" are relevant today.

This book examines African American politics and culture in Florida between the end of slavery and the presidential election of 1920 in order to understand why and how black Floridians created the first statewide social movement against Jim Crow. I build on an expanding body of work on African American lives and experiences in the segregating South.[10] Elsa Barkley Brown has unveiled the ways that African American women struggled to defend and expand the meaning of citizenship during Reconstruction and its aftermath. Brown has clearly established that African American women began participating in public life immediately after emancipation. Peter Rachleff's research on Richmond, Virginia, demonstrates that black fraternal and labor organizations helped forge sophisticated political ideologies and alliances after the Civil War. Earl Lewis has mapped out the institutional and economic bases of African American strategies for social change over several decades in Jim Crow Norfolk. Lewis also candidly delineates class tensions within black communities.[11]

Historians have continued to probe more deeply into differences along lines of class, gender, and politics in African American communities. In contrast to an all-encompassing idea of a unified black community during segregation, scholars are finding that competing strategies and perspectives may have made the African American freedom struggle more effective in the long run. Robin D. G. Kelley shows that black workers engaged in a creative array of maneuvers ranging from factory slowdowns to streetcar protests that white authorities—and black elite critics—found difficult to squelch in the name of order. Tera W. Hunter has pressed this insight of everyday resistance further to include black domestic workers who resisted the degradation of Jim Crow in white households and sought to express their feelings in churches, dance halls, and other public spaces they controlled. Kelley, Hunter, and others who have followed in their path have shown that African American workers created their own cultures and political goals outside the gaze of white racism.[12]

Equally important, Evelyn Brooks Higginbotham and Glenda Gilmore have illuminated the perspective of African American women who were active in churches, middle-class reform organizations, and other civic groups. Higginbotham has established that African American women created a "women's movement in the Black Baptist Church" by embracing the "politics of respectability," which they tried to teach to poorer African Americans as a strategy of empowerment. Glenda Gilmore's pathbreaking study of African American women's activism in North Carolina between 1896 and 1920 has caused a major reassessment of African American politics in the Jim Crow era. Gilmore argues that African American women seized the social space left by black men's forced departure from the political arena and took the lead in numerous organizing initiatives before and after the passage of the Nineteenth Amendment.[13] Cumulatively, these works have effected a revolution in the historiography of African American life and labor between 1877 and the Great Depression.

In spite of this pathbreaking work, social movement scholars in general have given the early years of Jim Crow a wide berth, depicting this period as a Lost Era of organizing. Assumptions of African American acquiescence to segregation adds dramatic flair to narratives that depict black southerners "awakening" to claim their rights at some point after World War II, *Brown v. Board of Education,* or the Montgomery Bus Boycott. One study of the modern civil rights movement claims that as late as the Great Depression, "the black masses were still ignorant of their rights, for the most part." Worse, "those who were not [ignorant] were also the ones most likely to be better off economically and educationally—and therefore the ones least inclined to rock the boat, to risk financial reprisals and perhaps violence by the white community."[14]

African American resistance in segregating Florida was continuous over time, but its effectiveness varied with changes in regional and national economic, political, and legal structures. African Americans did not resort to new strategies to create the Florida movement of 1919–1920. They called on preexisting institutions to mobilize a statewide campaign for social change. Organizing efforts were aided by national currents, especially the Great Migration, World War I, and passage of the Nineteenth Amendment. Nevertheless, the evidence of persistent resistance to white supremacy in Florida calls into question the thesis of the "New Negro" or a younger—largely male—generation dramatically appearing on the stage in the 1920s to fight white supremacy. In contrast, some of the key leaders in the movement had participated in Reconstruction-era politics. Decades-old mutual aid societies like the Colored Knights of Pythias provided tools and the foot soldiers for the movement. Black activists called upon African Americans to remember their history as a pathway to a liberated future. Some of the people who registered to vote in 1920 were survivors of slavery. In Florida the New Negro had gray hair.

Even more than serving as a harbinger of the modern civil rights movement, the Florida movement was intimately linked to the history of African American struggle dating back to slavery times. Indeed, what historian Charles Payne has referred to as an "organizing tradition" for social justice reached back several decades in Florida.[15] James S. Perry of Nassau County gave voice to this tradition in 1887:

> If we do not stand for our rights and remedy these evils, who do we
> expect to stand for us? The States and the United States governments
> have told us that they will not do anything for us, hence we must stand
> like men or die like dogs, and when they see that we are determined to
> have our rights, they will assist us in getting them.[16]

Perry's call for grassroots activism was issued a decade after the end of Reconstruction, and it expressed the determination of African Americans to energetically challenge oppression. Black Floridians raised the theory and practice of direct action to a high art. Urban communities organized streetcar boycotts against segregated transportation. Male and female workers battled for higher wages, respect, and safer workplaces. Groups of black Floridians took up arms to stop lynching and racial violence. Lodges, labor unions, and churches became vital sites of reciprocity that sustained hard-pressed members in good times and bad. These groups also created social spaces where black Floridians nurtured historical memories of African American achievements in slavery, the Civil War, and Reconstruction. Individuals who took part in these actions gained a heightened sense of self-confidence and identity that comes only from participating in shared struggle. Over time African Americans learned to build relationships of trust that linked them together in collective associations. In turn, these institutions formed the backbone of the Florida movement. The central lesson here is that social movements do not arise by chance: they require years of patient organizing and institution building.

I argue that the origins of the Florida movement may be found in the survival strategies that African American workers, women, and middle-class folk forged in the furnace of segregating Florida. Throughout the text, I ask three overlapping questions: What techniques did African Americans use to resist white supremacy? How did regional economic development and national politics impact the trajectory of the black freedom struggle? Finally, how did African American men and women define and lay claims to citizenship in an age of disfranchisement? In posing these questions, I do not assume that solidarity—among a people, a group, or a class—is an automatic reaction to oppression; I recognize that it must be *organized*. Coming of age in the all-black town of Eatonville, Florida, Zora Neale Hurston advised, "The Negro race was not one band of heavenly love. There was stress and strain inside as well as out. Being black was not enough. It took more than a community of skin color to make your love come down on you."[17]

This work is by no means a comprehensive history of African Americans in Florida; rather, the focus is on political and economic struggles for social justice. I begin with a discussion of slavery and the Civil War because of the formidable role that historical memory played in black—and white—politics. Chapters 1 and 2 discuss battles over suffrage, economic security, and the meaning of freedom. Former slaves and slave masters understood the pivotal role the elective franchise played in the region's development. While black Floridians demanded a "jealous regard for the rights of labor," employers and white officials schemed to disfranchise African American workers and inoculate white Floridians against inter-racial alliances. The bloody outcome of this contest set the stage for the coming of legal segregation, or Jim Crow.[18]

The next three chapters focus on the development of key African American survival and organizing strategies in Gilded Age Florida. These chapters unveil myriad efforts by African Americans to roll back the tide of white supremacy. Chapter 3 investigates the descent of Florida into racial terrorism and examines the tradition of black armed self-defense against white violence. Chapters 4 and 5 focus on the development of mutual aid, public commemoration of black history, and other institutions that would become decisive in the Florida voter registration movement.

The remaining chapters chart the emergence of the Florida movement. Chapters 6 and 7 describe how eruptions of African American resistance in the era of the Great Migration and World War I were actually rooted in decades of striving. Wartime migration, strikes, and Liberty Bond drives overlapped to create a new, more promising environment for older aspirations to be realized. Chapter 8 shows how black Floridians created the statewide movement, and chapter 9 describes the fate of the struggle. The conclusion comes to grips with the long-term legacies of the bloodiest election in modern American history.

Florida has too often existed on the margins of the literature on the Jim Crow South. With some exceptions, the Sunshine State seems to be barely in the South at all. There are some reasons for the omission. In contrast to

Georgia and Alabama, Florida had a relatively small and declining cotton belt. Tobacco was the real king of many a middle Florida plantation. Orange groves and phosphate mines rather than cotton fields contributed to the development of central Florida. Urbanization and the growth of the ports of Pensacola, Jacksonville, Tampa, and (later) Miami gave African Americans opportunities for occupational mobility not enjoyed in large parts of the South. Finally, regular infusions of migrants from Cuba, the Bahamas, and Central America contributed to the making of a complex cultural mix.[19]

Nevertheless, Florida exceptionalism does not square with the facts. The present study takes issue with V. O. Key's argument that Florida was "scarcely part of the South" and that race relations in Florida were "comparatively mild."[20] When South Carolina native Mary McLeod Bethune arrived in Daytona at the turn of the century to found a school for black girls, she found "racial prejudice of the most violent type."[21] Race relations in Miami were so bad in the 1910s that Bahamian immigrants hoisted the Union Jack as an act of defiance and petitioned the British Crown to save them from Jim Crow. By almost any quantifiable social phenomenon, including lynching, educational outlays by race, incarceration rates, or legislative statutes, Florida looks like a state in the segregated South.

Florida has had a decisive impact on race relations in the United States. African Americans in Florida carried out the largest slave rebellion in the nation's history at the outset of the Second Seminole War in 1835. No pantheon of American freedom fighters is complete without the names of Mary McLeod Bethune, James Weldon Johnson, T. Thomas Fortune, J. Milton Waldron, Howard Thurman, Harry T. Moore, and A. Philip Randolph. All came of age in the segregating South and all began their lifelong crusades against oppression in Florida. Each of them taught the world lessons about defeating injustice they had learned from their unheralded elders. This book is a chronicle of their—and our—ancestors in struggle. In the words of an African American soldier returning from France after the end of the Great War, black Floridians practiced "democracy in its fullest meaning."

ACKNOWLEDGMENTS

In the process of writing this book I have accrued debts that can never be repaid. I am thankful beyond words to the African American people in Florida who opened their homes, their lives, their stories, and their archives to me. In Tallahassee Laura and Samuel Dixie fed me, put me up in their spare bedroom, arranged oral history interviews, and introduced me to their beautiful family. After five decades of social activism together, Sam and Laura recently celebrated their fiftieth wedding anniversary. Sam's brother, Rev. A. I. Dixie, took me on a tour of African American history landmarks in Gadsden County that I will never forget. Ike Williams III, editor of the *Jacksonville Advocate,* opened up his private manuscript collection of the papers of Joseph E. Lee to a perfect stranger without reservation. Along the way we became friends, and I treasure the memory of late-night conversations with Ike about his recollections of Malcolm X and the movement years. Thanks also to the wonderful staff at the *Jacksonville Advocate,* who grabbed lunch for me on several occasions so that I could keep working through the noon hour. I'll never let my subscription to the *Advocate* lapse, Ike. In Gainesville local historian Joel Buchanan took me under his wing and introduced me to elders in the African American community who taught me their life histories. Several elders passed before this book could be completed. Malachia Andrews, Inez Stevens-Jones, Aquilina Howell, Mary Ola Gaines, Cornelius Speed, and Otto Gainey told me stories about Jim Crow Florida that need to be told and retold whenever possible.

In Durham, North Carolina, R. Kelley Bryant, Jr., offered decades of firsthand expertise about African American secret societies and taught me to pay very close attention to the work of black fraternal lodges in the South.

Archivists and librarians at several institutions offered invaluable guidance. Dr. James Cusick at the University of Florida, Gainesville, spent incalculable amounts of time introducing me to the rich holdings of the University of Florida's Special Collections Library. Just around the corner

Jo Talbird runs an excellent and accessible Microfilm Department at the Smathers Library. At the University of North Florida, Eileen Brady gave me access to the Eartha M. M. White collection and was kind enough to allow me to copy documents from that precious collection. Leslie Sheffield guided me through the remarkable photographic collection at the Florida State Archives. I am likewise grateful to the professional and work-study staff at Florida State University, the University of South Florida, and the Southern Historical Collection, UNC–Chapel Hill, for their forbearance. Thanks also to the staff at the Birmingham Public Library for their unfailingly kind and helpful attention. At Duke University's Perkins Library I am especially indebted to the staff of Special Collections as well as to Ann Miller and Mark A. Thomas of Public Documents and Maps, for helping me to locate several Florida contested election cases. I will always be grateful to the kind folks at the Perkins Library Interlibrary Loan department for establishing a special "Ortiz trouble file," wherein staff spent hours looking for long-out-of-print newspapers and other arcane items that form the foundation of this book. The staff at the Photographic Services Section at Wilson Library, UNC–Chapel Hill, expedited a critical photographic order for me. I can only marvel at the graciousness and energy of the staff at the Library of Congress and the National Archives, who do so much on such a tight budget. Finally, thank goodness for the Interlibrary Loan and Public Documents staff at University of California, Santa Cruz. Sorry for those last-minute calls, colleagues.

Florida is blessed with an abundance of outstanding scholars who have chronicled the state's history with great care and skill. James Eaton introduced me to African American history in Florida and provided an initial list of archival sources to mine. Samuel Proctor gave me an afternoon's worth of his inimitable knowledge of Florida history. Julian Pleasants introduced me to the oral history collection at the University of Florida, Gainesville. David Colburn has provided a critical ear and stimulating conversation, and he has kept tabs on the project as it wound its way to completion. Nancy Hewitt shared her remarkable research on Tampa with me, while Larry Eugene Rivers enriched my understanding of black struggles in Florida. Robert Cassanello offered insights from his own pioneering work in the history of African American working-class resistance in Florida.

Andrew Schneider, Alan Lipke, and Roger Beebe provided free lodging, friendship, intellectual stimulation—and directions to the nearest doughnut shops—during extended research trips to the Library of Congress, the

National Archives, the University of South Florida, and Gainesville, respectively.

A number of colleagues and friends have read, critiqued, and commented on parts of this work as it moved from dissertation to conference paper to book. I want to especially thank Florence Borders, Vince Brown, Kim Butler, Derek Chang, Pat Cooper, Angela Davis, Laura Edwards, Glenda Gilmore, Adam Green, Nancy Hewitt, Mike Honey, Paul Husbands, Walter Johnson, Ian Lekus, Leon Litwack, Catherine Martinez, Joseph Miller, Charles Payne, Eric Porter, Peter Rachleff, Larry Eugene Rivers, Lisa Rubens, and Julius Scott III for offering insightful commentary and ideas on the project. Larry Goodwyn flew all the way out to California to give me the benefit of his editorial eye. Dana Frank, David Wellman, and David Brundage graciously read the manuscript in its final stages and gave me sage advice on improvements.

My editor at the University of California Press, Monica McCormick, provided careful guidance through the entire process of preparing the book for publication. Associate editor Randy Heyman patiently fielded numerous questions, and Kay Scheuer carefully copyedited the text. Glenda Gilmore and David Roediger read the complete manuscript from start to finish twice. No author could ask for better readers. Both gave equal doses of strong criticism and endless encouragement. Glenda's readings were works of art; she uncovered numerous themes that remained undeveloped in the manuscript and encouraged me—much to my initial chagrin—to refine the organization of the book. David pushed me to think especially hard about the early parts of the narrative and the larger theoretical implications of the work. Dean MacCannell gave the penultimate draft a strong read and suggested improvements.

As a graduate student at Duke University, my intellectual life was enriched beyond belief by being a part of Behind the Veil: Documenting African American Life in the Jim Crow South, an oral history project based at the Center for Documentary Studies at Duke. Bill Chafe, Bob Korstad, and Raymond Gavins introduced me to the "BTV crew" at the outset of my graduate career and allowed me to work there for the duration. Association with the Behind the Veil Collective contributed enormously to my development as a historian, and being a part of the team that wrote *Remembering Jim Crow: African Americans Tell about Life in the Jim Crow South* was a learning experience I'll always treasure. At BTV and the Center for Documentary Studies I was inspired by a community of scholars and friends including Ramiro Arceo, Felix Armfield, Leslie

Brown, Alex Byrd, David Cecelski, Doris Dixon, Laurie Green, Mary Herbert, Homer H. Hill, Iris Tillman Hill, Blair Murphy Kelley, Libby Manley, Michelle Mitchell, Greta Niu, Robert Parrish, Aminah Pilgrim, Tom Rankin, Jennifer Ritterhouse, Keisha Roberts, Chris Ross, Mausiki Stacey Scales, Artie Smith, Annie Valk, Nicole Waligora, Tywanna Whorley, Melinda Wiggins, and Luba V. Zakharov. I look forward to years of joyous reunions and conference panels with y'all.

My dissertation committee was spectacular. Charles Payne graciously signed on in the final year of the dissertation project, agreeing to read reams of outlines and half-finished chapters. Charles has continued to have a profound impact on the manuscript and honored me by including a chapter of my research in his recently completed anthology on African American activism. Larry Goodwyn gave me the benefit of numerous readings. He also engaged me in conversations about democratic social relations, Populism, and *Solidarnosc* and treated me as a peer while paying the tab to boot. Raymond Gavins has now taught several generations of graduate students the field of African American history and deserves the highest praise for being an inspiring teacher and always lending a sympathetic ear to his students' concerns.

William H. Chafe served as my mentor and advisor from the very beginning. Bill patiently listened to more than one iteration of this project, told me what he thought was feasible, and turned me loose to make my own way. During my tenure at Duke, Bill ensured that I was immersed in the best intellectual environment that a graduate student could expect to find. Since then, he has continued to serve as my guide through the rigors of finding a publisher, getting a job, and becoming an assistant professor.

A strong group of comrades helped make graduate school an experience to remember. I want to especially recognize my friends Derek "D. S." Chang, Paul Husbands, Vince Brown, Ajantha Subramanian, Mary Wingerd, George Waldrep, Françoise Bourdier, Hasan Jeffries, Chuck McKinney, and Andrew Schneider for sharing on numerous occasions beer, dinner, basketball games, joy, sorrow, and gossip during and after our sojourn together at Duke. Never underestimate the power of friendship in the production of scholarly work.

During my undergraduate years, several key instructors challenged me to pursue my dream of becoming a historian. As a returning student at Olympic Community College fresh from a four-year stint in the U.S. Army, I found the counsel of Philip Schaeffer, David Toren, and Robert Ericksen invaluable. They told me exactly what I needed to know to move on to the next level. At Evergreen State College, Stephanie Coontz taught me how to write and to think in scholarly terms without losing touch with my activist roots. Stephanie, Beryl Crowe, and Tom Grissom were more than supportive faculty at Evergreen; by my senior year, they all but insisted that I apply for graduate programs in history. I only hope that I can emulate their examples as teachers.

Don Bidwell deserves a ton of credit for this book because he pushed me and three decades of Bremerton High School seniors in A. P. English to read Ellison, Wright, and Faulkner (and Shakespeare, for good measure). Chuck Semancik, Ralph Mantzke, and Arthur Luck were excellent teachers who helped me get my bearings in high school.

An ever-growing circle of erudite stalwarts have inspired me to become a better scholar, writer, and activist through their example: David Anthony, Bettina Aptheker, Andy Arnold, Katya Azoulay, Peter Bohmer, John Borrego, Pedro Castillo, Jack Cell (who is greatly missed), Jim Clifford, Stephanie Coontz, Angela Davis, Greta de Jong, Lisa Lindquist Dorr, Chouki El-Hamel, Betsy Ellsworth, Scott Ellsworth, Leon Fink, Tim Fitzmaurice, Dana Frank, Marge Frantz, Rosa Linda Fregoso, Barry Gaspar, Herman Gray, Steven Hahn, Jacquelyn Hall, Lisa Hazirjan, Karlton Hester, Nancy Hewitt, Mike Honey, Gerald Horne, Tera W. Hunter, John Jackson, Karen L. Jefferson, Will Jones, George Lipsitz, Alma Martinez, Scott Morgensen, Larry Mosqueda, Manuel Pastor, Kurt Peterson, Peter Rachleff, Carolyn Martin Shaw, David Sweet, Neferti Tadiar, Dana Takagi, Susan Thorne, Tim Tyson, Nick Wood, Peter Wood, Nan Elizabeth Woodruff, and Pat Zavella. You are my role models.

I want to thank my colleagues in the Department of Community Studies who welcomed me to UC–Santa Cruz with open arms and showed me how to thrive in the academy: Nancy Stoller, David Brundage, Bill Friedland, Deborah Woo, Carter Wilson, Pamela Perry, David Wellman, Mary Beth Pudup, Mike Rotkin, Joanie Peterson, Lisa Mastramico, Melessa Hemler, and Penny Stinson, the queen of department managers. My research assistant, Jenna Spears, provided critical database support and helped fine-tune the manuscript even as she embarked on her own promising research project.

Three individuals who have passed on played a critical part in my intellectual development. Joe Wood provided inspiration, editorial assistance, and friendship in the early years of this project. Joe: your shining example continues to invigorate the world. We will never forget you. Martin Glaberman shared precious memories of C. L. R. James, gave me the tract that provides the epigraph of this book, and was an exemplary scholar and activist. Dorothy Phelps Jones, the historian for St. Joseph's Historic Foundation in Durham, North Carolina, was a constant inspiration, a master storyteller, and a friend.

My students at Duke, N.C. State, and UC–Santa Cruz have been a source of strength. Their deep-felt desire for social change and their need for clarity have driven the attempt to write a book that presents its findings as concisely as possible. I'll be interested to see how they grade me.

The community-based historians of the Democracy Forum in Orange County, Florida, deserve recognition for their efforts to bring the 1920 Ocoee Massacre to light. I can only hope that this book aids in that effort. Never forget.

This project has been sustained by financial support including a Center for Documentary Studies at Duke University Graduate Fellowship from 1993 to 1999, a dissertation research travel stipend from the Duke University History Department, and Grinnell College's Minority Scholar-in-Residence Fellowship in the spring of 1999. At UC–Santa Cruz, I have received generous research grants from the Academic Senate as well as the Social Science Division. I am grateful to my department chair, Mary Beth Pudup, as well as the dean of Social Sciences, Martin Chemers, for granting me time off from teaching in order to finish the manuscript.

My father, Paul Pedro Ortiz, introduced me to the history of segregation and the art of oral traditions via his remarkable life story of growing up in Houston's Fifth Ward. My mother, Johnine MacDonald, insisted that I pursue the doctorate before she passed. My sister, Sophia Ortiz, has provided fresh inspiration as she moves at light speed through her own undergraduate studies. My mother-in-law and father-in-law, Evelyn and J. W. Payne, have been enormously supportive of my work and gave me a priceless gift in the form of a dependable automobile that carried me through thousands of miles of research. Sheila Payne has read and critiqued every word of this manuscript on more occasions than either one of us can remember. Her readings improved the final work beyond imagination, and her activist spirit has energized my life.

Paul Ortiz
Santa Cruz, California
October 30, 2003

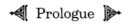

SLAVERY AND CIVIL WAR

The Van Buren and her entire cargo of 470 bales of cotton . . . was destroyed by fire the night of Dec. 5, 1834, while tied up at Martin's landing on the Chattahoochie river. The fire was set by a runaway negro who had been re-captured.[1]

THE PENSACOLA GAZETTE

ONE DAY early in the twentieth century an elderly woman is sharing a part of her life story with her grandson on the family's front porch. Reared in Daytona, the child has spent much of his life with this venerated midwife, reading passages of the Bible to her because she is illiterate. There is one part of the sacred text, however, that the young boy's grandmother, a descendant of African slaves and Seminole Indians, refuses to let him read aloud in her presence: the Pauline epistles with their injunction for slaves to obey their masters. By way of explanation, Nancy Ambrose recounts her life as a slave in Madison County and bristles with anger when she recalls, "Old man McGhee was so mean that he would not let a Negro minister preach to his slaves." Instead, McGhee directed a white pastor to teach "it was God's will that we were slaves and how, if we were good and happy slaves, God would bless us. I promised my Maker that if I ever learned to read and if freedom ever came, I would not read that part of the Bible." From a seat on his grandmother's front porch, the young boy—who will grow up to become one of the greatest Christian theologians of the twentieth century—listens, troubled by the ways that Christianity has been used to bolster tyranny.[2]

"The fact that the first twenty-three years of my life were spent in Florida and in Georgia," the Reverend Dr. Howard Thurman later recalled, "left its scars deep in my spirit and has rendered me terribly sensitive to the churning abyss separating white from black."[3] Nancy Ambrose tried to bolster her grandson's spirits by telling another kind of story about slavery, one that spoke of autonomy and dignity. Occasionally a black minister would somehow manage to hold services on Ambrose's plantation. The climax of *this* sermon was: "You are not slaves; you are not *niggers* condemned forever to do your master's will—you are God's children." The effect of the sermon on the slaves—and young Howard decades later—was electrifying.

> When those words were uttered a warm glow crept all through the very being of the slaves, and they felt the feeling of themselves run through them. Even at this far distance I can relive the pulsing tremor of raw energy that was released in me as I responded to her words. The sense of being permanently grounded in God gave to the people of that far-off time a way to experience themselves as human beings.[4]

These stories launched Howard Thurman on an odyssey to redeem Christianity for "the poor, the disinherited, the dispossessed." Nancy Ambrose's unlettered wisdom and her hatred of injustice prepared Rev. Thurman to become a spiritual advisor to a younger generation of activists including Martin Luther King, Jr. and James Lawson.[5] Thus, one branch of the river that became the modern civil rights movement runs deep through a slave plantation in Madison County, Florida. Tracing the course of this river means paying careful attention to the kinds of stories that Nancy Ambrose and others of her generation told younger people. Oral narratives of survival, war, and emancipation enhanced black pride and kindled a heritage threatened by lynch-law, poverty, and segregation.[6] Zora Neale Hurston found that African Americans in Florida amplified their oral traditions with songs and parables that emphasized the ingenuity of their slave forbears and the cupidity and sadism of their masters.[7] Gadsden County native Malachia Andrews was raised with stories of the Seminole Wars and slave revolts in Florida.[8] Historical memories of resistance gave hope for the future.

These oral traditions were rooted in slavery, and they open a window on a history of suffering and struggle. In the colonial period, African American slaves in the lower South who struck out for their freedom often fled to the thinly settled lands of Spanish Florida and established the region as a sanctuary of nonracial liberty. Africans fleeing slavery in the Carolinas built Gracia Real de Santa Teresa de Mose, or Fort Mose, two miles to the north of St. Augustine, in concert with the Spanish in the 1730s. Self-emancipated slaves from the British colonies willing to bear arms were granted conditional freedom by Spanish officials anxious to create a military redoubt against aggressive English settlers.[9] The Africans of Fort Mose pledged to expend their "last drop of blood in defense of the great Crown of Spain and the Holy Faith," and they inflicted severe losses on British armies and military adventurers from Georgia who sought to re-enslave them.[10] When slaves in South Carolina organized the Stono Uprising of 1739, Fort Mose was their destination.[11] After Spain ceded control of Florida to Great Britain in 1763, African Americans from the fort embarked for Cuba.

In the years between the American Revolution and the War of 1812, new generations of self-emancipated slaves from the lower South escaped to Florida seeking sanctuary.[12] Fighting alternately as soldiers in support of British and Spanish forces, African Americans formed their most critical alliances with bands of Seminole Indians, who had seceded from the Creeks or Upper Muskogees of Georgia.[13] Seminoles and their Muskogee kin were horrified at the brutality of American slave labor camps.[14] In the aftermath of a genocidal war that cost the Upper Muskogees fourteen million acres of land to the United States, the Seminoles welcomed fugitive slaves for the skills they brought with them.[15] Under the patronage of the Seminoles, Africans Americans became tax-paying farmers, interpreters, diplomats, and guerrilla fighters who helped their new allies challenge a slave republic that Alexis de Tocqueville called "the most grasping nation on the globe."[16] Historian Kenneth Wiggins Porter described the relationship between Seminoles and African Americans as a kind of "primitive democratic feudalism."[17] African Americans and Seminoles negotiated a relationship that allowed both sides to enjoy a level of autonomy and dignity that neither could have achieved alone, and it was viewed by the United States as a threat to national security.[18] George Washington's administration attempted to force the Seminoles to extradite black Floridians to their former masters by using the carrot of a federal slave bounty and the threat of military assault.[19] When diplomacy failed, Georgia deployed its state militia to Florida in order to force the Seminoles into compliance. The Seminoles and renegade African Americans soundly thrashed the Georgians.

In a pattern that would be repeated throughout the next century, the federal government intervened to enforce white supremacy in Florida. The United States of America waged three major wars to secure slavery and remove the Seminoles from Florida.[20] In the midst of these military campaigns, the United States purchased Florida from Spain in order to break the power of their antislavery foes, a task the Spaniards had failed, or refused, to accomplish.[21] The bulk of the Seminoles rebuffed U.S. offers to relocate to Indian Territory in the West largely because such a deal would mean the re-enslavement of their African American allies.[22]

At the outset of the Second Seminole War (1835–1842) hundreds of African American slaves in Florida rose in the Alachua and St. Johns River plantation districts to join the battle and strike for their liberation.[23] General Thomas Sidney Jessup observed that the Second Seminole War was "a negro, not an Indian war."[24] After the final defeat of the Seminole–ex-slave alliance, a candid white observer revealed the scope of the tragedy: "The Seminole made a desperate stand for his Florida home. He was exacting from the whites a terrible price for the acres they coveted. And even more desperately than the Indian, fought the negro fugitive. Defeat for him was not the loss of land, but of liberty; to yield meant not exile, but bondage."[25]

The most common path of slave resistance in antebellum Florida involved smaller-scale acts of insurgency.[26] Fugitive African American slaves escaped Florida's plantations to rejoin families and communities in the upper South that had been torn from them by the domestic slave trade that fed Florida and the Deep South with slave labor.[27] In 1829 a slave couple fled from the plantation of Robert Butler, "both about 40 years of age; and it is believed that they will make for Tenn[essee]" where the couple had originally come from.[28] In 1833, "Dick, a daring and artful villain . . . probably has procured papers to enable him to get to a free state, or to Virginia, where he was raised." In the same year, a married couple owned by Cornelius Devane stole their master's shot gun and fled his plantation with their three children and "are trying to get back to N.C. where they were raised. Pink will try to pass for [a] free woman. Has obtained pass for purpose."[29]

Authorities responded harshly to acts of resistance. Enslaved African Americans who participated in the Underground Railroad were beaten and mutilated.[30] Presaging the "Black Codes" of post–Civil War Florida, municipal officials hammered away at the fragile independence enjoyed by free blacks and slave artisans who hired their own time in port towns. During the Second Seminole War lawmakers in Apalachicola passed laws levying heavy poll taxes on free blacks who remained in Franklin County, empowered police to conduct sweeps and searches of black residences "without written permit," forbade the sale or gift of alcohol to slaves, and authorized the night patrol to inflict twenty lashes on "any slaves or free negroes found outside their own lodgings without written permit from owner, employer or guardian."[31]

This early history of struggle explains why enslaved African Americans did not wait for Abraham Lincoln's Emancipation Proclamation to strike for their freedom. In 1862, slave laborers escaped along the St. Johns River and sought refuge on Union gun boats.[32] African Americans played a critical role in the Union Navy's Atlantic blockading operations on Florida's coast in the spring and autumn months of the Civil War's second year. Using their knowledge of Florida's rivers, ports, and back roads, African Americans, classified early in the war as "contrabands," served as spies and scouts for Union forces. The Flag Officer of the South Atlantic Blockading Squadron alerted his commanders on March 1, "A contraband brings news that the enemy is abandoning Fernandina." This intelligence helped the Union Navy intercept Confederate forces while preventing the enemy from poisoning area wells and destroying military supplies.[33] Partisan slaves in Florida and Georgia kept Union forces apprised of Confederate troop and ship movements and warned of ambushes. U.S. Navy Lieutenant T. H. Stevens credited black intelligence for the survival of his forces then engaged in the St. Mary's River region.[34]

African Americans in Florida saw the Civil War as a war of liberation, and hundreds escaped from slavery to serve with Union regiments.[35] Black troops fought with distinction at Olustee, Florida's largest Civil War land battle. The aftermath of Olustee, where Confederate soldiers massacred wounded African American POWs, foreshadowed the racial violence to come in the late nineteenth century.[36] The First Battle of Gainesville ended on a more positive note. In February 1864, forty-nine Union cavalrymen carried out a raiding expedition on Gainesville, a town then behind Confederate lines. Hours after their occupation had begun, however, a black man approached the Union commander with grave news: two battalions of Confederate cavalry were bearing down on them. Newly liberated African Americans rushed to the aid of the beleaguered troopers and threw up a barricade of cotton bales on the outskirts of the town.

A witness to the battle marveled at how many blacks joined the out-gunned cavalrymen:

> Another, who had been a house servant, brought in an Enfield rifle, which his master had set up against a fence, while superintending the work of the field hands. Bringing the weapon into the town, he insisted on being allowed by Capt. Marshall to strike a blow for the liberation of his race. The negroes who were in the town procured clubs, and begged for permission to fight on the side of the Yankees.[37]

With the aid of these newest freed people, the 40th Massachusetts repulsed a Confederate cavalry force more than twice its size. As the Union detachment evacuated the following day, more than thirty former slaves from the county enlisted in the U.S. armed forces.

African American slaves who were not able to reach Union lines found their own ways to resist. Foreshadowing a conflict that would move to the center stage in the aftermath of the Civil War, black Floridians demanded more autonomy at work and a say over the products of their labor.[38] Catherine Hopley, an English governess for Florida's wartime governor, John Milton, charged that his slave laborers had become incorrigible, demanding high prices for the produce that they sold to Mrs. Milton and disobeying orders whenever possible. The enraged visitor began "cuffing" Milton's female domestic workers to restore order, but found that "the result of my 'cuffing' was wholly ineffectual. The negro was more dogged, stolid, and stubborn than ever."[39] After striking another female slave who refused to follow her orders, Hopley saw herself as the real victim of this highly charged conflict between mistress and slave, noting that "I came off so much the greater sufferer, that I concluded the means did not answer the purpose; and if I lived twenty years more in the South, nothing would ever induce me to strike a negro again."[40]

When the 3rd U.S. Colored Troops entered Tallahassee at the end of the Civil War, African Americans poured onto the streets to cheer their liberators. A black trooper tried to capture the glory of the moment: "The people of color were glad to see us, and cheer after cheer rent the air as we marched through the principle streets, led by the gallant Brevet Brigadier Gen . . . with colors flying and our band playing (John Brown's marching on.) The would-be rebels looked on in silence, not daring to speak above a whisper."[41] White observers noted with varying degrees of amusement (or chagrin) that black Floridians joyously sang, "We'll hang Jeff Davis on a sour apple tree, as we go marching on," to the tune of "John Brown's Body" when the Confederate president was captured by U.S. forces after the war.[42] African Americans would revive the memory of emancipation in their oral histories, public gatherings, and church ceremonies, and it was a moment that served as a catalyst for decades to come.

What did freedom mean to African Americans in the nineteenth century? A Key West man interviewed by Whitelaw Reid shortly after the end of the Civil War answered this question in an unforgettable manner. When the young journalist arrived at the Key in the entourage of Chief Justice Salmon P. Chase, locals insisted that the group visit the two-room cottage of Sandy Cornish, a former slave. Cornish hailed from Maryland and had been brought to Florida to work as a slave laborer on Florida's expanding railroad system.[43] His wife had purchased her freedom earlier and followed him to Key West in 1839. Nine years later, he had earned enough money to purchase his freedom, but before he and his wife could embark upon their new life, disaster struck. A gang of slave speculators abducted Cornish and determined to squeeze a profit from his remaining years. After beating and hog-tying him, the white men locked him in a jail to await the dreaded ship that would carry him down to the New Orleans slave market.

Sandy escaped from the jail and fled home, where he and his wife devised a plan to keep his freedom. Returning to the public square, he let out a great shout to rouse the local populace, including his captors. He then pulled out a knife and cut both of his Achilles tendons to shreds. He next drove the knife into his hip and cut a "hole ten inches long, and four inches deep, till my leg hung useless." Finally, Sandy took a hatchet and hacked his left hand to a bloody pulp. Showing his horrific scars to Reid, the former slave declared, "I would cut open my belly, and pull out de entrals before 'em. But dat I wouldn't go down to New Orleans for a slave agin, for I was free." Sandy mutilated his body to preserve the life he shared with his wife from a fate he judged to be worse than death. Freedom for this former slave was not an abstract proposition; it meant control over his body and his destiny. He understood how tenuous liberty was.

Cornish's plan succeeded: after he recovered, he and his wife rebuilt their lives, helped to found a church, and became two of "the most respected citizens of Key West."[44] The self-emancipated slave's chronicle signaled the priorities that freedpeople placed on rebuilding family ties that had been shattered by slavery as well as creating institutions that would serve their community in the uncertain times ahead. At the same time, Sandy's life became part of a rich collection of oral histories that survivors of slavery passed down to bolster the dignity and identities of younger folk. After the Civil War, Cornish's home attracted visitors from far and wide who came to the island to visit this man whose life became a testament to the meaning of freedom in America.

Sandy Cornish's history demonstrates that African Americans waged their most intense battles over the right to control their lives and labor. In common with former slaves in other post-emancipation societies, black Floridians would now struggle to expand freedom's promise just as surely as their former masters and others sought to limit it.[45]

◄ 1 ►

THE PROMISE OF
RECONSTRUCTION

The lawlessness in the South since the Civil War has varied in its
phases. First, it was that kind of disregard for law which follows all
war. Then it became a labor war, an attempt on the part of impoverished capitalists and landholders to force laborers to work on
the capitalist's terms.[1]

W. E. B. DU BOIS

NEWLY EMANCIPATED FLORIDIANS rapidly grasped the connection
between economic justice and electoral politics. African Americans
believed that access to inexpensive farm land, the right to bargain with
employers, free public schools, and the elective franchise were the keys of
liberty. This was a broadly democratic vision that subordinated the whims
of the powerful to the needs of the many. A black Floridian testified in
1867 that "[freedpeople] are all seeking lands for themselves and building
houses to live in. Some have been fortunate enough to make five or ten
bales of cotton and many bushels of corn. . . . We are all looking for the
day when we shall vote, to sustain the great Republican Party."[2]

The major outlines of the African American freedom struggle in Florida
emerged in the early moments of Reconstruction in Marion County. A Bureau
of Refugees, Freedmen, and Abandoned Lands agent, Jacob A. Remley,
observed that African Americans in that rural county were organizing
themselves "for religious worship [and] the mutual relief of one another in
sickness and pecuniary distress."[3] The agent noted that African Americans
held an Emancipation Day ceremony attended by over one thousand
black citizens in order to celebrate freedom and remember slavery.

African Americans sought the federal bureau's intervention to negotiate fair labor contracts with growers and to purchase land. Remley was clearly impressed: "I have daily applications from the Freedmen on the subject, and, it is the opinion of the Location Agent that at least five hundred Homesteads will be entered in this county."[4] In response to physical attacks by vengeful whites who would not accept the end of slavery, African Americans in Marion formed armed militia units to defend their communities. Remley was astonished to discover that "the freedpeople exhibit a knowledge of their political situation and their relations to it, which could scarcely be expected from a people heretofore prohibited from acquiring a knowledge of such matters." Large planters in the area were stunned that they could not persuade former slaves to vote as they directed them to.[5] African Americans emphasized mutual aid, labor struggle, historical memory, armed self-defense, and independent voting as cultural and political acts of survival and resistance in the years immediately following the Civil War.

Black Floridians chose the elective franchise as a primary weapon in the new war to guarantee their rights, and they initially looked to the Party of Lincoln to assist them. Shortly after the assassination of Abraham Lincoln, a former slave by the name of Joseph Oats was elected by his Tallahassee peers to participate in a national delegation of African Americans who petitioned President Andrew Johnson for the right of suffrage.[6] Oats and his counterparts asked the new president to remember that he walked in the footsteps of the Great Emancipator. Frederick Douglass, the delegation's leader, bluntly told Johnson: "Your noble and human predecessor placed in our hands the power to assist in saving the nation, and we hope that you, his able successor, will favorably place in our hands the ballot, with which to save ourselves."[7] African Americans believed that the right to vote was an indispensable vehicle in the long and difficult road they would have to travel to gain true freedom.[8] A black Union soldier stationed at Jacksonville at the end of the Civil War made his case succinctly: "There is only one thing I want, that is *my vote*."[9]

Powerful forces opposed democracy in Florida. Individuals inside and outside the state hoped to transform Florida into what the *Fort Myers Press* and others called the "American Italy," a center of tourism and a commercial gateway to the world.[10] Florida was to become a land of fruit groves, resorts, and industries built on the backs of the freedpeople, who would toil for low wages with minimal citizenship rights that would in any case be controlled from above. The Florida booster took many shapes and forms; nevertheless, whether he or she was Democrat, Republican, Wall Street financier, or state guidebook writer, the emphasis was on low wages, high profits, and white domination. As one white Republican official reasoned: "Colored labor is the cheapest, and therefore just the kind suited to the South in its present condition. This fact must have weight also with capitalists, for other things being equal, the returns from an investment must increase in proportion to the cheapness of the labor employed."[11] The state's boosters were obsessed with Florida's investment climate relative to other states'—especially California's—and touted cheap labor as the state's great selling point.[12]

Florida boosters conceived of suffrage restriction—the act of preventing black workers from voting—as a strategy to promote a version of economic development that would be controlled from the top. In this regime of white business supremacy, African Americans were to be kept as powerless and poorly paid as possible. A fierce battle raged across Florida as white Floridians dueled with African American men and women over the meaning of freedom and the shape of Florida's new economy.[13]

Transplanted northerners obsessed with creating a society that ran along "business lines" would over time help transform the Republican Party into a white-controlled organization that excluded black citizens from real political representation. Wisconsin immigrant Harrison Reed, who became Florida's first Republican Reconstruction governor, was the archetypal Florida booster. According to historian Richard Nelson Current, Governor Reed did not support black suffrage and "wanted to join with . . . other prewar Floridians to form a party that could reconstruct the state in the way that would be best for business."[14] Reed denounced black workers who refused to vote the way their employers did as "ignorant tenants" and sought to replace them with immigrants from "Minnesota and other Northwestern States."[15] After succeeding in the state's 1868 Constitutional Convention in limiting the number of elective offices in Florida, Reed wrote triumphantly to the conservative railroad magnate David Yulee, "Under our Constitution the Judiciary & State officers will be appointed & the apportionment will prevent a negro legislature."[16] Republicans and Democrats would increasingly join hands across the political divide to dilute the effectiveness of the ballot in Florida.[17]

When African Americans in Florida fought for higher wages, voted independently, or tried to buy good land, they were targeted for repression.

Florida boosters associated equal citizenship with insurgency, high taxes, and "wasteful" methods of small farming that interfered with an imagined future of tourism, large farms, and extractive industries (especially timber, turpentine, and phosphate mining). Politics, the workplace, and legal segregation were fatally intertwined. Prophets of the New South who urged diversified industry, outside investment, and an end to dependence on cotton succeeded in Florida as in no other state.[18] Racial oppression would underwrite this growth strategy and create a Jim Crow system as brutal as anywhere in the Cotton South.[19]

DEMOCRACY AND DEVELOPMENT

At the dawn of Reconstruction, Harriet Beecher Stowe journeyed to her newly purchased St. John's River plantation intent on building a new Florida. The author of *Uncle Tom's Cabin* noted, "My plan of going to Florida, as it lies in my mind, is not in any sense a worldly enterprise . . . My heart is with that poor people whose course in words I have tried to plead, and who now, ignorant and docile, are just in that formative stage in which whoever seizes has them."[20] Stowe believed ex-slaves needed the right to work more than they needed the right to vote. Like her brother Henry Ward Beecher, Harriet Stowe believed that reconciliation between former slave and slave master should take precedence over politics:

> Henry takes the ground that it is unwise and impolitic to endeavor to force negro suffrage on the South at the point of the bayonet. His policy would be, to hold over the negro the protection of the Freedman's Bureau until the great laws of free labor shall begin to draw the master and servant together; to endeavor to soothe and conciliate, and win to act with us, a party composed of the really good men at the South.[21]

The author asked her youngest brother, the Rev. Charles Beecher, to set up a "line of churches" along the St. John's River to train African Americans in the regimens of obedience and correct religious practice. The Episcopal Church, Stowe felt, was "the best system for training immature minds such as those of our negroes. The system was composed with reference to the wants of the laboring class of England, at a time when they were as ignorant as our negroes now are."[22] A white Episcopal minister from New York who settled in Florida concurred in Stowe's assessment, noting,

"I can heartily say that the colored man has my sympathy, that his condition commands it, and that I am anxiously solicitous to make him useful to himself and his employer. To effect this, kind feelings between him and the white man are essentially necessary; and I most earnestly hope that all who wish well to the poor African, will, in their efforts to benefit him, bear this in mind."[23]

Work discipline, racial reconciliation, and submission to white authority—this philosophy eventually united former abolitionists, clergy, Republicans, northern editors, and southern entrepreneurs into a common world view that emphasized varying degrees of black subordination. Harriet Beecher Stowe posed the question commonly asked by Yankee investors and plantation owners alike: "Who shall do the work for us? Is the inquiry in this new State where there are marshes to be drained, forests to be cut down, palmetto-plains to be grubbed up, and all under the torrid heats of a tropical sun."[24] Stowe assumed that African Americans were biologically better suited for toil in hot and humid weather than whites were.[25] The only problem, she believed, was that generations of toiling for no wages had destroyed the freedpeople's work ethic.[26] She was going to have to teach them.

Stowe quickly became embroiled in a dispute with two African American domestic workers, "Minnah" and "Judy." Neither woman was a stranger to the regimen of the plantation. Minnah's back was severely scarred with lash marks that were, as Stowe admitted, "the tyrant's answer to free speech." But Stowe was unable to compel Minnah to work properly. "Such a heap of clothes to be washed all in one day! It was a mountain of labor in Minnah's imagination," Stowe marveled, "and it took all our eloquence and our constant presence to keep her in good humor. We kept at Minnah as the only means of keeping her at work."[27] Stowe lamented that the newly emancipated domestic workers did not understand the value of a full day's work. "Democracy never assumes a more rampant form than in some of these old negresses," Stowe complained, "who would say their screed to the king on his throne, if they died for it the next minute."[28]

The author of *Uncle Tom's Cabin* portrayed Minnah as "kinky" and "argumentative" while referring to Judy as "a fat, lazy, crafty, roly-poly negress."[29] Judy incurred Stowe's wrath by downing her scrub brush and iron in order to fix regular meals for her husband, who was a foreman on the plantation. In Stowe's eye's, Judy had erred by letting family responsibilities take priority over domestic work. Stowe tightened up on work discipline and began her "lessons" anew. While Minnah and Judy saw domestic labor as only one component of the day's work rhythm—one that would have to be integrated with the tasks a black woman was expected to perform for her family and community—Harriet Beecher Stowe envisioned domestic labor as a total commitment.

Stowe demoted the troublesome Minnah to field labor and subsequently hired a "trained, accomplished, neat" African American cook from Jacksonville, but lost her also. The black woman left for Jacksonville to take up a better-paid position as a cook in a large hotel. "Such has been the good fortune of all the well-trained house-servants since emancipation," Stowe blustered. "They command their own price."[30] What the former antislavery advocate could not see was that the African American women were not interested in receiving lessons in how to work. They wanted fair pay, dignity, and a measure of control in the domestic workplace. After all, they were the ones doing the work. Most reform-minded whites seemed oblivious to this fact. "Instead of being teachable and submissive," another white employer in Stowe's neighborhood complained, "[Susy] is pert, makes answers and excuses—and still does not do what is required until after a good deal of insistence."[31] From a newly freed worker's perspective, however, this kind of negotiation over the terms of employment was perfectly logical. An African American minister affirmed, "It has been said that the Negro here will not work, that they are becoming indolent and vicious. The facts are, they have become tired of working without pay . . . those who have considered it their God-given right to swindle the negro out of the hard earned money due him are left without help."[32] African American women creatively tried to expand the meaning of freedom in their workplaces, and dared to test out the new possibilities of emancipation.[33]

Harriet Beecher Stowe's belief that African Americans were incapable of self-directed work coincided with the beliefs of native white southern employers.[34] W. E. B. Du Bois noted: "It was accepted as absolutely true by most planters that the Negro could not and would not work without a white master."[35] A year before Stowe arrived in Florida, the state legislature took this ideology to its logical extreme. In tandem with their counterparts in the former Confederacy, Florida's lawmakers passed a "Black Code" that subjected African Americans to forced labor as well as vagrancy and compulsory apprenticeship laws. The whipping post was the dominant method of punishment. Florida's Black Code also mandated segregation in public transportation as well as in religious and public meetings. Interracial marriage was forbidden, and assault on a white woman carried the penalty of death. White legislators denied black citizens the ballot, noting with satisfaction that their counterparts in Connecticut and Wisconsin had in effect recently done the same thing.[36] These infamous statutes would be struck down by the biracial democracy during Reconstruction. Nevertheless, the state would resurrect many of them as the foundations of legal segregation were laid in the final two decades of the nineteenth century.[37]

Harriet Beecher Stowe's pen once thundered with righteous indignation about slavery, but she was strangely silent about Florida's draconian Black Codes, calculated to bring a return to slavery in her adopted state. Conversely, Stowe was positively joyous about the potential of Florida, publishing her observations in widely read publications such as the *New York Tribune, Atlantic Monthly,* and *Harper's Magazine,* and encouraging northern migration to Florida. Stowe approved "all the money circulating in the State [that] comes from Northern immigrants," and she sought to provide these affluent immigrants with useful advice.[38] Like many of her northern contemporaries who were sympathetic to the freedpeople, Stowe could not envision African Americans as independent citizen workers with the ability to chart their own destinies. At best, she conceived of black people as a dependent working class. "We give the judgment of a practical farmer accustomed to hire laborers at the North and South," Stowe wrote, "and as a result of five years' experiment on this subject, he says that the negro laborer *carefully looked after* is as good as any that can be hired at the North."[39] Going one step further, an "Ex-Milwaukeean" farmer in Florida remonstrated, "They [black workers] are great, overgrown children, and the height of a darky's ambition is to sit on a jury or attend a political meeting."[40] He went on: "It is this uncertain condition of farm labor that has bankrupted very many northern men, who have come south since the war to raise cotton with 'free labor.'"

Democracy would have to take a back seat to development. James Woods Davidson, author of *The Florida of Today: A Guide for Tourists and Settlers,* lectured: "The future fortunes of the negroes are largely in the hands of the controlling race, and they themselves will probably have little to do in shaping it; and doubtless the less they have to do with it the better."[41] The Florida booster sold an image of Florida as the "Land of Flowers" where "sick Yankees" and wealthy Europeans would spend their money.[42] The *Edinburgh Courant* wrote: "What Italy is to Europe, Florida is to the States of America, but in a much more pronounced degree."[43] A developer from Leesburg boasted, "Our climate is unequaled by Southern

Italy, nor can Naples boast of bluer skies than ours, or Florence of sweeter moonlight than falls so softly on the unruffled waters of our lovely lakes."[44] At the bottom of this entrepreneurial plan rested a disfranchised and powerless black population whose low wages and hard work would underwrite the booming agricultural, service, and shipping sectors.[45] In this scheme, the new Florida was to rest on compulsion not cooperation. One Florida booster wrote, "Some of the niggers are industrious and are doing well—in many cases they are doing better than the whites as they stand this hot climate better than the whites, but take them as a class, they are lazy and worthless, and will not work unless compelled by necessity."[46]

In all post-emancipation societies the path of economic growth has had a decisive impact on the practice of democracy.[47] Just how "free" would newly freed black workers be? Larger industrial and agricultural interests sought to divert former slaves from exerting real political power because they believed that their investments were threatened by popular rule. The New York and Mobile Turpentine Company's 1866 corporate prospectus presented this argument clearly:

> The labor question, now nearly settled, has rendered all branches of industry in the South uncertain during the past year. This difficulty we no longer anticipate, as the freedmen, realizing that "liberty" does not mean "idleness," but that to work is a necessity, remain more permanently on the plantations. The Southern men themselves are ready to treat fairly with their former slaves, and Northern men understand more fully the proper way in which to manage the peculiar disposition of the blacks. . . . Politics yield to business, and every one is striving to rebuild his shattered fortunes.[48]

Oliver Martin Crosby's book *Florida Facts: Both Bright and Blue* epitomizes the philosophy of the Florida booster. *Florida Facts* was an investment guide for ambitious settlers and capitalists. Crosby wrote: "The Negro question in the South to-day is as unsettled as are the labor, socialistic, and emigration questions in the North, and with many characteristics in Unison. . . . The Negro Problem will assume a new form to even the most rabid abolitionist, after a residence in Florida."[49] Independent African American laborers represented a threat to economic development. "While the African is as necessary in clearing away forests and in hard manual labor as the Irishman is at the North, now that he is free he has no idea of working more than is barely necessary to keep him in pork and grits."[50] Citing a northern employer who had relocated to Florida only to face off with an uncooperative black work force, Crosby asserted, "With all the progress claimed for the colored man, it will be ages before the negro as a rule is a thrifty, honest laborer, and a town where negroes are in the majority has an 'incubus' indeed."[51] In Crosby's New South, race, labor, politics, and economic growth were intertwined. Like Harriet Beecher Stowe, the author of *Florida Facts* was not a native Floridian; he wasn't even a southerner. Indeed, Oliver Martin Crosby wrote "From a Northerner's Standpoint" in order to aid "Intending Settlers, Tourists, and Investors" hoping to make their fortunes in Florida. His work was part of an avalanche of guidebooks, corporate prospectuses, and travel narratives that contributed to an emerging white consensus that the economic expansion of Florida depended on the subjugation of black labor.

FIGHTING FOR THE RIGHTS OF LABOR

Freedpeople articulated a distinctive political philosophy during Reconstruction that contrasted sharply with that promoted by outside financiers, plantation owners, and corporations. Black Floridians emphasized landownership and labor mobility as bulwarks against oppression. In the port towns, black workers organized unions, enforced work rules, and fought for shorter hours.[52] African American farm laborers attempted to use the short-lived Freedmen's Bureau to bargain fair contracts with employers. African American workers believed that they would have to place firm limits on the power of former Confederate leaders, wealthy landowners (often the same individuals), and corporations in order to achieve a meaningful freedom. Leon County representative John Wallace invoked these values in an address he delivered before an audience of black union longshoremen in Pensacola. Wallace "pictured out, in glowing terms, the readiness of the rich to oppress the poor laborer. The [longshoremen] were present in large numbers, and declared that [former Confederate navy secretary] S. R. Mallory should not go to the Senate by their votes."[53]

Land, labor, and freedom were discussed in tandem, and black Floridians decried the trend of giving land and power to corporations and large landowners. African Methodist Episcopal minister and state representative Charles Pearce told congressional investigators that black farmers in Leon County "cannot get homes very well; the lands are owned by large land owners who are unwilling to sell their lands."[54] A black correspondent in Jackson County reported that African Americans there tried to secure land to build small farms, but were often displaced by railroads and larger landowners.[55] When state legislators considered a bill in 1872 that would give more privileges to corporations, African American legislators from black-majority Leon County thundered back as a body:

> Capital needs no legislation in order to provide for its use. Capital is strong enough to take care and provide for itself, but corporations are a dangerous power, especially large or consolidated corporations, and the American people fear them with distrust.
>
> We want no Tom Scotts, Jim Fisks or Vanderbilts in this State to govern us, by means of which they would influence legislation tending to advance personal interests. The great curse of Florida has been dishonest corporations, rings and cliques, with an eye single to their central interest, and if this bill is suffered to pass this Assembly, in my opinion we may look for a continuation of abuses and a usurpation of the rights of citizens who may be opposed to the evil machinations such as are generally exerted by consolidated bodies.[56]

This resolution touched the core of Reconstruction-era black politics. If African Americans could find a way to stop capital from crushing the people, then Florida—as in the days of the Seminole and African alliance—could become a sanctuary from the tyranny of modern-day slave masters. A black reporter enthusiastically wrote: "Florida is destined to become the Negro's new Jerusalem. . . . Her close proximity to Cuba, Hayti and Jamaica, makes her the great gateway between the negro tropical belt and the great Temperate Zone of the white race in the United States. . . . Here then the oppressed colored people of Georgia and intelligent and well-to-do colored men of the North must come and pitch their tents."[57] When Rev. N. B. Sterett's church was burned down by the Ku Klux Klan in Americus, Georgia, he found a safe haven in Quincy's black community, where he was protected from white violence.[58] The vision of a new land that would welcome the oppressed was part of the core ideology of the black freedom struggle in Florida.

African Americans based their hopes on Florida's large public domain—Florida had more than twice as much public land than any other southern state.[59] Black Floridians urged their counterparts to set up homesteads and find freedom. Bishop T. M. D. Ward of the African Methodist Episcopal

TABLE 1

Population of Florida, 1860–1930

	White	Black
1930	1,035,205	431,823
1920	638,153	329,487
1910	443,634	308,699
1900	297,333	230,730
1890	224,949	166,180
1880	142,605	126,690
1870	96,057	91,689
1860	77,746	62,677

SOURCE: U.S. Census Reports.

(AME) Church exulted during a visit to Florida: "The state is destined to be the home of the colored man and if the lust for power does not lead him to betray liberty, he will always wield an influence for good."[60] One correspondent wrote of black Floridians: "They all believe that there is a bright future to dawn upon this land of flowers, and they are doing all they can to encourage immigration from other States. Florida can afford homes for thousands of colored families, where they can have advantages which they cannot have in other states."[61] "I wish that the great mass of my own race, now struggling for a living in the cold regions of the North and West could be told of this land of promise," wrote Rev. John R. Scott; "here they may secure beautiful and happy homes, and the means for educating their children."[62]

Enhanced opportunities for landownership offered an alternative to white domination. When Francis Ellen Watkins Harper visited the state in 1870, she was told that nearly nine thousand African Americans had already become landowners.[63] "While I was in Florida a story was told to me," wrote Harper, "of a man whose mistress, no longer able to grasp his right arm as her property, took away his tools; deprived of them he borrowed others and went to work, and in a short time bought some for himself, and he, as I understood, was the possessor of at least seven hundred acres of land."[64] The sparseness of settlement in southern Florida provided opportunities even when landownership was not a possibility. Black farm workers were sometime able to negotiate higher wages in the southern part of the state and near the Everglades, where large landowners had difficulty recruiting labor.[65]

White Floridians believed that African Americans should become more faithful wage laborers—not landowners. Employers condemned ministers who preached about the iniquity of the wealthy, and Leon County plantation heiress Susan Bradford Eppes railed at one minister for teaching the verse: "It is easier for a camel to go through the eye of a needle than for a rich man to enter the kingdom of God."[66] After delivering a sermon in Alachua County, a black minister was accosted by two white men and criticized for the contents of his message. The minister's account is revealing:

> After he spoke to me he said, "I was just speaking to the Judge about your sermon last night and he said, 'I think you ought to have gone a little further and said to your people that they ought to be faithful to their employers.'" I then ascertained from him that he was running a large farm and had a great many of our people employed and he thought they did not do enough for the money they were getting. Then I understood why I did not go far enough for him.[67]

Members of the African Methodist Episcopal Church played an important role in rural communities by promoting small farm ownership, independence, and the dignity of labor.[68] The "Industrial and Political" platform forged by a state AME convention in 1871 unanimously adopted a resolution praising African Americans for their efforts to avoid plantation labor and achieve autonomy:

> Whereas labor is the basis of all wealth, and wealth is an absolute necessity of civilized society, and a peaceful condition of society, and security of life and property, a jealous regard for the rights of labor, are among the imperative duties of a well ordered government;
> Resolved by the convention of ministers and laymen of the African Methodist Episcopal Church in Florida, that we congratulate our people upon the rapid progress they have made in the past six years, and upon the increase of mixed industry, homestead and small farms in opposition to the ruinous plantation system. . . . we proudly point to these facts as a refutation of the slanders by our natural-born enemies, the democrats, that the freedmen do not work.[69]

African American ministers used the language of emancipation to exhort black Floridians to purchase their own homes and farms. Rev. Robert Brookens told his people in Baldwin: "In the first place a man without a home is a slave to the man that he rents from. . . . Now while our people are following up these lordly farmers they could all get settled on some Government land that is near them and build Good houses, and let their families stay there and improve them."[70] A white observer confirmed that black Floridians wanted to avoid toiling for Florida's lordly farmers: "He longed to purchase one of God's acres, where he could build his castle, and read his title clear."[71] Black Floridians struggled to become landowners and small farmers, but these endeavors were fraught with difficulties. African Americans never gained a majority in the state legislature, and successive white-dominated Florida legislatures deeded hundreds of thousands of acres of land to English land syndicates and railroads.[72] Would-be farm owners faced significant barriers to landownership, even during the life of the Reconstruction-era Southern Homestead Act.[73] "Our people are steadily securing small homesteads for themselves," wrote Rev. A. P. Miller from Lake City, "but not as generally as one might wish."[74]

Conversely, the state's boosters argued that black landownership discouraged wealthy growers from moving into Florida. The author of *A Guide into the South: An Open Gate to the Laborer, Large Returns to the Investor* tried to assure his readers that African Americans played no role in farm ownership or civic life in the state: "To those not understanding but who fear the presence of the Negro race we will state that the Negro is not in the way. He is not a land owner, except in a few instances, but lives, as a rule, in the quarter of the town set aside for him. . . . If you do not need him he does not bother you."[75] Financial observers claimed that African Americans who staked out their own homesteads robbed the state of export income. A Marion County booster griped: "The lands now under cultivation on these homesteads will probably average fifteen acres to the homestead, making 18,000 acres which have been brought under cultivation within the last four or five years, mostly by the freed people. Yet this has not added to the material wealth of the county, but has been the cause of a less production of agricultural products, especially of corn."[76]

Black Floridians also believed in the necessity of a strong, state-supported educational system that would help produce an autonomous citizenry. Education for all was to be a cornerstone of the Negro's New Jerusalem. William Cullen Bryant spoke with a teacher in St. Augustine who told him, "the colored people were so eager to learn that she gave, last summer, lessons to the washerwomen at ten o'clock in the evening, after the labors of the day were over, and found others waiting at her door for their daily lessons at six o'clock in the morning, before their work was begun."[77] Black Floridians working through church and civic organizations had to scrimp and scrape to supplement the state's educational system by raising money from hard-pressed members. By 1871, the African Methodist Episcopal Church alone had organized forty-eight Sabbath schools responsible for educating over 2,500 children.[78] After a fund-raising event held by the AME in St. Augustine in which church members pledged to raise $400 for education, a black correspondent wrote: "We are poor this year, but we hope in the future to be able to do more."[79] Emanuel Fortune reported that African Americans in Jackson County took up arms to defend their schoolhouse from whites who tried to physically destroy black education in their county.[80]

Conservative Democrats saw black education as a dangerous proposition because it led to bad work habits and high taxes. A white editor insisted: "No, education does not solve the [Negro] problem. This fact is now so well recognized that many of our people are getting tired of paying taxes to give the negro an education which tends rather to his ruin than to his betterment. He is spoiled as a laborer. He leaves the country to seek the town, and ekes out a precarious living 'in ways that are dark and tricks that are vain.' He looks upon ordinary everyday work as degrading, and hankers after a 'perfeshun.'"[81] The code phrase "getting tired of paying taxes" became a way of talking about race without mentioning race itself.[82]

INTELLIGENCE SHALL RULE THE COUNTRY INSTEAD OF THE MAJORITY

Conservative or "Bourbon" Democrats favored the same powerful institutions that African Americans most distrusted: plantations, large employers, and railroads. As a result, the Democratic Party failed to recruit large numbers of African Americans to its banner.[83] Democrats confirmed suspicions that they were the defenders of unearned privilege with crude depictions of slavery as a benevolent institution. A white political operative in Jefferson County explained why the Democrats repelled most black voters:

> A few of us have made an effort to direct political opinion among the newly enfranchised and if the old champions of Whigism and democracy of former days would give us the reins free and untrammeled, we could direct the storm but on the contrary we can never have a political meeting, that some political fossil does not regale the past with its political bearings (entirely unpalatable to the Negro). As well as Slavery and its blessings, generally winding up with a sigh for the good old days again. Thus every effort however well directed is lost by these vain regrets.[84]

African American women also foiled Democratic recruitment efforts. Like their sisters elsewhere in the South, black women viewed the elective franchise as a resource to be wielded for the good of the community, not just the individual.[85] Women defended polling places from white incursion, inflicted violence on black men who offered to sell their votes, and threatened would-be Democratic husbands with divorce.[86] When Gethro Robinson tried to vote for the Democrats in Madison County, "his sister pulled him out of line, and told him if he voted that way that she would get help and give him a good beating."[87] African American women also engaged in the art of public humiliation to shame black men into supporting the Party of Lincoln. On one occasion, female activists confronted a man leaning toward the Democratic ticket. Brandishing a black baby dressed up in chains, "they made a fearful noise, crying and screaming and told [the man] he was selling their children all into slavery."[88] African American women used their identities as mothers, wives, and sisters to convince black men that they too had a stake in electoral politics.[89]

Agricultural employers found that African American workers held distinctive political opinions that they could not effectively control. Some plantation owners halted operations, as one observer wrote, "chiefly because the planters did not wish to encourage more negroes to come into the country, as they were already so formidable a political element."[90] A transplanted New Yorker complained: "It is always something of an astonishment to find how well posted these otherwise ignorant negroes are on political matters, local events, or any important occurrence; they seem to have a secret sort of freemasonry by which they learn everything going on." This observer explained, "In all their camps were individuals who did the reading and writing; read the newspapers aloud, read the letters received by their less intelligent companions, and wrote the letter and postal-card replies." He then snarled: "Ignorant, but very cunning and unscrupulous, they would be a terribly dangerous element of society, were it not for their well-known fear of fire-arms, and their naturally peaceful disposition."[91] Frustrated in their bid for black support, conservatives turned ever more decisively in the direction of coercion and suffrage restriction.

The duel for labor control became an all-out war in Florida. At the forefront of the conservative scheme for economic improvement was the idea of a powerless and landless African American labor force.[92] One of the instruments chosen to achieve this goal was the Ku Klux Klan.[93] Black Floridians testified that KKK violence was directed by plantation owners against recalcitrant workers and ambitious black farmers who held land coveted by larger white landowners.[94] One Klan assassin in Jackson County "has been fitted out with arms and equipment, and rides a very fine horse around the county," and "There are continual . . . expressions throughout Middle Florida by men who approve of these things to this extent; They say they would give him the best horse on their plantations, if he needed it, to aid him in his operations."[95] State Senator Robert Meacham testified during the Ku Klux Klan investigation hearings: "I believe that there is some understanding with [white employers] that they will manage, in some way, to keep the colored people from having what they have justly earned."[96] Black Floridians swore that many employers refused to employ African Americans who were active in politics.[97] Rev. Charles Pearce testified that if white employers "were to concede to our people all their rights, and our people could be convinced of that fact; if they could create a confidence in our people in regard to that fact, I think it would change the matter materially."[98] However, employers who cooperated too closely with workers paid a price. Garth W. James, a Yankee farmer in northern Florida, felt satisfied that "we have fully vindicated the principle we started on, that the freed Negro under decent and just treatment can be worked to profit to employer and employee."[99] James was soon forced by vengeful whites to leave Florida for his own safety.

White Floridians used violence as a tool to show that they would rule the state by whatever means necessary. Secretary of State Jonathan Gibbs estimated that 153 black Floridians were assassinated in Jackson County alone between 1868 and 1871.[100] Emanuel Fortune, a member of the Florida House of Representatives, moved his family out of Jackson County after receiving numerous threats on his life. Testifying at the Florida Ku Klux Klan hearings, Fortune explained the conservative Democratic philosophy: "Intelligence shall rule the country instead of the majority."[101] The only way to achieve the rule of the few was through naked force. The *Palatka Daily News* yearned for the days of slavery because "the slaves who were governed strictly and evenly never gave trouble. The masters who broke the usual license on their plantations only by periodical savage punishments were always in dread."[102] Asserting "the Democrats possess all the wealth and respectability of the country," another white theorist argued that his race was justified in regaining domination over the society: "Ought not the intelligence and wealth of a State to rule the State? The 95 percent of the white voters who vote the Democratic ticket possess at least the same proportion of the wealth, intelligence and respectability of the

Gulf States, leaving for the 5 per cent of Republicans and all the negroes the remainder."[103] Black men and women who exercised leadership in their communities were targeted for reprisals. In 1873, Sister Cornelia McPherson, described as the "bone and sinew of the A.M.E. church," at Starke was assassinated—cut down at point blank range with multiple shotgun blasts—by the Ku Klux Klan.[104]

Growers in the plantation districts of middle Florida created a plan of action to seize control of the political system. Plantation owners used employers' meetings to educate each other about the scheme:

> Here are a few facts, which it would be well to state: 1st: the negro population of our country constituting the only labouring class of any importance are nearly all our political enemies & we are satisfied that the Chief reason why they have become such trifling workers is simply because they have so much to do *outside the field* to sustain the heavy weight of Radicalism & keep up the Radical Party.
>
> 2nd: Our circumstances are such that we cannot afford to allow our fields to remain uncultivated & if we are not able to get our friends as labourers we must of necessity take our enemies.
>
> 3rd: This is distasteful & repugnant to our feelings & yet we cannot afford to "cut off our noses to spite our faces."[105]

The plantation elite believed that they must achieve domination over their black political enemies before they would be able to institute a profitable system of agriculture. The main instrument for this plan was the "Black List," which targeted political activists and 10 percent of the work force for reprisal. Employers formed a club to institute the plan: "Let every member of this club bind himself to refrain from rent[ing] land or a house to, or to employ as a labourer for any consideration however small, any one whose name appears on the black List—Refuse shelter & employment to every one—Let them drift away silently from the neighbourhood by the *force of circumstances.*"[106]

ALL THE CONSIDERATION AND RIGHTS
THEY OUGHT TO DESIRE

The election of 1876 decided the fate of Reconstruction in the South. Nationally, Democrats hoped to use a national economic downturn and scandals in U. S. Grant's administration to capture the White House.

Across the South, conservative Democrats left nothing to chance in the months leading up to the election. They engineered campaigns of fraud, coercion, and violence against African American voters.[107] In Florida, large growers redoubled their efforts to intimidate plantation workers.[108] Democratic employers in Jefferson County vowed to ruin African American workers—and, implicitly, whites—who did not vote as they directed, and they published a circular to this effect:

1.   . . . we pledge ourselves, each to the other, by our sacred honor, to give first preference in all things to those men who vote for reform; and that we give the second preference in all things to *those who do not vote at all.*

2.   That we affirm the principle that they who vote for high taxes should pay for them, and that in employing or hiring or renting land to any such persons as vote for high taxes, in all such cases a distinction of 25 per cent., or one-fourth, be made against such persons. That merchants, lawyers, and doctors, in extending credit to such persons, make the same distinctions. . . .

4.   That in the ensuing year we positively refuse to re-employ one out of every three who may then be upon our places and who voted against reform and low taxes; and that a list of all such persons be published in the [newspaper], in order that we may know our friends from our enemies.[109]

African Americans in urban Florida also charged employers with pressuring them into voting the Democratic ticket during the election.[110] Employees of David Yulee's Florida Railroad Company in Jacksonville swore that the firm fired individuals who voted the "Radical ticket."[111] The railroad boss defended political coercion as a tool for improving Florida's business climate. Yulee told election investigators: "If, in view of its own interest, it was important to secure a certain government policy, as for instance, to remedy oppressive taxation and unfit appointments to office, there is no reason in morals or law why [the Florida Railroad Company] should not prefer in its services those who are disposed to promote and sustain its policy and interests."[112] The company, however, could not convince more than a small number of African Americans to vote for the party of white business supremacy. As one former employee, James Smith, testified: "I did not wait to be discharged, I quit."[113]

For decades afterwards, conservatives remembered the election of 1876 in heroic terms. The *Times-Union* crowed: "[The white man] violated the sanctity of the ballot box to save his State from shame and his community from destruction."[114] Black get-out-the-vote meetings were violently broken up. Black Republican leader Rev. John R. Scott was assaulted by a white man in the midst of a public speech in La Fayette County while gunmen attempted to assassinate Senator Meacham in Jefferson.[115] In Columbia County, "by a number of outrages on colored men before the election, and a systematic course of denying the right of others to vote on election day, many republicans were compelled to vote the democratic ticket, and others to refrain from voting at all."[116] In Levy County, "Samuel B. Hurlbut, a white man, who taught a colored school in Otter Creek precinct, had his house fired into, and frequent threats were made against his life if he should persist in voting the republican ticket at the precinct."[117] Hurlbut and his wife ultimately fled from Levy.

Braving violence and intimidation, thousands of black Floridians turned out to vote in the presidential election of 1876. This was no small feat, as groups of whites used every tactic imaginable to sabotage the election.[118] In Jackson, armed Democrats warned African Americans not to call on the local U.S. marshal for assistance, saying: " 'God damn you, let the marshal start, and there will not be a piece of him found as big as a rag, and there will not be a piece of you found as big as my hat.' "[119] Along with their beleaguered counterparts in South Carolina, Louisiana, and other southern states, black Floridians sacrificed tremendously for the principles of representative democracy. Black ballots in these states—and the electoral votes they delivered for the GOP—saved the Republicans from catastrophe. Democrat Samuel Tilden narrowly won the popular vote. However, the Republicans claimed Florida's contested electoral votes, which allowed their candidate to win the overall electoral vote. The GOP parleyed these electoral votes into a "Great Compromise" with the Democrats that gave the presidency to Rutherford B. Hayes in return for the withdrawal of federal support for Reconstruction in the South.[120]

George "Millionaire" Drew became the state's first post-Reconstruction Democratic governor in 1877. Drew was a New Hampshire man who came to Florida before the Civil War and made a fortune in the timber industry. He was a role model for northern whites who adopted "southern" attitudes on race and labor, and his election was the occasion for an exclusive interview in Horace Greeley's *New York Tribune*. Governor Drew told the *Tribune:* "The curse of this section is the thieving propensity of the blacks. . . . Only a few save any money. Out of over 200 in my employ I do not believe more than a half a dozen have laid up anything. They are great spendthrifts, and the worst thing is to pay them regularly."[121]

Millionaire Drew used the logic of racial inferiority to impose the company store system on his employees, paying them in scrip instead of real cash and reaping the profits.[122] The *New York Tribune* gushed, "The people have . . . cause for satisfaction that he is . . . an experienced business man, accustomed to dealing with large interests, and peculiarly qualified to place the disordered finances of the State on a good footing." Northern investors and southern employers were satisfied they had a man who would run the state along business lines.

In Florida, democracy was sacrificed on the altar of economic growth. A leading Democratic party historian noted that one of the most beneficial aspects of the restoration of white supremacy—ironically, called Redemption—was a rejuvenated market in state bonds.[123] J. Randall Stanley's *History of Gadsden County* explained why white entrepreneurs grasped for control of government:

> Following the war, they [Gadsden planters] wasted little time in "manor nostalgia" but directed their energies to the vital problem of recapturing political control of their state from the republican carpetbaggers and their negro satellites who, under the guise of Reconstruction, were plundering their country. With the return of white supremacy, the able descendants of the Gadsden pioneers led their state to a revival of agriculture, industry and business which today far surpasses the grandeur of the "Golden Age."[124]

While the state had hardly been "plundered" during Reconstruction, the restoration of white business supremacy spelled disaster for black Floridians. Plantation heiress Susan Bradford Eppes warmly depicted the white "supermen" who destroyed the "black Republican Serpent" by ushering in Governor Drew's inauguration in Tallahassee: "Louder and louder they grew, nearer and nearer they came. Some of these new-comers wearing red shirts, some waved red flags. Yelling like demons, they rushed into the square car-load after car-load of men, eager to help with the inauguration. Armed men they were, no idle threats and the Carpetbaggers and negroes recognized this fact and the inauguration proceeded quietly." Eppes continued: "When all was over and these men, who for ten years had been working for this end, realized that they had succeeded, that once again they had Home Rule—the famous 'Rebel Yell' went up like incense to heaven."[125]

Florida's triumphant "supermen" plunged parts of the state into chaos. Hernando County descended into virtual civil war as mass murder and courthouse burning became the stuff of everyday life.[126] Rev. Asa B. Dudley offered a harrowing account of Redemption in Jackson County:

> The democrats are now in possession of this State, and now they are showing their club foot. A few nights ago a crowd of them went to a colored man's house about three hours before day and called the man out. He came to the door—they caught him, but he got away from them, broke out the other door and made his escape. They then shot through the house but missed him; then burnt down all the dwellings on the place. His wife and six children came out, but every thing was burnt up. Now what will be the result?[127]

A white man in Duval County explained to the *New York Tribune* that northerners with money were now welcomed with open arms. Conversely, African Americans were targeted for assassination:

> There are some regions—and I speak from knowledge—where "the nigger" is not permitted to be; there are places where they have been obliged to leave their little holdings with only such things as they could carry away at a day's notice. . . . There are murders perpetrated in cold blood still unpunished and un-avenged, and it was only by a technicality—a question of jurisdiction that a certain number escaped trial and probably conviction the last year. A peaceable man was waked from sleep and taken out of his house and flogged severely, little more than a year ago. He has left the country, and the gang, well known, have never been punished. They are apparently too strong and powerful to be meddled with, and the secret organization, supposed to be of the Ku-Klux order, works its will.[128]

Harriet Beecher Stowe rushed in to defend her adopted state. In a rebuttal letter to the *Tribune,* she countered: "So far as they are to be observed in this county the Floridians are a remarkably quiet, peaceable, and honest set of people, who believe in the apostolic injunction, 'Study to be quiet and mind your own business.'"[129] Stowe reasoned: "As to the negroes, Duval County has a large population of them, who work for fair wages, and have all the consideration and rights they ought to desire." Finally, she warned that the earlier writer was guilty of ruining the state's business climate by scaring away northern investors. Stowe thought that African American labor and citizenship rights should be subordinated to capital. The bloody end of Reconstruction did not trouble her belief that all the rights that black Floridians "ought to desire" were safe with the triumphant Democrats. This belief tied Stowe to the dominant wing of the Republican Party and Rutherford B. Hayes's "Southern policy" of conciliation with the southern elite.[130] Stowe sincerely believed she was helping African Americans. Nevertheless, her dubious career as a reformer in Florida is a reminder that good intentions are not good enough, and that the ballot and political power are necessary antidotes to the paternalism of friend and foe alike. While Stowe had the last word in the *New York Tribune* debate on the end of Reconstruction, her published articles on Florida tarnished her reputation. The author spent her remaining years fending off the humiliating charge that she had recanted *Uncle Tom's Cabin,* and that she now found African Americans to be "degraded, ignorant and worthless."[131]

Northern investors applauded the triumphant march of white rule. A pamphlet put out by cotton brokers in Boston who sought to bring "Emigration and Capital" to the South published the letter of a white plantation owner in Florida who celebrated the fact that the northern Republicans were beginning to "see the folly of their ways. They see that no country can flourish under the domination of an ignorant minority, and that their best interests are to be gained only through an attempt to fix their own best security of lives and property."[132] The *Florida Times-Union* advised: "The immigrants . . . find that there is more money in being Democrats in Florida. They are generally employed by Democrats, and in two or three years it is intimated to them that Democratic is more acceptable than Republican service. They are treated better socially as Democrats and hence they go with the white majority."[133] The *Times-Union* failed to mention that transplanted northerners who persisted in genuine opposition politics became targets of less subtle forms of persuasion by prominent conservatives.

The Florida Railway and Navigation Company was heavily invested in the project of white business supremacy. The "Key Line" had carved out an important niche in Florida's rapidly expanding transportation network. With corporate headquarters in New York, the Key Line's board of officers included Wall Street giants such as E. H. Harriman, Benjamin S. Henning, and C. D. Willard. According to the railroad's lavish guide book published in 1884, the goal of the firm was to serve as a conduit connecting the sugar and coffee crops of Latin America to the consumer markets of the Mississippi and Ohio valleys.[134] Two of the company's top officers were W. Naylor Thompson and David Yulee, who had been accused by their workers of intimidating them to vote for company-approved Democrats in the election of 1876.[135] Now Thompson was the paymaster of the Key Line and Yulee was on the board of directors. The railroad's guidebook featured a story that provided white supremacists with a justification for their actions. Beginning with the "dark" era of Reconstruction, the story began:

> The "fortunes of war" worked a disastrous change in the conditions here, as elsewhere. The slaves were suddenly converted into "free American citizens," and lost no time in deserting from the great army of producers to engage almost *en masse* in the more congenial avocation of politics; the production of the staple crops ceased almost entirely; the plantation was deserted for the town and the cross-roads rendezvous, and its owner was left helpless and despairing, without an income, without capital, and without credit, but with a family to be supported, and a new future to carve out for himself under the most trying, disastrous and depressing circumstances which ever befell a prosperous and happy people.[136]

A northern-based corporation had issued an early manifesto of white Redemption in the South.[137] Investors constructed a powerful myth: Reconstruction had been a tragic era because African American workers downed their tools and deserted their plows in order to participate in politics. As a result, these propagandists argued, the state's economy had plunged into chaos. The perpetuation of this myth would serve as the most pervasive justification for the demolition of Reconstruction in Florida.[138] The same year the Key Line's guidebook was published, an apologist for Redemption asked: "Don't you remember, sir, how railroads and numberless other corporations were almost daily ground out by the carpet-bagger and negro Legislatures? . . . How different now."[139]

The forces transforming Florida into a southern state with low wages and racial oppression were not necessarily southern. It wasn't that northerners had "turned their backs" on southern blacks; indeed, they were obsessed with finding a way to control the fruits of their labor. In the same year that the Key Line published its interpretation of Reconstruction, T. Thomas Fortune, the son of Emanuel Fortune, published *Black and White: Land, Labor, and Politics in the South*. The younger Fortune argued that the oppression of black workers in the South was tied to the pauperization of labor throughout the nation. He bitterly critiqued land syndicates for taking land away from small farmers in the South, and he called out the two major political parties for falling prey to corporate influence. The Florida native asserted: "There is no fact truer than this, that the accumulated wealth of the land, and the sources of power, [are] fast becoming concentrated in the hands of a few men, who use that wealth and power to the debasement and enthrallment of the wage workers."[140] Florida's story was America's in microcosm.

In the first decade after the end of the Civil War, African Americans attempted to enlarge the meaning of freedom beyond formal equality to encompass larger questions of political economy. Black Floridians held that access to land, education, and the elective franchise and a jealous regard for the rights of labor were the keys to democratizing the New South. The foundational ideology of black politics was the belief that labor was the basis of all wealth. African Americans learned this truth in slavery, and they sought to transform Florida into a republic where powerful economic interests were subordinate to the needs of the people. In sharp contrast, white employers, investors, and the state's boosters believed that capital, not labor, was the source of Florida's prosperity. Conservatives schemed to deprive African American workers of political power in order to keep wages, taxes, and labor mobility low. Bourbons used terror, fraud, and coercion to elect governors and increasing numbers of white legislators, but they were unable to achieve their primary goal: the annihilation of black political aspirations.

⊰ 2 ⊱

THE STRUGGLE TO
SAVE DEMOCRACY

AFRICAN AMERICANS redoubled their efforts to build a democratic Florida in the final two decades of the nineteenth century. They faced enormous obstacles. Emanuel Fortune, Jr. lamented, "Southern Democrats think that the colored man who does not go to the polls to vote, who does not express his opinion when he has one is a fine fellow. But just as soon as he aspires to a political position, just as soon as he speaks up for his rights and condemns the injustice perpetrated upon colored people by the pretended preserves of law and order, he is pronounced an 'impertinent nigger.'"[1] The *Florida Times-Union* advised that one-party rule was good development policy: "The continuance of Republicanism as a distinct party in Florida is a standing menace to the State's prosperity and we should bury it out of sight."[2] Conservative whites refined an electoral system that used violence, fraud, and selective enforcement of the state's criminal codes to slash the voting rolls. In the 1880 election Cuffie Washington of Ocala was denied the right to vote because he had once been convicted of stealing three oranges, while his white neighbor A. J. Harrell was given a ballot even though he admitted "shooting a nigger."[3] Black Floridians who persisted in attempting to vote had to take up arms to defend themselves and their communities from terror on Election Day. Conservatives sought to wipe out black political activity because they realized that African American men and women were never going to accept an inferior place in the state's economic and social order as long as they could participate in the electoral system.[4]

While conservative Democrats tried to restrict the meaning of freedom, black Floridians fought to expand it. African Americans infused their search for political power with struggles for economic justice. Workers organized strikes and unemployed protests and asserted their self-respect in numerous ways. African Americans envisioned a new political party that would stave off disfranchisement, demand a "jealous regard for the rights of labor," and revive the unfulfilled promise of emancipation. Black Floridians interpreted the deal between southern Democrats and northern Republicans that ended Reconstruction as a betrayal. Civil War veteran M. M. Lewey argued, "We feel and know the many disadvantages to which colored men are subjected in this State, not only by Bourbon Democracy, but by the cold, selfish leaders of the Republican party whose only object is to have you vote for them on the day of the election while they fatten and revel on the spoils of office."[5] In order to break through this corrupt system, black Floridians forged a political alliance with dissident whites in 1884 that culminated in the creation of the Independent Party.[6] African Americans believed this interracial alliance would reduce racial violence, curb the power of corporations, and split the white vote. Lewey voiced the indignation—and determination—of black Floridians who were prepared to risk their lives in a struggle to save democracy: "those who are waiting for a realization of their imaginations when the colored man will voluntarily quit or be eliminated from politics; they will wait until the beginning of the next millennium."[7]

African American women workers led a renewed struggle for dignity even as the promise of Reconstruction crumbled. White employers and European tourists yearning to lord it over obsequious mammies and shuffling butlers were exasperated by the ways that domestics and hotel workers fought for respect on the job.[8] Black women resisted being called demeaning appellations such as "girl," "Aunty," or "nigger" at work.[9] Helen Harcourt, a columnist for the *Florida Farmer and Fruit Grower,* fumed that service workers insisted on calling each other "lady" and "gentleman" while referring to their white female employers as "women." Harcourt was offended by what she called this "ludicrous mistake."[10] She complained that African American domestics and laundry workers demanded higher wages and more dignity than white employers were willing to concede, and she sputtered: "Our chief troubles were to teach her the meaning of the words 'obey' and 'order.'"[11] A prominent English traveler bitterly criticized black household workers and advised his countrymen that they would have to bring their own "help" during their Florida vacation.[12] Domestics in larger cities such as Jacksonville organized unions to set terms of employment.[13] One disgruntled employer ran through a litany of complaints about African American domestics who he claimed "have a kind of secret society regularly organized, including both the men and women, and they meet regularly and fix their own prices for doing housework, cooking, washing, etc., and they stick right there and to the prices fixed, so you must either do your own work, not have it done at all or pay the prices."[14] Black domestics placed a higher value on the work they performed in their communities, families, and churches, and they shunned seven-day-a-week "live in" work in an employer's household whenever possible.[15]

African Americans who modified work hours to accommodate their community responsibilities angered employers, including one plantation owner who fumed: "Jack knocked off work at noon to go to Mandarin on important church business, more important than to stay and help me protect my grove from frost."[16] Managers looked for ways to impose total control over the labor force. T. Thomas Fortune gave a vivid portrait of a sawmill town on the Suwannee River that was dominated by a large plantation owner. "This man owns the entire town and all the land for miles around," noted Fortune.[17] The employer paid in "scrip," which forced employees to patronize the company store. Fortune observed: "The planters and storekeepers understand their mutual interest so thoroughly that few colored laborers on farms ever get their hands on a dollar bill."[18] Sharecropping was another weight tied around the neck of black labor. "I was informed in Florida that as a business proposition the crop-mortgage system was better than slavery," Clifton Johnson wrote. "A popular negro couplet sets forth the industrial situation thus: 'Naught's a naught, figger's a figger—All for the white man and none for the nigger.'"[19]

African Americans fought back by quitting, migrating, striking, and engaging in acts of sabotage.[20] Black Floridians were constantly on the lookout for higher wages in phosphate mines, naval stores, railroads, and the booming coal mines of Birmingham, Alabama.[21] One employer counseled: "The labor question in the South is getting to be a serious one. . . . If the planter pays moderate wages for housing his cotton, Sambo makes it high wages by the dirt and trash he will manage to pack into his picking, and swear there are none in it. Again he will pick early in the morning, to get the dew on his cotton, and leave the field early in the evening, because the cotton is dry, and won't weigh much." Growers objected to signs of initiative: "When a planter hires a number of hands to pick out his cotton, they are usually a jolly set, working like beavers as long as they find thick cotton, but as soon as it gets thin, by several pickings, or poverty of soil, they dodge off to some other farm."[22] The *Florida Dispatch* snarled: "The whole country has grown poor in the endeavor to draw an income out of the negro," and advised growers to institute more repressive measures of labor control.[23]

African American opposition to coercion and poor working conditions led some white entrepreneurs to look elsewhere for labor. Republican luminary Henry Sanford imported European farm laborers to drive wages down.[24] Jacksonville newspapers advertised plans to recruit docile "German girls" in the place of black women as domestic workers.[25] Outside firms began experimenting with the recruitment of migrant workers as a tool to keep costs down. "The best plan for securing labor, both as to cheapness and efficiency," noted the corporate prospectus of one phosphate company, "would be to carry all laborers needed to Florida from some of the Southern States. Negroes in any number would be very willing to secure employment in this way, and could be counted on to do good and efficient work. These laborers could be had for an amount not to exceed one dollar per day."[26] Good investment returns would be made by hammering down a *maximum* wage scale on African Americans. At the same time, phosphate firms paid higher wages to white workers in order to encourage separation of the races by segregating their wage levels.[27]

Lady Duffus Hardy, one of the foremost English writers of her day, visited the United States in the 1880s and became a vigorous Florida booster.[28] She proposed a colonial solution to the labor problem in Florida:

> Coloured labour is generally used, both in the house and in the fields, gardens and groves, but it is uncertain and unsatisfactory in its results; and the immigration of a few thousands of the quiet, industrious, reliable Chinese would be cordially welcomed throughout the State of Florida. They may have their drawbacks and be undesirable as citizens,

but as mechanical or field labourers or house servants they are unsurpassed, being quiet, civil, obedient and obliging; set against these their propensity for petty pilfering and lying; but these vices once acknowledge[d], you can prepare for or guard against them; their industry and faithful labour may always be relied on.[29]

What appealed to Lady Hardy and many entrepreneurs in Florida was a work force that had no political rights. "The Chinaman can't vote and doesn't drink whisky, but he could build the canal across the isthmus if called on, and do it well and cheap," one businessman argued.[30] Another booster wrote: "Politically, the Chinaman is no trouble, industrially he is a distinct gain, usually taking up lines of effort neglected by other nationalities."[31] Many of Florida's leading employers envisioned a disfranchised labor force as the key to Florida's development.

SEE HOW MANY OF OUR BEST MEN HAVE BEEN SHOT DOWN

Black Floridians struggled to hold on to the ballot in the 1880s. Their adversaries were formidable. White supremacists inflicted violence on would-be voters while conservatives used growing legislative majorities to sabotage the electoral system. Florida's newspapers provided editorial support for one-party rule and suppressed information about election improprieties. A Republican activist testified that the 1880 election in Leon County was plagued by "the use of . . . tissue tickets, violence, fraud in counting returns make the showing for the Democrats . . . the Mississippi plan was put into full operation and we were thoroughly cleaned up. Our honest republican majority of 5,000 reversed."[32] Fraud reached tragicomic proportions. A *Times-Union* report of voters' returns from Madison County in one election read: "Ballot boxes all stolen here. Can't find out a thing, but this county will surely be Democratic by about 300 majority."[33]

Terror endured well beyond Election Day. Black Floridians who gave testimony at the federal district court at Jacksonville about election fraud often paid with their lives. On his way back home to Madison County from giving testimony in a contested election case, John Bird was lynched by white vigilantes.[34] A group of African Americans who had direct knowledge of election improprieties in Jefferson and Leon Counties understood that if they testified in the circuit court, "Our lives would be in jeopardy unless we left the state."[35] After testifying in a contested election case,

Rev. H. C. Bailey of Bethel Baptist Church in Tallahassee requested armed protection from the governor:

> I have rec'd several letters, informing me if I return to Tallahassee violence and death await me. I have been advised to inform you of these things, and to know if you can guarantee protection to us. . . . My work is there, I have a congregation of six hundred members & wife & five little children. I am not afraid to come peaceably if I can, but if I can not I shall have to come & accept the situation. I am bound to be where those I love best.[36]

African Americans understood that they would have to defend themselves and their communities if they hoped to survive politically. Armed self-defense became an integral part of the black freedom struggle in Florida. GOP leader Joseph E. Lee received numerous death threats warning him to abstain from electoral politics. Lee, however, had taken precautions: "I am inhabiting a house in which we are guarded and vigilantly with lights burning . . . all that is necessary to bring the alarm bell and the tiger will be paralyzed."[37]

After Augustus Crosby testified against electoral fraud in Madison County at the district court, he was waylaid by a furious Democrat back in Madison and arrested. While he was sitting in the Madison jail, a lynch mob formed nearby. A group of African American women formed a human barricade around the jail and held off the would-be assassins until "colored men began to come armed, and the mob seeing them, went back up town to consult."[38] While African Americans were subsequently dispersed by the white militia, there was no lynching in Madison that day, and Crosby escaped to Jacksonville.[39] After his brush with death, Crosby declared: "A mild non-shooting Republican would be counted out in this election."[40]

Republican leader Malachi Martin learned firsthand the veracity of Augustus Crosby's insight by serving as a Republican poll watcher in nearby Gadsden County. While Martin attempted to count ballots inside the polling place, white "men stripped in their shirt sleeves brandishing their knives and swearing that they would kill every d—d son of a——of us . . . frequently came to the window of the polling place, shook their fists and knives at me, and calling me by the most vile names it was possible to utter, told me they would kill me as soon as I came out!"[41] While Martin watched the gathering mob with a sinking heart, African Americans from the plantation county hatched a plan to save the white man's life. "The Col[ored] men," Martin noted, "hearing the openly express[ed] determination of the

Dem[ocrat]s to kill me, sent for Arms and took position to strike the second blow. A large number of them un-armed, stood around the door and when I stepped out I was in a crowd of them who surrounded me and conducted me to a place of safety at the house of a friend where I stopped until daylight. My servants brought my team up on the street, the night was dark as pitch, a fellow whom we know, slipped up and cut their horses harness to pieces. In less than ten minutes the saddles and bridles of every Dem[ocrat] in the place was cut and the horses turned loose."[42] African Americans understood that their political survival depended on disciplined acts of self-defense.

Violence failed to corral African Americans into the party of white supremacy. On the eve of the election of 1882, a leading Democratic editor, C. E. Dyke, Sr., predicted that African Americans all over the South, including Florida, were planning to flock to the Democratic standard.[43] After the election, however, Dyke's paper grumbled that black Floridians had once again shunned his party.[44] In fact, Dyke and his allies nervously noted that in some areas the Republican vote in the state was actually *increasing*.[45] Most black Floridians continued to spurn Dyke's party as the party of privilege, railroads, and white supremacy.

African Americans employed sophisticated organizing strategies to hold out against the Bourbon onslaught at Key West. The island stood at the intersection of a brisk shipping trade in a variety of commodities, none more important over time than tobacco and cigars.[46] "We are on a little island here, cut off from the rest of the world, both civilized and uncivilized," local writer L. W. Livingston reported, "and absolutely dependent upon Havana, New Orleans, Tampa and New York, especially the last named place."[47] Migration from these ports brought a diverse working class together. Livingston noted: "There is such a conglomeration of American colored and white folks, Cubans, colored immigrants from Nassau and Conchs [white Bahamians], and such an admixture of them all that it is impossible to determine where the line begins and where it ends."

African American activists wove together a multinational alliance. The insurgent Knights of Labor formed a major presence on the island and gave local workers linkages to a potent national labor organization.[48] Republican meetings in Key West were boisterous and bilingual. As black newspaper editor John Willis Menard explained to Joseph Lee: "Clubs of Laboring men," consisting of Afro-Cuban and indigenous black workers, made up the rank and file of the Republican Party on the island.[49] "There is generally at least one speech in Spanish and at a Republican meeting I attended recently a Cuban delivered two speeches," noted Livingston, "one in English and one in Spanish."[50] White Republicans found themselves participating as junior partners in this coalition.[51]

L. W. Livingston called Key West the "Freest Town in the South."[52] Livingston wanted his readers in the North to understand what lay at the bottom of the Republican coalition's success: the ability of black Floridians on the Key to defend themselves from white assaults. Livingston affirmed that African Americans in Key West were "well equipped with the means of offensive and defensive warfare, as conducted in times of peace, with a good sprinkling of old soldiers among them, and the beauty . . . is that they are not the only ones that knows their power and invincibleness." Livingston was referring to black veterans of the American Civil War as well as immigrant veterans of the Ten Years War (1868–1878) in Cuba.[53] He noted that Key West had no white state militia company and that its unique geographical position shielded it. "The usual method throughout the South, as your readers are aware," wrote Livingston,

> when colored men attempt to defend themselves against outrage and murder is for some one to notify the governor of the State that the Negroes are "rising." The governor calls out by telegraph the militia of the town in which the little soldiers array themselves on the side of the whites, and they all fire into the Negroes. . . . Should the governor order out the militia here, it would take a day to get over even if the boat should be just starting, but the boat only makes two trips a week. . . . Only a man of war can storm Key West and, happily, they are owned and directed by a higher and little better power. We only want to show to the world how invincible we are, not that we anticipate any trouble whatever, for we believe all concerned are averse to it.

The political tensions that endangered this enclave of black political power did not escape Livingston's attention.[54] In his conclusion, however, he emphasized the connection between race, politics, and armed self-defense: "The idea I wish to convey is, that colored men here speak and act their sentiments, with none to molest or make them afraid, and there is nothing cowardly and servile about them."

The rest of Florida teetered on the brink of disaster as murder and mayhem spread like wildfire across the state. From Alachua County, former U.S. Representative Josiah Walls ruminated on the crisis:

> See how many of our best men have been shot down, for their lasting fidelity to some man, who is safely looking on, from some northern city

or some safe place in the State. I tremble with care for my wife and baby, when I reflect, and remember how near, an occurrence of nearly the same kind was at Arredonda for the same cause. And you may imagine, that is no pleasant information for me to read the manner in which our friends were murdered at Madison.[55]

THE INDEPENDENT PARTY

Over two hundred African American activists convened an emergency meeting in 1884 to confront the political crisis engulfing the state.[56] The delegates met in Gainesville and explained their purpose by recounting the state's descent into tyranny: "Let the last eight years of proscription tell. Let the hundreds of convictions in justice courts for the purpose of disfranchisement, tell. Let the frauds and counting out at the ballot box tell. Let the exclusion of colored men from the jury box, and all the other discriminations against colored men, tell."[57] Conservatives eliminated thousands of African Americans from Florida's voting rolls for minor criminal offenses including petty larceny, and poll observers in the 1880 election swore before a congressional committee that "they [white Democrats] challenged men who they said were convicted who they knew were not convicted."[58] Election officials frequently refused to allow African Americans their lawful right to take an oath swearing that they were residents of Florida—and hence, qualified to vote—while new European immigrants were "permitted to vote without exhibiting any written evidence of being a citizen of the United States."[59] An observer of state politics provided a grim portrait: "This is the situation. The State is really Republican, but by tissue ballots, false counts and violence in the back counties the will of the people is effectually frustrated."[60] At the same time, the Bourbon Democracy was helping railroads and land syndicates loot Florida's public domain at the expense of the state's small farmers, black and white alike.[61]

The Gainesville delegates suggested a new course of action to save democracy: an alliance with whites who were willing to break ranks with the business wing of the Democratic Party. Black Floridians looked with great hopes toward the interracial "Readjuster" coalition in Virginia that had recently:

abolished the whipping post; re-enfranchised the colored people of that State; made free speech possible; commenced the obliteration of the color-line in politics and in civil intercourse which was revived by the

Bourbons in the recent contest . . . put impartial judges on the bench, elevated colored men to the school board; and appointed colored teachers to teach colored schools.[62]

James Dean, a graduate of the Howard University law department and president of the Gainesville Conference, used his keynote address as a brief for equal citizenship. Dean itemized the lost wages that African Americans suffered in slavery and charged that these funds should be applied to rebuilding the state. He envisioned a new society where "education substitutes the teacher for the sheriff, the schoolhouse for the prison, and the workshop for the poorhouse."[63] Dean's address was a complete rejection of politics under white rule.

African American activists used the Gainesville Conference as a catalyst to launch a political coalition with dissident whites. This coalition grew into the Independent Party in Florida, which ran a full slate of candidates in the election of 1884. Black organizers believed an alliance with "Anti-Bourbon" whites would split the white vote and neutralize election-related violence.[64] It was also a rebuke of the Republican Party's retreat in the face of racial oppression. Josiah Walls supported the Independent cause because: "I see [African Americans] shamefully ignored by the leaders of the Republican organization; because I believe it is to the best interest of the laboring classes generally to free themselves from either of the old parties in the State."[65]

The Independent Party's platform was a direct challenge to eight years of conservative misrule. Independents proposed an overhaul of the state's educational system as well as the corrupt law-enforcement system that disfranchised blacks for stealing poultry while allowing white murderers to go free on a regular basis.[66] The party's central plank read: "We favor free and unrestricted suffrage, and sternly oppose any attempt to abridge it by imposing any educational or property qualification."[67] The Independents proposed a public commission to curb the power of railroads and other corporations. They attacked the pro-corporate bent of the Democrats: "We condemn the policy of the so-called Democratic party in selling lands to the speculator at 25 cents per acre, and denying them to the settler at the same price."[68] An African American from Columbia County asked: "How is it that the State authorities (Democratic) sell land to foreign millionaires at twenty-five cents per acre, and refuse to sell the same land to the poor whites and blacks who have squatted on these lands at not less than $1.00 per acre? And now it is next to impossible for them to buy it at any price. And we hereby demand the overthrow of the present Bourbon-Democratic Administration."[69] Black Floridians did not plan to be junior partners in this new coalition. As one observer noted: "They look upon the Independent movement as one calculated to lift them beyond the pale of white men's influence or dictation."[70]

African Americans envisioned a party that would eliminate white supremacy and restore popular government. J. Willis Menard of Key West wrote: "Independentism at the South means increased internal improvement, material development, increased facilities of popular education, the impartial administration of justice, better local governments, fair elections, and the elimination of the 'color line.' "[71] John Wallace reported from the heart of middle Florida that white men were threatening to leave the Democratic Party en masse: "I mean white men *who have* for years supported the democratic party, who declare that at least half of the white people will support the independent movements if the colored people will come out in convention and declare their willingness to support independent men that will stand by and protect *every right* that the Constitution guarantees to our people."[72] The possibility of shattering the Solid South before it had ossified seemed to be within reach.

Democrats counterattacked by defending land sales to outside investors, white rule, and the "Lost Cause" of the Confederacy.[73] Democrats referred to the Independents as "niggers," white outcasts, and the "Great Unwashed" of Florida.[74] Conservatives disparaged the premise of universal public education and promised lower taxes in order to rally their forces.[75] Democracy was seen as a threat to economic development and existing property relations.[76] A conservative theorist argued: "it is only reasonable for the good of all that laws affecting property should be passed only by those who are directly interested in the common welfare, and as society in Florida is now constituted, a controlling influence is often exerted at the polls by a class of voters who pay nothing in the shape of taxes for the privileges and protection awarded under the law. To establish the principle, 'No taxation without representation,' we cut ourselves loose from our mother's apron strings; we must now in self defense by measures strictly peaceful and entirely lawful establish the principle, equally important: 'No representation without taxation.' "[77]

The political initiative shown by African Americans and the defection of some whites into the Independent movement led conservatives to deliberate on ways to permanently disfranchise black Floridians. Democratic leader Richard Call Long premiered one of the new suffrage restriction strategies in a series of campaign speeches he made with the 1884 Democratic gubernatorial candidate, Edward Perry. Perry and Long identified the Independent movement as a grave threat to Florida's economic progress.[78] Long, the descendant of one of the state's antebellum governors, railed: "In this State we have a multiplicity of political parties, but out of all the isms or theories which are being advanced and advocated there can be but two words spelled—one of these is 'white man' and the other 'nigger'—and this practically is the only question which the white men of this State are called upon to solve at the coming election." Long symbolically shook his fist at black Florida and shouted: "One thing you might as well understand first as last, and that is you are not going to rule this government, and we are getting tired of having our minds diverted from questions which affect the prosperity and material advancement of the State by your pretensions at each recurring election in this direction. . . . You have opposed us in everything we have undertaken since your emancipation."[79] Long repeated the Democratic mantra that white Floridians were "tired of this school tax."[80] He argued that restricting the right to vote was the key to breaking the deadlock between white employers and African American workers in Florida:

> We are going to have a Constitutional Convention in less than eight months; that convention will be controlled by white men; no one but white men will be allowed a vote there; the angel Gabriel himself will not be allowed a vote; and don't you forget that the status of the nigger as a factor in the politics of this State will then be fixed. Then we want them to come. There are thousands of niggers in Georgia and Alabama who are working from 25 to 50 cents per day, while, in South Florida especially, we are being compelled to pay from one dollar and a quarter to two dollars a day.

R. C. Long promised something for every white man. If the business wing of the Democratic Party triumphed over the "great unwashed," employers would be free to pay low wages, landowners would pay less taxes, and the poorest white man would have more privileges than the angels themselves. If they proved their loyalty, white men would be repaid by full citizenship—but only if black Floridians were banished from the polity forever. Long tried to enhance the psychological value of racial supremacy by titillating his audience with the specter of race war. "There never has been any serious conflict in this State between the white man and the nigger," Long admonished. "That occurred in this county, and then we had a barbecued nigger. I don't want to see a recurrence of this, but don't you forget that we are not going to see this government go into the hands of anybody who promises you half of the offices." By appealing to male fantasies of masculine power unleashed, Long sadistically played the race and gender cards.[81]

The 1884 election was the ultimate test of the viability of interracial politics in Florida. In R. C. Long's scheme, white supremacy would be a precious resource that all white men in Florida would own; it would prevent whites from allying themselves with a politically and economically debased population of African Americans. The election returns were sobering. The Independent Party carried counties with large African American populations including Leon, Jefferson, Alachua, Marion, and Duval.[82] Once again, however, fraud and terror undermined the turnout. Whites who broke ranks with the Bourbons faced reprisals. "You know I am a Republican," wrote one white farmer, "but I did not dare to vote on Tuesday. If I had voted—voted the Republican Ticket—I would have put my life and my property in peril. So I kept away from the polls."[83] Most whites stayed with the Bourbons. The Independent movement went down to a crushing defeat.

The massacre of the electorate began in earnest. The Constitutional Convention that Long promised his constituents came in 1885. It empowered the state to institute a poll tax, the key strategy in suffrage restriction.[84] The new state constitution also required all county officers to be bonded, ensuring that only wealthier individuals or those who could procure bond money from the rich held state offices.[85] In the rural counties, white supremacists used a combination of fraud, violence, and the new voting laws to suppress voter turnout in the 1888 election.[86] The following year, the state legislature followed South Carolina in adopting a multiple voting box law. The new state poll tax law targeted low-income voters for disfranchisement while the confusing multiple voting box system discriminated against voters with lower levels of literacy. Stringent registration requirements also placed greater power in the hands of election officials who were eager to sweep African Americans off the voting rolls.[87] The *Quincy Herald* exulted in the triumph of one-party rule in the 1890 election: "Such a quiet election day has never before been known in this county. The entire Democratic ticket was elected without opposition, there being no republican candidates in the field."[88] The effective disfranchisement of African Americans in Florida's rural districts and small towns was nearing completion.[89]

THE JOY OF THE STRIKERS

Conservatives turned their attention to urban Florida. The *Times-Union* opined, "It is childish to think that the white vote of the State, being virtually solid for [the Democratic Party] cannot control a small per cent of at least of their negro employees, just as white employees are controlled in the north."[90] Yet, even as the ballot was being stolen in the hinterlands, black laborers in the port towns intensified their efforts to exert real political and economic power. African American dock workers, warehousemen, and tobacco factory operatives in Pensacola, Key West, and Jacksonville joined the nationally renowned Knights of Labor and led a series of strikes—sometimes in solidarity with their white counterparts—aimed at the state's most powerful employers.[91] While African American workers sought to influence municipal politics, state legislators searched for a way to destroy the black electorate in urban Florida.

In January 1887 a coalition of black and white longshoremen's unions struck Pensacola shipping firms in tandem with black fertilizer factory operatives who walked out of a major warehouse in the port.[92] Interracial labor activity in Pensacola was bolstered by a vibrant Knights of Labor assembly.[93] T. Thomas Fortune's pro-labor *New York Freeman* reported that the "Colored and White Workmen Unite[d] Against Oppression" walking out and demanding "better wages $2.50, $2, and $1.50 per day."[94] The fertilizer operatives formed their own union, the "Guano Association," to ensure that their demands were addressed within the biracial coalition.[95] This was more than a fight for higher wages. Longshoremen protested a change in work rules that made loading ships more hazardous to life and limb.[96] When the officers of Stevedores' Associations 1 and 2 directed a walkout against poor safety conditions, shippers responded by hiring nonunion employees or "scabs" to load and unload cargoes.

Over one thousand black and white longshoremen proceeded to Wittich's Wharf in Pensacola to present a carefully worded resolution to the shippers. When union officers attempted to present the document to businessmen David Lear and John Ward, the two drew their pistols and threatened to shoot the delegation. This was a very unwise decision. The unarmed longshoremen responded by pelting their bosses with a "volley of rocks and other missiles, one of which knocked Ward insensible and others

TABLE 2

Florida's Urban Population, 1860–1920

(totals by race)

	Jacksonville		Key West		Miami		Orlando		Pensacola		Tampa	
	African American	Anglo-American	African American	Anglo-American	African American	Anglo-American	African American	Anglo-American	African American	Anglo-American	African American	Anglo-American
1860	985	1,133	591	2,241	N/A	N/A	N/A	N/A	1,087	1,789	N/A	N/A
1870	3,989	2,923	989	4,027	N/A	N/A	73	1,018	1,264	2,083	222	574
1880	3,659	3,991	N/A	N/A	N/A	N/A	N/A	N/A	3,291	3,554	N/A	N/A
1890	9,801	7,372	5,654	12,390	N/A	N/A	1,031	1,822	5,743	6,001	1,607	3,900
1900	16,236	12,158	5,562	11,526	N/A	N/A	N/A	N/A	1,105	9,182	4,382	11,425
1910	29,293	28,329	5,515	14,409	2,258	3,209	1,416	2,478	10,214	12,758	8,951	28,790
1920	41,520	49,972	4,030	14,693	9,270	20,269	2,552	6,727	10,404	20,624	11,531	40,045

SOURCE: U.S. Census Reports.

struck Lear, badly bruising him about the head." Adding insult to injury, a loading crew of scabs deserted their patrons, jumping off the docks, "and from that moment were made the targets for rocks and stones whenever seen with their heads above water." Facing hundreds of determined unionists, Pensacola police joined in the retreat. The next day, the unions sought to reopen negotiations. Instead, the white state militia was deployed to escort a group of strikebreakers through the pickets. The white militia did not count on the interracial solidarity of the unions. A black journalist wrote: "Tuesday was a laughable day indeed. The Escambia Rifles (white) marched out with glittering muskets and bayonets to make the poor and oppressed colored and white men fall in submission; but they were badly mistaken, for as soon as they got as far as the workmen cared to have them come, they were surrounded. The workmen politely pointed out the way and they [the militia] willingly went back to their armory."[97]

Rev. G. W. Witherspoon, ranking elder of the Pensacola district of the AME Church and a member of the city council, appeared the following day to escort the scabs across the picket line. Not only did the strikers stop the scabs; African American workers reserved some very harsh words for Rev. Witherspoon, who quickly decided to leave the scene. As the *Freeman's* writer caustically noted, "It would make a government mule mad to see how quick some colored men, who say that they are leaders, hasten to do anything detrimental to the poor colored and white people, simply to please the bankers and railroad officials."[98] The picket line held another day, and employers capitulated. The *Freeman* celebrated: "Thus ended the strike, to the joy of the strikers and a majority of outsiders."

The following summer, African American timber and dock workers in Fernandina squared off against a powerful employers' association led by George "Millionaire" Drew, former state governor. Demanding higher wages and better working conditions, several hundred black workers formed a union in August and went out on strike the following month.[99] "The result was a complete tie-up of business," as the *Times-Union* raged; "the vessels lay idly at the wharves. Out of nearly five hundred men employed on the river front, only about twenty remained. A few of these were pounced upon by the strikers and severely beaten."[100] Governor Drew's association imported black strikebreakers from Madison County, but these men were curtly ordered by the union members to go home. The state intervened and Governor Edward Perry ordered the county sheriff to break the strike: "At any cost lawless men must not be allowed to prevent industrious ones from working and earning honestly their wages."[101]

When the beleaguered sheriff threatened to use force to end the strike, a delegation of three hundred union men responded: "They would allow no one to work but themselves, and told the Sheriff to bring on the militia and they would take their pop-guns away from them." This time, however, African American workers did not enjoy the support of white workers. Governor Perry ordered in units of the white militia and authorized mass arrests to crush the strikes and reopen the docks.[102]

The most important strike in Gilded Age Florida was waged at the Gulf Coast port of Apalachicola. On January 13, 1890, hundreds of African American sawmill, factory, and dock workers resolved to win the ten-hour day, regular payment in lawful U.S. currency, and collective bargaining rights. Workers and their allies, including West Indian immigrant labor leader E. P. Sanchez, met at the Colored Odd Fellows Lodge in early January to draw up a list of demands. The "Resolution for Arrangements of Labor by the Citizens" declared "that from and after the 18th of January, 1890, the working hours in all steam saw mills, factories and other working departments, shall be ten hours as is over the United States of America, and that no steam saw mills, factories, and other working departments shall work over that time."[103] Article three of the citizens' resolution demanded higher wages for all employees, "and that no common laborer shall work at any of the said steam saw mills, factories or other working departments for less than $1.50 to $2.50." The people of Apalachicola did more than demand equality. They called for an end to poverty wages, the right to regulate working conditions, and the power to institute these reforms. The workers' political vision extended far beyond the boundaries of their state to encompass "the United States of America."

The Apalachicola General Strike commenced on January 19. Hundreds of mill workers resolutely walked out of area factories and shut the port down. African American women deployed to the picket lines, to the horror of white employers who reported: "The negro women are violent in their denunciation of the action of the whites and are congregating on the streets."[104] Local support of the strikers was strong, because nothing less than the survival of the entire community was at stake. In one mill, two African Americans reported for duty on the first evening of the strike. One of the strikebreakers was killed by the strikers.[105] Deeming the situation at Apalachicola to be a seditious "riot," Governor Francis P. Fleming called out the Florida militia to restore power to Apalachicola's employers.[106] Defeated only three years earlier by an interracial force of strikers, the Escambia Rifles swept into Apalachicola and imposed martial law on the town. Mass arrests of strike supporters and leaders followed. By January 23, white militia and local law enforcement had broken the General Strike.[107] The dock strikes demonstrate that cooperation in African American communities was not a natural state of being; it had to be organized. Black strikebreakers were ostracized and even killed. The great port strikes revealed a growing class divide in black Florida.

The most important labor conflict in Gilded Age Florida did not involve a strike. Like their counterparts in Key West, African American Republicans in Jacksonville had entered into a coalition with the Knights of Labor and had successfully elected a reform slate of candidates who defeated conservatives and took office in 1886. Two years later, black political power continued to survive thanks to coalition building and African American women who played a decisive role in getting out the vote. On Election Day, 1888, black female activists gathered near polling places and assertively instructed their menfolk how to vote. The white elite was horrified at this demonstration of "disgusting" and "annoying" feminine behavior and deemed it responsible for democratically removing "good Democrats" from office."[108] The *Times-Union* lamented this "sad commentary on Unlimited Suffrage," which it opposed wholeheartedly.

The coalition government was faced with a devastating yellow fever epidemic that was depopulating the city. Those left behind faced grim prospects as entire industries closed down.[109] A special Committee on Sanitation (COS) was created to facilitate clean-up projects as well as to administer public work relief for unemployed workers. By the fall of 1888, the municipality employed over 1,400 African American workers on relief projects.[110] But on November 18, the Committee on Sanitation made a dramatic announcement. Citing dwindling funds, the committee decided to cut nearly half of its jobs.

Nearly one thousand unemployed black workers and family members gathered near the offices of COS executives and demanded the reinstatement of all public relief jobs.[111] City officials assured the protestors that there were no funds for extending the public works program. Unemployed workers persisted in their demonstrations and followed COS administrators through the town demanding jobs for those who had been thrown out of work by the epidemic.[112] Administrators responded that relief had to be severely curtailed, but the *Times-Union* claimed that "this class of laborers does not of course understand these things and can hardly be expected to."[113] The newspaper warned that Jacksonville stood on the verge of insurrection.

African Americans wanted jobs in order to keep their families alive, and they were certain that the city of Jacksonville should be responsive to their needs. Black workers engaged in a three-pronged campaign to save the municipal work relief program. They organized continuous public demonstrations, assembled each night to formulate strategy, and chose representatives to present demands to the city. The Jacksonville unemployed movement placed relentless pressure on the COS. On November 22, the city's relief agency finally relented: all workers who had been dismissed would be reinstated, albeit at a sliding pay scale depending on family size.[114] White COS officials congratulated themselves on their largesse, but African Americans understood that they had saved their public relief jobs through organization and agitation. Black workers held a meeting on the evening after the reinstatement of the jobs and reflected on their success. African Americans had gained a heightened understanding of their ability to influence municipal politics through disciplined protest. With the assistance of African American political leaders—including Joseph E. Lee—the assembly issued a public proclamation:

> The laboring men know very well that they are doing good service for a
> small consideration, and while the property-holders are being the
> greatest benefactors, after due consideration we know that it is working
> a serious hardship upon us to be compelled to give five days of labor
> and time for the sum of $3—a sum wholly insufficient for the support
> of men having families, or even for single men . . . and as we are loyal
> citizens and shoulder equally the responsibility with all others, We desire
> to submit . . . the following propositions.[115]

Black workers in deeds and words demonstrated that they were integral members of the polity. The Jacksonville unemployed movement highlighted the central conflict between black Floridians and white employers. The latter liked to imagine—in good times or bad—that they were "providing jobs" to indigent blacks. African Americans countered that labor was the basis of all wealth and deserved a place at the bargaining table of municipal politics.

Conservative Democrats across Florida viewed the Jacksonville protests with alarm. State officials rushed to find a way to make municipal governments in Florida as unresponsive to organized workers as possible. Nothing less than the future of white business supremacy was at stake. The key, conservatives decided, was to undermine the black urban electorate. Soon after the unemployed protests ended, the state comptroller rejected the bonds presented by the newly elected Republicans in Jacksonville, setting the stage for a Democratic coup.[116] In April, state legislators introduced a bill to revoke the charter of Jacksonville, thus giving the governor the power to replace elected officials with hand-picked individuals. The genius of the plan was that black voting power would be shattered by an ostensibly nonracial measure. The *Times-Union* was ecstatic: "Everybody favors the bill: lawyers, merchants, and businessmen."[117] The stakes were high: "If the present bill to amend the Jacksonville charter should fail, this city will get no relief whatever. Capitalists will not lend money to a municipality that can be bought for fifty dollars. At our next city election Jacksonville will be completely Africanized."[118] The *Times-Union* reiterated the conservative opposition to political pluralism: "The friends of the bill now pending to amend our city charter are warned to 'call a halt and reconstruct it to conform to the ideas of a majority.' The majority, to which reference is made, constitute the very 'majority' (so called) from which we seek to escape."[119]

The white-controlled state legislature revoked three city charters in the 1880s—all in cities with active African American labor movements, periodic interracial coalitions, and high black voter turnout. The purpose of revocation was to replace popular government with one-party rule and to silence the voices of black workers and potential white allies. Jacksonville's elected city government was deposed by the state in 1889. "This city which once elected its municipal officers," Emanuel Fortune, Jr. mourned, "will do so no more for the present. The right of suffrage has been taken away from the citizens of this city by a Democratic Legislature which does not represent the majority of voters in this city, because this majority is Republicans."[120] In the same year Key West's charter was revoked and James Dean, the first African American county judge in Florida, was removed by the state for allegedly licensing an interracial marriage.[121] Pensacola's elected government fell in 1885.[122] This coup was made possible by the refusal of white property owners to pay their taxes. This rebellion threw the city into a debt crisis that empowered the governor to remove Pensacola's elected officials.[123] In each case, state seizure of local government was carried out in the name of individuals the *Pensacola Commercial* referred to as the "intelligent, enterprising, business men."[124] Rarely had class warfare in the United States ever been so transparent.

African American workers in Gilded Age Jacksonville, Pensacola, Fernandina, Apalachicola, and other towns carried on the black Reconstruction-era belief in a "jealous regard for the rights of labor."[125] African American men and women endeavored to create a democratic society where they would be treated with respect, receive good wages, and exert a level of control in their workplaces whether they toiled on the docks or in an employer's household. In contrast, the white elite held that labor was inferior to capital at every level. The *Times-Union* instructed: "When the soldier represses disorder he serves labor first, though he shoot strikers and bayonet brethren of his own craft—all must be taught to obey the law or the weak will go to the wall, and labor is the weakest of all the factors that now uphold society."[126] White workers generally undermined the possibilities of interracial class solidarity. Seeking to maintain a fragile sense of privilege in a rapidly changing society, many white Floridians joined state militia units and became the tools of wage-cutting employers.[127]

THE VALUE OF CONVICT LABOR

White business supremacy's desire to keep labor "the weakest of all the factors" in society provided the engine for disfranchisement. Racial oppression and economic progress—as it was defined by Florida's elite—were two sides of the same coin.[128] Florida's lawmakers were now free to reinstitute and refine laws designed to limit labor mobility, ratchet down wages, and keep sharecroppers in debt. Vagrancy statutes, "after dark" laws (prohibiting sharecroppers from selling produce at night), and "anti-enticement" codes restraining employees from quitting work were aimed at locking African Americans into subordinate positions.[129] The *Gainesville Sun* swore: "We will be forced to force the negro to work," and authorities in Alachua County used the new laws to arrest black workers who quit jobs to pursue higher-paid work elsewhere.[130] Vagrancy statutes were unilaterally imposed to force African Americans in small towns to work for employers against their will.[131] County sheriffs, elected and bonded by an all-white constituency, reinforced the power of employers to pay miserably low wages to black workers. A Leon County sheriff posted a flier to African Americans "who seemed disposed to idleness," which read:

Take Notice! Fair Warning
Are you at work? If not, why not?
You will have to go to work or go to jail.
There is plenty of work for everyone and good wages
are paid in every line.

Take your choice; go to work and stay at work, or go to jail and stay on
   the county roads and work
there with stripes on under the gun. . . . Work is plentiful, wages good.
Find it quick or I will find you.[132]

A special report on Florida's agricultural future published by the *New York
Tribune* exulted: "Negro labor is cheap and abundant."[133] State boosters
touted this line as a drawing point, and Florida's lawmakers vowed to keep it
so. By the time that poorer whites discovered that vagrancy and other anti-
labor statutes would sometimes be used against them, it was too late.[134]

Convict labor became a lucrative enterprise in Florida. The state and
eventually county sheriffs garnered hefty bounties for providing African
American convicts to turpentine firms, phosphate mines, and road-
building firms.[135] An employer observed: "Were it not for the convict
labor there would be very little phosphate mined, naval stores manufactured and lumber cut."[136] Needless to say, the relationship between crime
and punishment in Florida became skewed as counties literally manufactured convicts for needy employers.[137] The state's newest slave laborers
were instrumental in building Florida's vast network of new roads at the
turn of the century. Road engineer Allan Rodgers boasted: "I will say for
the benefit of those interested in the good roads proposition that the
machinery used in my work in [Citrus] county is the kind that has been
known in the South for a couple of hundred years under the old fashioned
name of 'the nigger and the mule.' "[138]

The dream of New Jerusalem began to disintegrate into the nightmare of
an American Siberia of slave labor camps, the chain gang, and debt peonage.[139] In the wake of the Civil War, the *Christian Recorder* touted the Sunshine State as a promised land of freedom. Two decades later, the *Recorder*
mourned, "From Florida we have the newspaper report that absolute slavery still exists in certain sections in that State."[140] By 1910, Florida had the
highest incarceration rate of prisoners and juveniles in the Deep South.[141]
The state administered one of the most notorious penal systems in the
world, immortalized for decades to come in lurid films and exposés.

THE COLOR LINE

Disfranchisement paved the way for legal segregation, and the color line in
Florida hardened appreciably by the end of the 1880s.[142] Black Floridians
lost the right to a jury of their peers as local courts regularly excluded

African Americans from juries.[143] Funding for African American schools declined, and public school districts frequently limited black schools to three-to-six-month terms while offering nine months to many white pupils.[144] In 1883, T. Thomas Fortune observed: "The Georgia and Florida railroads have become infamously notorious for 'bouncing' colored travelers, and for taking decent fare and giving miserable accommodations to such—accommodations in smoking cars, where the vilest of impudent white scum resort to swear, to exhale rotten smoke and to expectorate pools of sickening excrementations of tobacco."[145]

Black Floridians did not silently acquiesce to these indignities. Sometimes their efforts halted or even rolled back the tide of segregation. In the same year that T. Thomas Fortune leveled his protest, African Americans in Pensacola won a lawsuit against local segregated transit.[146] When black Pensacolans were subsequently criticized for not supporting a scheme for railroad investment in Florida, they replied that the railroad discriminated against black passengers and should not expect their support.[147] After the state legislature passed a law in 1887 mandating segregation on Florida's railroads, the Pastors' Union in Jacksonville urged black Floridians to selectively boycott lines that refused to provide equal accommodations for all passengers.[148] African Americans were not asking to ride next to white passengers, but they wanted equal treatment on public conveyances.

White northerners were criticized for hastening the spread of segregation. An African American in Pensacola noted: "The colored people (or part of them) are beginning to question the conduct of some of our Northern 'good friends.' " A black man had tried to attend an opera and was thrown out: "Just here a thousand voices, more or less, shouted put him out!"[149] "The hardest thing for many of us to understand is the color line drawn in white churches," one black Floridian wrote. "The Negroes are permitted to sit with their white brothers in political caucuses, drink from the same glass very often, without thinking of the color. . . . Still, if you go to churches you are requested to take the back seats or skip up in the galleries or hop outside. What Christians!"[150]

Black Floridians did not reach consensus on the best way to deal with the march of segregation. T. Thomas Fortune issued a call for the formation of a national "Afro-American League" to fight for civil rights. African Americans in Pensacola quickly organized a branch of the League.[151] T. V. Gibbs, one of the state's last black elected representatives, opposed the Afro-American League, however. Gibbs believed that improved personal hygiene would defeat segregation: "When our people as a mass learn to ride in railway cars without eating water melons, fat meat, and peanuts, throwing the rinds on the floor;" he reasoned, "when our women leave their snuff sticks, greasy bundles and uncouth manners at home, railroad discriminations will abate much of their injustice."[152] Other African Americans echoed Gibbs's observations and blamed black workers' behavior for the onset of segregation ordinances. Segregation exacerbated class tensions in black communities. Nevertheless, the brutal ejection of AME Bishop Daniel Payne from a Florida train for refusing to move to the black compartment dealt a blow to middle-class arguments that "better manners" would avert segregation.[153]

DON'T EXPECT TOO MUCH FROM THE GOVERNMENT

A northern visitor stepped up to provide the justification for the tightening of white supremacy. Rev. Henry M. Field was among the many "sick Yankees" who visited Florida in the late nineteenth century to improve his health. Field was no common tourist. He came at the personal invitation of Henry M. Flagler, who was building the foundations of an economic empire in the state. A business partner of John Rockefeller, Flagler consolidated the Florida East Coast Railroad in the 1880s.[154] Eventually this line ran from Jacksonville all the way through the Florida Keys, making development of the Florida peninsula possible. Flagler was also a major beneficiary of two forms of slave labor that victimized African Americans and new immigrants: debt peonage and convict labor.[155] Flagler's "Key West Extension" was viewed as one of the great engineering feats in American history.[156] In fact, the rail lines leading into the Extension were first graded by black convict laborers and then, at the turn of the century, by individuals held against their will by agents working for Flagler's railroad.[157]

Rev. Henry M. Field's message to black Floridians must have pleased Flagler. Field advised African Americans to work hard and avoid politics: "I may not surrender a single one of my legal rights, and yet there may be reasons sufficient to myself why I should defer asserting them to a more convenient season. And so, my good friends, the less you talk and think about 'politics,' the better it will be for you."[158] "As to this whole political business," Fields continued:

one word of caution: Don't expect too much from the General [federal] Government! I know it is the most natural thing in the world, when you get into straits, to call on the power at Washington to help you out, and party papers echo the cry. Just now we hear a loud call upon Congress to secure to the negroes at the South "a free ballot and an honest count"—an admirable thing to do, if there were not several big stumbling blocks, veritable boulders in the way. . . . Meanwhile, is there something else to think about than going to election? Does it really make any difference in your corn crop? "De yam will grow, de cotton blow," no matter who is Governor.[159]

The New Yorker's "friendly advice" came at the moment that the U.S. Congress was debating the Lodge Elections Bill of 1890. The bill would provide a legal mechanism for investigating election irregularities. Senator Samuel Pasco from Florida was one of the bill's staunchest foes and argued that it was a pointless measure because white men were going to control the nation's political institutions forever. Pasco boasted to his Senate colleagues that "the Anglo-Saxon will be true to his history. In every quarter of the world where he has been placed side by side with people of other races he has ruled."[160]

As the Lodge Election Bill went down to defeat, Rev. Lyman Phelps of Sanford wondered: "How long shall I see a sheriff stand at the polls on election day and threaten a colored man who pays his taxes, owns real estate [and say] 'If you attempt to vote you will be arrested.'"[161] "The Republican party, as an organization," observed one Florida GOP leader, "is powerless to accomplish anything on account of the election laws, which we now have, and which were designed for the purpose of rendering the commission of fraud easily accomplished."[162] But the party's leadership must share much of the blame. "Lily White" Republicans worked to build an all-white and pro-business GOP.[163] Seeking to curry favor with the railroad interests in Florida, former GOP governor Harrison Reed told his friend Henry Sanford, "A Union League of the white republicans must be organized in order to bring together the intelligent & conservative who will not affiliate with or patronize negro mobs for office."[164] The Lily Whites did not understand that their platform was redundant. Florida already had an antiblack, pro-business party—the Democrats—who gleefully watched the GOP disintegrate.[165] At the same time, too many black Republican leaders—including Joseph E. Lee—retreated into "Black and Tan" politics and accepted patronage appointments from the national GOP instead of demanding rights for all.[166]

In Alachua County, where black farmers and laborers composed the backbone of rural Republican clubs in the 1880s, the Lily Whites delivered a lethal blow. On the eve of the 1888 congressional election, a white-controlled Republican executive committee deposed Josiah T. Walls, one of the most respected black Republicans in the South, from the county executive committee. Simultaneously, the committee purged both Walls and M. M. Lewey, a Civil War combat veteran, from the local ticket because white candidates refused to allow their names to appear alongside a black man's.[167] This move paved the way for GOP respectability in Alachua. In a subsequent contest, the election of three Republicans to minor offices in the county drew praise from the Democratic press because all of the men were conservative whites.[168]

White businessmen forged strategic alliances with their Democratic counterparts in order to make the state attractive to new investment. In Jacksonville whites formed the "Lincoln League," which was an "outgrowth of a movement to strengthen and make dominant white Republicans in the Republican party of the State."[169] Members were the quintessential men on the make. "The league will have social features to bring the members together," noted a report, "but the principal feature of the league[,] it is said, will be to promulgate the doctrine of the 'protective tariff.'" This strategy was designed to unite citrus growers moving into the state with "natives" who hoped to erect tariffs against foreign oranges and other agricultural commodities. White Republican businessmen found the Democrats to be benevolent rulers. The family of Reconstruction-era GOP Lieutenant Governor William Gleason was, by the 1890s, working with Senator Samuel Pasco to raise protective tariffs on pineapples and other tropical fruits that Gleason grew in Eau Galie.[170] The Gleason family repaid the favor by distributing campaign flyers for the Democrats.[171]

President Theodore Roosevelt's visit to Jacksonville in 1905 was a milestone in the remaking of Republicanism. Roosevelt came south to build ties of friendship and trust between North and South.[172] It soon became clear that the cost of sectional reconciliation would be paid mainly by black southerners, who were expected to relinquish their citizenship rights in the name of national unity. Roosevelt arrived in Jacksonville in the midst of the struggle over segregation on the city's streetcars.[173] Nevertheless, the *Florida Times-Union* was confident that "the President would hardly say anything to offend the white people of the South, who are giving him such warm and cordial reception, even in discussing the race problem."[174] Roosevelt did not disappoint. Speaking to members of the Jacksonville Board of Trade, the president expounded upon national unity and his theories of "race suicide" (white people needed to breed more prolifically, according to him). Roosevelt positively gushed over the possibility of building a canal through the heart of Central America that would benefit Florida's industries.[175]

The president addressed a separate assembly of black citizens at Florida Baptist College.[176] Roosevelt's speech in this setting was less optimistic. The president sternly lectured his audience to shun politics and that "duties precede rights."[177] He exhorted black Floridians to develop "morality" and to avoid entering the "professions."[178] The titular head of the Republican Party informed black citizens that, for them, the twentieth century was to be a profoundly limited epoch.[179] A Georgia Democrat gushed: "It is hard for me, a dyed-in-the-wool Democrat, to tell from President Roosevelt's talk whether he is a Democrat or a Republican. . . . He certainly said nothing in his speech here to the colored people but what Democrats had often said before."[180] The GOP's betrayal of black aspirations was complete.

Rev. J. Milton Waldron in Jacksonville spoke for many black southerners when he laid out the reasons for the GOP's demise in the region. While African Americans had expected the party to serve as a guarantor of equality, it had degenerated into the guardian of business interests:

> The republican party at the birth, and for fifteen or twenty years after was pre-eminently the party of human rights and loyalty to the union. . . . Human rights and freedom of body and mind are of far more concern to this nation than either free trade or free silver, and if those who put themselves forward as defenders of this freedom fail to keep their pledge to the people, the people will fail to support them. . . . [The party] has deserted the people and their rights for office and "trusts" and the people have arisen, Samson-like and crushed it.[181]

White Republicans' efforts to cultivate respectability paid off when Jacksonville Democrats invited them as well as Socialist Party members to participate in the city's white primary in 1907.[182] African American workers' egalitarian ideas and demands on the state were more threatening to white business supremacy than Socialism.[183]

The disfranchisement of black Floridians was a fatal blow to democracy. Conservatives promised that restricting the franchise to "white only" would purify the ballot. Instead, as some Democrats quietly admitted, the massacre of the electorate ushered in an era of political corruption. As one white editor noted: "In reality (in Florida) these railroad corporations and not the State Legislatures choose the Congressmen and Senators. They, and not the unbiased voice of the people control all laws and appointments, and make the State, in all its departments, simply the tool by which the will of the railroad corporations is registered, recorded and executed."[184] One-party rule allowed corporate interests to seize control of political appointments in county after county.[185] Florida's primaries and elections degenerated into orgies of vote buying and missing ballot boxes.[186] The segregation of African Americans (and later, Bahamian, Mexican, and Haitian immigrants) into low-wage labor and away from the ballot box became the linchpin of white rule in Florida.[187]

◀ 3 ▶

WE ARE IN THE HANDS
OF THE DEVIL

Fighting Racial Terrorism

I am impelled by a force of circumstance to inform the Christians of this civilized country of a concerted, and executed assassination of a colored preacher in the County of Hernando, Florida, a county wherein the life of a colored man is not worth two grains of corn since Reconstruction.[1]

THE CHRISTIAN RECORDER, 1877

[God] made the white into man, and implanted within his breast that determination to always be supreme among races of men. This is why the white man of the south, standing out boldly tells civilization: "I am a white man! I will rule!" Were he to do otherwise he would be a renegade to his race.[2]

THE OKALOOSA NEWS JOURNAL, 1920

IT IS IMPOSSIBLE to understand the African American freedom struggle in Florida without considering the toll that racial violence took on black lives. Between 1882 and 1930, African Americans in Florida suffered the highest lynching rate in the United States.[3] During those years, at least 266 black Floridians were lynched. In the same period, whites physically destroyed black communities, raped black women, and drove African Americans out of parts of central and south Florida designated by area residents as white homelands.[4] "Too late to talk about the 'suppressed vote' now," a black Floridian cried. "We are in the hands of the devil."[5]

Jim Crow's all-white juries allowed white citizens—and law enforcement officials—to inflict physical harm against African Americans.[6] An African American from Pensacola angrily noted in 1888: "A white man tried to commit a rape on a young colored girl Wednesday. Certainly no lynching."[7] At the turn of the century, the National Anti-Mob and Lynch Law Association promised a reward of $500 for the arrest of individuals who had burned an African American man at the stake at Bartow, but the organization's offer was met with contempt.[8] The guilty parties had not tried to hide their identities. The Bartow *Courier-Informant* exulted: "there is no jail in Florida that could hold the prisoner for twenty-four hours, nor is there a jury in the county who would convict him."[9] When a Jacksonville police officer shot Jesse Hall after Hall allegedly stole an umbrella, the *Times-Union* reported: "It was stated at the scene of the shooting that when the bullet entered Hall's neck he fell to the pavement, and did not even quiver. Life left his body almost immediately, and he died without a sound."[10] Jesse Hall's death adhered to the ideal script of Jim Crow. The central motif of this morality play was not about justice, right or wrong, or the punishment fitting the crime. It was about the maintenance of racial domination. The death of Jesse Hall served as a warning to all African Americans that the state of Florida judged their lives to be cheap and expendable.

On rare occasions when authorities showed an inclination to investigate incidents of antiblack violence the results were mixed. In 1920, two white men murdered an African American woman in Bay County by stabbing her nine times, shooting her in the back of the head, and dumping her body in a creek.[11] When local officials talked of bringing the men to trial, a group of white men burned the county courthouse—and the evidence pertaining to the case—to the ground.[12] A white individual who had lived in Florida for nearly a decade explained: "Southern white men use it as a by word that no white man is hung for killing a negro."[13] Jim Crow gave white men a monopoly on violence usually reserved for officers of the state, and they vigorously sought to maintain it.

White Floridians used lethal force to keep African Americans "in their place," but black Floridians did not suffer terror lightly. On numerous occasions, African Americans organized and took up arms in order to stop themselves from being victimized by white violence. African Americans in Florida established a practice that anti-lynching activist Ida B. Wells described as armed "self-help."[14] The primary goal of armed self-help was to ward off bloodshed and live to fight another day. Yet this form of social action was not merely defensive. When African Americans defended themselves, they often invoked the Fourteenth Amendment's language of equal protection under the laws. Black Floridians based their actions on the fact that the state had abrogated its responsibility to protect the lives and limbs of its black citizenry. African Americans linked the idea of armed self-help to their broader struggle for full citizenship. At the same time, black Floridians did not speak with one voice when it came to proposing solutions to racial violence. Some counseled passivity or patience in the face of racial aggression. After all, there was always the danger that self-defense would engender ferocious reprisals.

IT IS ALWAYS OPEN SEASON

Segregation and violence are inseparable. Daytona native Howard Thurman pointed out: "Segregation is at once one of the most blatant forms of moral irresponsibility. The segregated persons are out of bounds, are outside the magnetic field of ethical concern. It is always open season." The theologian observed: "Segregation gives rise to an immoral exercise of power of the strong over the weak, that is to say, advantage over disadvantage. . . . It is true that fear in the lives of the disadvantaged exposes them to be controlled by the advantaged. For generations fear has been the monitor, the angel with the flaming sword standing guard to make the pattern of segregation effective."[15] In 1887, S. D. Jackson of Pensacola illustrated the fact that segregation was ushered in by violence:

> Well, sir, I will tell you what they are doing with us down South. They
> are shooting us down as so many partridges; don't allow editors to speak
> the truth always through their papers to the people; kicking us off trains
> whenever they see fit to do so; distribute the school funds as their
> conscience directs, charging us very often as high as 24 per cent per
> annum for money when we are compelled to borrow it from them, and
> thousands of other things too numerous to mention.[16]

The goal of racial violence was to sever all African American claims to basic rights, dignity, and protection from the state. Black Floridians were killed for an almost unimaginable array of infractions including organizing unions, accepting lower pay rates, registering to vote, owning desirable land, failing to step aside on sidewalks when a white person approached, and failing to show deference to whites.[17] African American ministers and churches—especially those that promoted black autonomy—were targeted for reprisals.[18] After one black man allegedly handed an "insulting and obscene" note to a white woman near Fort Pierce, whites burned the man's church to the ground, "and forced all of the colored people to leave." The black press noted, "No effort has been made by the authorities to punish the guilty parties or to protect the people who are denied the common rights of a citizen."[19]

In 1883, white workers in Sanford responded to poor working conditions not by organizing against employers but by murdering a black worker for accepting lower than normal wages.[20] Four years later, when Knights of Labor union organizer A. W. Johnson was assassinated near Milton, a black reporter observed: "one 'poor trash' said to a colored man here: 'If that nigger had kept his mouth shut he would have been alive today.' "[21] Attempts by African Americans to exert authority over white Floridians were not met kindly. In the early twentieth century, a black building contractor's family home in Palatka was dynamited on five separate occasions because he tried to employ white labor. His family finally left the town.[22]

Violence became the watchword of Jim Crow Florida. A black worker in Madison County was "literally shot to pieces" because "from what could be learned, he was a very impudent and fearless negro, and gave his employers, as well as the entire community a great deal of trouble and uneasiness."[23] Another Madison resident was murdered for stealing a hog. Later the dead man was found to be innocent, but a local citizen noted: "Of course the white murder is unmolested, the voice of 'justice' is stifled."[24] A wealthy planter and his son killed an elderly African American worker because he had left their employ owing a five-dollar debt.[25] Allegedly, the aged debtor had been guilty of displaying "impertinence" toward the planter. African Americans were supposed to defer completely to whites. "Talking back" was an offense punishable by death. One writer conveyed the results:

> Not a great while ago at the River Junction, 22 miles this side of
> Quincy, a young man by the name of Allison, a native of Quincy,
> employed by a railroad at the junction, had some words with an
> employee of the same road, when another clerk said . . . "Here, take my
> pistol & kill the black son of a bitch," this he did, deliberately walking
> up to the colored man and blowing his brains out! For this crime
> Allison was never arrested. I am told this by a *Democrat,* an eye witness
> to the affair. Such dastardly outrages are of daily occurrence in the
> South of which you hear nothing, and we are powerless to prevent it.[26]

White Floridians believed that African American communities should pay the price for crimes allegedly committed by black individuals. In the aftermath of a gun battle between white policemen and African Americans at Kissimmee, south of Orlando, an English travel writer wrote:

the citizens of Kissimmee arose, raided the coloured quarter, fired several houses, and drove out a large number—it is to be presumed and hoped only such members as were deemed objectionable and disorderly—of the coloured population; or, as a witness, in describing it to us, tersely put it, they "went through Nigger town and ran out the niggers." The expelled negroes thereupon took the train for Orlando. Kissimmee telegraphed the news to her sister city (Orlando), and when the train arrived at the depot of the latter town, a deputation of the citizens of Orlando were there ready to meet it. They met it with leveled revolvers. . . .[27]

The system of Jim Crow did not rest upon the consent of the governed; instead, it relied on everyday acts of brutality to maintain itself. A hack driver was gunned down by white youths on a Jacksonville sidewalk after he failed to move out of their way quickly enough.[28] Another black driver told James White, a newspaperman, that he owed him additional cab fare. White shot the driver through the head, killing him instantly.[29] Jacksonville police rescued White from a group of African Americans who had gathered—allegedly—to lynch him. An all-white jury excused the crime, noting that the assailant was depressed and had been drinking heavily for several days. Worse, the hack driver had "applied a vile epithet" against the white man. The *Pensacola Daily News* noted with satisfaction that a black porter who insisted on taking his lunch break at the same counter with white patrons was beaten to death. The newspaper reported that the murder "gives somewhat of an idea as to how a black man endeavoring to force his way in the matter of social equality is treated, especially around the Flomaton settlement."[30]

The lynching of black men in segregating Florida was frequently extolled as a civic virtue. The *Times-Union* lectured: "In the South, ever since the emancipation of the Negroes there have been occasional instances of summary punishment meted out to men of the colored race who perhaps inherited the savagery of their ancestors and defied all laws."[31] In 1895, Sam Echols, Sam Crawley, and John Brooks were abducted by a group of white men in Lafayette County. Despite protesting their innocence in the death of a local white woman, the three men were taken to the woods to be punished. Pleading for their lives, the men were tied to stakes. An eyewitness reported: "They were scalped, their eyelids and their noses cut off, the flesh cut from their jaws, their bodies scraped and their privates cut out. The blood flowed in streams from their ghastly wounds, and their screams rent the air only to be silenced by the tearing out of their tongues by the roots."[32] The men were burned at the stake. Two other African Americans were lynched near Pemberton Ferry but cut down from the tree before they died because the mob had forgotten to ask if they were guilty. Once confessions were extracted from the dying men, they were re-lynched and incinerated.[33]

Lynchings were designed to strike fear into the broader community. Wash Bradley of Bronson was accused of murdering a white woman. Bradley was taken from the custody of the local sheriff to the nearby woods. From there, "his ears were cut off, his back slashed with knives, while the blood spurted and the victim groaned. His arms were nearly severed with buckshot, and other indignities are no doubt unfit for publication."[34] Only after they had tortured Bradley and fired additional shots into his body did his tormentors lynch the man. Afterwards local whites turned their fury on a black minister named "Parson Pitts," who had been "giving considerable trouble among negroes in that section, by paying twenty-five lashes with a buggy trace."[35]

In many white minds, gender, political, and economic tensions were mixed together into a lethal brew of resentment against black Floridians. Insecure in their ability to maintain disfranchisement, some whites fantasized that African Americans were plotting revenge. In 1898, a writer from Holmes County wrote to Governor William Bloxham that African American workers were using the Spanish American War as a pretext to plan a general uprising:

They are holding secret meetings and are plotting together to kill out all the white people after a little when the war gits a little hoter and a little more of the men gits off to the war and take everything to themselves and are continually trying to rape the young white women and threatening to kill them if they dont submit . . . now shall we jest let them go on and rob and run over and ravish our wives and children and kill us out and take the young women like they are fixing to do or what shall we do [?]. . . . we have a lot of men out of any employment and the turpentiners and other pub works wont hardly hire a white man if they can git a Negr."[36]

The letter demonstrates that even though the benefits of white supremacy were not being shared equally—witness the reference to unemployment—the writer's resentment was trained on African Americans. Like his counterparts throughout the South, the Holmes County writer used race and sex fears to fix white women in a subordinate position, helpless and dependent on male protection. Simultaneously, African Americans were relegated to the bottom of the social and economic pyramid. Any efforts by black Floridians to improve themselves were tantamount to revolution. If the state would not preserve the status quo, the white men of Holmes County would have to do the job.[37] Later that year, local whites threatened African American turpentine workers with death, and many of them fled from the county.[38]

THE DISCIPLES OF VIOLENCE

Reconstruction-era violence was rooted in the determination of white Floridians to keep African Americans as close to slavery as possible. Gilded Age terror was a central part of employers' schemes to cement one-party rule and black powerlessness. Sociologist Oliver Cox held: "there is an inseparable association between Negro disenfranchisement and lynching. Disenfranchisement makes lynching possible, and lynching speedily squelches any movement among Southern Negroes for enfranchisement. In the South these two are indispensable instruments in the service of the status quo."[39] The *Times-Union* explained the ground rules of white supremacy:

> In the South, the negro in politics is not tolerated—in other sections he must obediently follow. There are lynchings so nearly everywhere that the rule is established, but the South does not forbid the black man to earn a living as do our neighbors. If the negro be wise he will respect the limits set for him as does the elephant and the tiger and the others who accept rules and make no pretense to reason.[40]

The march of one-party rule in Florida mirrored that of other totalitarian societies in the modern period. Philosopher Hannah Arendt explained that in one-party regimes, "Terror is lawfulness." Arendt observed that in such polities, "Guilt and innocence become senseless notions; 'guilty' is he who stands in the way of the natural or historical process which has passed judgment over 'inferior races,' over individuals 'unfit to live,' over 'dying classes and decadent peoples.' "[41] Any serious effort to challenge the "natural or historical" processes of white authority in Florida was viewed as heresy and punishable by extreme force. A union organizer, a troublesome employee, and even an assertive minister were subject to lethal retaliation. While black southerners fell prey to the institutionalized violence of convict labor, the chain gang, debt peonage, and other forms of oppression, the fate of those who engaged in oppositional politics or resistance was equally bleak.

White elites repeatedly emphasized the linkage between one-party rule and terror. Historian J. Randall Stanley wrote that prior to the Civil War, whites in the plantation districts of middle Florida had been "conservative" and peaceful. During Reconstruction however, the same people "became *the disciples of violence* because it had become a necessity—if not righteous—in combating white and black radical domination."[42] The disciples of violence ensured that stories of political terror from Reconstruction endured in written history and popular memory. The Ku Klux Klan was deified.[43] Tales of political violence were told and retold with relish in order to short-circuit challenges to white rule. When African Americans in Sumter began registering to vote over four decades after Reconstruction, an older white Floridian by the name of Murden raised the specter of mass violence as a cautionary tale for prospective African American voters. Murden claimed that during Reconstruction, "northern negro lovers" had incited black citizens of Sumter to plot an uprising against the white population. In response, a mounted white posse rode into Wildwood, where the plot was said to have originated, and drove all of the African Americans out of the settlement. According to Murden, "While not all of the colored ministers and school teachers were mixed up as leaders of the attempt at assassination, many were and they disappeared."[44] As late as the Great Depression, Sumter County whites told a chilling story about an enormous sink hole near Sumterville: "During the tragic and stormy reconstruction days, the strange hole was said to have been a convenient receptacle for disposing of too obnoxious people of color."[45] Folk memories of physical savagery became tools of social control.

The disciples of violence also targeted white individuals who were deemed threats to the system. C. M. Hooper was an elderly Confederate veteran who lived in Jackson County. Hooper uncovered a "political assassination Association" formed in the late 1880s to crush black and white dissent in Florida. He began working on an exposé titled "A Voice from the Solid South." Local whites abducted Hooper and took him to the woods to be lynched. Hooper managed to flee, and he noted with anger: "I had to hide in swamps to escape Ku Klux."[46] Hooper begged Republican Senator William Chandler to allow him to testify before the U.S. Senate about the collapse of democracy in Florida, but his offer was never accepted by the Republican leader. Like the Seminole Indians, the Confederate veteran was driven into the swamps of Florida because he had allied himself with African Americans and against the forces of white progress.[47]

In 1890, F. G. Humphreys, the collector of customs at Pensacola, warned Senator Chandler that the assassination of a white U.S. marshal in Quincy was viewed as an acceptable act of violence in Florida.[48] The marshal, W. B. Saunders, was said to be an "impudent" Republican who did not defer to the Panhandle's Democratic elite. U.S. Senator Wilkinson Call told his colleagues in Washington that the marshal was a "meddlesome man" and implied that he deserved to die.[49] If a law enforcement official could be assassinated with impunity, no one was safe. Humphreys had lived in Florida for nearly fifty years. He begged Senator Chandler to understand that federal martial law would be needed to restore order in Florida.[50]

The sanctioning of violence against African Americans had an impact on the entire society. Corruption became generalized. Once white officials—particularly law enforcement officers—tasted complete power over black communities, they were tempted to extend their reach beyond the disfranchised. In 1900, a group of white citizens in Hernando County petitioned Governor W. S. Jennings to stop a sheriff who had launched a local civil war: "You are requested to suspend Sheriff A. M. White. He is a drunkard and has a [whiskey still] in his office. He and his deputies are whipping and killing niggers and driving good citizens out of the county. He has threatened to kill Leo Morper, Orvil Higgins and his enemies and to burn Brooksville."[51] Jim Crow Florida lurched from one catastrophe to another.

Economic oppression and racial violence were also bound together. African Americans who toiled in regions with heavy concentrations of timber, turpentine, and phosphate businesses were more vulnerable to outbreaks of racial terror than black workers in most other occupations. The business cycles of these industries were inherently volatile, subject to extreme fluctuations in supply and demand as well as profitability.[52] Profit margins were slim. Turpentine operators denounced outside investors and financial agents (or "factors") as well as the Standard Oil Company, which they blamed for controlling profits and prices in the industry.[53] Local operators claimed that industry factors denied credit to turpentine operators who paid anything but basement wages.[54] Hence, employers in these fields treated workers' demands for higher compensation with extreme hostility. Finally, workers in these industries were often migrants and perhaps less rooted in local communities that could mobilize to defend them during emergencies.

Industry operators formed employers' associations and vowed to keep wages down.[55] The Turpentine Operators' Association stated: "This is an age of organization and cooperation," but the benefits of organization were to be limited to employers only.[56] When turpentine owners met in Bartow to "combine for mutual protection," the major items on their agenda were establishing tighter labor control and shattering the existing wage structure. In essence, turpentine operators combined to set a maximum wage rate, stretch out pay periods, and deal "with the present unsatisfactory condition of labor, and to prevent as far as possible, the losses sustained by promiscuous advances and credits."[57]

Employers demonstrated contempt for their employees. Florida turpentine operator J. B. Crosby boasted of his own work ethic but claimed, "its different with the niggers. They seem to be able to live in affluence without working. The trouble is this, there are no blacks left in South Georgia and Florida. They are all 'Mister blackman' these days. You've got to be kind to them for it suddenly develops that all of them were born of sensitive parents and have been raised pets."[58] White employers turned their anti-labor ideology into public policy through Florida's promiscuous expansion of the vagrancy laws.[59] One employer stated that "idlers" were refusing to work, and that convict labor was the guarantor of economic progress in Florida.[60] A worker responded that it was foolish to "think that an honest laboring man will put himself on the market to work eleven, twelve, and thirteen hours a day for $1.25 a day, and at the end of the week have nothing to show but $2 or $3 and a batch of commissary checks."[61] African Americans in these industries were subjected to white business supremacy at its most ruthless stage.[62]

The state's phosphate and turpentine regions resembled battlefields as workers struggled with woods riders (foremen) and bosses over wages, company store debts, and issues of respect.[63] An employer in Baker County ordered Edward McRae, a black turpentine worker, to kneel down before him. McRae's refusal to humiliate himself angered the white man, who "pulled his revolver and endeavored to make the negro kneel to him." McRae pulled his own pistol. At the end of the fray, both men lay dead.[64] In 1903, T. L. Marquis, a phosphate employer in the Bartow area, killed an African American employee because "it seems that the negro got into a dispute with Strother Booth, bookkeeper for Mr. Marquis and became very abusive." Marquis claimed that when he saw the laborer "in the act of drawing his gun, he fired at him, killing him instantly."[65] An argument erupted in Wakulla County when a woods rider engaged in a heated conversation with African American workers gathered at a company store. The argument escalated into a gun battle with workers and company managers arrayed on either side. Both the foreman and the employee who allegedly shot him were killed.[66]

African American workers defended themselves from white incursions. White debt collectors tried to crash a festival organized by African American turpentine workers in Hamilton County on their payday. After a harsh exchange of words, a gun battle ensued leaving at least six dead.[67] At a point when there had "been bad feeling between the whites and desperate negroes employed at the mines" in Alachua County, African American workers near Williston engaged in a shoot-out with a group of armed whites.[68] African American survivors of these local race wars were invariably delivered up to county officials for punishment, whereas their white antagonists walked away free men. After the smoke from Williston cleared, "the live negroes had fled, but the whites followed and succeeded in capturing one, whom they delivered to the sheriff."[69]

The desire of some whites to reserve areas of the state as white homelands fueled acts of racial violence. In 1893, the *Bartow Courier Informant* promised: "One race or the other must leave and the whites are going to remain."[70] African Americans were excluded—sometimes upon the pain of death—from traveling and working in certain parts of Florida. "It is emphatically a white man's country," a reporter for the *Tribune* wrote. "In Lafayette County, to use the expression of an old settler, 'a nigger goes through on the run with his hat off.'"[71] In 1883, a black linesman attempting to repair a faulty telegraph wire between Tocoi and Palatka was gunned down by whites in Moccasin Branch because he had crossed a racial "dead line" beyond which no African American could work.[72] A crew of African American cross-tie cutters was fired upon in the vicinity of Ocala by local whites who had taken an ironclad vow in 1886 "not to allow black people in the area."[73] After whites in West Pasco County massacred African American sawmill workers on the Cotee River, a sign hung near the entrance to Elfers as late as the early 1920s that read: "Nigger, don't let the sun set on you, hear."[74]

W. J. Bell was a northern investor who came to western Florida in 1903 to start an all-white town. "You see, the 'dream,' as you call it, of 'A White

Man's Empire,' " Bell lectured, "is not altogether utopian, chimerical or unreasonable."[75] "White labor will not come South to work side by side with the black man," Bell claimed. He planned to build "a colony where every man will own his own property, but he must be a man without one drop of negro blood in him. I propose to have a God-given section where the black man is not welcome." Whites in central and south Florida far outpaced their counterparts in the northern part of the state in imposing residential apartheid. A white "Christian colony" in De Soto County put out the word that "No Negroes, No Dagoes" were wanted.[76] African Americans were also warned to stay out of Gulfport well into the 1920s. Gulfport became national news when a group of contractors tried to bring in a crew of black laborers to work in the town, "but they soon received a letter explaining that the white laborers did not mean to have the colored men about and if they were not sent away there would be some dead negroes."[77]

THE SOONER WE ORGANIZE, THE BETTER

Black Floridians did not come to a consensus on how they should react to white violence. Some echoed T. Thomas Fortune's 1887 call for the creation of a national civil rights organization. James S. Perry shared a harrowing story with readers of Fortune's *New York Freeman* of how he and his brother had taken up arms in Nassau County to stop drunken whites from assaulting his family. Perry advocated armed self-defense because: "the sooner we organize the better; for our people have been suffering insults, mobbing, ku kluxing and lynching too long, and instead of growing less it is becoming worse."[78] Above all, Perry believed that T. Thomas Fortune's proposed national Afro-American League would help address these injustices.[79]

J. Willis Menard disagreed with Perry's advocacy of armed defense and the Afro-American League. In contrast, the first black man elected to the U.S. Congress promoted an idea of black nation-building whereby the federal government would "furnish free transportation and homesteads in the Western States to at least 1,000,000 colored people," promising that from this point on, "the race question in the South would be reduced to its simplest elements."[80] From Palatka, T. L. McCoy acknowledged the attractiveness of emigration, but he believed that another strategy was needed: "Some advance the idea that emigration is the best method to pursue. I am opposed to emigrating to foreign lands. I believe that this race problem must be settled here, peaceably or otherwise; I care not which, so long as it is settled once and for all."[81]

Some black Floridians talked of leaving for Africa. Rev. C. H. Pearce, a pioneer of the AME Church in Florida and a highly respected political leader during Reconstruction, told AME bishop Daniel Payne that he was thinking of becoming an advocate of black emigration to Africa. "I am frank to acknowledge that I am in favor of the movement [to Africa]," wrote Pearce, "and were I a young man I would not stand the insults of the American white people; and above all this we have a higher and grander object in view, namely the civilization of benighted Africa."[82] In the same year, a small group of African Americans in Tampa boarded a steamer bound for Liberia.[83] A Chipley newspaper noted: "A negro preacher lectured here last Sunday and Sunday night to the negroes, and offer[ed] them great inducements to go to Africa. We learn that a good many of them signify their willingness to go."[84]

Others counseled more patience, faith, or legal measures to deal with racial brutality. The *Evangelist,* a leading black newspaper in Jacksonville, advised against armed resistance due to the numerical superiority of white citizens.[85] R. S. Quarterman of Orlando asserted that the best way to stop racial violence was to address the issue in churches: "This sin is raging in this country because the colored and white ministers are afraid to preach against it."[86] S. D. Jackson looked to the state's legal system to reverse its course, asserting: "We want a judge who will hang those who band themselves together and shoot us to death by the dozen."[87] At its annual meeting in Ocala, the Inter-Denominational Ministers' Union resolved to ask the state legislature to enact an anti-lynching law.[88] The law was never enacted, and some black Floridians resolved to take matters into their own hands.

AND MAKE A MILITARY COMPANY OF THEM

In 1888, James Austin, a black prisoner being held in the Palatka city jail, allegedly handed an insulting note to Deputy Sheriff W. Lowring. In response, the angry jailer entered Austin's cell to beat Austin, a practice becoming increasingly common in Palatka's jails.[89] In the midst of this thrashing, the prisoner grabbed Lowring's police stick, whereupon the deputy sheriff pulled out his pistol. In the scuffle, a round from the pistol discharged into Lowring's stomach. By the time Lowring died, a crowd of white people had gathered and, according to a *New York Age* correspondent, "The cry, 'lynch the nigger' was heard on every hand."[90]

Under the cover of darkness, a group of African Americans spirited James Austin away on a wagon to provide the endangered man with medical attention and physical safety. Black citizens in Palatka raised a twenty-four-hour armed guard on Austin and vowed that he would not be lynched. At the same time, black citizens approached white Republican leader George P. Fowler for advice.[91] The attorney reportedly stated: "You colored people should go home and desist from trying to defend a villain who shot down a white man in cold blood. He ought to be lynched and the sooner he is gotten out of the way the better for you and the community in general." Fowler's words angered the delegation, who replied that their votes had supported a Republican who now supported lynch law.

The county sheriff vowed that if black Palatkans did not surrender, he would call the white militia out to "kill every one of them." In response, the *Age*'s reporter wrote: "The colored citizens banded together, waited upon the sheriff and told him that they were determined not to submit quietly to lynch law, and if an attempt was made to lynch the prisoner they would resist it to the bitter end."[92] While the fate of James Austin after this incident is unclear, one thing is certain: he was not lynched.

African Americans' practice of organized self-defense was based on their dogged belief in equal citizenship. During Reconstruction and well into the 1880s, black Floridians resorted to self-defense in order to protect themselves from white violence during elections. African Americans' belief in the right to bear arms was fortified by the ways that they remembered the Civil War. Black Floridians emphasized the revolutionary character of the war and dramatized the ways they had helped to save the Union by military service. No Emancipation Day ceremony was complete without the Grand Army of the Republic veterans and a Volunteer Colored Militia unit.[93]

Black militia companies had been mustered into service by the state during Reconstruction.[94] African Americans were exceedingly proud of their "home guard" units. During the 1870 Emancipation Day ceremonies in Tampa the volunteer black militia led a march of enthusiastic citizenry to the county courthouse singing "John Brown's Body," a song sung by African American soldiers during the war.[95] Two decades later, a black militia company formed the first major rank of the Jacksonville Emancipation Day parade.[96] The march was succeeded by patriotic messages and eulogies of Frederick Douglass and William Lloyd Garrison. The political symbolism was transparent. Black Floridians linked their right to bear arms with their memories of the Civil War and their struggle to become full citizens in the new republic.

Throughout most of the 1880s, African Americans served in separate militia units in larger towns such as Pensacola, Jacksonville, and Tallahassee.[97]

But the collapse of African American political power led to the demise of the state-sanctioned black militia in Florida. In 1891, most African American militia companies were purged by the state even as white militia companies grew exponentially.[98] In 1896, Jacksonville newspaper editor W. I. Lewis asked Senator Chandler to block the federal appropriation for state and naval militias because African Americans were excluded from state militias in the South. Lewis told Chandler that several southern states, including Florida, "have laws on their statute books prohibiting the organization of Negro militia companies & making it illegal for a man or person of 1/8th Negro blood to have a gun in his or her house or to carry the same upon the highway."[99] Lewis indignantly pointed out that the federal government was arming the white South at the expense of African Americans.

Used to break strikes and enforce the dictates of Florida's employers, the state militia became Jim Crow's strong arm of authority. Militiamen frequently clashed with black Floridians during their annual encampments. During the 1904 encampment at St. Augustine, troops exchanged harsh words with African American hack drivers, and a fight broke out between them. Soon a riot erupted, with the hack men and their allies flinging stones at the militiamen, who fixed their bayonets and called for reinforcements.[100] Looting broke out in the city that evening.[101] Likewise, James Weldon Johnson left Florida soon after he barely escaped a beating by white militiamen who mistakenly thought his female acquaintance was a white woman.[102] Ostensibly called on to "preserve order," the white militia often did the exact opposite.

White Floridians went to great lengths to enforce the monopoly of force that white militia fighters enjoyed. In 1896, a group of twenty black teenagers in Tallahassee began marching in formation and drilling after a military fashion, using brooms to simulate firearms.[103] The Leon County sheriff formed a posse and confronted the youngsters as they were allegedly "going through their manual of arms." White riflemen fired into the group and killed "one negro boy about 15 or 16 years of age," and seriously wounded another. A coroner's jury was formed, and its verdict was "that the deceased came to his death by a gunshot wound from the hands of unknown parties." Black Floridians were outraged. M. M. Lewey cried: "If the boys were committing any offense against law and order by practicing boyish parades on the streets of Tallahassee, every one of them could easily have been arrested and dealt with according to law."[104] Lewey voiced the angry refrain that swept over the South: "Will the day ever come when white men in the South will cease their inhumanity to Negroes?"

The following year, "the Colored Citizens of Lawtey" in Bradford County petitioned the governor to allow them to form a militia company because they had suffered repeated assaults on their neighborhood "by the wicked and cruel people of Bradford County." Delegated by his neighbors to write the letter of protest to Governor William Bloxham, C. C. Ellis complained, "the white mens are shooting and killing up the Col[ored] people on Cold blood then they say they was justifible in doing so." Ellis told the story of a white man by the name of Roberson who shot down a black man in broad daylight. When the dead man's cousin asked the deputy sheriff of Bradford County why he refused to arrest Roberson despite the presence of multiple witnesses to the murder, the lawman drew his gun and threatened to kill the inquisitive relative. Ellis reminded Governor Bloxham that "the black Man payes their taxes like the white man so the law ought to provide for the black Man as do white in this case." He bluntly asked: "And now we want to no will you chose or take the Citizens good Sobered men of their Col[or] and make a military company of them[?]"[105] African Americans in Lawtey stubbornly adhered to the idea of equal justice. The governor's office stamped Ellis's letter "No Reply."

NOT TO SUBMIT QUIETLY TO LYNCH LAW

Innumerable incidents of racial violence in Florida arose over disputes between African American workers and white bosses. The conflict between an Anheuser Busch teamster Benjamin Reed and his supervisor Frank Burrows in 1892 was unusual only in the fact that it led to armed insurrection in Jacksonville. According to Reed, he had been sent out by Burrows to deliver a wagon load of beer. Thinking that the wagon driver had tarried in his delivery, the supervisor berated Reed upon his return to the warehouse. The men traded insults and both began fighting, grabbing boards and other available objects to strike at each other. Burrows claimed that Reed called him a "black———," and struck at him first. By the end of the fight, Burrows had fallen, wounded from a blow to the head.[106]

After the fight, Benjamin Reed was sent out to make another delivery. When the gravity of the white manager's injuries became apparent, the police were called in to investigate. Reed was arrested in the middle of his delivery, and by dusk the manager was pronounced dead. Talk of retribution swept through white Jacksonville. The *Times-Union* warned of "rash white men" carrying on "talk about lynching," and the newspaper fanned the flames of racial conflict by referring to Burrows as "a quiet, hard working young fellow, popular with everybody who knew him," while characterizing Reed as a boozing hooligan.[107] As angry white men began to gather around the courthouse, the Jacksonville police department quietly vanished.[108]

African Americans organized to prevent the lynching of Benjamin Reed. By 11 P.M. armed sentries were patrolling the immediate perimeter of the jail and questioning every white man who approached the area. Whites with no business near the courthouse were asked to leave. Eventually, dozens of African Americans filled the approaches leading to the jail.[109] This emergency militia was solidly working class or, in the *Times-Union's* preferred phrasing, "this negro mob was composed of the riff-raff of the colored population."[110] But this mob was well organized:

> Sentinels stood on each corner, and when a white man would pass they would ask him about where he was going, etc. A whistle signal would then be passed on to the next corner and the pedestrian would be surrounded and followed. If he went in the direction of the jail the negroes would close in upon him and he would soon find himself covered by fifty or more cocked revolvers.[111]

How did African Americans organize this self-defense operation so rapidly? One of the members of the armed resistance was Dan Treavan, a cook. According to the police reports, "Treavan says he was sent out by one of the colored secret societies of which he is a member."[112] Another person arrested was Ben Dilworth, a local minister who was accused of "making an incendiary speech in front of the post office."[113] Alonzo R. Jones, "a coal black negro" who had served in the police department before Jacksonville's city government was deposed by the state legislature in 1889, was also incarcerated. These three leaders of the emergency black militia represented a cross-section of African American institutions: secret societies, churches, and civic officials. They had connections to wider networks of solidarity that could be mobilized rapidly and efficiently.

Furthermore, the black working class in Jacksonville was itself well organized. Lower-income workers were members of groups such as longshoremen's associations and washerwoman's unions as well as burial societies. It was not unusual for a laborer in Jacksonville to hold simultaneous memberships in a union (e.g., the Knights of Labor), a fraternal order (the Knights of Pythias), and a church. It is not the case that African Americans in Jacksonville were not divided to a certain extent along lines of class, gender, and neighborhood—they were. Still, the practice of belonging to overlapping institutions made community mobilization against lynching possible.

As the white militia poured into Jacksonville and began arresting the "ring-leaders" of the emergency militia, the city's African American middle class joined their voices to those of white authorities who asserted that blacks should put down their weapons.[114] Led by William Artrell, a former Key West assem-blyman, the black "committee" presented their resolution to the public:

> Resolved (in the name of all good colored citizens), that while there are extenuating circumstances in connection with the assembling of the colored citizens on Monday night to prevent lynching, the congregating of these men together on the other night after the militia appeared to protect the jail is highly reprehensible, and meets our unqualified condemnation. Resolved, That we regret that military companies have been brought [to] Jacksonville from various parts of the state when the Jacksonville military companies were perfectly able to put down any uprising among the people.[115]

The black committee's critique of African American armed self-reliance was complex. On the one hand, they criticized black workers for taking up arms, but only *after* militia units had arrived to reinforce the police, who were now able to halt the lynching. The committee's resolution implicitly supported the initial African American network of self-defense that had been organized when Benjamin Reed's life was threatened by vigilante action. Furthermore, the committee made clear that it did not support the idea of bringing white militia companies from other Florida cities to Jacksonville. Indeed, their resolution went on to state that if the city of Jacksonville had called upon African Americans to help with the situation, such a crisis would never have arisen in the first place: "The colored citizens of Jacksonville are ready and willing at any moment to assist in putting down and quelling any disorder," stated the committee, " . . . and had they been called upon at the outset the disorder would have been instantly removed." African Americans in Jacksonville offered an effective way of preventing lynching. While this strategy would have kept the peace, however, it would also have undermined white rule. It was rejected out of hand by Jacksonville's authorities.

Ida B. Wells lauded African Americans for stopping the lynching of Benjamin Reed. Wells drew on the episode in Jacksonville to formulate her doctrine of armed "self-help" as an example for black Americans across the country to emulate. Wells observed: "Of the many inhuman outrages of this present year, the only case where the proposed lynching did *not* occur, was where the men armed themselves in Jacksonville, Fla., and Paducah, Ky. And prevented it." [116]

In June 1897 Sylvanus Johnson was accused of raping a white woman in Key West. In the midst of Johnson's arraignment at the county courthouse, former Knights of Labor leader C. B. Pendleton, a white, rose and exclaimed: "Are there enough white men in this room who will help me in lynching the brute?" Immediately, a group of African Americans in the courthouse made a rush to defend Johnson and temporarily foiled Pendleton's plan. However, the *Times-Union's* man on the scene remained hopeful: "Your correspondent would not be surprised to learn in the morning that the brute had met his deserts during the night." [117]

African Americans surrounded the jail and the courthouse to prevent Sylvanus Johnson from being lynched. [118] Throughout the evening, emergency militia patrolled the approaches to the courthouse and forbade any white man from entering the area. The *Times-Union* complained: "If a lynching is attempted trouble will follow, as there are not enough whites here at present to cow the tough negro element that is at present making the trouble." The Monroe County sheriff wired Governor Bloxham: "Negroes greatly outraged, and threat[s] to burn and kill whites openly made." [119]

Governor Bloxham wired President William McKinley for U.S. troops to crush what white officials now viewed as an insurrection. The governor remonstrated that Key West was "Too far from mainland to secure necessary State Troops." [120] One cannot help but notice the irony of a "states' rights" Democrat begging a Republican president for federal intervention. Once again, white Floridians had misjudged African American aims. The goal of the "Negro rioters" was to stop a lynching, not to overthrow the state. As soon as authorities demonstrated a willingness to guard Johnson, African Americans dropped their armed guard. [121]

The fate of Sylvanus Johnson illustrates the possibilities and limitations of insurgency against lynch law. While armed resistance earned a trial for Johnson, it could not ensure a fair hearing before a jury of his peers. A little over a month later, Sylvanus Johnson was tried and found guilty by a jury of white men. His trial took all of one hour and forty minutes, and his court-appointed counsel was not allowed to cross-examine the witnesses. Visibly disgusted with the charade of justice, the condemned man turned to the jury and exclaimed: "If God was black and came before this jury you would find him guilty. You may hang my black body, but you cannot harm my innocent soul." [122]

Two years later, African American phosphate miners in Dunnellon tried to stop the escalation of racial violence in the phosphate boom region by organizing the "Anti-Lynch and Mob Club."[123] In contrast to the middle-class reform organizations that undertook Progressive Era initiatives, the miners left behind no records. The only surviving descriptions of the group characterize the members of the Anti-Lynch and Mob Club as coming straight out of the "Dunnellon Phosphate Mine." Dunnellon was a brutal town, even by Florida standards. Judge E. C. May recalled one day in the 1890s when seven African Americans were assassinated, their bodies "piled on the depot platform, like cordwood. Exactly nothing was ever done about it, and I never knew who killed any of them, or why."[124]

In June 1899, a black man who was in jail facing trial for allegedly shooting the town marshal was taken out of his cell and lynched.[125] Subsequently, it was rumored that African Americans in Dunnellon had assassinated two black men who were said to have been hired to carry out the initial lynching. Authorities called out white posses from Citrus and Alachua Counties to restore order.[126]

Soon afterwards, the white press retracted its claim that African Americans had killed the two black men said to be implicated in the initial lynching.[127] A local correspondent's report to the *Richmond Planet* adds some depth to this story. This writer reported that the two black men had been taken along by the white mob and forced to aid them in the initial lynching. "Hearing this some of the colored men proceeded to search for the lost man," wrote the correspondent, "and signs being favorable some of the men returned to town with arms and arrested the two colored men who were with the white mob."[128] After making citizen's arrests, Anti-Lynch and Mob Club members took the two black collaborators to the city jail for incarceration. The armed group of African American miners also solicited a description of the white men who had taken part in the lynching. Not knowing that the black miners had acted with such dispatch, the local white press printed its initial claim that African Americans from Dunnellon had lynched the two men. The *Planet's* writer stressed that whites were angry that the truth about the initial lynching was out and that the white posse that came to town actually sought to eliminate the two black witnesses. "The county sheriff came from Ocala," wrote the *Planet's* correspondent, "investigated matters and gave the colored men credit for protecting the law. Not one gun has been fired for signal of riot nor has there been, since the finding of the lost man." Two more lynchings had been prevented.

A world of different experiences separated African American miners in Dunnellon from their counterparts in Jacksonville and Key West. The great majority of these miners were migrants from the Carolinas who came to Florida during the phosphate boom of the 1890s.[129] Phosphate miners tended to live in isolated camps segregated from both white neighborhoods and older, more rooted African American communities. What the miners did have was a sharp sense of grievance against the phosphate mining companies. While phosphate mining was a step up from low-paid farm labor, it was still a tough occupation. Lives and limbs were frequently lost to dynamite blasts, workers inhaled toxic fumes for long stretches, and miners rarely made the wages promised them by labor agents.[130] Operating in a hypercompetitive environment, mining companies sought to boost profit margins by enforcing low wages, scrip payments, and company stores. Routinely the object of police violence, phosphate miners were known for carrying Winchester rifles, banding together, and defending themselves from company harassment as best as they could.[131]

White authorities in Dunnellon had no intention of tolerating the existence of an organized body of working-class African Americans dedicated to the prevention of lynching. The Anti-Lynch and Mob club was too effective, and it is certain that the members of the organization understood that it was only a matter of time before local officials moved decisively to crush them. The day of reckoning came in early October 1899, when members of the anti-lynching association engaged in a pitched gun battle with Dunnellon marshal J. J. Stephens and several of his relatives and friends—all "marshals" of varying ranks. Marshal Stephens, according to local reports, "while treating all the negroes well, was very strict and on one or two occasions had to shoot one of them."[132] White residents remembered that Stephens and his brothers were brutal men who boasted of killing and torturing African Americans.[133] Whether Marshal Stephens provoked the fatal gun battle that destroyed the Dunnellon Anti-Lynch and Mob club or whether the miners themselves initiated the fight is not clear.[134] The result was the same: the anti-lynching organization ceased to exist.

TO PROTECT THE WHITE MAN FROM HIS OWN TEMPER

Armed self-defense was always fraught with danger. Manatee County farmer Jack Trice was faced with as terrible a decision as any father has ever had to make. His son had gotten into a fight with the son of Braidentown city marshal John Hughes. Hughes deputized a posse and came to Trice's house to "regulate" the fourteen-year-old boy. Seeing the armed men approaching his home, Trice barricaded the door. When Hughes demanded that Trice send out his son to meet his punishment, "Trice refused and the whites began firing." Trice's marksmanship was superb. Each time a man advanced to break down the door or set the house afire, Trice fired a shot that found its mark. The white posse fled for reinforcements and vowed to burn Trice and his son at the stake.[135] The Trices, however, left the county under cover of darkness.

A wave of terror swept over Manatee County as white mobs burned down homes and shot down African Americans who were accused of being in the Trice home during the gun battle. Employers were warned by the "President of the Whitecappers" that "all negroes and whites who defend them must leave or be killed."[136] The local press claimed that another group of African American workers had refused to step aside when a white man approached them on a pathway. When a warrant was issued for their arrest, this group of black workers resisted and barricaded themselves in houses where they fought off white attackers.[137] African Americans fled the region in droves. The Manatee County race war illuminates the terrible dilemma that confronted black Floridians. There were occasions where armed self-help seemed to be a necessity. Nevertheless, armed resistance evoked draconian responses from whites, who could rely on local law enforcement officials to support them.[138]

African Americans made the linkage between the right to bear arms and equal citizenship in the letters they sent to Governor Bloxham asking for the right to form citizens' militia units to participate in what they believed would be the liberation of Cuba in 1898.[139] In Tampa, J. J. Hendry petitioned to raise a company of troops for *Cuba Libre,* and told city officials: "Don't think for one moment that we have forgotten the stars and stripes. We love the flag for it stood for Union and freedom."[140] The connection that Hendry made between military service and freedom for all was odious to individuals who were building a one-party state. In contrast to North Carolina and Virginia, Florida would muster no African American regiments into service for the Spanish American War.[141]

John Mitchell, Jr., the influential editor of the *Richmond Planet,* lauded armed self-help in Florida as a strategy to be emulated by all African Americans.[142] In contrast, white leaders in Florida warned that a new breed of black Floridian was emerging: the revolutionary "Winchester Negro," who had no fear of any white man. White Floridians framed black armed resistance in political terms because they had seized control of the state through armed violence and understood that African Americans claimed the right to defend themselves from white incursions. "It looks, my countrymen," wrote a white columnist in Jacksonville, "like a return to the days of 'old John Brown,' and I see again the picture which appeared thirty-one years ago in a northern paper. . . . The time has come when we must arm against a foe within, and settle this question for all time."[143]

State officials sought new ways to permanently end African American claims to equal citizenship or inclusion in the society. State Senator John Beard introduced a bill in 1907 to nullify the Fourteenth and Fifteenth Amendments to the United States Constitution in Florida. The state senate passed the nullification bill by a resounding margin.[144] In the same year, Governor Napoleon Bonaparte Broward proposed in his annual address that Florida work with the U.S. Congress to expel African Americans to a foreign "territory purchased by the United States."[145] The governor pointed to the state of racial warfare in Florida: "The negroes today have less friendship for the white people, than they have ever had since the civil war, and the white people have less tolerance and sympathy for the negro." Broward claimed that an African American had "less inclination to work for one and be directed by one he considers exacting, to the extent that he must do a good days work, or pay for the bill of goods sold to him," and that "civilization and Christianization" were being destroyed. He argued that "to protect the white man from his own temper," black Floridians should be removed from the state. The governor's address extended the open season decree on African Americans in Florida.

The year after Broward's address, African American timber workers in the Panhandle town of Millville faced a new crisis. One evening black laborers engaged in an argument with a white shopkeeper that escalated into a gunfight. Two African Americans were arrested and lynched. "This aroused the negroes who feared further attacks," stated the *Panama City Pilot*, "and it is said that they bought a large number of cartridges, and threats were made by both negroes and whites."[146] This conflict robbed the local lumber factory of an entire shift when mill operatives, both black and white, took up opposing defensive positions "on the railway and at Southport so that by Monday the mills could only operate one side owing to these desertions." Once again, African Americans had taken up arms to defend themselves. There would be no more lynching that year in Millville.

African American traditions of armed self-defense in Florida challenge the standard chronology of black resistance. It has often been assumed that a younger, more aggressive generation of African Americans came onto the stage in the wake of the Great Migration to do combat with white mobs in the East St. Louis Race Riot of 1917 as well as the 1919 race riots.[147] As we have seen, however, black Floridians on numerous occasions openly took up arms to defend their communities between the end of Reconstruction and the turn of the century. The role of armed self-reliance in the anti-lynching movement also needs reappraisal in light of the evidence from Florida. Long before the rise of the better-known Progressive Era anti-lynching organizations, black Floridians created the basis of an anti-lynching struggle—at the high tide of the lynching years, no less—that at times successfully prevented racial violence. African American armed self-help suggests a more continuous black struggle against racial terror than scholars have generally posited. Certainly, excluding Dunnellon miners and others who fought lynching in the trenches from the narrative of the anti-lynching movement is the equivalent of excluding slaves from the antislavery movement. A striking characteristic of these episodes of armed self-help is the large number of individuals involved and the absence of a single leader. Indeed, Florida's authorities arrested dozens of African American "ringleaders" in the wake of these episodes. This is a testament to the democratic nature of self-defense as a mode of resistance. Armed self-defense was a critical component of the African American freedom struggle in Jim Crow Florida and would be a vital part of new battles to come.

⫷ 4 ⫸

TO GAIN THESE FRUITS
THAT HAVE BEEN EARNED

Emancipation Day

HISTORY WAS one of Jim Crow's fiercest battlegrounds. African Americans invoked memories of slavery and Civil War to emphasize their claims on citizenship while white Americans used history to show that African Americans had done nothing to earn a stake in the society.[1] When a group of African American Civil War veterans from Florida attempted to participate in a remembrance day ceremony near Fitzgerald, Georgia, in 1911, a crowd of nearly one hundred white men ripped the military insignia off the men's jackets and ordered them to leave the area.[2] Nothing was more threatening to the maintenance of Jim Crow than the idea that African Americans had been active participants in the struggle to save the Union in its darkest hour. On a national level, prominent academics produced a literature heavily influenced by eugenics and social Darwinism that promoted white nationalism and black inferiority.[3] Historians presented slavery as a benevolent institution and Reconstruction as a tragic descent into Negro Misrule.[4]

White Floridians erected monuments with state sanction that paid homage to antebellum slave holders, the nobility of the Confederacy, and the Lost Cause. Indeed, the past was intensively present in Florida. Carl L. Crippen was struck by the ways that white Floridians mourned Jefferson

Davis's death in 1889. Crippen noted that official society would not tolerate any dissent from a blind homage to the Confederacy: "Talk about the New South, One Country & one Flag, its all bosh, they would sink the Ship of State, today as quickly as they did when the lamented Lincoln was at the helm had they the opportunity & could. They talked here of Jeff Davis's death—*Our* President's death—they could not forget the [Civil War] & do not desire. . . . P.S.: Don't expose me as I do not wish to be 'A Silent Voter.' "[5] Stoking the memory of the Lost Cause paid handsome dividends to white folks. Black and white Floridians were assessed taxes on what reportedly became the most generous Confederate pension plan in the South.[6]

Public school books in Florida taught that newly freed African Americans acted like buffoons. A typical primer read: "Many of the negroes loved their old masters and stayed on the old plantations, but others wandered away. Some thought that because they were free they would never need to work any more, so they dressed up in their best clothes and went to picnics and had a good time."[7] Florida's curriculum in Jim Crow history was much the same as that nationally described by historian Leon Litwack: "The treatment of emancipation depicted blacks passively waiting for Massa' Lincoln to strike off their shackles. And Reconstruction saw the enthronement of black ignorance and inexperience, with the Ku Klux Klan in some accounts redeeming Anglo-Saxon civilization from alien rule."[8] Florida's history books made one thing clear: African Americans were completely unfit for equality or citizenship. The *Florida Times-Union* promoted a history tailor-made for racial imperialism:

The two races have existed on earth as far back as knowledge can reach. The white man without a helping hand has steadily climbed upward. The civilization of the twentieth century is of his unaided building. The negro, where he has had to depend on himself, has advanced not a step in all the centuries. Individuals have surmounted difficulties but the negro has not climbed except when he has been helped up by association with the white man. The negro today is as much of a savage as he was thousands of years ago except in "the white man's country."[9]

In contrast, African Americans fashioned democratic narratives honoring slavery's survivors, the Union Cause, and the egalitarianism of Reconstruction.[10] These lessons enhanced black pride by providing examples of black accomplishments. Politically charged memories also helped to shape black identities and aspirations for social change. Born in 1889, Crescent City native Asa Philip Randolph recalled that his father's stories of the revolutionary heroes of black history and the positive legacy of Reconstruction taught him to stand up for his rights at a young age.[11] Mary McLeod Bethune based her doctrine that African American women were the equals of their male peers on her grandmother's and mother's accounts of resisting the sexual advances of their slave masters. In 1904, Bethune founded the Daytona Educational and Industrial Training School for Negro Girls. Black history was at the top of the curriculum, and segregation was banished from school grounds.[12]

African American elders attempted to pass on to their children what will be referred to here as a testimonial culture, a way of testifying to the dignity of individuals in the segregated present while weaving together a history of striving reaching back to slavery times. Black Floridians organized public activities and rituals including Emancipation Day, veterans' ceremonies, and public rituals emphasizing African Americans' contributions to the republic. African Americans created a popular (and frankly political) history accessible to a broad audience, and they invoked this history in their struggles for social change.[13]

MEMORIES OF SLAVERY

Black testimonial culture was rooted in the ways that African Americans remembered their experiences of bondage. In 1882, a Republican activist named S. W. Anderson explained how he shamed another African American into joining the party:

> I ask him "Sir what principal does you support[?]" [He replied],
> "I always generally vote a Democratic ticket for the last 15 years & have not seen the point where I can have pleasure in voting on any other principal." Yet then as a moment I call his attention & replied to him: "Dear Sir, as far as my supreme abilities will allow me I will now give you a friendly advice" & said to him "can you realize the day when you was under bondage?" His reply was "yes" and immediately I then said "take consideration & think where you are now & if you continued your course where will you be then.["] Then he look sorrowfully and well my Sir the Stranger said "I never was enlighten." Then I said to him: "Will you consider your self a converted Republican?" He said "yes," then I said now from this rule depart the strict rules of the said state."[14]

African American oral traditions of slavery emphasized the institution's severity. In Pensacola, residents spoke in hushed tones about those who had been physically mutilated for participating in the state's Underground Railroad.[15] Survivors spoke of generations of rape, psychological cruelty, severe floggings, and violence so endemic to antebellum culture that even in the depth of the Great Depression former slave Samuel Johnson remarked that "even the best masters in slavery couldn't be as good as the worst person in freedom, Oh, God, it is good to be free, and I am thankful."[16] Ex-slave Taylor Gilbert recalled how slave owners' sons "would go 'nigger hunting' and nothing—not even murder was too horrible for them to do to slaves caught without passes. They justified their fiendish acts by saying the 'nigger tried to run away when told to stop.' "[17]

Stories of suffering endured long after slavery's demise. Wakulla County resident Martha Harvey Farmer remembered that during the 1930s, "My grandfather used to tell about the slaves. They was treated, some of them, terrible. They were beaten."[18] Gadsden County native Malachia Andrews recalled the stories that his own grandfather told about slavery:

> He has told us from time to time how their master, the slave driver who really took care of his slaves and kept them working. He'd tell how they used to do them when they, regardless to how cold it was, rainy, he got them slaves up in the morning and put them out to work. If they didn't work they beat them. He told a story how one young man who told him that he was sick and they accused him of just trying to resent work. They took him and they hung him up by both hands and they took a rawhide whip and whipped him, beat him and beat him and beat him. As a result, when they carried him back home he died in the woods.[19]

The Day of Jubilee was enshrined as a sacred moment of liberation. "I remembers the day when the word came, that word that made free men an' women of our black peoples," a survivor told one northern visitor.[20] After crying of the "whippin's the black people's had," and "the death blows the runaways got" during slavery, this informant went on to contrast white and black reactions to emancipation: "I remembers that day well, when them black men an' women an' lil' chillun were a-crowdin' roun' each other, an' cryin' fo' joy, an' a shoutin': We's free, we's free! Glory! Glory! We's free, we's free!' An' I sees the [masters] a-scowlin', some of them as pale as death. I hears them cussin' mad, so mad that they cannot bear it, an' go shoot themselves like cowards."[21]

The survivors lived with the consequences of slavery for the rest of their lives. With time as their enemy, African Americans desperately sought to reunite with family members who had been torn from them by the domestic slave trade. In 1900, Mary Ann Harris was still searching for her mother:

> Information wanted of my mother, Jane Fields. When I left Jeffersonville, Ky., my mother had a number of children. I do not remember the name of any but Jack, Gabe, Sallie and Rebecca Fields. I was brought from Jeffersonville, Ky to Sherman, Tex., by my owner, John Field, Jr. The rest of my family belonged to his father, John Field. My name at that time was Mary Ann Fields, but now it is Mary Ann Harris. Any information of said people will be gladly received by Mary Ann Harris, 206 Field Street, Jacksonville, Fla.[22]

Calls for slavery compensation became a recurrent theme in black discourse. In 1884, the State Conference of the Colored Men of Florida presented an argument for slavery compensation and municipal reform:

> It is sometimes asked that, aside from all questions of public policy, is it just and equitable that the white people should be taxed to educate the colored, as they are under our present public school system? My answer to this is most positively in the affirmative; and I further assert that the reasons why it should be so, from an equitable standpoint, are stronger by far than any that can be urged in favor of it upon grounds of public policy. It is a settled principle that runs through the entire business transactions of the world, that when a person renders to another something of pecuniary value, he is entitled to a quid pro quo, or something of equal value in return. This principle is well founded in law, constitutes a bed rock in equity, and is taught by the holy writ in the living language that "the laborer is worthy of his hire."[23]

The conference's keynote speaker, James Dean, went on to create a formula for estimating the unpaid wages owed to black Floridians during slavery. (Modestly, he included only the final thirty-five years of slavery in his calculations.) Dean explained how he would apply this fund to rejuvenate education and state government:

> From 1830 to the close of the war in 1865 there was an average laboring population of 29,000 colored people in this State. In equity and justice

they were entitled to their earnings; and if they had been allowed wages during this period at the low rate of 40 cents a day, and board, their earnings would have aggregated the sum of $145,000,000—a sum equal to more than four times the assessed valuation of property in the entire State of Florida to-day. This amount could have been judiciously invested, and under the present tax law we could have raised an annual sum of $145,000 for school purposes, $435,000 for the expenses of the State government, and $435,000 for the interest on the State debt. This Conference should take some steps looking towards a more liberal support for education, and petition the Congress of the United States for national aid for the same.[24]

Black Floridians continued to believe in the essential justice of the principle of slavery compensation.[25] At the turn of the century, a visitor to Florida remarked: "It is often claimed by Southern men that the negroes were better off as slaves than they are now, with regard to physical comfort and all essential needs, but this view finds no endorsement among the negroes themselves."[26] As late as the 1930s, aging former slaves were still trying to gain remuneration for their unpaid labor. The "Ex-slave Club" of Miami was organized by Rev. J. W. Drake, at St. John's Church, in 1932. Members of the organization, "being from 85 to 97 years of age, have vivid recollections of the emancipation and of their living on the plantations. In some instances, these children were separated from their parents while they were so small as to have no recollection of their own father or mother."[27] As the Great Depression deepened, these former slaves organized, and "one of the objects of the club is to secure a pension for the members, as they are nearly all in very needy circumstances." The survivors waited in vain for their recompense.[28]

EMANCIPATION DAY

Emancipation Day was the centerpiece of black testimonial culture, a day to commemorate liberation as well as to mark the progress of the race. From the very beginning, African Americans transformed a day of remembrance into a public event that stressed their rights of citizenship. Soon after word of the Emancipation Proclamation reached Union-occupied Key West in 1863, African Americans organized a massive celebration and invited Sandy Cornish to be the keynote speaker. Cornish was a legendary figure on the island who had physically mutilated himself decades earlier to avoid being sold back into slavery.[29] His enormous personal sacrifice was adopted by his peers as a reminder of what they had endured for generations. Twenty-five years later, Rev. R. R. Downs told readers of the *Christian Recorder:* "I was by the hospitable Pensacolians invited to participate in the Emancipation celebration. They celebrate the 20th of May because on that day, they were liberated from slavery by the order of the Union Generals. . . . they truly celebrated on a grand scale." [30]

In a typical Emancipation Day ceremony, "there were special seats provided at the front for the men and women who were survivors of slavery, and many reminiscences of the dark days . . . given by them served to make us more appreciative of our present liberty and opportunities."[31] Program committees invited keynote speakers to discuss the intersection between past and present struggles. In 1906, Pensacolans asked C. F. Call to be their main speaker. Call had been a lead organizer of the city's streetcar boycott movement against segregation the prior year.[32] Joseph Lee, who had served as an elected official during Reconstruction, was invited to speak at numerous events ranging from St. Augustine's 1881 celebration to one at Valdosta, Georgia, in 1914.[33] African Americans chose Lee at least in part as a reminder that they had once participated on a mass level in electoral politics.

The Day of Jubilee generated massive turnouts, and women often took center stage. In 1891, "Several hundred of the leading colored citizens of Ocala" gathered to hear Miss M. J. Brydie deliver a speech on "Lincoln" while Mrs. F. L. Williams spoke on "Freedom," as part of the day's events.[34] The following year, "hundreds of colored people from all over the state of Florida commenced to arrive in [Jacksonville] last night and continued to come in on every train this morning to take part in the emancipation proclamation celebration."[35] The Ocala day of remembrance generated large turnouts through the rest of the decade. At the 1896 event the audience sang patriotic songs, and participants heard a variety of speeches including one by Hattie F. Bryant noting that "the history of the race . . . attested of wonderful success under conditions so unfavorable since emancipation days."[36] Over a quarter of a century later, the tradition of celebrating emancipation in Ocala remained intact, and African American women played a central role in making the event successful.[37]

Male and female organizers toiled over the choreography of the ceremony. "In the beginning we have been told," a Florida WPA interviewer noted in the 1930s, "the main portion of the Emancipation program consisted of singing, praying and giving thanks to God and a few speeches by

Negroes who were more enlightened than most of the others, and they would teach."[38] As black communities grew, emancipation observances became more complex:

> As time passed the celebration became more elaborate. Parades with numerous floats and bands of music passed through the streets. The floats were set up to represent the progress of the negro. These showed him on the plantation, out in the cotton field, etc. [T]he women wore cotton-checked dresses and bright colored bandannas tied around their heads. . . . The overseer wearing his broad brimmed or tall crown hat, his leather boots and carry the familiar bull whip was always necessary.[39]

Emancipation Day celebrations combined elements of high drama, pageantry, and storytelling. This was the methodology of black public history: the young and untutored were introduced to history via parades, dramatic role playing, and participatory learning. The cruelty of slavery was not forgotten—witness the personage of the overseer with his whip—but the hard-fought progress of African American communities was also displayed:

> A parade depicting the progress of the race from slavery, along the lines of profession and trades is held. After the parade a mammoth mass meeting is held and many speakers of interest and note are heard. After the mass meeting a banquet is tendered the speaker. The banquet is made possible by personal donations, collections from churches and from various other sources.[40]

African Americans tried to stay alert to the ways that past struggle was related to current striving. An integral part of Emancipation Day was the taking up of a collection to benefit the local community. It was noted that "during one of these affairs the money collected was enough to extend the school term of the public school."[41]

Emancipation Day also allowed African Americans to relax, let off steam, and renew contacts with old friends in other parts of the state. In 1889, black residents in Jacksonville traveled to Quincy to share the day's ceremonies with African Americans in Gadsden County. According to a local report, "The Quincy Brass band paraded the streets and as usual the day was wound up with a game of base ball. A large picnic was had at the rock spring, south of town."[42] At Sanford's 1886 celebration, brass bands from Tampa and Jacksonville performed.[43] At the turn of the century, it was not uncommon for African Americans who lived in the timber town of Milton to travel to nearby Pensacola to celebrate the Day of Jubilee.[44]

When Rev. D. S. D. Belliny spoke to an African American audience at Macclenny during an Emancipation Day gathering, "there was scarcely a dry eye in the audience as the speaker told the story of the hardships and struggles the race passed through during the dark days of slavery, but how God, through his own goodness, guided it through the darkness into the new dawn of Christian civilization."[45] Rev. Belliny used the stories of shared oppression in the past to call for increased "race unity" in the present. After prayer, the participants sang patriotic songs, played baseball, and had a banquet. One participant enthusiastically noted: "The eloquent address of Prof. Belliny is still the talk of our town." This was more than a holiday. Black Floridians enriched Emancipation Day ceremonies with joy, spirituality, self-reflection, and a desire for social change.

REMEMBERING THE UNION CAUSE

After helping to lay flowers on the graves of departed African American soldiers and sailors buried in a Jacksonville cemetery, a participant in the memorial service urged: "Emancipation Day and Decoration Day are two days above all others which should ever be remembered by colored people."[46] To enshrine the sacrifices that African American Civil War veterans had made toward the liberation of all, black Floridians created a tradition of observing Memorial or Decoration Day in a manner that clashed with surrounding customs of the Lost Cause. In their memorial services, African Americans contrasted their service to the nation with the sedition of their ex-Confederate antagonists. "Decoration day was the usual one-sided affair," a black correspondent from Pensacola wrote in 1888. "An excursion left here for the national cemetery to decorate the graves of those who fought for what they considered right; also the ones who fought for what they knew was wrong."[47]

In Jacksonville, African American Union veterans organized their own Grand Army of the Republic post, Charles Gabriel Post No. 6, in 1885 to avoid discrimination in the white-controlled GAR post. The veterans were celebrated as heroes by the black community, a writer noting: "The cause which made it possible for such organizations as colored Grand Army Posts to exist was the struggle for the union and for liberty."[48] The same correspondent celebrated the sacrifices of black Civil War soldiers "who, when the call was made to do battle for this country rushed into the field and fought with the zeal of the Romans and the courage of the Spartans." While white Floridians were decorating graves with Confederate flags, African Americans conducted their own solemn services:

> The ritualistic service of the Grand Army of the Republic was closely followed in the decoration services, led by Post Commander Andrew Solomon. The fifty or more graves of war veterans were strewn with flowers by the members of the Women's Relief Corps and children, and the members of the Grand Army post placed a miniature flag at the head of each soldier's grave. There are several soldiers buried in Mt. Hermon Cemetery. A detachment of the Grand Army post went there yesterday in the forenoon and decorated them.[49]

Veterans and community speakers used these forums to exhort African Americans to hold their heads high. At one Decoration Day memorial service in Jacksonville, M. M. Lewey, a combat veteran of the 55th Massachusetts Infantry regiment, discussed black sacrifices at Fort Wagner, Olustee, Honey Hill, and other battlefields of the Civil War. "Mr. Lewey grew eloquent while relating reminiscences of the war," wrote a correspondent; " . . . valuable were the deductions he made and the applications ending in strong exhortations to all to live up to what has been achieved."[50] Another speaker at the memorial service lectured on the role of African American soldiers "from colonial times to the present day," and "America" was sung with the national flag flying conspicuously. John Wallace, a veteran of the 2nd United States Colored Troops, "spoke with much enthusiasm." Among other things, Wallace said: "he rejoiced to know that ten million people armed in the holy cause of the struggle to reach the topmost round in the ladder of Christian civilization are invincible against all forms of injustice and oppression."[51]

African American women kept these celebrations alive even as the ranks of surviving Union veterans dwindled. At the 1903 Memorial Day services in Jacksonville, Miss Eartha M. M. White and members of the Woman's Relief Corps led a procession "bearing flowers which were placed on the graves of the sleeping heroes."[52]

African Americans laid claim to equal citizenship by fashioning a historical past that emphasized black service to the republic. A determination to keep the memory of African American sacrifices to the Union Cause alive is manifest in the letter of a black Republican to Joseph E. Lee in 1879. This correspondent contrasted African American devotion to the

Union Cause with white treachery: "Some of the Republican bigots who believe when we broke the slavery chains in 61 and 5 we should rely on vassal servitude. They think the colored man should always bow the servile knee to their deliverer. . . . now nine out of ten of those big blowers done in the time of Battle but very little in the great cause of Union and Emancipation."[53]

DEBATING SLAVERY'S LEGACY

In spite of a general consensus about the importance of remembering past defeats and victories, African Americans did not agree over which cultural practices from slavery were appropriate for carrying into the present. Nowhere is this conflict more evident than in disputes over worship styles in the post-Reconstruction South. Historian Evelyn Brooks Higginbotham argues that college-educated African Americans were critical of the older religious culture, noting that the "men and women of the Talented Tenth" believed that "gaining respect, even justice, from white America, required changes in religious beliefs, speech patterns, and manners and morals."[54] Discussing the "Progress and Drawbacks of the Race," in 1888, H. T. Tanner explained this conflict in generational terms: "The old folks believe in the shout still and a long experience, while the model church discountenances such and believe in using the organ in religious services."[55]

Most older black Floridians believed that the kind of liturgies that the Talented Tenth wanted them to adopt would compromise their struggle against white supremacy. An African American writer in Palatka complained about expressive practices in local churches and described the attitude that the typical black church member expressed toward worship: "He does not believe that the religion white men claim to possess is 'true religion.' A religion that does not make one shout or respond to what the preacher says, is worthless in his estimation."[56] The same observer remarked, "He likes to give vent to his spiritual feelings in loud exclamations and shouts. To disapprove of his manner of worshipping God, brings down his utmost contempt, accompanied with the assertion that your religion is 'book larnt' and will not do 'to die' with."[57] A supporter of the newer, more formal style of worship in Pensacola remonstrated, "Some people find fault with Rev. R. D. Dunbar because he cannot 'moan' like others."[58]

This effort by the church hierarchy to alter African American worship styles into more "progressive" directions met concerted resistance. Hezekiah Butterworth, a travel writer who visited Florida in the 1880s, transcribed performances of the ring shout as well as slave spirituals and work songs. An ex-slave, "Aunt Jane," told the inquisitive writer that African Americans of her generation performed the old-time spirituals because they had carried them through bondage, and she complained that younger people did not seem to fathom this. "'We sings 'em 'mong ourselves . . . we old folks, but dey don't sing 'em at meetin' no more,'" this former slave protested. She went on to explain that:

> We's got pow'ful fine preachers, but dey sings mostly outer pra'r-books, new hymns; an' de young folks, dey follers 'em. Dey says as how our ole hymns ain't got no sense in 'em; but, bless you, dey's got a heap ob sense to us. Dey kin lift us up high as de golden chariot, and dat's 'nuf fur me I reckon.

Butterworth was moved by these sacred performances, but northern black church officials were less impressed.[59] Efforts by AME ministers to replace the "old-fashioned" slave spirituals with the new songs were denounced by women of "Aunt Jane's" generation, who referred to them disdainfully as "white people's hymns."[60] Later, Zora Neale Hurston argued that class tensions between "high-brow" and "primitive" black Floridians resulted in the Sanctified Church movement. Members of the Church of God in Christ and Saints of God in Christ were highly critical of ministers who drew their sermons from learned theological texts. "They say of that type of preacher," Hurston observed: "'Why he don't preach at all. He just lectures.' And the way they say the word 'lecture' makes it sound like horse stealing."[61]

Northern black church officials also tried to abolish the ring shout in Florida, a practice that emerged in the synthesis between West African spiritual beliefs and Christianity in slavery. Again their efforts met with strong resistance.[62] AME bishop Daniel Payne railed against "Voodoo Ring Dances" in northeastern Florida, but admitted their persistence, noting that "this 'heel and fist' mode of worship which was imported from Africa was cherished during the reign of slavery and has been encouraged by unprincipled pastors who have more respect for animalism than for Christianism."[63] Bishop Payne worried that the ring shout reinforced racist stereotypes of black behavior that discredited the entire race. So did William Artrell in Key West, who complained that during one revival, "one of the converts had to fall down on the floor in church & join the others in their maniacal performances. As long as this way of worshipping is continued among the colored people, the whites, can never respect us. . . . I have raised my voice openly and fearlessly against it."[64] Artrell was not able to continue vocalizing his disgust with African American religious practices, however, because he had aspirations to run for political office, and he told Joseph Lee that such public utterances would ruin his standing in the black community. Shortly afterwards, the frustrated middle-class leader cried: "I am tired of the life I am leading in Key West. I long to be able to attend my Church once more & partake of the Holy Sacrament, and to be among intelligent people. I have resolved on leaving Key West as soon as I possibly can."[65]

ECHOES OF RECONSTRUCTION

Battles that joined historical memory and contemporary politics became a regular feature of segregating Florida. The state legislature openly supported the nullification of the Fourteenth and Fifteenth Amendments to the U.S. Constitution. The Reconstruction experiment of guaranteeing equal protection under the laws and voting rights to African Americans was recognized in polite society as misguided.[66] In sharp contrast, African Americans in Fernandina created a "Fifteenth Amendment Day" celebration to mark passage of the law that formally guaranteed their voting rights. The celebration included a parade, speakers, recreation, and other festivities. In calling their community to prepare for the 1897 celebration, organizers stated:

> The Fifteenth Amendment Association of Fernandina will celebrate the anniversary of the adoption of the Fifteenth Amendment to the Constitution of the United States of America. . . . We call upon every society, the presidents, Sunday-school superintendents, benevolent societies, barbers' associations, stevedores, pastors of the several churches and all societies and kindred organizations to participate in the grand parade on that occasion.[67]

While white authors argued that the end of Reconstruction had brought a just "Redemption" to their state, African Americans taught the opposite lesson.[68] Frank Berry offered a memory of Reconstruction that could not be reconciled with segregation: "Berry recalls the old days of black aristocracy when Negroes held high political offices in the state of Florida, when

Negro tradesmen and professionals competed successfully and unmolested with the whites. Many fortunes were made by men who are now little more than beggars."[69] African Americans remembered Reconstruction as a democratic moment and blamed white violence and GOP cupidity for its demise.[70]

While white Floridians may have honored the memory of the Reconstruction-era Ku Klux Klan, black Floridians reserved harsh judgments toward whites who used terrorism to undermine democratic government. Harriet Jefferson, reared in rural Leon County, was given instruction by her elders in the ways that white Democrats had attained power:

> Yeah, they talked about hanging people. I know papa said he used to tell us about the first sheriff was a black sheriff in Tallahassee and said I imagine when they got ready to get rid of him or something they just come to talk with him about him. Just come in and he was sitting down to his table, but said they just come in and shot him in the mouth. He was sitting down to his table to eat and instead of just firing him if they didn't want him or something like that they just came in and shot him. Shot him in the mouth into his head.[71]

The lesson that Mrs. Jefferson's elders taught her was likely told as a cautionary tale to avoid white people whenever possible. On another level, this lesson challenged the legitimacy of white Democratic rule. Is political power attained through terror legitimate? What type of government allows this to happen? Not every story of this type was designed as a lesson in civics; nor were these stories necessarily accurate. Nonetheless, what Harriet Jefferson learned about Reconstruction in her own neighborhood was more useful to her than anything she would learn about the period in a standard history text.

GRASSROOTS HISTORIES

Black Floridians transformed remembrance days into theaters of universal democracy. When African Americans in Pensacola held a mass celebration for the William Lloyd Garrison Centenary in 1905, the editor of the *Florida Sentinel* asserted: "There is no man, living or dead, to whom the American Negroes owe so much and to whom we are indebted for so noble a life's service in our behalf, as to William Lloyd Garrison."[72] When Mrs. L.J. Madison read a paper titled "Frederick and Freedom" to commemorate Douglass's ninety-seventh birthday in Jacksonville, black Floridians were asserting the righteousness of their struggle for dignity in America.[73] African Americans in Jacksonville organized the Crispus Attucks Suffrage Club, in honor of the black seaman who fell in the Boston Massacre, a key event in the making of the American Revolution.[74] In January 1906 the Crispus Attucks Club held a meeting discussing "The Law Governing the Qualification of Voters," and also heard a lecture titled "A Sketch of the Life of Crispus Attucks," making the link between black history and equal citizenship explicit.[75]

African Americans treated the fiftieth anniversary of their emancipation as a sacred moment of popular celebration. Black Floridians formed program committees months in advance of Emancipation Day, 1913. Committees in towns including Crescent City, Lakeland, Miami, Arcadia, Titusville, De Land, Daytona, St. Augustine, and others had decades of expertise to draw upon.[76] On January 1, African Americans across the state remembered where they had come from, where they were, and where they wanted to go in the future. The survivors of chattel bondage took center stage to share their stories with each other and the young.[77] In Bartow, "Hon. C. L. Livingston, an old veteran of slavery days, made the opening speech" to an audience of approximately one thousand people.[78] In Daytona, former slaves rode in a parade float of honor "which contained four old mothers who were eye witnesses to the liberating of the race. . . . The parade was one of the grandest ever witnessed here."[79] In Gainesville, African Americans held a torchlight parade, and sang "The Battle Hymn of the Republic" and the "Star Spangled Banner."[80] At Fort Pierce, A. J. Kershaw gave the primary oration titled "Claim of the Negro to American Soil." At St. Joseph's Church in Jacksonville, the speaker of honor "reviewed with credit and pleasure to his anxious hearers, the United States History in that he showed that the negro has a reasonable, merited and legitimate right to claim America as his country."[81] African Americans used the fiftieth anniversary of their emancipation to make claims on the state. James Weldon Johnson wrote a poem for the occasion that was read in emancipation ceremonies throughout Florida and the nation:

A few Black bondsmen strewn along
The borders of our eastern coast.
Now grows a race, ten million strong.
An upward, onward marching host.

Then let us here erect a stone,
To mark the place to mark the time;
A witness to God's mercies shows,
A pledge to hold this day sublime. . . .

This land is ours by right of birth,
This land is ours by right of toil.
We helped to turn its virgin earth
Our sweat is in its fruitful soil. . . .

To gain these fruits that have been earned.
To hold these fields that have been won.
Our arms have strained, our backs have burned.
Bent bare beneath a ruthless sun. . . .

That for which millions prayed and sighed,
That for which tens of thousands fought.
For which so many freely died,
God cannot let it come to naught.[82]

The raw material for James Weldon Johnson's poem may be found in the desires of ordinary African Americans to finally gain the full measure of freedom. They had fostered a testimonial culture that undermined white efforts to glorify slavery and denigrate black character. Black Floridians did not believe that their stories of suffering, heroism, and endurance merely added to the nation's historical record; rather, they believed that their experiences in slavery, Civil War, and Reconstruction changed the meaning of the nation's history altogether. Black southerners wove the institution of Emancipation Day into the first universal narrative of freedom that existed anywhere in the country. Black Floridians were preserving a chronicle of striving that strengthened affective bonds between the generations and deepened the culture of survival. Equally significant, a careful study of black testimonial culture shows that African Americans learned their politics through their experiences with slavery, Civil War, and Reconstruction. Black Floridians cited their own histories as the foundation for their demands for equal citizenship, and they chose days of remembrance as the tie joining the struggles of the past to the challenges of the future.

TEN DOLLARS REWARD.

RAN AWAY from the sub-
scriber, a *Negro man* named *Charles*, and a *Negro woman* named *Dorcas*. The man
is about forty years old, and
the woman thirty-eight. The
man is very black—about five
feet nine inches in height,—
with the African marks on his face of his native country. The woman is about five feet
nine inches, and rather thick set. Any person returning them shall receive the above
reward.   **HENRY W. MAXEY.**
Cedar Point, March 4.   1w10

1 ▶ Advertisement for runaway slaves (from the *Jacksonville Courier*, April 16, 1835). *Source: Department of Special and Area Studies Collections, University of Florida Libraries.*

2 ▶ Matthew M. Lewey. A Civil War combat veteran, M.M. Lewey began his polit-ical career during Reconstruction when he served as mayor of Newnansville. He subsequently became a newspaper editor. He was a leader of the 1905 Pensacola street-car car boycott and helped organize African American vot-ers in 1920. *Source: Florida State Archives.*

3 ▶ James Dean, n.d. Dean argued for the justice of slave reparations at the State Conference of the Colored Men of Florida in 1884. Four years later, he was elected Florida's first black county judge. He was deposed by the state the following year for allegedly licensing an interracial marriage. *Source: Florida State Archives.*

4 ▶ Domestic worker, Apalachicola. While most African American women toiled in low-wage occupations such as laundry and personal service, their struggles against workplace oppression infused black politics with demands for dignity and economic justice. *Source: Florida State Archives.*

5 ▶ Harriet Beecher Stowe. The author of *Uncle Tom's Cabin* purchased a Florida plantation shortly after the end of the Civil War and subsequently published accounts of her bitter disputes with African American domestics over work rules. *Source: Florida State Archives.*

6 ▶ Mary McLeod Bethune, ca. 1904. Bethune established the Daytona Educational and Industrial Training School for Negro Girls in 1904. She was an ardent promoter of black history and a leader of the Florida Federation of Colored Women's Clubs. She famously told black Daytonans in 1920, "Eat your bread without butter, but pay your poll tax." *Source: Florida State Archives.*

7 ▶ Women on ox-drawn cart near Willie Plantation, Lloyd, Florida, in 1907. *Source: George S. Baker Photo Albums, Willie Plantation, Lloyd, Florida, Department of Special and Area Studies Collections, University of Florida Libraries.*

8 ▶ Richard A. Twine photographed this Annual Emancipation Celebration in St. Augustine around 1922. African Americans turned Emancipation Day into a day to honor the survivors of slavery and reaffirm their right to equal citizenship. The "GAR" banner in the foreground was the standard of the black Civil War veterans. *Source: Florida State Archives.*

9 ▶ Celebrating Emancipation Day at Horseshoe Plantation, Leon County, ca. 1930s.
Source: Florida State Archives.

10 ▶ "An Afternoon Meal—Miami, Fla," 1905. Postcards and novelty items depicting African American children being devoured by wildlife were mass-produced in segregating Florida. They were purchased and disseminated through the mail by tourists from the North and Europe. *Source: Florida State Archives.*

11 ▶ Convict laborers. The convict lease was profitable to the state, county sheriffs, and northern-based firms alike. By 1910, Florida had the highest incarceration rate of prisoners and juveniles in the Deep South. The state administered one of the most notorious penal systems in the world, immortalized in decades of lurid films and exposés. *Source: Florida State Archives.*

12 ▶ African American miners at a mine face of the Dunnellon Phosphate Company mine no. 2 in 1890. Workers at this mine organized an anti-lynching association in the 1890s and employed armed self-defense in order to prevent lynching. *Source: Florida State Archives.*

13 ▶ Eartha M. M. White and her mother, Clara White. Eartha White was
a leader of the Florida Federation of Colored Women's Clubs, a teacher,
and a legendary community activist in Jacksonville. She co-founded the
Colored Citizens' Protective League in 1900 in order to promote black
political activity. *Source: Florida State Archives.*

14 ▶ Carpenters, Jacksonville, ca. 1900. African American carpenters in Jacksonville were union-ized, periodically struck for higher wages, and promoted a strong practice of mutual aid between members and their families. *Source: Florida State Archives.*

Jacksonville, Fla. Bethel Baptist Institutional Church

15 ▶ Bethel Baptist Institutional Church, Jacksonville, 1911. Bethel played an important role in Jacksonville's black neighborhoods and provided meeting space for the 1901 and 1905 streetcar boycotts against segregation. *Source: Florida State Archives.*

RESOLUTIONS IN CONDEMNATION
OF THE
INIQUITOUS "JIM CROW" STREET CAR LAW.

PASSED BY THE INTER-DENOMINATIONAL MINISTERS'
MEETING OF JACKSONVILLE AND
DUVAL COUNTY, FLORIDA.

WHEREAS, the Legislature of the State of Florida recently
enacted a "Jim Crow" street-car law which aims to humiliate all
Negroes who do not travel in the capacity of servants, and which is
calculated to create further friction between the races and destroy
the selfrespect of our people;

THEREFORE, be it resolved that we, the members of The
Inter-denominational Ministers' Meeting of Jacksonville and Duval
County, Florida, do most unqualifiedly denounce said Law as unjust,
barbaric and promotive of caste distinctions; and we condemn the
spirit which prompts this and all similar legislative measures as
being contrary to the "Golden Rule" and opposed to the principles
upon which the American Government is founded, and is calculated only to engender ill-will and strife between the races.

RESOLVED 2ND: That in order to retain our self-respect and to
show our utter condemnation of the above mentioned unjust and
cowardly measure, and in order to preserve the peace of the community and to avoid possible clashes between our people and the
street car conductors and motormen, we advise the members of our
race not to ride on the street cars;

RESOLVED 3RD: That these resolutions be printed and distributed as widely as possible among our people.

Respectfully Submitted;

REV. J. MILTON WALDRON, D. D., Chair.
" S. A. WILLIAMS.
" W. D. CERTAIN,
" H. C. WILLIAMS,
" L. B. ELLERSON, Sec'y.
Committee on Resolutions.

REV. J. S. TODD, D. D.,
President,
The Inter-denominational Ministers' Meeting of Jacksonville, and
Duval County, Florida.

REV. L. B. ELLERSON,
Secretary.
Jacksonville, Fla., June 12th, 1905.

16 ▶ 1905 Jacksonville streetcar boycott broadside. African Americans in
Jacksonville and Pensacola organized effective boycotts against segregation
in public conveyances and temporarily turned back the tide of Jim Crow.
*Source: The George Baldwin Papers, Southern Historical Collection, Library
of the University of North Carolina at Chapel Hill.*

17 ▶ Governor Napoleon Bonaparte Broward. Broward held office from 1905 to 1909. In his 1907 speech to the state legislature, he called for the expulsion of African Americans from Florida. *Source: Florida State Archives.*

18 ▶ Jacksonville longshoremen taking a lunch break in 1912. African American dock workers in Florida's port towns established strong unions in the late nineteenth century and organized for shorter hours, better pay, and safer working conditions. *Source: Florida State Archives.*

19 ▶ Turpentine workers chipping pine trees, ca. 1890s. Turpentine was a volatile industry that suffered from extreme swings in supply and demand. Employers banked their profits on pushing workers' wages as low as possible. *Source: Florida State Archives.*

20 ▶ Joseph E. Lee, probably around the turn of the century. Lee served as an elected official during Reconstruction. He later practiced law, became an ordained minister, and was appointed to numerous Republican patronage positions in Florida. After World War I, Lee turned his full attention to black voter registration. *Source: Florida State Archives.*

21 ▶ James Weldon Johnson. The Jacksonville native was principal of
Stanton School, where he composed "Lift Ev'ry Voice and Sing" for his
school's choir to perform for a 1901 celebration of Lincoln's Birthday.
Johnson became executive secretary of the NAACP and testified before the
U.S. Congress about election improprieties in Florida's 1920 presidential
election. *Source: Florida State Archives.*

22 ▶ Colored Knights of Pythias State Lodge Building, Jacksonville, 1919. The Pythians became one of Florida's premier mutual aid institutions. By the end of World War I, one out of every six adult black men in Florida belonged to the secret society. *Source: Florida State Archives.*

23 ▶ Wedding of Dr. W. S. Stevens, February 8, 1910. When Stevens finished his medical internship in Gadsden County in 1905, area residents
begged him to stay. Stevens became a successful businessman, a leader of the
Knights of Pythias, and a key organizer of the Florida voter registration
movement of 1919–1920. *Source: Florida State Archives.*

24 ▶ Ku Klux Klan parade, Brooksville, 1922. The Ku Klux Klan terrorized African Americans and white dissenters in Florida during Reconstruction. The Florida Klan was resurrected in the summer of 1920 and became the most powerful paramilitary force in America. *Source: Florida State Archives.*

Map 1 ▶ Florida Counties and Cities in 1910. *Source: Based on U.S. Census, Population Reports by States*, 1910.

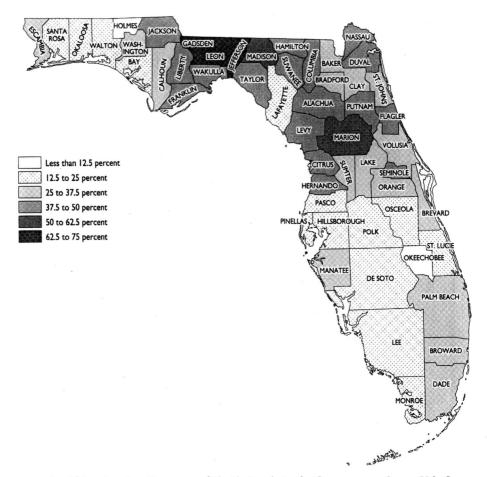

Map 2 ▶ African American Percentage of Florida Population by County, 1920. *Source: U.S. Census, Population Reports by States*, 1920.

5

TO SEE THAT NONE SUFFER

Mutual Aid and Resistance

Societies have progressed insofar as they themselves, their subgroups, and lastly, the individuals in them, have succeeded in stabilizing relationships, giving, receiving, and finally, giving in return.[1]

MARCEL MAUSS, *THE GIFT*

We share our mutual woes,
Our mutual burdens bear;
And often for each other flows
The sympathizing ear.[2]

ODD FELLOWS OPENING ODE

DAYTONA NATIVE HOWARD THURMAN observed, "It is clear that for the Negro the fundamental issue involved in the experience of segregation is the attack that it makes on his dignity and integrity."[3] African Americans throughout the nation organized institutions of mutual aid, especially secret societies, lodges, churches, women's clubs, and labor unions, in order to sustain black dignity, testimonial culture, and economic security.[4] Black fraternalism in America originated in the struggle to survive slavery.[5] In post-emancipation Florida, black cooperative associations elevated the practice of civic fraternalism—public acts of fellowship that advanced African American solidarity and public struggles against oppression—to a high art. The national leader of one of Florida's chief secret societies, the

Colored Knights of Pythias, proposed mutual aid as a force to challenge oppression:

> I am one of those who believes that since we are Negroes first, and seeing that the line of prejudice is being more tightly drawn each day, it is the duty of every individual, every school, every church, every organization and every lodge to do all in its power to help ameliorate the condition. . . . There is no way of estimating the power and influence we would have, if we act in union for common interest of our ten million people and use the same methods that are used by other intelligent interests. . . . It is for this reason that I so strongly endorse the movement for the friendly society union or anything else that has for its object the bringing of better conditions for us as a people.[6]

African Americans taught civic fraternalism through the practice of organized reciprocity. Rank-and-file members of lodges and fraternal orders took solemn oaths to assist each other in times of crisis. A keen observer of African American mutuality noted, "In sickness and at death the case is rare where some society, organization or church does not come forward with relief. Sometimes the amount is small, but still enough to keep the name of the unfortunate from the pauper list."[7] One's dues (or tithes) paid for sick benefits and an honorable burial as well as ensuring the survival of the association. In 1902, an organizer with the Independent Brotherhood in Orlando proudly declared: "This organization has added more than 3,000 members to its rolls during the year in this state. It has paid to sick members $2,500 in the past twelve months."[8] Novelist Sutton E. Griggs commented on the ubiquity of benevolent societies in the Jim Crow South and affirmed: "the aid furnished by these societies during sickness, and their public displays upon the occasion of the burial of their members are strong attractions for the Negroes of limited means and of little note."[9]

Being a member in good standing of a mutual aid association often meant the difference between life and death, dignity and shame. African Americans also gained an enormous amount of self-confidence and community organizing experience as they shepherded these institutions through the harsh decades of legal segregation. This is the key to understanding the resilience of the freedom struggle in Florida: African Americans drew upon the secular and sacred ties they had forged with one another in their organizations and used these ties as a starting point for creating new political insurgencies. This was politics based on experience and strategic relationships of trust. African Americans ultimately invoked civic fraternalism to challenge the power of white supremacy and to demand justice from the state.

A secret society recruitment notice in Jacksonville read: "The Universal Brotherhood is spreading and is an ark of safety for all who may join."[10] The religious imagery of an ark sheltering its battered passengers from rising flood waters was an apt metaphor in segregating Florida. In the Jim Crow South, one's safety depended on mutual assistance—coming to the aid of a brother or sister in need—and African Americans learned the practice of mutuality in their secret societies, labor associations, churches, and fraternal lodges. "When I say more race unity," Florida native Emanuel Fortune, Jr. emphasized, "I mean [African Americans] should form strong organizations among themselves for mutual and effective protection in time of need. The existence, the objects and the aims of these organizations should be known only to the members of them, and they should be appealed to and used at the right time and in the proper manner."[11] Secrecy and solidarity were the watchwords of institutions trying to ward off the blows of racial oppression. The centrality of fraternal organizations in African American life may be gauged in part by their sheer size. By the time the Prince Hall Masons convened their 1906 Grand Lodge meeting in Palatka, they boasted 250 state lodges and twelve thousand members. The following year the Grand Lodge reported fifteen thousand members in good standing.[12] The Colored Knights of Pythias and its sister organization, the Courts of Calanthe, claimed similar numbers.

THE CONSOLATION OF KNOWING THAT HE WILL BE DECENTLY BURIED

Wage earners formed the base of these institutions, and it is necessary to turn to their experiences in order to understand how and why African Americans transformed secret societies into vehicles to advance community organizing. Jim Crow relegated black Floridians to the most dangerous jobs that paid the lowest wages.[13] This was an era where labor safety regulations were rejected by the nation's courts as unfair impediments to employer prerogatives.[14] African Americans depended on their mutual aid organizations to promote cooperation and to serve as a buffer from the worst impacts of unregulated capitalism.

African American workers suffered grievously in Florida's workplaces. The state's railroads were especially treacherous. H. C. Gilchrist worked as a machinists' helper on the Atlantic Coast Line in Lakeland. He was working underneath a seventy-five-ton engine when it collapsed, mortally crushing him.[15] Around Christmas of 1902, a porter on the Atlantic Coast Line from St. Petersburg "was killed . . . by the train mashing him to pieces; he was brought home in a barrel and buried by Rev. P. R. James. He leaves a wife and several children and brothers to mourn his loss."[16] Florida's booming timber and agricultural sectors also claimed many lives. Wesley Bird, working in a Gadsden County sawmill, "accidentally came in contact with the saw and had his arm cut off. He was brought to town and Drs. Lamaer and Munroe did all in their power for him, but he died in a short time, from loss of blood."[17] Two days later, a black worker in a nearby mill was severely maimed by the power machinery.[18] Agricultural workers and day laborers perished in farm accidents, heat waves, and lightning strikes.[19]

An enthusiastic state official claimed: "It is said that a cargo of cotton shipped from Fernandina, or Jacksonville, or St. Augustine will often reach Liverpool before a vessel from New Orleans or Texas will have reached the Caribbean Sea."[20] An untold number of African Americans died or suffered crippling injuries while handling those goods. Arthur Philips, "quite well known among the negro longshoremen," slipped off the Washington Street dock in Jacksonville while loading timber onto a steamer and drowned before his fellow workers could save him.[21] A terse announcement in Pensacola told the tale of another tragedy: "A negro had his head seriously crushed on Commandancia wharf this morning. It is thought he will not survive the injuries."[22] "To the man of capital," one Florida booster exulted, "Florida offers a large variety of specialties to employ it surely and profitably, whether as an investment looking to the future for increase, or present employment and quick returns."[23] Little thought was given to the value of African American workers' lives in this system.

Black labor organizations struggled to maintain the élan and self-respect of their members in the charnel house of Florida employment. In 1887, Archie Williams was buried alive when the ditch he was digging caved in. Williams was also a member of the Knights of Labor in Pensacola, and, "being a Knight of Labor, the number of people that attended [his funeral] was one of the greatest ever witnessed here."[24] The KOL ensured that their brother received a dignified funeral and that services were held at a local Baptist church. Nothing less was satisfactory to these men who lived every day of their lives with the specter of workplace catastrophe. To his employers, Archie Williams was a "ditch digger." To his union brothers and fellow church members, he was a human being worthy of respect.[25]

The African American longshoremen's union in Pensacola established a tradition of stopping work and shutting down the docks whenever a comrade was being buried. Union members wanted to ensure that each brother's passing was marked with solemnity and honor. The longshoremen asserted their humanity against employers who viewed them as factors of production. Pensacola's shipping magnates entreated the unionists to see reason:

> Gentlemen—We, the undersigned shippers of timber and lumber of Pensacola, beg to ask you if you cannot possibly arrange so as to obviate the entire stoppage of work in the harbor whenever a member of your association is buried? Under the present charter-party, recently adopted by English steamship owners, this works a great hardship and loss on us, and besides placing Pensacola at a great disadvantage in competing for tonnage with some of our neighboring cities.[26]

Few African Americans had the kind of workplace power that unionized longshoremen exerted. The longshoremen's remarkable tradition, however, demonstrates the point that fraternal-based organizations prided themselves on their ability to provide a befitting funeral service for their members.[27]

African American organizations strove to maintain a culture of dignity for both the living and the dead in the community. Labor unions, male and female lodges, churches, and other organizations combined the functions of mutual assistance and burial society. Efforts to secure linkages with the past invigorated efforts in the present to spread the benefits of civic fraternalism throughout the wider community. An African American newspaper correspondent in Pensacola observed, "All the churches that I have named have societies, whose object is to bury the dead, take care of the sick, and help the destitute generally."[28] An African American in Palatka observed of his average fellow citizen: "Next to his church duties come his society duties. He believes that every one should be connected with some secret society, if for no other purpose than to look after his remains when breath leaves the body. The consolation of knowing that he will be decently buried is sweet to his thoughts."[29] These collective bodies formed the bedrock of African American culture and society in Florida's cities and towns.

The same was true in rural Florida. A. I. Dixie, a lifelong resident of Gadsden County, began learning about black secret societies as a child during the 1920s. African Americans in rural Gadsden created the Order of Emancipated Americans as part of their search for autonomy. Prior to the order's existence, if a family member died, Dixie noted, "you had to go to your boss man to get a casket, and these black folks went together and started this little lodge, and you'd pay twenty-five cents a month, and get a hundred and twenty-five dollars 'long then that would bury you [and] you was carried to the cemetery in a wagon."[30] The Order of Emancipated Americans flourished in Gadsden, Leon, and Jefferson Counties by practicing reciprocity: "If you was a farmer and your mule died," Mr. Dixie recalled, "the farmers in the community had to give you a day's work 'til you get . . . another mule and that's it."[31] Rules-based solidarity proved very effective. In 1927, African Americans in Gadsden maintained no fewer than seventeen secret societies including Frederick Douglass Lodge No. 37, Colored Knights of Pythias.[32] Secret societies promoted African American self-respect in life and in the transition to death. Six decades later, A. I. Dixie was still a member of the Emancipated Americans.

African American women organized their own associations. A member of a women's secret society in Live Oak encouraged others to sign up because "those who have joined it would not take anything for their membership. We care for our sick ones and bury the dead."[33] The Courts of Calanthe, the sister lodge of the Knights of Pythias, affirmed that in Palatka, "the Calanthes take good care of their sick."[34] Louise Perry Haile recounted that her mother-in-law and other women in rural Alachua County created the Female Protection mutual aid society in 1904:

She was a midwife and she felt that some of the people were very, very poor. Everybody couldn't take care of their own, just like today. She had gone to South Carolina with some of her people and they were having organizations up there. When she came back, she began thinking of those people who couldn't pay me. Those who pay me with syrup or chicken. She decided that she would ask the neighborhood to come together, the ladies, and give their dimes and nickels so when these people got sick, they could pay somebody to go in and help them. They could help them by giving them money to help themselves.[35]

The Female Protection society expanded to four lodges in Alachua County with a membership of four hundred people. The association offered death benefits to impoverished members. "The men would get together and make the casket for different people when they died," recalled Mrs. Haile, "especially for the poor people." When Mrs. Haile was interviewed in 1983, the Female Protection society was still in existence.

African American associations marked the deaths of their members with a dignified moral significance no less important than the material benefits they provided. In April 1901, David Hall, a young African American dock worker, was straining along with a gang of laborers to load cargo onto a Clyde steamship when he was struck by a falling piece of timber and driven deep into the St. John's River. Despite his fellow workers' efforts to rescue him, Mr. Hall's body was not recovered from its watery grave until the following morning. The white press cited Hall's death, but misspelled his name and quickly moved on to other matters like promoting the region's export shipping trade, for which David Hall had sacrificed his life.[36] African Americans reacted much differently to Hall's death. "The untimely death of Bro. David Hall is quite a sad blow to the pastor and members of Ebenezer M. E. church, as he was among the most pious young men," grieved a member of the church. "He was a faithful steward and prominent member of the normal class of the Sunday school. His funeral sermon will be preached on next Sunday night and resolutions from all of the departments with which he was connected will be read."[37] David Hall was also a member of the black Millmen's Union, and the workers of that organization attended their fallen brother's memorial service en masse.[38] Ebenezer Church was packed with mourners that Sunday. David Hall's church and union brothers and sisters wanted to ensure that their deceased friend would be memorialized with the dignity and respect that Jim Crow Florida denied black citizens.

Such memorials were deeply rooted in African American history. Students of slavery in the Americas observe that black funeral rites were based on traditions that reached back to West African beliefs stressing obligations between the living and the newly deceased.[39] Black Floridians sustained the African emphasis on the connection between the living and the dead and adapted it to a new context. A white travel writer unwittingly encountered the echoes of a West African religious practice in a Jacksonville cemetery during Reconstruction. Mistakenly framing the practice of grave decoration as one "savor[ing] very much of desecration," the writer described the sacred headstones: "The colored people have the greatest variety [of grave decorations] consisting of china doll heads, legs, arms, glass bowls . . . broken vases . . . pieces of fine china pitcher handles, lamp stands and mustard jars giving more the appearance of a child's play house than the repose of sacred dust."[40]

One pathway to the roots of black testimonial culture in Jim Crow Florida leads to a cemetery "reached by a series of winding country trails" in Jackson County, where African Americans buried their dead during slavery. "On these rustic monuments are inscribed crude words of farewell," remarked a WPA folklorist in 1937. "These are often written in longhand in many of the stones, some of them appearing to have been painfully spelled out by the survivors of the person whose grave they mark." Black residents of Jackson County told the folklorist that the slaves

> were buried in the cemetery only with the greatest secrecy. Sometimes, they say, the slaves had to disinter the bones of a loved one after dark, after a slave holder had buried it somewhere on his plantation or in a shallow hole in the woods, and re-bury it in the "slaves' graveyard." One of them explains, "Mary's" stone in this manner; he states that "Mary" was the much-loved wife of a slave from whom she had been taken after the pair were sold in the Jackson County area, and that she died shortly thereafter. It was her husband who learned to write her name, and later put it on a rock he dug or found in the woods. . . . Another stone has on it merely "Good-bye Timothy."[41]

When enslaved African Americans disinterred bodies to provide appropriate burials, and offered "words of farewell" to recently passed loved ones, they were creating narratives of death that countered the slave owners' propensity to view chattel slaves as less than human.[42] In the post-emancipation period, labor unions, secret societies, and churches formalized the practice of ensuring a proper burial for their dead. In 1905, B. B. Banner, a member of the Bricklayers' Union, died in Jacksonville and was buried by city authorities in a paupers' cemetery. As soon as Banner's union brothers discovered what had transpired, they scraped together a collection of money and did what their ancestors had done in slavery: "The union, on last Sunday, had the body exhumed and re-interred in Mt. Hermon Cemetery, with proper ceremonies."[43]

Funeral eulogies reaffirmed the dignity of the deceased, promoted a positive vision of the community, and not infrequently offered stinging critiques of racial oppression. "When a Negro funeral is to be held, every friend or well-wisher of the deceased one must get off from work that particular day to attend the funeral," wrote an observer in Lakeland. "The funeral services are long. . . . Every friend must read an obituary. These are the customs of the average colored funeral."[44] The triumphant and sorrowful testimonials offered to those who had been slaves reminded black Floridians where they had come from. A eulogy given in honor of Rev. C. B. Simmons in 1883 noted, "He was first taken to Key West as a slave, but being among that heroic few who[,] struggling with the adversities and cruelties of slavery, yet had that craving of spirit, that greatness of soul and nobleness of ambition, by his own exertion freed himself, paying in gold for what the laws of his country should have secured him."[45]

A eulogy to a recently deceased leader of a Masonic lodge served as part personal tribute, part history lesson:

> He was born in the dark fifties, at a time when it was a penalty to be
> born in the South, and a chain-gang offense to be educated. He was
> nursed from the lap of a slave mother and nurtured on the coarsest of
> food. Coleman was one year old when the Supreme Court of the
> United States rendered this infamous decision in the Dred Scott case,
> signed by nine justices, that no African, whether slave or free, could be a
> citizen of a State or of the United-States. . . . John Brown was at this
> time teasing in his den the lion that we sometimes call slavery.[46]

Black organizations did not just offer words of respect to their deceased members; they created narratives of death that bolstered their surviving associations. When Allen Robinson died in 1907, his brothers in the Carpenters' Union took pains to amplify the idea that Mr. Robinson's life had a transcendent meaning:

> Inasmuch as it has pleased our All-Wise Creator to remove from our
> midst our esteemed brother, Allen Robinson, and, Whereas, His long,
> useful and intimate relations with us make necessary and befitting that
> [we] record our appreciation of him; therefore be it Resolved, first, That
> we shall ever hold in grateful remembrance the ability which he showed
> in helping to construct and maintain this organization; second that the
> sudden removal of such a one from among us causes a vacancy and casts
> a gloom that will be long felt by each member of the union.[47]

The rites of death bestowed a shared dignity upon funeral participants and the deceased that the larger society denied. Furthermore, while association members might hail from different class backgrounds, the death rituals of secret societies had a leveling tendency. When Anthony James died in a railroad accident on his way to work, members of his Odd Fellows lodge recited the same burial creed that would be invoked for any member in good standing:

> The great and small; the rich and poor; the sovereign and peasant; the learned and illiterate; the high and the meek and low in heart must bow to His divine will. Teach us then, oh Lord, to do Thy will and be ever ready for Thy call. To those who come to this order, first and last, "Lay down thy arms, the battle is fought, the victory is won, henceforth and forever rest from thy labor."[48]

African Americans' deep concern over maintaining their dignity in this life—and the next—spawned efforts to bolster and maintain ties between past, present, and future generations. Black Floridians created narratives of death that infused their lives with meaning. This was testimonial culture at its deepest level.

The practice of visiting sick or injured members and offering them succor and financial relief was another pillar of civic fraternalism. Such practices enhanced a sense of trust and obligation among members. Private ailments became collective concerns. A typical notice announcing the illness of an African American in Jacksonville read: "Mr. Floyd, who was badly hurt while at work in the shipyard some time ago, desire[s] his brethren of the Odd Fellows to call and see him at No. 1054 West Church Street."[49] After she had lost her beloved husband, Mrs. J. W. Burgess publicly thanked her Rose of Sharon lodge sisters as well as her husband's brothers in the painters' union "for their kindness shown to her late husband during his illness."[50]

Black trade unionists forged labor solidarity on the anvil of mutuality. When D. I. Robinson, an African American carpenter in Jacksonville, fell seriously ill and could not work, he called on his brothers in Carpenters' Union Local 224 as well as fellow lodge members of the Odd Fellows "to call and see him" through his illness.[51] A few months later, Robinson's union went out on strike against city building contractors, who discovered to their chagrin that "no colored man will work outside of the union after he has been approached by a colored member of the organization."[52] Rather than cross picket lines, the carpenters sought employment as common laborers on railroads. "A contractor . . . referring to the strike . . . said that he had learned from this experience that the colored carpenters will stand together, regardless of reason or argument."[53] The carpenters built labor solidarity on what anthropologist Marcel Mauss would have called the "stabilizing relationships" they had created with each other on and off the job.

Secret societies adopted rigorous rules and procedures for ensuring that sick members were not forgotten. In towns where two or more Knights of Pythias lodges existed, members were required to organize a relief committee "to look after sick or distressed brothers, to pay them their benefits or make donations or loans."[54] Each lodge was required to form a "committee to visit the sick," usually consisting of five members who would look in on afflicted members to ensure that their needs were being met. Such visits were undertaken to bolster the morale as well as the material condition of the afflicted, and the Pythian manual advised: "Let your conversation be such as to cheer him up and make him forget his pain."[55]

J. R. Hawkins, a resident of Orlando, was effusive in his praise "to his friends for favors shown him during his illness. His lodge and his church also remembered him. . . . The physician now attending him says he can cure him."[56] Hattie Johnson's Gainesville lodge, the Household of Ruth, called on their ailing sister with a basket of "many valuable articles, such as oysters, tomatoes, rice, flour and many others."[57] Mrs. Gussie E. Capers, "a long and patient sufferer" of an undetermined illness in Palatka, was "tendered a surprise . . . by her brother and sister members of Emanuel Church. She was made to feel good with the spiritual consolation given, as well as being the recipient of a goodly supply of edibles and a purse of several dollars."[58] Serving ailing members in their time of need was viewed as one of the noblest pursuits by church members, and the informant of this sick visit articulated the religious dimensions of civic fraternalism: "God will help those who remember the afflicted."[59]

Black Floridians created institutions that boosted members' morale, kept families intact in moments of crisis, and delivered benefits in emergencies.[60] Collective action was the midwife of civic fraternalism. "The negroes carry their race contest into every department of life and of business," reported a Florida newspaper in the midst of the 1888 yellow fever outbreak. "Not only this, but they organize as a race in all cases of public and common calamity. They have formed a colored auxiliary committee in Jacksonville to control the supply of the [yellow] fever fund and provisions to the negroes of that city."[61]

Secret societies, labor unions, and churches were rooted in local communities. However, their affiliations with larger organizations put black Floridians in communion with state and national bodies, thus alleviating the isolating impact of Jim Crow. In 1881, black Masons in Palatka welcomed Amos Webber, a Civil War veteran, civil rights advocate, and a fraternal brother from Massachusetts, to their town by hosting a rousing celebration.[62] In the aftermath of the Great Fire of 1901 which destroyed Jacksonville, Knights of Pythias lodges—as well as other secret societies, churches, and labor unions throughout Florida and the nation—sent emergency relief funds to beleaguered members.[63] The Independent Afro-American Relief Union of Gadsden County urged members to think how their organization placed them in touch with a community that reached beyond their rural county:

> The general nature of the business to be transacted by said corporation shall be to help raise fallen humanity; to conduct and carry on a benevolent endowment department; to bury the dead; to create, establish and organize subordinate associations and local assemblies of said corporation throughout the state of Florida and other states of the United States and in foreign countries whenever the board of directors shall think necessary.[64]

Black Floridians named their fraternal lodges, clubs, and secret societies for individuals linked with crusades against racial oppression. African Americans yoked themselves to ancestors in struggle who had fought for abolitionism and Reconstruction and against tyranny of all kinds. Lodges were named for J. C. Gibbs (the highest-ranking black political leader in Reconstruction-era Florida), Frederick Douglass, John Brown, William Lloyd Garrison, Paul Laurence Dunbar (who had written a poem eulogizing the black Civil War heroes at Olustee), Richard Allen, Ulysses S. Grant, Antonio Maceo, Wendell Phillips, Phillis Wheatley, Crispus Attucks, and others.[65] Black Floridians chose these names to strengthen their connections to a legacy of egalitarianism opposed to the nation's nostalgic embrace of chattel slavery and the Lost Cause.[66]

Black civic fraternalism's emphasis in ensuring the dignity of the dead as well as the living brought it into open conflict with white supremacy. In 1904, a white Alachua County man shot and killed Rev. J. L. Shaw, a neighboring black farmer, over a fence boundary dispute. The white farmer was exonerated by the coroner's jury of any wrongdoing.[67] Black lodges and churches in Gainesville did not accept this judgment. They mobilized to seek justice for J. L. Shaw, stubbornly pursuing his case in the courts. Secret societies including the Masons and Odd Fellows raised funds and petitioned a lawyer from Jacksonville who managed to revive the murder charges. While this concerted effort did not change the outcome of the case, it at least reminded white Floridians that African Americans were human beings, and not animals to be shot down in cold blood.[68]

In the same year that J. L. Shaw was murdered, Julia Ward, an African American laundry worker in Jacksonville, engaged in an argument with her white landlord who arrived at Ward's apartment to collect the rent. What happened during the argument was open to dispute, but the outcome was dreadfully clear: S. C. Taylor shot Julia Ward, who died soon afterwards.[69] In line with the prevailing etiquette of Jim Crow, this was an open-and-shut case. When the coroner's jury convened, witnesses claimed that Mrs. Ward exhibited superhuman strength in her fatal encounter with Taylor and that the landlord had only been defending himself from a crazed black woman. Ward's death was ruled a "justifiable homicide."[70]

This verdict did not sit well with most African Americans in Jacksonville.[71] Churches and fraternal associations contested the judicial devaluation of black life. A delegation of ministers from the Interdenominational Ministerial Alliance approached the county sheriff and "respectfully, but urgently, asked that officer to use his best endeavors to have S. C. Taylor located and arrested for shooting and killing Julia Ward on last Tuesday evening."[72] At the same time, the ministers "went to a prominent law firm in the city and engaged them to prosecute the case." Soon after, Taylor was indeed arrested.[73] While he was subsequently acquitted, the ministers' actions and the mobilization of the black community signaled a determination to vindicate the name and reputation of Julia Ward.[74]

At the same time, Julia Ward's union sisters mobilized to ensure that she received a decent burial. Ward had been a member of Ladies' Union No. 946, and the women of that organization, led by Alice Jackson, a laundry worker, scraped their dues money together and visited African American churches in the city as well as charitable individuals to gather donations to defray the expenses of Ward's funeral.[75] To aid the survivors of Mrs. Ward's family, Eartha White, a co-founder of the Colored Protective Association, spearheaded efforts to raise money to "assist the five small children" of Mrs. Ward and her sick husband, who was confined to the hospital.[76]

Lodges, unions, and other self-help institutions were designed to be focal points of striving and struggle. Building from the base of providing burial insurance and sick benefits, black institutions were sometimes able to challenge the prerogatives of Jim Crow and engage in a broader array of activities such as raising funds for schools. An African American from Lakeland captured the ethos of civic fraternalism:

> Co-operation is the key note of the age. In this highly developed twentieth century civilization an individual counts for less than formerly; not because his personal worth is discounted, but because social obligations are more intelligently realized. The efficiency of the individual is redoubled by co-operation. "We are members one of another" is just as true in our civic as in our spiritual relations. . . . "We must hang together or hang separately." There are many things we need which will come to us only as we work conjointly. Some of these things are better schools, better churches and a more edifying moral environment.[77]

THE LIMITS OF SOLIDARITY

The benefits of mutuality were not universally shared. Fraternal organizations operated on shoestring budgets that depended on membership dues, and these institutions were vulnerable to economic downturns that dried up their treasuries. They simply could not afford to carry the entire community. In 1881, a fraternal leader lamented that an economic slump in Key West and high unemployment were draining the coffers of the island's fraternal orders, observing, "If business would only [pick] up a little I think our lodges would be all right again."[78]

African Americans singled out individuals who had no ties to church, labor union, or secret society to teach each other stark lessons about the price of living outside of the bonds of organized reciprocity. One negative example involved an African American woman once "reckoned among the well-to-do people of their race." Upon her demise in 1901, however, this woman's secret society "could not find her name among those of the members who are in good financial standing."[79] The implication was clear: a formerly wealthy woman would not receive "that respect in burial to which she was entitled," because she had let her ties to the sisters of her secret society lapse. An Ocala resident lectured: "The young men of the city should take warning as to the sad fate of Will Green who dies so poor that the city had to bury him as a pauper."[80] An African American in Jackson

County was equally severe, noting publicly that the widows of two deceased former members of a fraternal order would not receive death benefits because their spouses had let their membership dues lapse.[81] Black Floridians stressed rules-based solidarity as a mechanism to shelter the individual from the indignities of Jim Crow.[82]

At the same time, not every African American organization was concerned with the broader struggle for justice. The Knights of the Roslyn Castle seem to have been primarily concerned with throwing elaborate balls and dressing up like the nobility of medieval Scotland.[83] Outside of the mass-membership secret societies, some fraternal orders used highly selective criteria—including skin color and financial status—to bar potential recruits. A group of light-skinned African Americans in Pensacola wanted to start a "blue blood" society that would have excluded darker-skinned applicants. When local residents discovered what the so-called blue bloods were up to, they "promptly entered a boycott against the applicants, who are professional men. . . . Negroes stated that if the applicants are too exclusive in their associations, they are also too good to receive their money."[84]

Segregation has been credited with enhancing black togetherness, but it also created destructive tensions among African Americans.[85] "We have a class of men who delight in tearing down any enterprise controlled and owned by men of their own race," one black Floridian complained.[86] Church congregations squabbled, ministers were summarily dismissed, and fraternal lodges bickered over jurisdictional boundaries.[87] Pastors assisted labor organizations in honoring deceased members, but sometimes joined hands with white employers when these same unions fought for higher wages.[88] Gossip destroyed bonds of trust. "It is rumored around the city that I am doing business for a white undertaker in this city," funeral director Lawton L. Pratt stated, "and I want my customers and friends to know that this is an absolute falsehood, and the parties whom anyone hear say anything of this kind about me are that much prejudiced toward me."[89]

Black Floridians nevertheless wove together a culture of civic fraternalism resilient enough to weather most intraracial conflicts. African American cooperation was based on organized reciprocity. Black Floridians well understood Eatonville native Zora Neale Hurston's proverb: "The Negro race was not one band of heavenly love. There was stress and strain inside as well as out." Therefore, accountability to the larger collective was not taken for granted—it was written into lodge, union, or church bylaws.

The dedication of women such as Alice Jackson and Eartha White who came to the aid of a deceased sister's family, the presence of groups like the Female Protection association in Jonesville and the Order of Emancipated Americans in Gadsden County, pointed the way to a kind of freedom struggle that the architects of Jim Crow had not counted on.

THE COLORED KNIGHTS OF PYTHIAS

By the end of World War I, the Knights of Pythias and their sister organization, the Courts of Calanthe, ranked as the most powerful secret societies in Florida. The Pythians were destined to play a pivotal part in African American political insurgency, and it is critical to understand this secret society's development. The first Florida lodge was organized during Reconstruction.[90] The Knights' sacred oath pledged members to "destroy caste and color prejudices; to relieve the needs and afford succor to a brother; to elevate man to a higher plane of intelligence, morality and social equality; to administer to the sick and suffering."[91] The Pythian endowment, built by the nickels and dimes of membership dues, became a lifeline sustaining widows and survivors of members who died from work accidents, yellow fever, and other tragedies.[92]

Each brother Knight was pledged to carry the work of the lodge to the wider community and promote the work of civic fraternalism:

> Do not think that when the Lodge closes your work is done. The work in the Lodge room is very little when compared with that which you are expected to perform outside. It is but the preparation room, where lessons of charity and benevolence are instilled into your mind, that you may practice them toward your brethren and toward the outer world. . . . You are to visit the sick and distressed; the widow and orphan are to be attended to; they may need aid or counsel, perhaps both. It is your duty to see that none suffer.[93]

The Knights became a wellspring of democratic striving. The Pythian *Manual* stated: "Every member, however humble he may be, has the same right with every other to submit his propositions to the Lodge, to explain and recommend them in discussion and to have them patiently examined and deliberately decided upon by the Lodge."[94] Lodges contained elements of hierarchy—most KOP leaders tended to be older men, many of them clergy or successful businessmen. However, important lodge decisions were

TABLE 3

Knights of Pythias Endowment Claims Paid, September 28, 1918

Name of Payee	Residence	Benefit Amount
Lizzie Owens	Jacksonville	$100
Emma Harris	Fort Myers	$100
Marion Jones	Interlachen	$100
Addie Cohen	Alachua	$100
Charlotte Shackleford	Orlando	$200
Viola Tate	Gainesville	$100
Georgia Johnson	Ft. Lauderdale	$100
Susanna Trey	Ocala	$100
Georgia Hall	Jensen	$100
Celia Epps	Eustis	$100
Hagan Cohen	Delray	$100
M. A. Curtis	Orlando	$300
Elnora Griffin	Green Cove Springs	$300
Sallie Powell	Glenwood	$100
Annie Valentine	Clearwater	$100
Rosa Andrews	Tarpon Springs	$100
Alice Wooden	Dunnellon	$100
Olivia Norman	Tallahassee	$500
Emma L. Townshend	Orlando	$100
Ruth Borden	Orlando	$100
Bertha Epkins	Croom	$100
Mollie Stewart	Sorrento	$100
Susie Gilham	Tampa	$200
Della Farmer	Palmetto	$100
Alice Garett	Tallahassee	$500
Elvira Williams	Ocala	$100
Ida Clark	Jacksonville	$100
Essie Gammon	Palatka	$100
Addie Wells	Jacksonville	$100
Orin Ida	Ocala	$200
Anna Belle Wynu	Carrabelle	$100

SOURCE: "Pythian Endowment Claims Paid," NCP, *Florida Metropolis,* October 1, 1918.

decided by democratic means; on this point, the *Manual* was explicit: "As the business of the Lodge interests all, no member should fail to express his views or choice by voting on every subject that may arise. . . . No one has the right to avoid share of responsibility. The secret ballot was instituted to allow each individual the utmost freedom in the expression of his will."[95]

Each Knights of Pythias lodge was an island of egalitarianism in a sea of racial oppression.[96] As the order grew and thrived, members developed a level of collective self-confidence that allowed them to challenge white supremacy. In 1899, members successfully fought an effort by their white counterparts to make them surrender the title of "Knights of Pythias" to members "exclusively of the white race."[97] In 1913, S. W. Green, the Supreme Chancellor of the order, was waylaid by a white mob in Santa Rosa County for insisting that he had the right to purchase a berth on a Pullman car. Green's humiliation was compounded when he was arrested and fined by a local judge for his insolence. In response, the Knights issued a stinging critique of Florida justice:

> The entire Order of the Knights of Pythias suffered indignity, insult and injury, while in the mistreatment of S. W. Green as a man and a law-abiding citizen, because of his color is an imposition upon us as a race, and an infringement upon our rights as Americans. . . . we . . . do pledge ourselves to lend all assistance in our power as a fraternal organization, and as individuals, for the uplift of not only our own race, but for the betterment of our country, but at the same time we insist that we be given a citizen's chance and a free man's opportunity.[98]

The Florida KOP embarked on a dual program of recruitment and political agitation beginning in 1915. In that year, the lodge presented a resolution to Governor Park Trammell protesting the state's efforts to impose a grandfather clause that would further restrict voting rights. The Knights also fought the state legislature's efforts to bar African American attorneys from practicing law.[99] The Knights' democratic philosophy and effective mutual assistance programs made membership drives highly successful. In Florida's smaller towns and rural communities, the KOP drew upon and strengthened traditions of mutuality.[100] A. I. Dixie noted that during his youth "about all the Colored folks" in Gadsden County were Pythians. "They covered Florida like water covered the sea," recalled Mr. Dixie.[101] In 1920, the Pythians boasted over fifteen thousand members in good standing in Florida. One out of every six adult black males in the state was affiliated with the order.[102] The KOP's emphasis on black autonomy and egalitarian values set it on a fateful collision course with Jim Crow Florida.

THEY OBJECT TO THE TANGIBLE EXPRESSION OF THE COLOR LINE

The United States Supreme Court's 1898 *Plessy v. Ferguson* decision rubber-stamped the idea of "separate and equal" on a nation that understood that Jim Crow was anything but.[103] African Americans did not silently accept *Plessy.* Black southerners launched boycotts against the imposition of streetcar segregation in almost every major southern city between the 1890s and 1910s.[104] African Americans in Pensacola, Jacksonville, and Tampa launched their own protests against segregated streetcars. Urban transit systems provided affordable transportation options to tens of thousands of black working people. Segregation laws on these public conveyances transformed streetcar conductors into deputy law enforcement officials. Hereafter, conductors would enjoy "full police power" and gain the right to expel, humiliate, or arrest black passengers who violated the ordinance.[105] For black Floridians segregation in public conveyances represented the ultimate public insult to African American self-respect. Rev. E. J. Gregg entreated Mayor Duncan Fletcher to veto Jacksonville's 1901 segregation ordinance: "The conductors are mostly irresponsible men, and to clothe them with police power will mean friction between the races. They are already insulting to the colored people, and the new law will have the tendency to make them more so."[106] Black Floridians did not care if they sat next to white passengers. Nevertheless, they wanted absolute equality on urban public conveyances.

The base of every social movement is made up of relationships of trust knitted together by individuals who spend time establishing the foundations of collective self-confidence needed to challenge power. African American institutions that promoted mutuality and reciprocity played critical roles in the streetcar boycott movement. Bethel Baptist Institutional Church in Jacksonville provides a case study. Bethel served as a beachhead of protest against streetcar segregation after 1900.[107] In 1895, however, Bethel's greatest challenge was to build a new church. Bethelites submitted themselves to strict discipline to raise funds for their new sanctuary: "The membership has been styled 'Bethel Baptist Brigade,' with officers from lieutenant up and divided into companies," noted one account of the drive. "A small badge will be worn as the brigades' uniform till after the new building is completed and paid for."[108] Bethel's flock gained a sense of shared sacrifice from participating in this demanding fund-raising exercise. Most important, they had rebuilt a social space for their faith community.

Bethel's institutional charter allowed its members to undertake a variety of programs including vocational training schools, recreational programs for youth, and Emancipation Day events.[109] In short, Bethel was an integral part of the community. Bethel's pastor, J. Milton Waldron, used his base at the thriving church to take a leadership role in antisegregation efforts.[110] Rev. Waldron informed his white counterparts at a 1905 meeting of the General Convention of American Baptists in St. Louis that segregation was a sin against God and humanity. He inveighed against Jim Crow in a language his congregation sanctioned: "It is not a question of whether you will eat with the negroes or whether you will sleep with them. But a question of whether you will treat them as Jesus Christ wants you to treat them."[111] J. Milton Waldron was an effective leader; his leadership, however, was premised on the sweat and sacrifices of his flock at Bethel Baptist.

In Jacksonville, the 1901 and 1905 streetcar boycotts were marked by a diversity of tactics and organized solidarity. Working-class African Americans initiated the movement and enforced boycott discipline. "Many servants have this week notified their employers that they will work no longer than this week," the *Metropolis* reported, "as they cannot ride on the cars after next Saturday."[112] Teams of sentinels patrolled streetcar stations and used a variety of methods ranging from quiet persuasion to threats of violence to keep black passengers off the cars.[113] A writer for the *New York Age* reported, "your correspondent has not seen a dozen Afro-Americans on the white car lines. It is said that an Afro-American who rode on these cars a few nights ago was taken off the car by a number of Afro-Americans and severely beaten as an example to all his kind."[114]

Black women spearheaded the campaign against Jim Crow. In the 1901 Jacksonville struggle, "the backbone of the opposition originated with the women, who threatened a boycott of the men of the race if they dared to ride in the separate cars. . . . Too much praise cannot be given these women."[115] African American women understood that they would be the first to suffer depredations at the hands of newly empowered white male conductors, and they were determined to win the boycott.[116] The *Christian Recorder* marveled: "The courage and self-sacrifice shown by these people as a whole during the contention for their rights was really remarkable. Women and children would walk miles day and night rather than submit to the outrage which was ratified by the city council. They were so wrought up over the indignity that they ceased to patronize the cars even after the offensive restrictions were withdrawn."[117]

The success of the 1901 boycott movement may have been aided rather than hindered by class differences among African Americans. Boycott activists in Jacksonville used an array of tactics including moral persuasion, direct action, legal threats, and sabotage. These tactics boosted the momentum of the boycott because they were launched from different social locations in the community and kept white authorities off balance. On November 7, a group of African American clergy and councilmen from Jacksonville's black wards begged the mayor of Jacksonville to veto the segregation ordinance. The following day, the mayor announced he would be signing the bill. That same evening, over eight hundred African Americans met at St. Paul's AME and resolved to initiate a boycott of Jacksonville's streetcars.[118] On Sunday, November 10, the cars "were practically vacant." The Hackmen's Union organized an alternative transportation network for African American passengers that shadowed existing car lines.[119] The mass action campaign was enormously successful.

Simultaneously, other groups of African Americans engaged in a hit-and-run campaign of firing into streetcars, harassing conductors, and vandalizing company property.[120] The second week of the boycott was marked by more incidents of streetcar sabotage.[121] Black middle-class leaders denounced the extralegal tactics; nevertheless, they reminded city authorities that the chaos had been ushered in by the segregation ordinances. The "Respectable Colored People" also informed the beleaguered city council that they were now preparing a constitutional challenge to the ordinance.[122] African Americans engaged in legal, extralegal, and mass action tactics to oppose streetcar segregation. The cumulative impact of the boycott stunned white authorities. A correspondent for the Indianapolis Freeman wrote: "The Negroes are 'standing pat' against the [segregation] measure, and it would be extremely risky for a Negro to patronize the lines under existing conditions. The darkies mean business, and are out for blood."[123] African Americans were able to show Jacksonville's officials that streetcar segregation would cost the city dearly, and the mayor quietly dropped enforcement efforts. Black Floridians had repudiated *Plessy v. Ferguson* and struck a blow against segregation.

The state legislature intervened to impose segregation on black Floridians. In 1905, state representatives crafted a bill to force African Americans—with the exception of black nurses tending white babies—to sit in separate compartments.[124] Black Floridians organized even as the bill was being deliberated. African Americans in Pensacola held a mass meeting at Tolbert Chapel AME and drafted a set of resolutions that M. M. Lewey, C. F. Call, and other leaders elected by the assembly would present to state legislators. The petitioners reiterated that they did not seek to "intermingle" with white folks. They had learned, however, "by past experiences [that] the actual operation and enforcement of the laws intended to separate the races upon public conveyances have operated at the injury of your petitioners, and discriminated unjustly."[125] The Pensacola deputation's resolutions were ignored, and the Jim Crow law, known as the Avery Bill, passed both houses of the state legislature unanimously.[126]

Black Pensacolans struck back with direct action. Local streetcar managers reported to their Boston parent corporation, Stone & Webster, Inc., that African Americans initiated an ironclad boycott against the streetcars in May even before the Jim Crow law had passed: "In Pensacola 90% of the negroes have stopped riding even though the company has not issued an order or intimated anything as to what they intend to do. The negroes have appointed Committees who meet negroes visiting their city at the train and present each one with a button to be worn in the lapel of the coat. This button bears the single word WALK."[127] "A number of negroes have been noticed on the cars," the *Pensacola Journal* noted, "but in each case when they are seen by persons of their own race they are subjected to taunts and cries of 'Jim Crow.'"[128] A white editor fumed, "They get as good accommodation as the whites in the street cars, but they object to the tangible expression of the color line."[129]

African Americans in Jacksonville launched their boycott when the Avery Bill took effect on July 1. Boycott organizers used the 1901 campaign as a model. Almost two weeks into the struggle, an African American testified: "They are holding meetings in the different parts of the city three times a week and they are largely attended. The newspapers pooh! pooh! and say that we will all be riding soon but this is the 10th day and even women and boys are forming clubs to keep any of our race from riding."[130] Again, hack drivers were unsung heroes of the boycott. The *Atlanta Constitution* explained that the wagon drivers sacrificed their small profits for the sake of winning the boycott: "The usual fare for a trip of a few blocks is twenty-five cents, but since the enactment of the Jim Crow law the negro cab drivers have cut the fare to ten cents for people of their own race, though they still charge the customary price for white people. This has been a great factor in enabling the negroes to carry on a sort of a boycott on the street car company."[131]

The boycott was effective. A Stone & Webster operative counted a total of 90 black passengers on Sunday, July 23. This was compared to 3,552 black passengers on the first Sunday after the end of the boycott—when ridership was still very low.[132] "Those Jacksonville Afro-Americans are terribly in earnest in their resolve not to ride on the 'Jim Crow' street cars," reported Thomas H. Malone, who related the power of the boycott:

A friend of mine visited that city last Sunday and as he emerged from the station he was met by two determined colored men. "You are a stranger here," said one of the men to the man with the grip in his hand, "and we just wanted to say to you that we all refuse to ride on the cars that compel us to take the rear seat: we ask you to do the same while you are in town. There's a colored car line here and we hope you will use it. Before you get on the 'Jim Crow' line think hard a little while and then—walk." My friend promised to do as he was asked, and for the three days he was in town he never had occasion to be "Jim Crowed."[133]

Some middle-class African Americans were lukewarm in their stance toward the 1905 movement.[134] From Boston, Stone & Webster, Inc., engaged in a secret campaign of bribery to buy off black leaders in Jacksonville.[135] Praising the white manager of the Jacksonville Street Railway company, a conservative black voice complained, "strange to relate, an alliance of some of the pastors of city churches, prematurely as well as unwisely, has had printed and propogated a circular, announcing a boycott of Afro-Americans on the street cars."[136] Class tensions in Jacksonville flared as working-class African Americans suspected prominent clergy and editors of betraying the black community. Indeed, a number of prominent leaders were summoned to a popular tribunal and forced to issue public statements of support of the struggle.[137] African Americans were not about to take black solidarity for granted.

Even as the Jacksonville boycott was gaining momentum, African American lawyers engineered a legal challenge to the Avery Bill. Acting on a prearranged plan, J. E. Cashen boarded a streetcar, refused to move to the white section, and was arrested. Attorneys J. Douglass Wetmore (who also served as a Jacksonville city councilman) and I. L. Purcel planned to use the case to prove that the law was unconstitutional.[138] Their legal strategy hinged on proving that Section 7 of the Avery Bill—the exemption for black nurses caring for white children—was a clear violation of the equal protection clause of the Fourteenth Amendment.[139]

When the Florida Supreme Court struck down the Avery Bill barely a month after its passage, African American activists took the credit, arguing, "The decision in this case was brought about by the colored people of Jacksonville boycotting the streetcars after the law went into effect on July 1. They one and all determined to stay off the cars, and the slogan was: STAY OFF THE CARS AND WALK."[140] African Americans had again used a variety of tactics to beat back de jure segregation. In Pensacola, African Americans received the news with joy, knowing that it was their sacrifices that had made the great victory possible. As they triumphantly resumed riding the streetcars, a chagrined *Pensacola Journal* reported, "The negroes began to ride early and it was noticeable that they almost invariably occupied the front seats."[141]

Black Florida's stunning victory over Jim Crow was fleeting, however. Soon after the Supreme Court's decision, the Pensacola Chamber of Commerce sponsored a new model segregation ordinance that modified the Avery Bill's discriminatory language in Section 7. The ordinance was validated by the Florida Supreme Court in 1906.[142] Streetcar segregation triumphed in Florida because it was relentlessly promoted by institutions of power including the U.S. Supreme Court, the state legislature, the Pensacola Chamber of Commerce, a northern-based streetcar firm, police, and municipal authorities.

Nevertheless, black Floridians continued to resist segregation. African American women frequently challenged the police powers of white conductors. When Mary Jackson boarded a streetcar a year after the segregation ordinance had been passed, she found that all the "black seats" had been taken, so she sat down next to a white woman.[143] "When requested to sit in one of the seats reserved for colored people she refused to move," according to one account, "and then proceeded to curse the conductor and use profane epithets to express her opinion of the Jim Crow law in general."[144] In the same year, two African American women, a mother and daughter, challenged a streetcar conductor and were spitefully referred to by authorities as "Amazons," when the mother aggressively came to the aid of her daughter who was being arrested.[145] When Beulah Wilson refused to make way for a group of white women on a streetcar in 1911, she was arrested and her bold action was caricatured by police: "Dat cracker says git oud de way of dem white wimmins, an hit made me mad."[146] African American women's resistance to segregation illuminates the gendered contours of Jim Crow. White male authorities tried to downplay black female acts of assertion against white women whose very persons had become markers for segregation, but they could not hide the fact that many African American women did not display the proper respect for white "ladies" or Jim Crow.

This was illustrated one Monday morning in Pensacola when Olivia Morgan, a young African American laundry worker, went to the home of her employer, Bell Clark, and allegedly "cursed her out because payment for laundry work was refused."[147] Clark responded to the laundry worker's demands by grabbing a broom and assaulting Morgan. When a police officer tried to arrest Olivia Morgan, the young woman fled but soon returned with her mother, Eliza Johnson. Johnson did not take kindly to her daughter's wages being withheld nor the spectacle of her being arrested. Johnson struck the police officer in the face "for no other reason than that he had the girl under arrest." During their court hearing, the two women were supported by members of their community, who testified so energetically on the behalf of Johnson and her daughter that they "came near being arrested for their conduct about the box." The case ended with Olivia Morgan paying a five-dollar fine for using profanity toward her employer. Black women's resistance hit segregationists especially hard, because it confounded male notions of female deference in the public sphere.[148]

Jim Crow found no easy resting place anywhere in Florida. While whites tried to assert their state-sanctioned authority, black Floridians reasserted their dignity. Clashes in small-town commercial spaces arose when white store owners attempted to put black customers "in their place." An argument between a white storekeeper and a black patron in Miccosukee in 1903 ended in the clerk giving "the negro a sound thrashing, perhaps just what he needed," according to the area white press.[149] Local African Americans seem to have disagreed with this assessment, however, and a large crowd of black people congregated outside the store after the man's beating. "Some women joined in the pow wow and threats were made," noted the *Weekly Tallahassean,* "so much so that some of the people became alarmed at the outlook and closed their places of business and armed themselves for trouble." One rumor was that "the negroes left town about 2 A.M. Sunday, avowing that they would return and burn the town on Sunday and saying by Monday morning there would not be a white person alive in the place."[150] In a society where race relations were on a hair trigger, such a conflict represented nothing less than an impending insurrection in the white mind. The sheriff rode into Miccosukee with an armed posse and arrested at least fourteen African Americans including two women said to be among the "ring leaders" of the conflict. The *Weekly Tallahassean* gravely warned that African American men had recently come to Leon County and were "inciting the negroes" to rise against the whites. The press of the state's capital took this occasion to repeat a warning:

> The negroes are treated right, they are given everything that they are entitled to, but the past testifies eloquently to the fact that our people will brook no meddling by them, and they would be fools to commence a riot, for it could mean nothing to them but extermination, and that in the shortest possible time. This statement is made in no threatening spirit, but simply to *repeat the warnings of the days of reconstruction,* when it would not be permitted even while they had white leaders.[151]

In 1910, black Floridians began circulating, selling, and wearing Jack Johnson buttons weeks in advance of the black heavyweight boxer's racially charged match with Jim Jeffries, "the White Hope," on July 4.[152] Moments after Johnson triumphed, elated African Americans celebrated while white Floridians seethed. In Jacksonville, African Americans clashed in the streets with whites enraged over "their manner and manifestations of joy" after Johnson's victory.[153] Authorities in Pensacola resorted to mass arrests of African Americans who celebrated too vigorously in order to avert the kind of rioting that broke out all over America in the wake of the Johnson-Jeffries match.[154]

In 1914, black Miamians initiated a boycott of white businesses operating in the Negro section because they refused to hire black clerks and managers. Led by a Baptist minister, Rev. J. T. Brown, the boycott held firm until "it was found necessary for white people to withdraw, and some of them who had large stores, just placed their business in the hands of our people."[155]

The following year, African Americans in Florida organized to halt the showing of D. W. Griffith's film glorification of the Ku Klux Klan, *Birth of a Nation.* African Americans in Pensacola protested against the film, but their campaign failed.[156] African Americans in Palatka successfully banned the antiblack film from being showing locally. The difference between Palatka and Pensacola was that the latter city had no black elected officials. Since they were able to regularly elect two black councilmen—albeit councilmen confined to the two black residential wards—black Palatkans were able to maintain their local Republican club and more effectively negotiate with the city's white power structure. African Americans in Palatka asserted, "The Birth of a Nation contains scenes which breed contempt for the Colored Race by misrepresentation and straining of facts."[157]

In addition, African Americans used their political strength to agitate for better schooling. The year after they stopped *Birth of a Nation*, the editor of the local black newspaper proudly noted that black citizens had carried on a sustained campaign to increase funding for public education: "Public demonstrations have been made and strong appeals presented to the white tax-payers and voters to this end already and the most forceful methods used to arouse their people to see Palatka's need in its true light in comparison to other cities and towns, and they are aroused."[158] Three years later, African Americans in the town presented a petition to the city council demanding that a railroad be prevented from laying tracks through the middle of a local black school.[159]

By the eve of the Great Migration and America's entrance into World War I, black Floridians had established a tradition of defying Jim Crow in myriad ways ranging from individual acts of resistance to organized boycotts. African Americans called on their mutual aid institutions to maintain the one thing that legal segregation always threatened to destroy: their dignity. Black secret societies, churches, labor unions, and other collective associations struggled to preserve their memberships' autonomy and self-respect. At times, these organizations also mounted open challenges to white supremacy. In no way should black political power be exaggerated in what was quintessentially a one-party state. Nevertheless, African Americans sustained models of community organizing and protest that would serve them well in the years ahead. Mutual aid allowed African Americans to survive the bitterest years of racial apartheid. Protests against segregation kept the spirit of resistance alive.

◀ 6 ▶

LOOKING FOR
A FREE STATE TO LIVE IN

I worked out too in the public. And I worked at they houses and cooked and took care of their children and washed and ironed their clothes. Yes! It was a lot time they *did not* pay. You'd work a whole week and they wouldn't *pay at all but $3.00 a week for all day long!* . . . you see my daddy worked all week and he worked in a sawmill and they earned seventy-five cents *a day!*[1]

GERTRUDE WILLIAMS
Tallahassee

AFRICAN AMERICANS IN FLORIDA had engaged in decades of struggles against Jim Crow by the time that World War I erupted in Europe. This history explains why black Floridians were so quick to seize the opportunity provided by labor shortages in the North. Black working families were pioneers of an exodus out of the South into northern wartime factories that became known as the Great Migration.[2] Leaving the South en masse challenged the power of white business supremacists who sought to keep African Americans immobile through vagrancy statutes, convict labor, and poverty wages. The migration disrupted southern labor relations and gave black workers who remained—if they seized it—more bargaining power vis-à-vis their employers. The exodus also disrupted class relations within African American communities. Potential migrants confronted "race leaders" who urged working people to stay South and trust the good white folks to take care of them. Workers renounced these "Representative Negroes" and demanded that they cease kowtowing to the white elite. In contrast to most treatments of the Great Migration, the focus here is on the impact the exodus had on the great majority of black southerners who ultimately stayed in the South.[3] While African Americans dreamed of better opportunities in the North, they began anew the struggle for justice in the South. Black migration set in motion new organizing opportunities and was a step toward mounting a larger struggle against Jim Crow.

HEADING NORTH

The good news spread like wildfire in the summer of 1916: shade-tobacco growers in Connecticut were paying $2.50 for ten hours of labor, a stupendous increase over agricultural wages in the Sunshine State.[4] Thousands of African American workers in Pensacola, Quincy, St. Augustine, Jacksonville, and other cities determined to leave the poverty of Jim Crow behind and assembled to catch trains heading north.[5]

Black workers and their families made their decisions against a backdrop of severe oppression. In Gadsden County, the shade-tobacco industry was dominated by the American Sumatra Tobacco Corporation, which owned over thirty thousand acres of prime land in Florida and Georgia.[6] A. I. Dixie, who worked as a day laborer for American Sumatra, recalled working conditions on the company's farms vividly. "We was treated very cruel, working for very low wages, seventy-five cents a day, and the [boss] Man would sometime whip mens. They had the biggest of the farms in Gadsden County and they growed more 'bacca than anybody else at that particular time. The headquarter was up North but they had men from the South operatin' it, and them was the men that was rough on the folks, was the man who was operatin' the farm." Overseers brutalized workers who talked back. A. I.'s younger brother, Sam Dixie, mused: "All I could see was they *didn't* want you to be together." Most crucially: "They didn't want you to get organized." Workers who questioned white authority were hauled off to the dreaded "Campbell Field" in Quincy. There recalcitrant field hands were "dressed down" or whipped.[7]

Decades later, A. I. Dixie still remembered the cold Monday morning that his best friend and co-worker Lonzie Dean was abducted by his overseer and taken to the Campbell Field: "When I got up, I saw Lonzie in the car with his boss and his boss's brother pass my house just as I was coming out the door. And when I come from town getting ice for the 20th of May, they put him out and his britches was striped where they whipped him and then he couldn't go to work." The moment that Lonzie Dean recovered, he "stole away" from Gadsden in the night and went north. "I ain't ever seen him since," Mr. Dixie lamented.[8]

Hidden beneath chronicles of punishment and departure was a history of relentless struggle that constituted the reality of daily life in the segregated South. Planter coercion took many forms, most of it designed to break any semblance of black economic mobility. In Gadsden County, African American sharecroppers were constantly trying to find a way to break out of the cycle of poverty. Malachia Andrews recalled: "We were paid from fifty to seventy-five cents a day." The Andrews family did not rest easy with economic oppression, however. Andrews's father challenged the white landowner for a larger share of the profits during "settling-up" time, but resistance was costly. "We left Havana because they resented us challenging about our share of the crop, so we had to hunt other places to share," Andrews remembered. "This was dangerous. Black folks as far as they thought wasn't supposed to talk back, challenge the big boss. I'll say about the harvesting, and sometimes it would cause house burning. Sometimes it would cause flogging, hanging and different things." When African American plantation workers in Gadsden struck out to farm on their own land, the consequences were severe: "The big farmers burnt them all out, burnt out the fields, set them afire, corn fields and all these types of things in order to break them down, to have them come back to the big farm."[9] Back on the "big farm," the lines of authority were clear. Sam Dixie stressed: "The boss men had power 'bout like the sheriff."[10]

Conditions weren't much better in Alachua County. Alvin Butler's family had lived in rural Alachua since his grandfather had been hauled there as a slave from South Carolina shortly before the Civil War. Butler grew up in the Kirkwood community, several miles east of Micanopy. There, African American landowners and sharecroppers alike were caught in an economic vise. While landowning farmers saw their land melt away or "disappeared for taxes," sharecroppers were hit even harder. "While their crop was growing up," Butler noted, they "would get a little money from 'em [white landowners] and they wasn't able to read or write too much. And at the end of the year, they say they owed them . . . and when they'd get the crop and then they would have no money."[11] African American women who toiled as laundry or domestic workers cited the nonpayment of wages as a chronic problem.[12] Segregation piled insult upon injury. The Butler family children could not attend the closest school because they were black.

Persistent violence stalked African Americans in Alachua County. Newberry was a phosphate mining town notorious for racial conflict. A resident from nearby Gainesville reported that white authorities in Newberry had passed "strict regulations" against carrying weapons, but aimed this ordinance solely against black people: "Colored men who are caught with weapons are given up to nine months in the chain gang. You know what that means. Whites carry arms openly, and are rarely held in jail."[13] One day in 1916, two deputy sheriffs engaged in a gunfight near Newberry with a black man, Boisy Long, over the alleged theft of a hog. When Long shot and killed one of the deputies, local whites organized a vigilante committee to track him down. Long disappeared, and whites turned their fury on the African American settlement in Newberry. White gunmen seized and lynched five African American men and women. Another black resident was murdered the next day.[14] As usual, the white perpetrators operated without fear of incarceration.

As African Americans took stock of their lives and assessed the safety of their families, they looked north, where wartime labor shortages mounted. Black Floridians paid close attention to the Hartford Valley tobacco crop of 1916.[15] An African American wrote a letter to the *New York Age* which captured a renewed spirit of determination:

> When spring opens we want to come North. We see through the columns of THE AGE very encouraging words for those who want work. We are enthused over this intelligence. Have been reading in THE AGE about employment offered at Holyoke, Mass., and in the tobacco fields of Connecticut. Let us know how we can get our tickets to come North, so we will be ready when the time arrives for our departure.[16]

In July, African Americans in Leon County welcomed a labor agent recruiting for the Connecticut Leaf Tobacco Association.[17] As black workers weighed their options, they knew that they were looking at the chance of earning between $1.50 and $1.75 *per day* more in wages harvesting the Hartford Valley tobacco crop.[18] At the same time, however, Gadsden farmers were raving over the predicted value of the local tobacco crop.[19] The *Daily Democrat* boasted: "The shade crop this year will probably reach two million dollars to be distributed among all the people of Gadsden county."[20] Agricultural workers, however, were skeptical that profits would be equitably distributed "among all the people" and planned their next move.[21]

On Sunday evening, July 30, hundreds of African Americans from Gadsden and Leon Counties gathered together at a major rail depot in Tallahassee to say farewell to the Sunshine State.[22] Tobacco growers and state officials, however, had no intention of surrendering to black aspirations. Farmers asked their northern counterparts to stop labor recruitment, and sheriffs' deputies began shutting down railway depots.[23] Mayor Lowry of Tallahassee telegraphed the Connecticut Leaf Tobacco Association (CLTA), asking the organization to stop recruiting in Florida and to refrain from paying the transportation costs for African American laborers. On August 1, 1916, the CLTA obliged and sent Lowry a return telegram, "notifying him that the recruiting of labor here, and in this territory would cease."[24] The mayor thanked the CLTA and "gave notice to the colored men who had congregated here from Gadsden and other counties, that return transportation would be furnished to all desiring it and he wishes the *Democrat* to state that he will do so for any who are still here and who wish to return to their homes."[25] Defying great odds, African Americans continued to leave Florida.

Jacksonville, aptly named the Gateway City, became the most popular point of departure for the North. In late July, labor agents circulated handbills in the city's streets:

Wanted! Trackmen
for work on Pennsylvania Railroad in Pennsylvania, New York and Maryland. Wages $1.80 Per Day—Positions Permanent—Free Transportation—Coffee and Sandwiches furnished to destination. . . . No fees charged.[26]

The Pennsylvania's message addressed African Americans' yearnings for better wages and more dignity. The *Times-Union* reported that hundreds of black workers sought to exit the state through Jacksonville and that "all carried suitcases, bags, sacks and bundles and talked unceasingly of their departure from here to join thousands of others who have left Florida to work in other sections of this country."[27] Some African American men "hesitated at first, but the women got behind their husbands and insisted, that they at once leave the south henceforth and forever."[28] Most of the workers gathering at Union Depot shared the sentiments of one railway man who fired off this letter to the *Chicago Defender:*

i am now imployed in Florida East coast R R service road way department any thing in working line myself and friends would be very glad to get in touch with as labors. We would be more than glad to do so and would highly appreciate it the very best we can advise where we can get work to do, fairly good wages also is it possible could we get transportation to the destination. We are working men with familys. Please answer at once.[29]

White officials moved again to stop the exodus. Invoking the vagrancy statute, Jacksonville Mayor J. E. T. Bowden issued orders to Chief of Police F. C. Roach to stop black Floridians from leaving the city.[30] City police began attacking and beating African Americans at Union Depot with clubs and night sticks.[31] Groups of would-be migrants melted away during police assaults, only to reassemble later near the depot. On August 2, Chief Roach ordered a new police sweep of the station. The first target of the raid was three white labor recruiters. To the surprise of authorities, however, the arrests of the recruiters did nothing to disperse the workers, who remained near the depot.[32] About an hour later, the police waded into the ranks of black workers with clubs and batons swinging.[33]

If Jacksonville police hoped to end the labor exodus by violence, they failed. African American workers continued to defy police authority by finding ways to leave the state via Jacksonville well after August 2. "The following night upon the rumor that a special train would leave," reported the *Defender,* "about a thousand gathered at Twenty-first street and Railroad avenue, but the police, who drove up in automobiles, scattered them with the threats to shoot."[34] For several weeks after the police riots, working-class African Americans patiently watched and waited for the best chance of escape out of Jacksonville. A tense and sometimes deadly game of cat-and-mouse ensued between white police ordered to halt labor migration and black workers determined to leave Florida.[35]

Learning from the debacle at Union Depot, black laborers outwitted police by trying other points of departure from the city's congested rail yards. Jacksonville authorities could not fathom how African Americans were organizing. "The police believe that either the negroes assemble to leave the city after listening to false rumors or that someone is fooling them," sputtered the *Times-Union.*[36] Jacksonville's labor newspaper, the *Artisan,* claimed that 1,000 black workers successfully fled from the city in a matter of a few weeks.[37] On other occasions, the police dispersed would-be migrants.

The *Afro-American* stated that in Florida "Southerners like Pharaoh loath to let Colored folks go."[38] How did black Floridians beat Pharaoh? Travel writer C. W. Johnston stumbled onto one of the organizing centers of the Great Migration. Four miles outside of Jacksonville city limits, African American migrants and white labor agents colluded in setting up a safe haven and jumping-off point for prospective migrants that was well out of the reach of the police. They created "an underground passageway to a hill known as 'Four Mile Hill.' This was so called because it was four miles outside of city limits." Here, a remarkable convergence of humanity took place. As families gathered at the hill, "Some were laughing and some were crying. Families separated for the time being, bade each other good-bye. . . . They went out peaceably and full of hope, ready to go anywhere in this their own country in order that they might make a new habitation under better conditions and among people whom, though strangers, they considered as their friends. As darkness came on, two trains with twelve coaches each were filled with the race that has suffered much from the hands of the whites."[39]

African Americans were carrying out an *organized* labor exodus out of Florida. A Daytona newspaper reported: "The platform at the railway passenger depot Sunday morning at the time of train No. 86, due north bound at 9:24, presented the appearance of a colored excursion, and was such for between 30 and 40 of the men who were leaving, in charge of a government recruiting agent, for government work at Brunswick, Ga." According to the Daytona *Gazette News,* "The high wages paid has drawn heavily upon both the skilled and the unskilled labor of this vicinity and it is becoming difficult for even the essential business to retain a necessary number of employees and much shifting is in evidence."[40]

Black Floridians attempted to carry the institutions they had worked so hard to build with them to the North. Noting that "there is a moral reaction against ill treatment by the whites," Adam Clayton Powell stated that an Ocala minister, Rev. A. L. James, "discovered last week that his entire parish had moved to New York. He followed them and is preparing to organize them in a church in Harlem."[41] Two years later, H. W. Mills, a Mason and a stevedore, wrote back to Florida from Philadelphia: "I have organized in this city a choice lodge, composed of Masons from Florida. . . . I have also organized a court of the Heroines of Jericho. . . . Tell the craft we are leading right on for success of our temple on Broad street."[42]

One African American newspaper in Florida observed: "There is a cause . . . for this immigration. [T]he European war has greatly affected the tide of foreign immigration to our shores. Then again, the Negro has a horror [of] lynching, he wants the protection of the law, which he is called upon to obey, when he fails to get this, he, to a certain extent, loses interest in everything else."[43] Increased war production in the South proper also created new positions that needed to be filled, and black Floridians were quick to take advantage. At the end of April 1918, white employers in Jackson and Bay Counties were infuriated to discover that *five hundred* African American workers had left the region in less than one month in order to work at the federal nitrate plant at Muscle Shoals, Alabama.[44]

African Americans explained their reasoning for leaving the South by expressing their desire for economic justice *and* political freedom, something they had been doing since emancipation. "I will say at this junction [St. Petersburg] that there are more than 250 men desire to come north," stated one worker, "and for a little assistance they will come at once for the condishion there is terrible the low wage and high cost of living and bad treatment is causing all to want to come north."[45] From Sanford, an African American worker wrote: "The winter is about over and I still have a desire to seek for myself a section of this country where I can poserably better my condishion in as much as beaing assured some protection as a good citizen under the Stars and Stripes."[46] One young man wrote: "I am anxious to get North not to get rich, but in search of better treatment."[47] African Americans frequently wrote their letters anonymously, fearing retribution from whites.[48]

From Pensacola, black people wrote letters to the *Chicago Defender* and other newspapers expressing their desire to leave Florida. "Please send me at once a transportation at once. I will sure come if I live," pleaded a bricklayer in April 1917. "Send it as soon as possible because these white men are getting so they put every one in prison who are not working. I can not get any [work]. I can do any kind of common labor."[49] "*Sir:* You will give us the names of firms where we can secure employment. We will come by the thousands," a Pensacola laborer promised the *Defender.*[50] James D. Reese wrote: "I am a poor colored man 42 years of age and looking for a free state to live in and work to do that I can get some wages for as the wages are poor down here and no privlodge at all and if you will instruct me in some way I will thank the League and its members lookin for an early reply."[51]

African Americans in Florida had been trying to break through the barriers of racial oppression in their state for generations, but labor shortages in the wartime industries in the North gave them new weapons. The Great Migration enhanced black southerners' confidence that it was possible to change the social relations in the region. Authors of the exodus understood that much more was at stake than wage levels. African American workers and white authorities were locked in a bitter ideological battle over the very meaning and value of black life and citizenship.

Florida's employers fought to regain the upper hand. State officials were determined to suppress the Great Migration and to freeze existing race relations (and wages) at Jim Crow levels. Governor Sidney Catts warned an audience of African Americans to stay in Florida because "The colored people . . . should live in the warm climates and where they leave and try to live in cold climates they are going against destiny."[52] The Jacksonville Chamber of Commerce extracted oral promises from northern capitalists to stop recruiting black workers in northeastern Florida.[53] County sheriffs redoubled their arrests of labor recruiters.[54] After the black exodus from Jackson and Bay Counties, Governor Catts issued an executive order authorizing county officials to summarily arrest all labor agents who did not carry special licenses.[55]

Like their counterparts elsewhere in the South, Florida's employers depended on the state to pass laws designed to limit black labor mobility.[56] In 1903, the state legislature required a $500 license fee for a person "who shall seek to influence and by such persuasions cause the removal of any inhabitant from this State, or who shall seek to entice away from the State labor. . . ."[57] In 1916, the labor recruiting fee skyrocketed to $1,000. By 1917, "any person, agent, solicitor or recruiter engaged in the business of hiring, enticing or soliciting laborers or emigrants in this State to be transported and employed beyond the limits of this State" had to pay a $2,000 license fee. Failure to procure such a license could lead to a $5,000 fine or twelve months in a county jail.[58] When even this legislation did not squelch the flow of African American emigrants, Florida state authorities begged U.S. senator D. U. Fletcher to find a solution to their crisis.[59]

Sensing that physical coercion was a losing strategy, the Jacksonville Chamber of Commerce changed gears and called an interracial "joint conference" to confront the exodus. Chamber leaders invited noted black professionals and businessmen to confer about the best way to keep the African American working class down in the South. Black invitees included Joseph E. Lee, former judge and collector of customs, N. W. Collier, president of Florida Baptist Academy, and G. W. Wetmore, a lawyer who had played a pivotal role in the fight against the city's Jim Crow streetcar ordinance fifteen years before.[60] Mayor Bowden was joined at the conference by many of Jacksonville's chief employers.[61]

Not a word was spoken at the conference about improving the living conditions of African Americans in Jacksonville. The chamber of commerce insisted that area firms couldn't afford to pay better wages, and claimed that the departure of black workers would lead to "the closing down of plants, bringing great hardships on the laborers left behind." One executive sought to garner sympathy by claiming that he was just "breaking even" and stayed in business only in order to serve his employees.[62]

The "Representative Members of the Negro Race," as they were called by the *Times-Union,* pledged to support the employers. The venerable Joseph E. Lee stated that African Americans were too weak to endure the northern winters. J. H. Ballou "felt that the negro race fares better, all things considered, in the Southern states. He pledged his service in speaking to laborers whenever possible and outlining the difficulties they might expect to experience by going to a colder climate." N. W. Collier offered to teach a stay-put message to African Americans. The participants in the interracial conference affirmed: "it will be an economic blunder for negro laborers to go North in a wholesale manner to engage in railroad construction work on promises of much higher wages than are being paid by the industries in Jacksonville."[63]

The black leaders' public support for the Jacksonville Chamber of Commerce seems to conform with Carter G. Woodson's negative appraisal of the black middle class. "Denied participation in the higher things of life," Woodson argued, "the 'educated' Negro himself joins, too, with the ill-designing persons to handicap his people by systematized exploitation."[64] Jacksonville's "Representative Negroes" placed the burden of racial harmony on the backs of the black poor, who were expected to forgo opportunities in the North in order to maintain peaceful race relations in Florida. In a scathing article attacking "the weak-kneed leaders of the Race" who attended the interracial conference, the *Chicago Defender* intoned: "The wages [in Jacksonville] are a dollar and ten cents to a dollar and a quarter a day. [A]nd then the laborer is cursed and dogged around." Mocking the ineffectiveness of Florida's black leaders, the *Defender* wryly observed: "Thousands have left and many are planning to leave."[65] African American workers were leading the way to a better future while "race leaders" were holding the community back.

On the other hand, it is almost certain that from the perspective of Joseph Lee and the others who attended the interracial conference it was impossible to achieve concrete improvements in black life without appealing to white businessmen.[66] Indeed, Lee and his counterparts used the small space opened by the interracial conference to urge Mayor Bowden to order his police force to stop brutalizing African Americans trying to leave the state.[67] Next, the black conference participants issued a public statement titled "Words of Advice." The document began on a tepid note. "We condemn this wholesale exodus as injurious and unwise," the authors stated. Joseph Lee and the other signers of the document lectured: "Jacksonville is our home. We are property owners and tax payers here. In many respects it is the best city for us and for our people."[68] After sounding a note of conciliation toward white employers, however, black leaders critiqued them: "The wages paid our laborers by some firms are not adequate for them to live comfortably and support their families. In this day of high prices, how can any man support himself and his family upon the low wages of $1.10 per day?"[69] The authors also insisted: "The wages should be commensurate with the services required and adequate to support the laborer and his family." Black migration was now given qualified support: "We believe that any man who has ascertained beyond all question that by leaving now he will receive higher wages, that he will be employed for a long time, thereby making his condition and state in life better, does himself an injustice to remain." "Words of Advice" was penned in the context of Jim Crow's etiquette, whereby middle-class African Americans acted as racial brokers between parsimonious employers and impoverished workers. Ultimately, the authors of "Words" undermined their credibility by placing the solution to the labor crisis in the hands of the very individuals who had created the problem.

African American union representatives in Jacksonville immediately denounced the "Words of Advice." Black union activists countered with their own resolution denouncing the dialogue between area employers and "representative Negroes" as a sham. African American trade unionists denied that the middle-class "leaders" who participated in the conference could speak for black workers. Union leaders contrasted their own positions as *elected* officials of black labor organizations with the unrepresentative character of the middle-class leaders essentially hand-picked by white businessmen: "We take the method of informing the public, that the undersigned [union activists] are the only authorized leaders of the labor organizations of Jacksonville (colored) and, we have in no wise participated in any of the meetings, nor given our consent to any of the sentiment expressed in any of the meetings, nor have we in any way given authority to anyone to represent us in the expression of opinion in the matter."[70] Instead of holding meetings with nonelected officials, African American union leaders suggested that "all labor troubles or controversies should be submitted to labor organizations." Black labor leaders continued by criticizing "the persons alleged to have signed the resolutions or advice published recently in the daily papers to which the names of: Rev. John E. Ford, Joseph E. Lee, John H. Ballou, L. H. Myers, John R. Scott, N. W. Collier and others were signed." Union leaders concluded by stating: "We are unalterably opposed to any person or persons acting as our agent or counselors, without our consent." This was a devastating critique of the foremost black leaders of Florida.

African American trade unionists had issued an open statement of protest against the undemocratic forms of dialogue that prevailed between whites and blacks in Florida. As the Great Migration gained momentum, black Floridians continued to break ranks with their unelected leaders. S. W. Jefferson of Pensacola demanded "a square deal" and "democracy" for black people in Florida:

> Plenty of "sound advice" is given him [the black worker] about staying in the South among his friends and under the same old conditions. The bugaboo of cold weather is put before him to frighten him: of race antagonism and sundry other things, but not one word about better treatment is suggested to lighten the burden, no sane and reasonable remedy offered.
>
> The world war is bringing many changes and a chance for the negro to enter broader fields. With the "tempting bait" of higher wages, shorter hours, better schools and better treatment, all the preachments of the so-called "race leaders" will fall on deaf ears.[71]

"Representative Negroes" who depended on white patronage continued to lose their authority. As a Department of Labor report found, black Floridians were finished with the Old Regime:

> They rarely consult the white people, and never those who may exercise some control over their actions. They will not allow their own leaders to advise them against going North. A Rev. Mr. Carter, of Tampa, Fla., who was brave enough to attempt such advice from the pulpit, was stabbed next day for so doing. They are likely to suspect that such men are in the employ of white people.[72]

The Great Migration had a major impact on the lives of the black majority who "stayed behind." The initial movement of labor took the form of an exodus *away* from oppressive economic and political conditions. Migration undermined the state's ability to guarantee a pool of impoverished, low-wage labor. Before long, African Americans began to call for a renegotiation of the terms of employment *in Florida*. By launching the Great Migration, African American workers took the leading role in a new and revitalized struggle for justice. They demanded that their more educated "race leaders" rethink their dependence on white business interests. As employers raged and as the state tried to clamp down on the mobility of black labor, African American workers opened up vital social spaces for new political organizing to occur.

By the end of 1916, approximately twelve thousand African Americans had left Florida, and James Weldon Johnson sensed a revived spirit of hope in the South:

> I was impressed with the fact that everywhere there was a rise in the level of the Negro's morale. The exodus of Negroes to the North . . . was in full motion; the tremors of the war in Europe were shaking America with increasing intensity; circumstances were combining to put a higher premium on Negro muscle, Negro hands, and Negro brains than ever before; all these forces had a quickening effect that was running through the entire mass of the race.[73]

Johnson believed the Great Migration opened possibilities to organize in the South. Now a top NAACP official, he embarked on a whirlwind tour of the region to build association branches in Florida and other states. Johnson raised the NAACP's credibility among black southerners by emphasizing its crusades against debt peonage, lynching, and disfranchisement. He used his hometown of Jacksonville as a base on his way to other points in the South.[74] Success was not immediate. White supremacy made the NAACP's doctrine of interracial cooperation problematic in the Deep South. Efforts to start a new branch in St. Augustine failed because the organizers invited "white gentlemen" to participate. A local organizer explained the problem: "Please note that the white gentlemen are of the opinion that the prime object of the organization is to make the Negro a better citizen, while the colored gentlemen are of the opinion that their interests are to be protected in every way possible."[75] Segregation bred too much distrust for interracial organizing to work easily. Later, African American activists in the Ancient City transformed the group into an all-black organization, and the branch thrived.[76]

In Jacksonville, African Americans held their first NAACP meeting in February 1917 at James Weldon Johnson's behest.[77] George H. Mays, a retired letter carrier who served as the branch's treasurer, gave the NAACP a direct link to Reconstruction. Born in 1849, Mays served as a constable in Jacksonville in 1873 and later was a city marshal before embarking on a thirty-three-year career in the post office. He also helped organize the Grand United Order of Odd Fellows in Florida.[78] His participation in the

NAACP symbolized the intergenerational character of the black freedom struggle.

The NAACP owed its existence to the recent momentum generated by the labor exodus, but it also tapped into deep roots of African American striving in Florida. As the nation became ever more enmeshed in World War I, black Floridians prepared to strike at tyranny abroad and Jim Crow at home.

⫷ 7 ⫸

ECHOES OF EMANCIPATION

The Great War in Florida

BOLTON SMITH, a white southerner, felt the need to warn his countrymen that World War I had spawned an insidious enemy from within. The writer claimed that African Americans were subverting the tenets of white supremacy and segregation. Smith offered the example of a black chauffeur who pointedly refused to be served in the rear of a segregated restaurant. Citing this and other cases, Smith argued that since blacks had long accommodated themselves to white rule there was only one explanation for these insurgencies: German spies must be spreading anti-American propaganda among the Negroes to foment a rebellion in the United States.[1]

James Weldon Johnson challenged Bolton Smith's rhetoric about the impact of the war on race relations. "Now, it is not that the war and German propaganda have worked any sudden change in this chauffeur," Johnson asserted:

it is rather that the war and the bogey of German propaganda have worked a change in Mr. Smith. It is that Mr. Smith now notices some things to which he has hitherto been blind. He says that he has known this colored man for years; yet the thing which this man had long carried deep in his heart, the thing for which he was ready to undergo privation and pain was something that Mr. Smith knew nothing about. . . . The fact is, the white man in the South knows a good deal *about the Negro,* but he does not *know* the Negro. He is familiar with the Negro's habits, his mode of speech, his peculiarities and whims, his humor and good nature; that is, he knows the Negro from the outside. But of the bitterness and anguish of soul that the race so often passes through, of its hope and yearning and aspirations the white man of the South knows almost nothing.[2]

As Johnson so eloquently stated, African American resistance was rooted in aspirations that white supremacists had failed to stamp out. African Americans in the South had fought streetcar segregation, starvation wages, racial violence, and other forms of oppression for decades. African American activism was boosted by the Great Migration and the nation's mobilization for a war ostensibly waged against oppression. Black labor unionizing was on the rise, and the NAACP was in the midst of a national organizing drive. W. E. B. Du Bois encouraged African Americans to "close ranks" and support the war effort, but Du Bois also vowed at war's end: "By the God of Heaven, we are cowards and jackasses if now that the war is over, we do not marshal every ounce of our brain and brawn to fight a sterner, longer, more unbending battle against the forces of hell in our own land."[3] Black struggles in wartime Florida must be placed in the context of a national effort by African Americans to win a just peace at home.[4]

While historians have stressed the impact that returning black veterans played in citizenship struggles after war's end, they have often missed the ways that African American men and women on the home front prepared the way for those struggles even prior to direct U.S. involvement in the war. Equally important, the traditional narrative of postwar black activism focuses on male agency at the expense of the work done by African American women in the midst of the conflict.[5] In Florida, women played enormous roles in mobilizing African American communities across the state to support the Allied war effort. This was not a blind, sunshine patriotism, however. Black Floridians stressed their contributions to the republic past and present, and they voiced the expectation that Jim Crow would share the same timely demise as "Kaiser Bill." African Americans demonstrated that they were aware of the irony of "fighting for democracy" abroad while living under tyranny at home, and they brought this contradiction to the nation's attention.

SUPPORTING THE WAR FOR DEMOCRACY

A week after President Woodrow Wilson announced America's entry into World War I, African Americans in Quincy convened at Mt. Moriah Baptist Church to discuss the coming conflict. One hundred participants deliberated on the kinds of roles black Floridians might play in the Great War. Next they settled down to the business of drafting public resolutions. W. S. Stevens, Quincy's black physician, read the first resolution aloud:

> *Whereas,* Our country is now involved in the greatest war the world has ever known, and
>
> *Whereas,* The serious situation demands complete preparedness to protect and maintain the rights of its citizens, and
>
> *Whereas,* Our race constitutes a part of the citizenship of this great commonwealth and has always shown its patriotism and loyalty in all of its struggles from the revolutionary war down to the recent trouble with Mexico, be it
>
> *Resolved:* That we pledge our country our faithful service in this critical period and stand ready to aid our government in any movement it deems necessary for the safety of its citizens and the honor of our flag.[6]

The Mt. Moriah assembly also petitioned the state for a charter to organize a black "military company" to serve in the war. White southerners justified disfranchisement in part with the dogma that African Americans had done nothing to earn the rights and privileges of citizenship. The congregation at Mt. Moriah pointedly disagreed. Before a U.S. regiment embarked for France, African Americans in Gadsden County staked a claim for citizenship on the rich soil of black patriotism and military service.[7] African Americans across Florida were determined to prove their loyalty on one condition: the state's barbaric treatment of its black citizenry had to come to an end.

African Americans in Florida entered into the war with a great determination to reap the fruits of service. A black newspaper pointedly noted that African Americans in Putnam County had heavily out-registered their white counterparts (341 to 254) during the nationwide military registration in June 1917.[8] As the first group of black conscripts from the county marched off to war, "the departing boys were given a rousing send off, as there was a great gathering of friends at the station to bid them farewell. The colored school children sang patriotic songs, and as the train pulled out a mighty cheer was given."[9] Similar events were organized for departing recruits from other locales.[10] Composing about 30 percent of Florida's population, African American communities provided over half of the state's citizen soldiers.[11]

Black Floridians served in segregated regiments that became some of the most highly decorated Allied units. Leo P. Dennis, a member of Bethel Baptist Institutional Church in Jacksonville, fought with the 350th Machine Gun Battalion.[12] Dennis's unit helped rescue a white infantry regiment from annihilation by German forces the day before the Armistice was signed.[13] Jacksonville musician Eugene F. Mikell served with the 369th Infantry, "The Hellfighters," who fought for 191 straight days, the longest stretch of any U.S. unit in the Great War.[14] Some black Floridians volunteered for the armed forces of other Allied nations including "Private R. Gilbert, a colored soldier in the Canadian army, [who] has sent home an iron cross which was given him by a German officer whom he captured single handed."[15] Despite their valor (the French awarded the Croix de Guerre to the 369th for extraordinary courage in battle), African American soldiers were frequently vilified by white officers who warned French citizens that black troops were bestial by nature. W. E. B. Du Bois remarked that "American white officers fought more valiantly against Negroes than they did against the Germans."[16]

While shouldering the responsibilities of American citizenship during their country's hour of need, black Floridians simultaneously worked to secure their rights. One fraternal lodge leader urged his order to contribute to the Allied cause because "the whole country is at war to down autocracy and set up the kingdom of wide world democracy, not to the rich or poor alone, white or black, but for all."[17] J. D. Avent, lead organizer for the Victory Boys' Division in Florida, framed his statewide call for support within the dual frameworks of race pride and citizenship:

Boys, the 400,000 colored soldiers in the camps, in embarkation points, on the high seas and on the other side ready to render their last full measure of devotion to homeland in the fight for universal freedom are looking to you and the rest of the folks back home to back them in delivering the goods. They must have comfort and cheer, recreation and religious administration to keep them fit to fight the hun. . . . I tell you boys, its an opportunity to show yourselves valued little citizens. Rally and help Florida to help put the boys over the top.[18]

The Colored Knights of Pythias mobilized its growing membership base for the task of supporting the war for democracy. One Pythian observed,

"More than a thousand of [the order's] members are either on the firing line or in camps awaiting the coming of the overseas transport, and thousands more are at home, with their satchels packed, awaiting the call, eager to join their brethren and offer up their sacrifices that democracy may reign and the world be made safe for all men and all men made citizens."[19] At Pythian rallies across Florida, Grand Chancellor W. W. Andrews urged lodge members to contribute to the war effort.[20] Pythian ceremonies culminated with the unfurling of ornate war service flags, stitched with one star for every local lodge member in the military. One such ceremony was performed by the members of Garrett Ward Lodge No. 17, who stressed "the contribution which the Pythian order has made to the nation in the great war."[21]

African American men in Gainesville formed a singing group called the High Speed Quartet to boost the sale of Liberty Loan bonds in order to help pay for the Allied campaign.[22] The group was popular with both black and white audiences. The quartet sang a unique mix of spirituals that they modified to fit the moment. "Go Down Moses" became "Go down soldiers—way down in Europe Land. Make old Kaiser let them Belgians go. . . . We're the sons of Ham and we know no loss. No Kaiser Bill can be our boss."

Black businessmen and promoters of the Liberty Loan drive in Jacksonville urged African Americans to "Subscribe through your own Colored Committee or Your Own Bank so that the race will get credit for our share."[23] W. I. Lewis agreed: "If there is any one doubting as in whether or not he should buy bonds, let that doubt fly with the winds. . . . The loyalty of the colored citizens from Jacksonville must not be questioned on account of lagging in this drive."[24] The Victory Loan Committee promised: "What has been achieved has proved a revelation to all, and from now on, a stiffening will be put into affairs, looking to justice and fair dealing in all things civic."[25]

African American women spearheaded the Liberty Loan drives and also played a central role in framing the meaning of black service to the nation. Mary McLeod Bethune, president of the State Federation of Colored Women's Clubs, was a key leader in these efforts.[26] Bethune taught her students at Daytona Educational and Industrial Institute to see themselves as equals of the campus's white visitors. Wilhelmina W. Johnson, an alumna of Bethune's school, recalled: "In the afternoon services that we would have, Mrs. Bethune would say, 'This is a democracy working in the South. White people, you sit where you can. If you don't want to sit beside

a black person, sorry. I am sorry because we do not discriminate here.'"[27]
At the onset of the war, Bethune was in her early forties, a peerless organizer. She led Red Cross drives and recruited black women in Daytona to
donate thousands of cans of fruits and vegetables and "many articles for
the comfort of the soldiers."[28] Bethune also used Daytona Normal as a
forum for events that paid tribute to black patriotism. Her students performed a play titled "Echoes from France." Students played "the big soldier," "little sister," and "the brave mother," acting out the work that each
character had to do in order to win the war. Bethune proudly noted that
"the last scene in which the returned soldiers told of their experience and
the winning of the *Croix de Guerre* was pathetic and filled the hearts of
the audience with patriotism and pride."[29] The great educator choreographed a vision of expansive citizenship where women, men, and children alike acted out their roles in winning the war for democracy abroad
and on the home front. No ambiguity here: democracy was for women
and men.

Eartha Mary Magdalene White was also a leader of the State Federation
of Colored Women's Clubs, a teacher, and a revered community activist
who spent many of her hours ministering to black prisoners in Duval
County jails and agitating for improved living conditions for county
inmates.[30] During the war, Miss White became the state chair and organizer of the Colored Women's Council of Defense, charged with coordi-
nating black war work throughout Florida.[31] White toured the state in
1918 to solicit funds for the war effort from black institutions and also
established in the same year a "Liberty Kitchen" in Jacksonville that taught
food-preservation techniques.[32] The war personally touched Miss White.
Fifty-five of her fellow Bethel Baptist Institute Church members—including Leo P. Dennis—served in the armed forces. Five would be buried in
France.[33] As White traveled across the state doing war work, she spread
news about the other organizations that she was involved in. Like Mary
McLeod Bethune, White was a pioneer NAACP member. She was also the
president of the Jacksonville "Colored Citizens' Protective League, whose
chief interest is to see that colored men qualify for voting. This association
at different times has protected citizens who have been unjustly treated.
This branch of work has been in existence for eighteen years."[34] Eartha
White pragmatically combined war service work with an emphasis on
equal rights. Meanwhile, less heralded but equally energetic women across
Florida led Liberty bond campaigns and collected clothes, medical supplies, and other necessities for the troops.[35]

White Floridians denied that African American contributions to the war effort should in any way alter race relations.[36] To this end, white newspapers generally refused to list the names of black soldiers and sailors who were killed or wounded in their war casualty columns.[37] Black Floridians worked to set the record straight. In preparation for the 1918 state fair, A. C. Porter, director of black exhibits, sent out a call for photographs of African American service members. Porter emphasized, "Pictures in uniform are preferred, but if you haven't one send the other. . . . Hurry now and let us show that the colored men are as numerous in the war as the white men. This is your opportunity; don't let it pass."[38] When General John Pershing praised the gallantry of black soldiers, W. I. Lewis published the letter in "News of the Colored People," even though the white press did not print the statement.[39]

Families who lost their loved ones in war refused to allow their sacrifices to go unacknowledged. Bereaved relatives published letters of condolence that they received from the government in order to emphasize the price that was being levied for the nation's freedom. The family of Private Thomas Butler memorialized his life in a poem published in the black press:

He left his home in perfect health,
He looked so strong and brave,
We little thought how soon he'd be
Laid in a soldier's grave.

Somewhere in France they buried him.
Within a quiet lonely grave;
Unknown save by his fighting mates,
Who shared the cause he died to save,
And for his sacrifice the stars
And stripes proudly wave,
Somewhere in France.[40]

CONFRONTING THE GOVERNOR

The "Encouragement Meeting" held in Jacksonville on July 16 to honor the success of black Liberty Loan drives and stimulate further efforts revealed the gulf in black and white perceptions over the meaning of the war. Speakers for the event included Governor Sidney Catts and noted individuals from the federal government including George E. Haynes, director of the Division of Negro Economics. This was a branch of the Department of Labor created to coordinate black labor in wartime industries.[41]

The meeting, held in the spacious Duval Theater, began on a festive note. Afro-American Life Insurance Company founder A. L. Lewis discussed the substantial amount of funds that African Americans mustered for each of the Liberty Loan subscriptions. In turn, each speaker praised African Americans for their contributions to Red Cross drives, War Saving Stamp programs, and other initiatives.[42] George Haynes commended black workers for boosting America's industrial capacity, and his white Department of Labor counterpart urged peaceful labor relations for the duration of the war.[43]

James Weldon Johnson provided a firsthand account of what happened next. Sidney Catts rose to give the keynote address of the evening. The governor was sick and tired of all of this talk about African American patriotism. In his mind, black Floridians were incapable of making constructive contributions to the society. In any case, these contributions would dangerously imply that the state's Negro population deserved something in return from the state. So Governor Catts began bullying the gathering. He told African Americans to get jobs, stop loafing, and cease selling bootleg whiskey. Catts boasted: "You are looking into the face of the most powerful man in Florida," and warned them that he was going to force them to work harder.[44] Catts was just getting warmed up:

> At one place in his speech the Governor seemed to imagine that he was talking to a crowd of gamblers and loose women. . . . He enlightened his audience as to why the Indian had vanished. He said it was because the Indian would not bow to the white man, and that no race could hope to survive along with the white man unless it bowed. He also stated that if he were a Negro he would be ashamed to be a brown one or a yellow one, he would be ashamed to be anything but a black one. He spoke of keeping Negro labor in the State as though Negroes were peons. He spoke of soldiers and venereal diseases as though most of the women in the audience were to be held responsible. . . . Had he not been the Governor he would most likely have been hissed.[45]

The governor's diatribe stunned the audience. After an awkward silence, J. H. Blodgett, a successful black businessman and a leader of Jacksonville's black Liberty Loan Executive Committee, took the podium.[46] "Mr. Blodgett began timidly by saying that he 'could not be expected to make a regular speech because he was nothing but an illiterate man.' At this," James Weldon Johnson continued, "the Governor lay back in his seat and beamed on Blodgett, evidently in anticipation of a real 'good nigger' speech." What followed was anything but Jim Crow. Blodgett moved African Americans to applause, laughter, and tears by saying out loud what they had been saying among themselves for generations:

> He said that it was a waste of time and energy for the white people to hold meetings to urge the Negro to be loyal; that the Negro's loyalty was not on trial; that he had been proving it ever since the time he helped the white man take this country from the Indian, and he was still proving it; that what the Negro wanted to hear was how the country intended to reward him for his loyalty. He then went on to tell the Governor why so many of the faces he looked into were brown and yellow; and he told him why so many Negroes had left and were leaving the State; and about lynching and "Jim Crow" cars and political inequalities.[47]

The governor was seized with fury. Springing from his seat, Sidney Catts shook his fist and "declared that Blodgett was assailing him, had insulted him, and made him the butt of ridicule." The man who had bragged during his election campaign that he had "killed a nigger" sensed a challenge to white supremacy in Blodgett's rebuttal.[48] Johnson observed: "After five minutes of charges and rebuttals exchanged between the Governor and Mr. Blodgett, the latter abruptly closed his speech and sat down. The audience sang 'My Country, 'Tis of Thee' and the meeting was dismissed."[49] This exchange indicates that much had changed since the "Interracial Conference" of 1916, where black middle-class leaders had said exactly what the Jacksonville Chamber of Commerce expected them to say. Now the Great Migration and African Americans' active participation in the Allied effort gave black Floridians new weapons to wield in the war against segregation. Indeed, had Blodgett acquiesced to Catts on this occasion he might have become the target of black ridicule and scorn. Kowtowing to white authority was now distinctly unfashionable. Johnson noted that the governor had been presented with an opportunity to acknowledge black patriotism, but "could do nothing except rehash the old stock charges against the race about laziness and loose living." The fact that the governor felt insulted simply because Blodgett stated the case for black dignity and citizenship illuminated the unresolved conflict between democracy and white supremacy. State officials believed that the war would not upset the racial status quo. African Americans staked their lives on it.

WE FEEL THAT THERE SHOULD BE NO DISCRIMINATION OF WAGES

African American women seized the moment and began fighting for better pay and improved working conditions. Domestic workers whose husbands served in the military used the leverage earned from military allotment checks to quit white households in order to find higher-paying employment.[50] Black women sought to renegotiate the terms of employment, and, like domestic workers in other southern states, they confronted the wrath of white female employers who tried to resist changes in race and labor relations.[51] City authorities passed "work or fight" ordinances and targeted African American women who left employers in search of better jobs. Methodist bishop John Hurst reported: "colored women in most cases demanded an increase in wages, this increase being necessary because of the increased cost of living, which applied in Florida as well as in other parts of the country. When these demands for an increase in wages were denied by their employers, they quit, and were arrested when their employers reported the cases to the police authorities."[52] On one occasion, a white woman in Tampa demanded that an African American woman work for her because she had been unable to find a cook. The NAACP's Walter White observed: "The colored woman informed her that she had experienced the same difficulty, and at the time the white woman asked her to come and cook for her, she had been upon the point to ask the white woman to come and cook for her (the colored woman). The white woman, thereupon had the colored woman arrested."[53]

African American railroad workers searched for a way around racist managers and state authorities by joining national unions and appealing directly to the federal government. Ingeniously recasting job discrimination as a political question, railway men welded the language of equal citizenship to the discourse of wartime service to demand federal intervention in the workplace. Petitioning the government became a viable strategy when the Wilson administration took control of the nation's rail lines as an emergency war measure.[54] First, black railroaders organized unions and created workers' committees to petition federal authorities.[55] In Sanford, High Springs, Pensacola, Lakeland, and New Smyrna, African American railroad laborers organized locals of the Railway Men's

International Benevolent Industrial Association, a union based in Chicago. In Tampa and Jacksonville, railway men joined the National Brotherhood Workers of America.[56]

Jim Crow barred African Americans from the better-paying crafts. White railroad unions also banned African Americans from membership.[57] Since they were officially denied employment in the "operating crafts," African Americans did not enjoy the benefits of the newly passed Adamson Act.[58] While white workers in these jobs profited from federally mandated wage increases, the eight-hour day, and seniority provisions, black railway men were excluded.[59] Black railroaders invoked their wartime service on the nation's most vital internal transportation system in order to link citizenship claims with their struggles for better pay and an end to job discrimination. Sixty Florida East Coast Railway firemen petitioned W. G. McAdoo, a member of President Wilson's war cabinet in October 1918. The firemen stated: "We feel that there should be no discrimination in wages on account of color. We all do the same work."[60] Petitioners enclosed a wage schedule showing that black firemen were being paid lower wages than their white counterparts. This was a violation of General Order No. 27 of the Railroad Administration, which stated that African Americans "should be paid the same rates of wages as were paid white men in the same capacities."[61] The petitioners couched their appeal in terms of the wartime sacrifices they made:

> We are subscribers to all the Liberty Loans and certain amounts are deducted from our wages each month to pay the same. We have authorized deductions from our wages to pay our subscriptions in the Thrift Stamp drive, and other war funds. . . . We therefore find it increasingly difficult to live upon our wages as reduced by the Florida East Coast Railway and in defiance to your order No. 27. We are certain that if this company pay us according to the spirit of your order, we not only could meet the advanced cost of living, but could pay all our subscriptions to the several war funds.[62]

Black railroaders stated that they were routinely ordered to do unpaid craft work such as braking and switching cars and that they should be covered under the Adamson Act and receive overtime pay. African American workers saw federal control as a way to redress years of injustice. In a union petition from Tampa, including signatures of workers "just returned from France," the railway men who were classified by their bosses as "porters" pointedly referred to themselves as "colored brakemen," carefully detailing the skilled work they were performing.[63]

Railroad managers invoked the timeworn chimera of black inferiority to counter the avalanche of African American petitions to the federal government. One white manager asserted: "In handling the negro in the South there are certain restrictions that must govern him; otherwise he becomes ungovernable. . . . We believe that none of these complaints deserve more consideration than we have already given them. Our officers understand the negro and he is being treated well."[64] Stalled by federal officials who deferred to local management, black railroad workers sent their grievances straight to the president of the United States.[65] African Americans believed that economic exploitation in Jim Crow Florida had to be addressed as a political problem in the nation's highest councils.

John Taylor, leader of the National Brotherhood Workers' local in Tampa, was fired for his union activities after he signed a petition addressed to Woodrow Wilson. Taylor explained that his boss had told him that "if you will not fight these wages any more I will put you back to work." Taylor went on to make a case why the federal government should concern itself with his plight:

> I have been with the S.A.L. for a long time, working for a little wage up to government control; worked for the government during the war to help move trains over the road, at this high cost of living for $60.00 per month. Live on that at both ends of the road and take care of my family. At that I have lost my health serving you as a loyal American citizen to help win the war. Now at this age of mine after I have worked both before and since government control, and made to perform the duties of brakemen on a passenger train, and just on account of asking for more money to live on at this high cost of living now I must be put out of service. . . . Gentlemen of the Board of Division of Labor, sirs, to your Honors, there is no justice. . . . Will [you] ask the board to consider this matter, if you please, at once and let me hear from you at the earliest date possible.[66]

The federal government stood firmly on the side of white business supremacy. The State Department bent immigration law in favor of Florida's growers, keeping a pool of reserve labor in the state.[67] The U.S. Department of Agriculture supported agribusiness by acquiescing to "work or fight" laws rather than advocating higher wages to keep farm workers in the fields.[68] When George Haynes, director of the Division of

Negro Economics, refused to deter African Americans from unionizing, Governor Catts convinced the Department of Labor to halt the division's war mobilization work there—making Florida the only state where this occurred.[69] The governor reminded federal authorities that white businessmen did not negotiate with black workers. Catts warned Secretary of Labor William Wilson that African Americans were demanding equality and that Florida was on the verge of a new civil war. The governor made it clear which side he was on: "Of course it may be that I am looking upon this question from the standpoint of a white man, and being a Southern born man I could look upon it from no other viewpoint than that of the white race, for this race will always dominate and control the South."[70] Subsequently, the U.S. Department of Labor ceased its work with black Floridians.[71]

Florida's employers also tried to stop black workers from leaving the state to work in defense factories. An administrator with the U.S. Employment Service complained that Florida's officials were interfering with labor recruitment for the government's defense plant in Muscle Shoals, Alabama, where "the need for labor . . . is great and immediate." The same federal official noted, "We have had numerous obstacles placed in the way of recruiting labor in Florida for Army projects by the State Administration. This particular complaint would seem to be part of the same policy of hoarding labor in the State."[72] White business supremacy triumphed over patriotism. The federal government deferred to employers in Florida even when Jim Crow hampered the war effort.

WELCOMING THE TROOPS HOME

Despite wartime setbacks, African Americans demanded a share in the fruits of victory: the demand for equal citizenship was back on the table. Black Floridians quietly began organizing a new voter registration campaign during the first Emancipation Day ceremonies after the Armistice. At one Jacksonville ceremony, Daytona minister S. G. Baker asserted: "The great heart of the United States is too just and fair to allow our boys who have been greatly instrumental in bringing about world-wide peace and making it possible to make the world safe for democracy, their dependents and their posterity to have anything else but a fair chance in the great battle of life."[73] Rev. Baker understood that something more than the good will of the federal government was needed in order to achieve equality: "To be a full-fledged citizen one must be a taxpayer and a registered voter," the minister concluded.[74] W. I. Lewis noted: "At least two of the speakers on Emancipation Day laid the strongest emphasis on the duty of every man of the proper age paying his poll tax and registering. This one prime duty of every citizen must not be neglected."[75]

Rev. R. C. Ransome received thunderous applause at an AME conference in West Palm Beach when he "admonished the people that there was a new era about to dawn. The boys from overseas would be coming home, and as they had been fighting for democracy abroad, they would expect to have the same brand of democracy at home—freedom of thought, equal opportunity and [an] open door for every man. If democracy means anything, it means just this."[76] Black Floridians organized numerous ceremonies in honor of the collective sacrifices that the race had made in the national war effort. "The great welcome home celebration for colored soldiers of Leon County will take place Tuesday, May 20th, at Bethel Baptist church at 4 o'clock," announced an African American in Tallahassee. "They were not too proud to fight for us, and we are proud to welcome them home." The date for the celebration was no accident: African American communities in middle Florida traditionally set aside May 20 as Emancipation Day, a time to celebrate the end of slavery and to honor the institution's survivors.[77] A month after the ceremony in Tallahassee, nine members of the event's committee became charter members of the town's NAACP branch.[78]

"Emancipation Day was enthusiastically celebrated in St. Petersburg, under the auspices of the Colored Citizens Advancement Association, Prof. R. H. Graham, president." Mrs. P. T. Chaney read the Emancipation Proclamation. "The colored soldiers took a prominent part in the big parade, and a big chorus, directed by H. E. Richardson and Mrs. M. L. Fields rendered patriotic music."[79] African Americans in Suwanee County set aside a day of "patriotic rejoicing" with a parade, barbecue, and rally at Florida Memorial College in honor of "every young man who served in the army and navy in the great war."[80] T. S. Harris, a GOP leader at Live Oak, gave the keynote address.[81]

Black Floridians drew from a rich testimonial culture to emphasize connections between history, education, culture, and politics. Black organizations did more than commemorate black service in World War I. They made connections between slavery, the Civil War, and the Great War, tying these histories of struggle to the reconstruction of democracy after the Armistice. Mary McLeod Bethune's students at Daytona Normal staged a "joint celebration of the birthdays of Washington, Lincoln and the Negro orator and abolitionist, Frederick Douglass." The Normal's students made a giant diorama depicting the presidents, Douglass, and black slaves as well as "scenes showing the evolution of the Negro from a slave in chains to the Negro of today as teacher, Red Cross nurse, soldier and patriot. And over all waved the beloved flag of our common country." Bethune emphasized that men *and* women had shouldered the burdens of citizenship in the war, and she forged an even stronger link between the present and the past by inviting R. A. Scott, a former slave, to address the audience. Scott's talk was titled "Echoes of Emancipation."[82]

Echoes of emancipation rang out all over Florida. A reception given at Laura Street Presbyterian Church in Jacksonville in honor "of the young men who are members of that church and have returned from overseas" featured the "brief and highly interesting" speeches of the congregation's returned heroes from France. But Laura Street also reserved a place of honor for the aging freedom fighters: Matthew M. Lewey, a combat veteran of the 55th Massachusetts Infantry Regiment in the Civil War, "who has a record for individual bravery on the front, was introduced and given a respectful hearing, while he spoke with much interest of the days of his youth fighting the battles of his country."[83] Lewey had been an elected representative during Reconstruction. In 1884, he served as a delegate from Alachua County to the statewide conference of African Americans who forged the Independent movement. Twenty years later, the *Indianapolis Freeman* referred to the fiery newspaper editor as "Florida's most polished diplomat and peerless leader."[84] The grand old man now broke bread with a younger generation as determined to claim freedom's wreath as he had been over a half century earlier.

This joining of historical struggle with contemporary striving served as a reminder that African Americans had for many generations proved their loyalty to America. Such a message served as an organizing tool. At an NAACP meeting in Jacksonville held in April 1919, African Americans began the proceedings by singing the "Battle Hymn of the Republic." Mrs. C. C. Lewis read Paul Laurence Dunbar's tribute to black Civil War veterans, "The Colored Soldiers." Dunbar's poem had special significance for black Floridians as it memorialized the bloodiest Civil War battleground in Florida, Olustee, where scores of black soldiers had fallen. At the conclusion of the meeting, seventeen new members were added to the Jacksonville NAACP branch's roster.[85]

African Americans celebrated the past in a way that bolstered their contemporary claims to equal citizenship. An African American correspondent reporting on the Newman Methodist Episcopal Church's annual memorial service in Key West noted that this ceremony was "their annual memorial services for the unknown dead and also other heroes who fought for freedom during the Civil War." Surviving black Civil War veterans were honored at the service. The keynote speaker, the Rev. D. W. Demps, chose as the text of his sermon the belief that "if the son therefore make you free, ye are free indeed." Rev. Demps freely mixed religious text with African American political history:

> The speaker vividly pictured many historical facts that occurred on the battlefield during the Civil War. Because of the noble part played by the negro during the Civil War, also that of the recent war with Germany and the allies, he exalted us as a race to stand together to sustain the freedom for which the negro so nobly fought, bled and died that we not only live, but while living enjoy the rights, principles, and freedom of our country. He also placed great stress upon the word slavery by saying "As long as we fail to recognize negro enterprises we are yet holding ourselves as slaves."[86]

In coupling the memory of the Civil War with the part played by African Americans in the Great War, Rev. Demps reinvigorated the democratic covenant of the Emancipation.[87]

African Americans in Jacksonville staged the largest black war victory celebration held in Florida since the end of the Civil War. The "Welcome Home Parade" was a carefully planned and orchestrated act of political assertion. On the surface, it resembled the storied march of the 369th Infantry held in New York City the previous February. There, thirteen hundred black infantry soldiers and eighteen white officers, fresh from active duty in France, marched down Fifth Avenue saluting white dignitaries amidst roars of applause from spectators both black and white.[88]

The Welcome Home Parade in Jacksonville was a more sophisticated tool for social change than its New York counterpart was. Black Floridians used the event to publicly and explicitly promote the idea that they had made enormous contributions to their nation and that they were no longer willing to endure the tyranny of Jim Crow. Each detail of the parade was designed to emphasize black dignity and steadfastness in the face of adversity. This was a carefully scripted, black-controlled event (neither Governor Catts nor the chamber of commerce was invited to participate). The event was organized by the black Public Safety Committee, an organization chaired by Joseph E. Lee, Florida's senior African American political leader. Lee had regained his poise after his humiliating performance before the 1916 chamber of commerce where he had promised to help stem the tide of black workers out of Florida. African American social activism in the war pushed the venerable Lee to craft a public event that stated the case for equal citizenship in Florida. His organizers ensured that, in contrast to the New York marchers, the soldiers that marched in the Jacksonville parade would be led by *black* officers. More important, the Jacksonville parade was designed to involve thousands of African Americans as active participants rather than passive onlookers. The Public Safety Committee recruited numerous black organizations to march with the soldiers. Secret societies, labor unions, civic organizations, businesses, groups with histories of sustaining mutual aid in black neighborhoods and subscribing to the war effort were given major roles to play in the parade. The point was to show that the entire community had contributed to the Allied war effort. Children were asked to gather flowers for a memorial to the fallen soldiers. Black schools and businesses created ornate floats, while others donated automobiles to use during the parade.[89]

After weeks of planning, May 1 finally arrived. At 7:00 on Thursday evening, the city's premier black brass bands struck up a martial tune and seven hundred war veterans started to march crisply from State Street west through throngs of cheering onlookers. "There they came," marveled W. I. Lewis, "that long olive brown column, those boys who suffered so much in far away France, and upon the high seas; men who had learned to give a hand to the fellow farther down in bivouac, in the trench, on the field, on the hike; who displayed real humanity, forgetting silly race distinctions, loving country and flag."[90] Captain E. W. Latson, mounted on an Arab charger, led the veterans onto Davis Street, where they were joined by members of the city's leading fraternal orders including the Knights of Pythias, the Odd Fellows, and the Masons. Members of the Pythians' uniform rank regularly drilled for occasions such as this, and their uniforms, hearkening back to the garb of the Union Army soldier, reinforced the intergenerational theme of the day. As the marchers approached the intersection of Julia and North to "volleys of applause," black labor unionists swung into line and added their strength to the burgeoning procession. As the vanguard of soldiers and sailors approached Lee and pivoted south onto Forsyth, "Younger people rent the air with all sorts of jubilation," and spectators were treated to the sight of ornate floats that had been funded by the Afro-American Insurance Company, Walker's Business College, and other black-owned institutions. While the veterans sharply executed a column left north onto Laura Street, members of the city's black clubs and civic groups swelled the march's ranks. A delegation of black veterans from St. Augustine, led by D. M. Pappy, a black Reconstruction-era official and founding member of the Knights of Pythias, marched in solidarity with their Jacksonville comrades.[91] W. I. Lewis exulted: "Aged men and women who had not seen so large a number of soldiers of their race since the Civil War overran with a joy that showed itself in yells, mingled with tears. . . . Ultimately there were so many participants that it took an hour and a half for the parade to pass a given point."

The Public Safety Committee had planned the final destination of the march with care. The marching contingent, now some five thousand strong, made their way from Forsyth onto the campus of Stanton Public School, an institution that rested "on a tract of land that was bought by the fathers shortly after they were freed from slavery." These were the grounds where the Stanton High School choir first performed the song now known as the Negro National Anthem: "Lift Every Voice and Sing." Stanton's most illustrious headmaster, James Weldon Johnson, wrote the song for a celebration of the birthdays of Frederick Douglass and Abraham Lincoln in 1900.[92]

The speaker's podium was flanked by a mammoth pyramid-shaped display of flowers gathered by children and their teachers as a memorial in honor of African American soldiers who had been killed during the war. African Americans were determined to remind each other—and their white counterparts—that they had suffered in the name of democracy. After the audience sang the "Star Spangled Banner," Dr. J. A. Gregg, president of Edward Waters College, president of the Jacksonville NAACP, and a delegate to a new statewide civil rights organization, the Negro Uplift Association, delivered the keynote address. "Today marks an epoch in the history of the colored citizens of Jacksonville," intoned Dr. Gregg. He reminded the assembly, "Black men have fought in wars before in this country; black soldiers have so fought for right and justice, and have so maintained the honor of the stars and stripes in other days, that their bravery and loyalty have become traditional."[93]

The keynote speaker asked his listeners to think back on the opening days of the Great War. Was it not evident that they had entered into the war "to make the world safe for Democracy"? Subsequently, "new visions of liberty and justice and righteousness were seen, and men, grim visaged and determined, yet withal with their faces lighted by the sacred joy of sacrifice and devotion for a cause that was to bring a larger degree of privilege, came forward and willingly made themselves sacrifices upon the altar of this new hope, ready to suffer to the utmost that they and theirs might enter into this new freedom." Dedicating the flowers to black Jacksonville's "sacred dead," Gregg turned to the men who had passed through the rigors of service: "We welcome these returned soldiers with outstretched arms and bring to them the garlands which they see tonight, but for those who died for the cause, either in the cantonments or on the battlefield, we dedicate this pyramid." Pausing for a moment of silence, Gregg promised, "Their bodies tonight are buried in the soil of France, their last resting place made hallowed by the traditions of the land where they fell and sanctified by their own sacrifice, and though they are not here in person, I fully believe that their spirits commune with ours tonight."

Now gesturing to the massive assembly, Dr. Gregg observed, "Over here our people have willingly met every call of the nation in self denial and giving, and over there the two most outstanding things in the whole war are that black men are the first Americans to have gained the highest honors of war, the *Croix de Guerre*[,] and on the day of the signing of the Armistice, the black troops were nearest the German lines before the fortress of Metz." After reciting a passage from Lincoln's Gettysburg Address, Gregg prayed for the newest generation of war dead: "May the sacrifice of those dear boys be indeed not in vain. May we catch the spirit they have exemplified and dedicate ourselves here tonight to the task of keeping inviolable the institutions of this free and mighty nation that promises freedom to the oppressed and life, liberty and the pursuit of happiness to all." Speaking of the great battle before them all, Gregg concluded: "Let us not become disheartened, but give, as they have done, of the best we have that the best may come back to us. Someone said, 'Load a gun with bullets and you kill a tyrant; load it with ideas and you kill tyranny.'"

The Welcome Home Parade was a declaration of war on Jim Crow. African Americans on the home front had initiated the call for a major offensive against segregation. Now, returning veterans bolstered the crusade. Corporal L. A. Alexander, an artilleryman from West Palm Beach, demanded a redemptive outcome for himself and his comrades. Proudly noting that "we played our part in the great struggle for Democracy," Alexander sharply observed:

> It was not until after the armistice was signed that we really saw our hardest times overseas. The majority of our officers were white, and I must say that some of them were real gentlemen, but on the other hand, there were those who doubted them, that did not have the welfare of the colored soldiers at heart whatever, but I voice the sentiment of every colored soldier in the United States when I say that we are hoping and expecting to reap the benefits of our toilsome struggles and that Democracy in its fullest meaning will be for the betterment of the negro race as it will be for all other races.[94]

Pioneer infantryman Henry Thomas agreed with his comrade from West Palm Beach. After returning to Gadsden County to work on his parents' farm, the young veteran became a charter member of the Greensboro NAACP chapter.[95] That chapter would soon help spearhead a voter registration drive in Gadsden. Political activism was nothing new in the Thomas household. Henry's father had served as the Gadsden County Republican Party alternate delegate for the GOP's 1916 statewide convention.[96]

The war against racial violence and segregation was foremost on the minds of returning soldiers in Jacksonville who organized the League for Democracy, a black veterans' organization. Among the League's foremost goals were: "securing a just, fair and unprejudiced record of the achievements of the colored military in the histories used in the public schools and to fight against the arch enemies of the race—lynching, jim-crowing, disfranchisement, discrimination, inequality in educational advantages as well as for justice in the courts and economic and industrial freedom."[97]

On the other hand, white Floridians were determined to return to the racial status quo as soon as possible. The duel for labor control was ever present. The *Jasper News* opposed a veterans' aid bill because it might also benefit African American veterans: "Give to the nigger who saw service in France one hundred dollars and forty acres of land . . . and the white man will have to hew all the wood, and draw all the water."[98] Congressman Frank Clark ridiculed the idea that black Floridians had played any meaningful role in the Great War and desecrated the memories of African American casualties. "This, according to Mr. Clark, was the extent of the work done by the negro to make the world safe for democracy," the *Times-Union* chuckled. "He said that no more were killed in the war than in an ordinary riot."[99] One of Clark's constituents countered black hopes with lethal warnings:

> The Negro returned soldier who is full of the "equal rights" treatment he got in Europe during the past months will do exceedingly well to remember that for every one of him there are about a thousand white returned soldiers who were completely fed up on the same equal rights stuff over there, and they are not going to stand for one moment any internal rot started by any yellow-faced coon who has the hellish idea that he is as good as a white man or a white woman.[100]

THE POSTWAR STRIKE WAVE

African American workers in Florida launched a series of postwar organizing drives and strikes that simultaneously drew from and bolstered rising expectations of social and economic justice.[101] African American workers, reinforced by a cohort of returning veterans, created their own interpretations of the meaning of the Great War upon their lives.[102] In St. Petersburg, "the union idea, having been stirred up here lately, is spreading and now the negro women who do washing and ironing and general housework . . . are to demand $3 a day, no matter what is their employment."[103] At the end of October 1919, Crescent City "Negro orange pickers connected with the Sawyer & Godfrey packing house went on strike last week, demanding 10 cents per box for picking."[104] African American farm laborers in Palatka began organizing a similar campaign for higher wages. From a worker's perspective the relative labor shortage brought about as a result of the Great Migration was a blessed thing. One black newspaper exulted: "Everywhere we hear the cry for labor almost at its own price. Minors are paid $2.00 per day in the potato fields while skilled labor is being offered 80 cents per hour and more."[105] One white man complained that his fellow farmers "are showing a total loss of effort to get together. Floating negro labor has demonstrated greater ability to this end then we."[106]

African American farm and forest workers battled to raise the hourly wage rate as high as possible.[107] Beating a tactical retreat, some local growers' associations began offering $3.50 a day for field labor, a major increase over the wages current just two years earlier, but still lower than what turpentine and timber workers were demanding.[108] The *Florida Grower* admonished: "When the citrus fruit grower is called upon to divide his possible profits with the men who hoe his trees or pack his fruit we imagine that the weeds will grow tall in his grove and we cannot imagine much development taking place either here or anywhere in the world under such a plan."[109] "Outside agitators" were blamed for labor strife, and Democratic newspapers warned that strikes were being orchestrated by white political forces. "Race relations are ticklish enough now," lectured the *Jasper News*. "The American Federation of Labor has decided to organize the unorganized labor of the South. All the radical forces of the labor world have their minds intent on organizing the negro farm labor of the South."[110]

Organized labor now had a golden opportunity to forge an interracial alliance of working people in Florida. W. M. Watson, a black union leader from Tampa, helped to draft the resolution on interracial cooperation that was passed at the AFL's 1919 national convention.[111] But the resolution had little impact on AFL affiliates such as the Boilermakers' union in Pensacola, which called for the expulsion of black workers from skilled trades in the spring of 1919.[112] By that summer, the Florida State Federation of Labor (FSL) tentatively extended an olive branch to African American workers. FSL president Richard B. Lovett answered a Florida newspaper that criticized interracial cooperation by arguing that "he [the black worker] is over-worked and under-paid, and has no chance whatever to improve himself or his family because, with rare exceptions, he is not permitted to earn more than will keep body and soul together."[113] At the FSL's convention however, the Miami building trades delegation threatened to walk out if two black union representatives were seated. The state federation cut a Faustian bargain with segregation. The *New York Age* observed: "The labor federation of Florida made itself ridiculous by its cowardly surrender of the first principles of the equality of labor, at the sight of two dark skins. And yet these same workingmen want the support of the colored laborers in their contests with capital and blame them when they are forced into an attitude antagonistic to union labor."[114] Skilled trade unionists from Pensacola to Miami were determined to exclude African Americans from well-paying jobs and apprenticeship opportunities. Ironically, organized labor fell on the very dagger it had aimed at African Americans as one strike after another went down to defeat. A working class divided against itself had no hope of holding its own against Florida's powerful employers.

Meanwhile, growers struck back. In response to black unionizing efforts, packinghouse owners in Crescent City as well as Eustis vowed to operate on an "open shop basis," or shut their plants down altogether.[115] Farmers in Seminole and Manatee Counties united to slash the daily wage rate for farm labor, and citrus-belt growers agreed to impose a maximum pay scale in their industry.[116] Law enforcement officials aided and abetted labor repression. When farm workers at one Leesburg grove quit after the employer refused to pay $3.50 a day, they were arrested by a Lake County sheriff.[117] Law enforcement officials in Palatka arrested a black "labor agitator," charging him with "vagrancy and disturbing labor." At the same time, an African American woman was seized for trying to recruit Putnam potato workers for better-paying work in Jacksonville.[118] When African American waiters in Palm Beach threatened to strike, a sheriff threatened the men with arrest, vowing that the strikers "would be put to work, as peons, on the roads" and "stated that if any trouble arose he, the sheriff, would not get hurt, but [warned] the Colored waiters might."[119]

Union organizing fueled class conflict in black communities. When African American miners around Fort Meade began to join the International Union of Mine, Mill, and Smelter Workers, some black clergy aided phosphate employers in impeding the effort.[120] Rev. Mays, an area minister, was given a car by a mine owner to aid in the mission of paying anti-union propaganda visits to black miners' homes. Once black mine laborers discovered the purpose of his visits as well as his source of income, however, they shunned him as a traitor to his race.[121] Not one to admit defeat easily, Mays called a public meeting for the "Welfare of the Colored People." The white press noted with approval that the minister is "endeavoring to carry out the mines' idea of bettering the present condition of all colored citizens, especially the working man."[122] African American miners rejected this overture. The *Fort Meade Leader* noted: "Saturday night on Broadway, Prof. Mays, the colored orator, delivered one of his good lectures to the members of his race. Only a few of the colored people were out, however, but a large number of white citizens listened with appreciation to the speaker's eloquence in behalf of patriotism and the colored race."[123] The lack of an African American audience did not stop a few ministers at this meeting from drafting a statement of gratitude to area mine owners. The obsequious resolution was silent on the issues that were actually central to the African American miners: wages, working conditions, and squalid company housing.

Over time, African American labor actions carried stronger overtones of political insurgency. Black workers understood that their ability to organize was circumscribed by their lack of political power. Tampa's leading black trade unionist, William Watson, proclaimed: "admission into labor unions carries with it the prerequisite of the applicant being a registered voter with his poll tax paid up."[124] An African American from nearby St. Petersburg wrote: "There is much talk of a general strike by the colored laborers of all classes. . . . Pamphlets have been circulated among them urging that they demand equal rights with the white people, and it is claimed that the [Knights of Pythias] is behind the movement which resulted in so many colored men qualifying as voters by paying poll taxes."[125]

At the onset of the Great Migration, black workers had sought to escape the repressive conditions of Florida; now they struggled to change those very same conditions. In doing this, African Americans increased their knowledge of organizing. In activities ranging from petitioning the federal government, unionizing, going out on strike, or paying their poll taxes, black workers contributed to an upsurge in collective action and self-activity among African Americans in Florida. Along the way, black working people pushed "race leaders" who collaborated with employers off the stage of leadership. Now it was possible to forge an authentic political movement.

Capitalizing on the momentum generated by African American activism, a group of black leaders issued a call on February 5, 1919, for a statewide civil rights convention to assemble in Ocala. Convention organizers issued the call so "that we may formulate . . . and agree upon some workable program whereby we may secure to ourselves and to our children the enjoyment in larger measures the rights and privileges which are ours by right." The Negro Uplift Association was born. The NUA's call mixed religious and secular imagery:

> Our god is marching on. And out of His conquests surely something of
> the good things for which we have labored and prayed shall be ours to
> enjoy. . . . Let us be reminded that the world can go forward in the way
> of ordered justice and right only as it shall concede and guarantee to us
> Negro people more and more the enjoyment of life, liberty and pursuits
> of happiness. So self-evident is this truth that there can be no better
> proof of our patriotism and devotion to national ideals than is shown
> by our earnest insistence upon the enjoyment of these blessings by
> ourselves and our race.[126]

The NUA sought to end lynching and to effect "the removal of individual political discrimination." The organization wanted "fairer economic and industrial conditions" and "adequate provisions for education and better protection and care for delinquent children." Leaders of the organization would be elected as delegates from their local communities. The "Representative Negro" would now owe his or her position of leadership to the people and not the white business establishment.

African Americans across the state began meeting to elect NUA delegates in March.[127] "The Negro Uplift Association movement is a live wire in this St. Lucie County," wrote a black correspondent on March 13. "Prof. H. R. Jenkins, chairman, has held several meetings, and every one of them drew out large crowds of interested people." The correspondent discussed the election of the delegates to the convention in Ocala and noted that "there will be a mammoth mass-meeting held at Fort Pierce, the county seat of St. Lucie county and at which time the delegates and other citizens will be present."[128] St. Lucie's black communities in Viking, Jensen, Wabasso, and Fort Pierce energetically collected NUA dues for the cause.[129] A correspondent from Gifford urged black Floridians to support NUA goals: "If you have race pride, if you are loyal, if you want better opportunities, if you want better citizenship, you can be depended upon [to] be present."[130] In Tallahassee, a "very enthusiastic mass-meeting was held" for electing NUA delegates, and "the chairman gave a very interesting address laying stress upon the importance of the rural districts organizing in order to get the desired results."[131]

The Negro Uplift Association delegates and officers were men with deep roots in their communities. At the local level, many of the NUA's elected delegates were members of new NAACP branches, older Republican Party organizations, and political and fraternal orders. The NUA's secretary, S. H. Savage, was a prominent AME minister from Daytona.[132] Lieutenant R. E. S. Toomey, who appointed the initial NUA county chairs, was a Spanish-American war veteran and a highly respected community leader in Miami.[133] J. S. LaRoche, NUA delegate from Marion County and a state officer of the organization, was a senior member of the Grand United Order of Odd Fellows in Ocala.[134] Rev. S. H. Betts was an AME minister known throughout the Panhandle as an outspoken advocate for black education and civil rights.[135]

Delegates were often members of activist organizations. R. D. McLin, from the St. Petersburg Civic League, a civil rights group, was the NUA chair for Pinellas County. J. S. Pottsdammer, an officer with the Tallahassee NAACP and a member of the Knights of Pythias, was the NUA chair for Leon County. D. J. and B. J. Jones, brothers, businessmen, Pythians, and organizers of the Lake City Republican Party, were NUA delegates, as was Dr. W. S. Stevens, a member of the Knights of Pythias and a leader of the Republican Party in Gadsden County. J. A. Gregg, president of the Jacksonville NAACP, was a delegate from Jacksonville, as was W. W. Andrews, Grand Chancellor of the Knights of Pythias. AME bishop John Hurst, a strong advocate of civil rights and a national board member of the NAACP, was a delegate at-large. The Pensacola Southern Protective Association, a group active in the fight against Jim Crow on the city's streetcars, affiliated as a body with the NUA.[136]

African American women were conspicuous by their absence in the upper echelon of association leadership.[137] On the local level, however, evidence from two chapters suggests that they played a critical role in the development of the organization. In the St. Lucie county NUA, four of the seven elected officers were women.[138] In Tallahassee, women served on all of the branch's committees.[139] Still, women remained underrepresented in the major positions of NUA leadership. Perhaps as a way of addressing this weakness, Mary McLeod Bethune, president of the State Federation of Colored Women's Clubs, organized a "reconstruction conference" during the Federation's 1919 convention where NUA, NAACP, and "various women's organizations in the State" conferred and listened to addresses by Eartha White and R. E. S. Toomey among others.[140] Bethune provided a space where organizers could meet and confer with the women of the Federation.

The Negro Uplift Association convention opened on April 23. Lieutenant Toomey's gavel brought the assembly to order, and a reporter noted: "There were expressions of great surprise on every hand at the large number of delegates in attendance." The convention was organized into workshops, break-out sessions, and plenary talks, held in Ocala's Metropolitan Theater. N. B. Young, president of Florida A & M College (and a member of the Tallahassee NAACP), was a keynote speaker. Dr. Young had always been a staunch opponent of disfranchisement, and his position at a state-sponsored college was embattled as a result.[141] Now he declared that the South's segregated school system "is fast dying out, and, with very few exceptions, is a failure. He further said that some of the schools would be far better off if they did not exist."[142] Dr. Young's militant address set the tone for the conference.

Dr. J. A. Gregg discussed the "status of the negro when he returns to America from the blood-washed fields of France," and Rev. A. L. James also gave "a glowing tribute to the valor of the negro soldiers in France." J. D. McCall of Ocala spoke on "The Economic Status of the Negro," and "urged a higher wage scale for negroes and a diversification of negro interests." The only female speaker listed on the agenda of the convention, Mrs. Evans from St. Lucie County, gave a presentation which summed up African American thoughts on the present state of Florida politics: "This Jim Crow Law Ain't Right."[143]

The Ocala convention deliberated on a course of action to bring their anti–Jim Crow message to the Florida State Legislature. Delegates chose several representatives to deliver a resolution to Governor Catts and Florida state representatives in Tallahassee. The NUA representatives "plead for better railroad conditions, protection against lynching, a longer school term, and a colored superintendent for the State Industrial School." The NUA resolution called "attention to the part Negroes played in winning the war by serving their country both at home and abroad," and argued that "the adoption by the legislature of the recommendations of the petition would help to stem 'the continuous, though quiet, exodus of the Negro from the South.' " NUA representatives who presented the memorial to the state legislature were men who exercised leadership positions in black organizations throughout Florida: H. Y. Tookes, a Masonic lodge officer and AME elder from Jefferson County; Rev. S. A. Owen, an AME minister and political leader from Daytona; C. C. Manigault, a former city council member from Jacksonville; Rev. Betts from Jackson County; NUA state organizer Toomey; and R. G. Lee, NUA president and resident of West Palm Beach.[144]

The NUA committee formally presented the memorial to the Florida State Legislature in May. As the Senate clerk was in the act of reading the NUA petition however, he was stopped by legislators when they discovered that the petitioners were African Americans. " 'Offense was taken at the signatures of persons who signed themselves 'Lt.', 'Rev.', and 'Mr.' "[145] These were titles reserved for members of the white elite. The clerk was ordered to purge the petition from the Senate record.[146] An African American newspaper angrily noted: "The effrontery of the legislature in Florida is regarded as one of the grossest insults ever perpetrated upon any people, even in the darkest days of Russia and the 'Hunniest' days of Germany."[147]

The abysmal failure of the Negro Uplift Association petition was an important experience for black political organizers. Black Floridians had presented a statement asking the governor and the state legislature to acknowledge the dignity of African Americans, their contributions to the war effort, and their rights to citizenship in the state. Had this petition been presented in a more deferential spirit, with fewer controversial themes, the legislature would likely have been willing to hear it. The NUA delegates had failed to stoop and truckle sufficiently in order to gain an audience with the white representatives. Unlike the 1916 staged meeting between "representative Negroes" and the Jacksonville Chamber of Commerce, the NUA memorial was driven by a grassroots protest movement. However, NUA delegates had made one strategic error. In truth, the Florida legislature had little incentive to consider any petition from African Americans. Outside of a few scattered areas, black Floridians had been barred from voting or participating in state politics for decades. Now, they were proposing changes in race relations without possessing any political power. Asking for an extra appropriation for segregated schools was one thing; asking for a longer school term and black control over the school system (thus implying that the current system was dysfunctional) was out of bounds.

Equally unacceptable was the NUA request to end lynching in the state. Governor Catts countered an NAACP request to investigate a lynching in Madison by responding: "You ask me to see that these lynchers are brought to trial. This would be impossible to do as conditions are now in Florida, for when a negro brute, or a white man, ravishes a white woman in the State of Florida, there is no use having the people, who see that this man meets death, brought to trial, even if you could find who they are; the citizenship will not stand for it."[148] Catts couldn't accept black Floridians as citizens because if African Americans were included in the "citizenship," they would legislate against lynching.

This "newest era of Reconstruction," as Mary McLeod Bethune called it, required that concepts like citizenship, democracy, and economic security be redefined and fought for. African Americans confronted the grim reality that the sacrifices they had so recently made in European trenches, in their workplaces, and in war support drives were being willfully ignored by white Floridians. Worse, state officials used the absolute political power they enjoyed as functionaries in a one-party state to oppose the struggles of black workers on every front. Historian Rayford Logan observed: "When Armistice sounded on November 11, 1918, few Negroes believed that their country appreciated their services on the battlefield, behind the lines or on the home front. . . . Negroes soon learned that the war by which the world was to be 'made safe for democracy' would not revolutionize their subordinate status in American society."[149]

African Americans would have to make their own revolution, and the first step in this process was regaining the ballot. Black Floridians interpreted the rejection of the NUA's petition as a signal to carry their struggle to the next level. The battle to end one-party rule in Florida began in earnest.

◄ 8 ►

WITH BABIES IN THEIR ARMS

The Voter Registration Movement

My experience in the South has convinced me that no coming together of Negro leaders to discuss anything that is not in confirmation of what the South has already fixed for the Negro is going to bear fruit. The one thing to my mind that is going to be effective in dealing with the South is the use of *force* and always *force*.[1]

REV. JOHN HURST
AME Bishop of Florida, January 1919

Men must register and pay their poll tax. This duty is absolutely imperative on the part of every man. . . . Peace is here, and the citizen who shirks from this elementary duty is not worthy of the name and privilege of being a citizen. Now is the time when the ballot is mightier than the bayonet, and every citizen should arm himself with the ballot to do battle in the mighty conflicts coming.[2]

W. I. LEWIS

IN THE SPRING OF 1920, Clem Gandy tried to return a bottle of flavoring extract that she had purchased at a store in Fort Meade. The white proprietor brusquely refused to offer a refund. Feeling that she had been discriminated against, Gandy contacted a local group, the Negro Welfare League, for assistance. The organization sent a letter of protest to "practically every business and professional man" in Fort Meade "asking the white people to reply to questions on how they stood in regard to the matter and their opinions regarding the relations of the white and black races."[3]

White businessmen in Polk County called a meeting to deal with the situation. Their power to exercise domination over black consumers had been challenged, and they resolved to drive Gandy as well as G. B. R. Grant and Lafayette S. Hankins, two officers of the Welfare League, out of town, "and they did leave as quickly as possible."[4] The local press reported, "White people here also decided that as far as they were concerned there would be no more 'Negro Welfare League' nor would another circular letter similar to the one sent . . . be considered for a moment." The school board shut down the school that Mr. Hankins served at as principal because "Hankins' activities in connection with the Negro Welfare League were against the best interests of the school and community." Seeking to widen the growing purge, whites sent threatening letters to other African Americans, ordering them to leave the region.[5] The Fort Meade Terror underscored white southerners' grim resolve to maintain their domination over black people.

African Americans interpreted incidents like these as confirmation that the only way to end the humiliation of Jim Crow was to break down one-party rule in the South. On January 1, 1919—Emancipation Day—African Americans in Jacksonville issued the first public calls to start a voter registration movement. African Americans had always used Emancipation Day as a time when they reminded each other and their white neighbors that they had earned their citizenship, and now they used this day of remembrance to plan for the future. Over the next several months African Americans in twenty-eight counties organized voter registration campaigns that congealed into a statewide movement aimed at shattering white supremacy. Black Floridians believed that if they could decisively participate in the 1920 presidential election they would be taking the first steps toward regaining their rightful role in the republic. The Florida movement was rooted in the history of struggle that African Americans had forged between the end of slavery and the coming of World War I. African Americans did not share identical ideas on politics, religion, and a host of other issues; nevertheless, they broadly agreed on the necessity of defeating the Jim Crow system.

African American women played a decisive role in the Florida movement. Black Floridians were able to launch the voter registration movement largely because the Nineteenth Amendment changed the fulcrum of southern politics. African American women were more than ready to exploit the opportunities that expanded suffrage offered.[6] Mary McLeod Bethune, Eartha White, and other female activists in Florida understood that this was the moment they had been working for all their lives. History and historical memory played an animating role in the struggle. One African American woman in Florida explained to the NAACP why she risked her livelihood to vote: "My Dear Father helped to fight three years [in the Civil War] to raise children as [R]epublicans and this year was the first year I voted and it was cast for Harding. . . . All that is needed is to let the southern white man know that the War of [18]63–4 and 5 has made us free, and the negroes are no longer their slaves, and have the right to be protected by our laws."[7] African Americans had preserved oral traditions of slavery and service to the republic that reinforced their claims to equal citizenship. This woman demonstrated a commitment to destroy Jim Crow, a commitment sustained by her sisters in decades of struggle against abusive employers, streetcar segregation, and disfranchisement. Black women were confident that this was their time. Florida became the pivotal battleground state in the struggle to end white supremacy.

FORGING A MOVEMENT

The Jacksonville branch of the National Alliance of Postal Employees, a union of African American railway mail clerks, met at the home of A. J. Gillis, a senior clerk, for their monthly meeting during the final week of May 1919.[8] D. H. Dwight, the union local's president, recalled that the older workers had organized the Alliance "to help our younger brother coming into the service," after all new black clerks were racially barred from the Railway Mail Association, an American Federation of Labor affiliate, in 1913.[9] Building on the soil of black fraternalism, the union became a cornerstone of mutual aid, establishing a benefit fund that members in good standing as well as their widows and children could depend on during hard times. Dwight's narrative of the union's history emphasized the grievance procedure that the clerks had negotiated with management as well as the patriotic service that members had rendered during World War I.

After opening with prayer, members discussed union business and plans for the Alliance's national convention to be held later that year in Jacksonville. The meeting's final agenda item heralded a new day in Florida. As the union's recording secretary noted, "The committee appointed to see that each local clerk had paid his poll tax and was duly qualified as a citizen, and registered voter . . . reported that every clerk, with one exception, possessed the proper credentials, and the one clerk mentioned who had just become of age, gave assurance of obtaining the necessary qualifications real soon."[10]

In a society where younger folks are often identified as the catalysts of social change, the image of older African Americans urging a young black man to vote may seem odd. The clerks' union was able to call upon its members to risk the dangers of engaging in politics in Florida because the union had woven together personal relationships of trust and reciprocity that allowed members to survive Jim Crow.[11] Senior unionists had earned a level of respect among younger workers that gave their resolution on paying poll taxes credibility. This credibility did not stem from the leaders' race or their charisma or even their age; it was based on sustaining a labor organization that served the needs of its membership.[12]

African Americans across Florida drew on bonds of solidarity nurtured by organizations such as the National Alliance of Postal Employees and others to create a statewide voter registration movement. The struggle was forged by African Americans working in the kinds of institutions that had guaranteed survival in a harsh social order: secret societies, unions, women's clubs, churches, and other groups that bolstered black dignity and civic fraternalism. Since the end of Reconstruction, black Floridians had used these organizations to cultivate the kinds of intergenerational affinities that must exist for a large social movement to emerge.[13] Taking advantage of the momentum they had generated during the war years, male and female activists transformed these organizations into spaces where they set about redefining the meaning of citizenship in Jim Crow America.[14]

The barriers standing in the way of an honest election in Florida were staggering. "I have talked with a great many of the negros, and they all want to vote the Republican Ticket," Louis J. Brinkman, an Aucilla resident noted, "but they tell me they fear their votes will be throwed out."[15] Florida's election machinery was in the hands of unabashedly corrupt officials. Political violence also loomed as a barrier to participation. NAACP official Walter White traveled to Florida incognito—he was able to pass for white—to report on the obstacles faced by the Florida movement. He testified that African Americans in Orange County were mocked by white registrars: "A White lawyer told me laughingly of how a Negro would approach a registration booth in his county, Orange, and ask if he could register. The officials there, in most cases of the poorer order of whites, would reply, 'Oh, yes, you can register, but I want to tell you something. Some God damn black ——— is going to get killed about this voting business yet."[16]

Organizing a movement in the shadow of terror requires a means of recruitment, a shared commitment to take risks, and a social program based on the needs of the aggrieved. Black Floridians conceived of the ballot as a mechanism for launching a decisive struggle against racial oppression. This assertive approach to politics—addressing the most pressing social issues of the day instead of shrinking from them—is one key to understanding why so many black Floridians would risk their lives and livelihoods to participate in this campaign. Rev. E. J. W. Day in De Soto County informed Warren G. Harding that he would be organizing on Harding's behalf because he and his people expected the GOP to do something about lynching in the South.[17] The editors of the Pensacola *Colored Citizen* answered the question "Why the Negro Should Register 3,000 Votes" with reasons grounded in the experience of black workers:

> Another law that works against the black man, is the one wherein a labor agent is compelled to pay a license of $2500, if he gives him transportation to another place; if the man is out of work, and some one wants to send him to another place where he can make an honest living at good wages, he must sneak here and there like a hunted criminal to meet the agent who will furnish transportation. Can not the Negro see that this law, a relic of slavery is against him? Why not register and vote some one to the legislature who will work for the repeal of this old time slavery law.[18]

The *Colored Citizen* framed voting as a way to smash a repressive labor system that had all the hallmarks of slavery. African American workers had carried this burden since emancipation, and their latest efforts had borne fruit in the guise of the Great Migration and the postwar strike wave. Now, a distinctively pro-labor political agenda was at the heart of black politics. An AME Zion church official in Pensacola offered equally meaningful reasons to join the movement:

> We are urging our folks to register and vote for the same reason that other people are registering and voting. We want full protection of the law, representation where we are concerned, decent public accommodations; for equal pay, better schools and a living wage for our teachers, womanhood respected regardless of color, good roads, a fair share of public improvements and the free and unabridged right to vote like any other American citizens.[19]

Black Floridians expanded the idea of democracy to encompass concerns and issues that impacted the entire community.[20] African Americans achieved this sophistication by organizing discussion forums known in

Jacksonville as "citizens' meetings" to generate face-to-face conversations about politics. At these meetings, African Americans discussed women's suffrage, black history, and the recent war, and they learned how to pay their poll taxes and register to vote. These were not meetings where a pedantic elite taught the masses about politics. Participants in these gatherings voiced their own desires and ideas about a democratic future where their families and communities would be respected and treated with dignity. Individuals who were planning to vote for the first time in their lives were able to imagine themselves transforming the social fabric of American society.[21] African Americans simultaneously tried to transform the Republican Party into a vehicle that would end one-party rule in Florida. This meant shaking the GOP loose from its Lily-White moorings, and uncoupling southern Republicanism from patronage politics.

African American women took the lead in building the Florida movement. Female activists created a shared language of political struggle that drew from their decades of experience in promoting mutual aid and combating white supremacy. Black women used their statewide connections in religious organizations and the Florida State Federation of Colored Women's Clubs to help spread the word about tactics used in local organizing drives. A month after the first public call to register to vote had been issued, Mrs. Louise Genwright announced that the Allen Christian Endeavor City Union would sponsor a "series of Christian citizenship meetings." Genwright insisted that in this initiative, "the officers are determined that these organizations shall be of real benefit to the race in a political as well as a spiritual way." The topic of discussion at this first Christian citizenship meeting was: "How to Make Every Colored Man in Duval County a Qualified Voter."[22] Invoking imagery from the New Testament, Louise Genwright exhorted African Americans by pointing out that "Jesus Christ fed the hungry, gave sight to the blind and helped men physically as well as spiritually and we must help others and thereby help ourselves as this is our only hope."[23]

Women's clubs mobilized to spread the voting drive. The Brooklyn Citizens and Improvement Club met at the home of Mrs. Sadie Ash Bordner to hear "Rev. A. P. Postell deliver a very interesting address which was enjoyed by all. Many men have qualified themselves to vote through the activities of this club since its last meeting."[24] These men became qualified voters thanks to the efforts of a club whose members did not yet even enjoy suffrage rights. The Brooklyn club was a part of the City and State Federation of Colored Women's Clubs, and for many years emphasized equal citizenship, voting rights, and the commemoration of Emancipation Day.[25] In a previous election, Jacksonville's black women's clubs had "placed slides in public places appealing to men to pay their poll taxes and register so as to be qualified to vote and won support from the city for a black playground and addressed Duval County Commissioners for better treatment for prisoners."[26] African American women were determined to expand the Florida movement.

On May 24, a week after the Negro Uplift Association's petition for justice was rejected by the state legislature, the Knights of Pythias convened their State Lodge meeting in Tampa. Approximately one out of every six adult black males in the state belonged to the order.[27] After discussing the KOP's role in the Great War at home and abroad, the Pythians passed a historic resolution by universal acclamation. Members solemnly bound each other to pay their poll taxes and register to vote in their home communities.[28] Any member who failed to do this by the end of the year would be expelled from his lodge. Fifteen thousand African American men joined the Florida movement. The Knights' resolution flowed logically from the organization's time-honored principles: to "destroy caste and color prejudices; to relieve the needs and afford succor to a brother; to elevate man to a higher plane of intelligence, morality and social equality; to administer to the sick and suffering." As KOP members returned to their home counties, what had started as a series of important local voter registration campaigns solidified into a statewide movement.

The KOP oath had such a powerful effect in Florida because it was based on years of sick visits, shared labor, and democratic practices. If such a resolution had been issued by an organization that did not have the confidence and respect of Florida's African American communities, it would have been meaningless. In St. Petersburg, the Associated Negro Press reported: "Pamphlets have been circulated among them urging that they demand equal rights with the white people, and it is claimed that the K. of P. society is behind the movement which resulted in so many colored men qualifying as voters by paying poll taxes. The lodge practically ordered the members to pay up, and qualify as voters."[29] In Jacksonville, W. I. Lewis reported that in W. P. Ross Lodge No. 7, KOP, "nearly every man in this lodge is a registered voter. . . . For some time it has been made a prerequisite in this lodge for all members to be qualified voters, and with the main reminders now afloat, this requirement has gained greater emphasis." The Knights' resolution had a snowballing effect as other secret societies began to require or at least urge their members to register to vote.[30]

W. E. B. Du Bois published a letter detailing the impact of the KOP's resolution on voting in the *Crisis:*

> This revival of the Negro's interest in becoming registered and paying his poll-tax began last May when the Grand Lodge Knights of Pythias passed a resolution prohibiting any member from entering the lodge in the state of Florida after January 1, 1920, until he had registered and paid his poll taxes. The Knights of Pythias has a membership of fifteen thousand men of voting age. It is a question in my mind whether this resolution could have been enforced had any member objected in the courts but no one objected, hence the other fraternities followed suit and as a result we have a heavy registration of Negro voters which has already had a telling effect on the attitude of white men toward the Negro.[31]

While the impetus for postwar political activism has often been credited to a younger, more radical generation—the New Negro—the story in Florida is much different. The idea of the New Negro has always rested on the assumption that postwar militancy replaced decades of African American acquiescence or accommodation. This heroic narrative has almost always favored the romantic image of a future-oriented vanguard, primarily male, mainly based in the North, who used their individual talents to lead the race beginning in the early 1920s. From the very beginning however, black Floridians collectively fought unequal treatment in numerous ways ranging from acts of armed self-defense to protests against segregated streetcars to strikes. The intensity of the struggle ebbed and flowed with the vicissitudes of time, but it was continuous nonetheless. In fraternal organizations like the Knights of Pythias, African Americans created relationships of trust and social spaces necessary for a social movement to emerge. These relationships were knitted together through the practice of mutual aid. This rules-based solidarity meant that older African Americans who ushered newer members into unions, secret societies, and women's clubs played leading roles in local movements. Black Floridians were building an intergenerational social movement that drew from the creative energies of young and old alike.

In the midst of this great political revival Joseph E. Lee returned to the grass roots. The grand old man of Florida politics had served in political office in one capacity or another going back to the time of Reconstruction. He had once served as municipal judge in Jacksonville and later benefited from the politics of federal GOP patronage.[32] Lee held the federal post of collector of internal revenue in Jacksonville until 1913, when Woodrow Wilson's purge of southern black office holders began in earnest.[33] Things went from bad to worse when Lee was excoriated by black trade unionists for cooperating with the Jacksonville Chamber of Commerce's drive to stop African American workers from leaving the state. The nascent Florida movement convinced Lee that mass black politics were once again possible, and he sought to transform the moribund Republican Party into the "party of human rights" that Jacksonville minister J. Milton Waldron had envisioned three decades earlier.[34] At age seventy and in failing health, Lee knew that this would be the final crusade of his life.

In March 1919, Lee convened a meeting at his law office to organize the "Central Republican Club of Duval County" (CRC).[35] Over the next few months, Lee brought together veteran organizers and community activists to take part in the new association. The "citizens' meetings," one-part voter education seminars and one-part discussion group, were the linchpin of the CRC's recruitment efforts. These meetings were designed to build the base of a new African American–led Republican Party as well as to stoke the fires of the voter registration campaign.

The citizens' meetings were generally held in churches. On June 8, the club met at Mt. Zion AME, which was led by Rev. R. A. Grant, a charter member of the Jacksonville NAACP. At the meeting, "there was a good attendance of members of the church, friends from different parts of the city and club members, who occupied reserved pews and wore badges."[36] I. L. Purcell, a legal strategist of the 1905 streetcar boycott in Jacksonville against segregation, facilitated the meeting. The meeting began with singing. Eartha M. M. White led a discussion on women's suffrage. Newspaper editor W. I. Lewis answered questions on "Poll Tax and Registration." Joseph Lee gave an address, "The Colored Man, His Prerogatives and Duties."[37] Lee expressed his excitement at the energetic participation of the audience, and after receiving a wave of applause, he made a call for new members. Membership requirements were clear: all prospective applicants had to bring their poll tax receipts to the meeting. The CRC welcomed fifty new members into the organization that evening.

Over the next few months, the Central Republican Club continued to build its membership base while strengthening its connection to fraternal, religious, and political organizations that enjoyed statewide and national ties. Eartha White's participation linked the club to the Florida State Federation of Colored Women's Clubs. In addition, speakers with ties to the

Negro Uplift Association and the Florida NAACP participated in Republican Club gatherings. Other visitors to Republican Club meetings included Nathan B. Young, the president of Florida A & M College and a secret NAACP sympathizer.[38] These connections helped African Americans in Jacksonville spread the word about what they were trying to do to activists throughout the state.

At a citizens' meeting held at Grant's Memorial AME Church, a familiar figure from Florida's past took the podium. It had been over thirty years since M. M. Lewey had been treacherously stricken from his party's ticket by white Republicans in Alachua County. Now, the Civil War veteran spoke to the participants of the meeting about the intricacies of the poll tax and voter registration.[39] At the same meeting, I. L. Purcell led a discussion on the Thirteenth Amendment to the U.S. Constitution, and S. H. Hart, Jr., a lawyer (and World War I veteran), talked about "Citizenship under the Fourteenth Amendment to the Constitution of the United States."[40] At another citizens' meeting, newspaper editor Lewis led a discussion on Frederick Douglass, and "many men in the audience afterwards gave their names to become members of the club, and all were delighted to know the nature and aim of the club."[41] Club speakers redoubled their efforts to educate young and old alike about politics and American history with the goal of urging them to make history in the present by registering to vote.

Speakers at the citizens' meetings facilitated discussions on more recent political history, giving concrete reasons why participants should reclaim their citizenship. R. P. Crawford answered an address titled "Why Our People Should Qualify for the Presidential Election of 1920" by remarking on "the peculiar incidents and events relating directly to his race in the attitude of the national government and its administration in the past seven years."[42] By February 20, 1920, when club members gave speeches celebrating the birthdays of Frederick Douglass and Abraham Lincoln, 350 African Americans were members of the Duval County Central Republican Club.[43]

Joseph E. Lee and his organizers had created a public forum where energetic discussions on politics could take place. Using the citizens' meetings as a participatory vehicle, African Americans democratized the Republican Party. The new party that they were building pledged itself to the defense of the Reconstruction amendments, political equality, and full participation in contemporary politics. In the process, African Americans had jettisoned the "Black and Tan" patronage politics that delivered token appointments to a few black middle-class leaders in favor of grassroots democracy.[44]

The core organizations of the Jacksonville movement—including the clerks' union, women's clubs, churches, and the CRC—succeeded in recruiting new members and building the voter registration campaign because they had created a *space* for organizing to occur. Within these spaces, African Americans talked to each other about social change and crafted the techniques to make change happen. In sum, these organizations sponsored what civil rights activists of a later era might have termed "citizenship schools." These schools taught members the rudiments of voter registration, sponsored talks on political issues, and provided African Americans with forums to define their own agendas.[45]

The Jacksonville movement was based solidly in the black working class. While no complete record of voter registrants exists, it is possible to partially recover a sense of who registered to vote in Jacksonville by crosschecking a set of NAACP affidavits submitted to the U.S. Congress in 1920 with census and city directory records.[46] Out of this list of 682 African Americans who tried to vote in 1920, the greatest number—224—came from households headed by common laborers. One hundred and fifteen African American female voter registrants came from households headed by laundresses or domestic workers. The bulk of the registrants were employed as manual or low-wage service workers. After laborers and domestics, porters, railway firemen, and hack drivers headed the list of voters. A smaller number of teamsters, building trades workers, cooks, barbers, and teachers rounded out the group.[47] Jacksonville had been a major way station for the Great Migration out of the South. Now, African American workers planned to deal with Jim Crow on its own turf, and their weapon was the ballot.

The voter registration movement took a toll on Joseph Lee's health. At age seventy, he was taxing his body severely. In the heady days of 1919, he delivered numerous addresses that stressed the passing of leadership to the younger generation of black Floridians.[48] By the end of the year however, Lee's health had deteriorated and he began missing citizens' meetings.[49] As the new year dawned, Lee again took ill and was confined to his bed for two weeks. But there was too much work to be done to allow infirmities to take over. Lifting himself out of his sickbed in mid-February, Judge Lee presided at the state Republican convention in Palatka. While at the convention, he contracted a severe cold. A few weeks later, Joseph E. Lee was found dead at his office desk. Condolences to his family poured in from across the state.[50] Lee's life spanned three generations. As an elected Reconstruction official in Florida, he had seen black political power flow and ebb until the shroud of Jim Crow fell over African Americans in the state. With his people, he had spent forty years in the political wilderness. Along the way, Lee had abandoned popular politics for the patronage politics of the southern GOP. But safety had its own costs. By the era of the Great Migration, Lee's cautious style of leadership was being openly challenged. As African Americans struggled to regain the ballot, Joseph Lee returned to the fray, providing an inestimable blend of leadership, organizing skills, and élan to black Republicanism. He believed that the GOP should consist of ordinary people and not just wealthy businessmen moving into the state. Judge Lee would not pass over with black Floridians to the promised land, but he had helped them find a path out of the desert.

GAINING MOMENTUM

If the voter registration campaign was to gain momentum across the state, activists had to grapple with the fact that many African Americans did not possess the resources needed to pay their poll taxes. The state of Florida imposed an extra burden on the poor by requiring two years' payment of poll taxes before giving the applicant a voter registration certificate.[51] The Civic League for Colored People of St. Petersburg, organized in April, 1919, solved this problem. This group, led by Rev. R. D. McLin, pastor of Bethel AME and chair of the city's Negro Uplift Association chapter, pooled resources in order to provide funds for poorer black citizens to pay their poll tax. The Civic League help pay poll taxes for nearly four hundred voters.[52]

Like their Jacksonville counterparts, Civic League activists convened meetings where African Americans talked about politics and learned the intricacies of voter registration. The League built the St. Petersburg movement by agitating on behalf of education and economic justice. To save the city's failing black schools, the organization proposed to "make efforts for a longer school term by every man paying his poll tax, that our strength may be considered by the school board when lining up for the next term of school."[53] Women played a leading role in the Civic League. Clara Blackman and other local organizers helped African American women prepare to engage in electoral politics through voter education workshops and by closely studying local and national political issues. Building on the increasing pace of black labor activism, Blackman noted that the Civic League helped spur the growth of an "Organized Women's Labor Union."[54] The League's activism paid large dividends. A year later when black organizers created the St. Petersburg Harding-Coolidge Club, five hundred African Americans immediately joined the organization.[55] When women's suffrage came to St. Petersburg, African American women were ready. More than one hundred domestic workers registered to vote in a single day.[56]

The oath that members of the Colored Knights of Pythias took to pay their poll taxes and register to vote had a deep impact on the voter registration movement in smaller towns and rural communities where the KOP drew upon and strengthened existing practices of mutual aid. In Sanford, which featured a "flourishing Pythian lodge," the white press reported that black men were out-registering their white counterparts in two precincts as late as September 24, 1920.[57] Black voter registration was also particularly strong in Starke, the seat of Bradford County, which dedicated a new KOP Lodge in September 1920.[58] African Americans in Tallahassee, another bastion of the Pythians and the Courts of Calanthe, were likewise on the move. In two city precincts at least 287 African American women would register to vote.[59]

Gadsden County was at the heart of the Florida movement. A. I. Dixie recalled during his youth that "about all the Colored folks" in the rural county were Pythians, and observed that the Knights played a crucial role in the voter registration struggle in Gadsden.[60] Nearly three-quarters of a century later, the Colored Knights of Pythias pledge lives on in Mr. Dixie's memory: "Well, the black people were trying to get together for equal rights, and this preacher that my brother was telling you about well he was a Knight of Pythias (that was an order) and he told the boys, he said, 'we took an oath to stand together,' and they did."

The state Vice Grand Chancellor of the Colored Knights of Pythias, Dr. W. S. Stevens, lived and worked in Gadsden County. Stevens arrived in Quincy in 1905 fresh from Meharry Medical College, planning to serve out a brief medical apprenticeship in the tobacco town and then set up a practice in a larger, more promising city. Dr. Stevens was intimately acquainted with the mores of white supremacy. His mother died when he was a small child, and his uncle, who lived in Tallahassee, adopted him. One Sunday afternoon after coming home from church, Stevens's uncle was summoned to the door by a group of white men. For a reason never discovered, the white men shot and killed Stevens's uncle in front of his wife and children in broad daylight. No charges were filed. Under the dictates of Jim Crow, the white men had committed no crime.[61]

Dr. Stevens had not planned to stay long in Gadsden County, but when he packed up to leave, local African Americans, suffering from a severe lack of access to health care—a grim hallmark of legal segregation—begged the county's only black doctor to stay, saying, "No Doc, we need you right here."[62] W. S. Stevens stayed in Quincy for the rest of his life. Combining his medical practice with a sharp business acumen, he gained the trust and respect of local black residents. White residents, however, were ambivalent about "Doc Stevens." On the one hand, he provided the only reliable medical care system for the region's tobacco plantation workers. On the other hand, he enraged the area medical establishment when he attempted to open a black hospital. White vigilantes bombed the hospital (which never opened) and shot into Dr. Stevens's house. Stevens's assertiveness endeared him to local African Americans, and he assumed a leadership role in the local Pythian lodge. In 1916 he was elected a delegate to the state Republican convention.[63] In 1919, Stevens was elected a delegate from Gadsden to attend the Negro Uplift Association convention in Ocala.[64]

Dr. Stevens plunged his lodge's resources into the local voter registration drive. His daughter remembered: "The Knights of Pythias was behind the drive for voting," and "Daddy said they [white people] didn't want the people to be educated on their own voting and their rights, they didn't want them to have a hospital, didn't want them to have nothing."[65] Dr. Stevens understood that he was in a race against time. Once local Democrats caught word that the lodge was promoting the registration drive, retaliation was certain to follow. Pythians as well as members of their sister organization, the Courts of Calanthe, gathered under the guise of local lodge meetings in order to hold workshops on voter registration.[66] In this endeavor, Stevens was assisted by Rev. T. Phillyaw, a pastor and leader of the local KOP.[67]

As the struggle gained momentum in Quincy, two critical allies emerged in the countryside. T. L. Sweet, secretary of the Harding-Coolidge Club in nearby River Junction, began to facilitate voter registration meetings there.[68] The Greensboro NAACP branch, which consisted mainly of farmers and farm laborers, took up the same work in their locale.[69] J. T. Smith, a farmer and the president of the Greensboro NAACP, explained the barriers that African Americans in rural Florida faced when trying to register and vote: "The white peoples are very hot here on the account of the election. Some says they will be blood spilt here that day, and some say they will not let us vote they close out the Redistration Books A head of time as to keep some of our Peoples from redstring."[70] The sheriff of Gadsden

County also warned that special deputies would be waiting at the polls on Election Day with handcuffs in order to arrest "ex convicts, who have registered as qualified voters."[71]

Nevertheless, with the NAACP covering Greensboro, the Harding-Coolidge Club at River Junction, and the KOP in Quincy, the Gadsden County movement flourished. In late September, a terrified white resident reported: "Quite a number of our women were at [River] Junction registering Monday afternoon, but we feel that something should be done quickly to arouse the white women of this and all other places and to help them see [and] realize the vast importance of registering to vote. . . . To date, of 112 who have registered here, only 36 are white; while the books show 76 newly qualified negro voters and only 8 white men."[72]

Black Floridians continued to approach registration officers despite threats from white officials. The methods that African Americans used in this struggle illuminate the ways in which social movements may emerge in repressive societies. Black Floridians mobilized primarily through the two institutions most central to their communities' survival: their secret societies and their churches. These institutions played a pivotal role in the statewide voter registration struggle in part because their internal operations were not accessible to white Floridians. Rev. W. N. Mitchell, a Madison County pastor, told GOP presidential candidate Warren G. Harding, "Your Nomination for the Republican President braught Rays of Sunshine to the Colored Voters of Florida. . . . We are sending you hearty congratulations. I have organized a Club in my church named the Harding Club. We meet every Thursday evening to discuss plans for the coming Nov. election which we hope you will win."[73] This transformation from church to political club made the task of organizing all the more easier.

Further to the south in phosphate country, black political organizing would require an equally high level of internal cooperation. Democratic officials valued white supremacy as much as they treasured the powdery mineral that made their benefactors rich. Polk County judge Kelsey Blanton was enraged that African Americans were trying to regain their citizenship rights. In an "Open Letter" to the state Democratic executive committee, Judge Blanton sounded the alarm:

Many millions of black men in a country where social equality is denied them can only be a menace to the whites under any circumstances whatsoever. There can be no such thing as the exercise of political rights by the negro without threatening and disturbing the white man's social

status and the continuous occasion for racial conflict. Rape and riot
have followed in the wake of this disturbance of the social status. . . .
The Anglo-Saxon possesses greater genius for government than any
other people and no thoughtful person could expect him to surrender
one of the chief objects of his pride to junglemen from Africa or their
near offspring.[74]

The corollary of Judge Blanton's white supremacist logic was violence.
When a black railroad porter was lynched in the county for possessing
knowledge of an affair between a white railroad porter and a married white
woman, a white citizen acknowledged, "It was a terrible tragedy. Yet no
more than what goes on all the time."[75] African Americans in Lakeland,
the county seat, held out hope for a better day. In 1913, hundreds of black
residents from the county had energetically celebrated the fiftieth anniversary of their emancipation. "The success of this celebration," remarked a
Lakeland correspondent, "bespeaks great credit to the willingness of our
people to co-operate in a good movement and carry it through to a successful conclusion."[76] A year later, members of Harmony Baptist Church
had joined in a national day of protest against segregation on the nation's
railroads, staging a special prayer service against Jim Crow.[77]

Six years later, Lakeland became a hotbed of African American political
activity. The *Lakeland Star* shrieked: "There is one thing happening in
Lakeland right now that is causing too much of this color line elimination
business to be shown, and it don't set very well with the white people of
the South."[78] Two weeks after the passage of the Nineteenth Amendment,
the *Star* fumed that black women were out-registering their white counterparts.[79] Democrats searched the town for mysterious white organizers
who were said to be "coercing" black people to register. They promised
African Americans that they would drive these white troublemakers out of
town, but received no cooperation from the black community in this
search.[80] In the meantime, over five hundred African Americans in Lakeland registered to vote.[81] On the eve of the election, the truth finally
dawned on the Democrats: black citizens in Polk County had used the
local Pythian lodge as their primary organizing vehicle.[82] The veil of
secrecy confused white Democrats in Lakeland and other towns across the
state, who repeatedly failed to cut off local registration efforts at their
source.

Conservative officials across the state heard shocking rumors about resolutions that were being passed in black secret societies and churches, but

they did not understand how African Americans were organizing. Hamilton County Democrats faced an upsurge in black voter registration and wailed that "the negroes are being led to believe that they have as much right to rule the country and dictate the officers thereof as does the white people of this county," but they could not discover the source of the local movement.[83] Unable to pierce the veil of secrecy that governed African American organizations, the Democrats foolishly went looking for white "race agitators" or the "mysterious forces" said to be behind the struggle. Meanwhile, black organizers redoubled their efforts.[84]

In Suwannee County, fraternal lodge leader T. S. Harris traced his political activism back to the early post-Reconstruction years.[85] In 1890, Harris had been a member of the "Colored Man's Political Protective League," an organization that vowed that "No Longer Will They Be Used by a Handful of White Republicans."[86] In 1916, Harris served as a delegate to the state Republican Party convention.[87] Now, Harris was conducting voter education meetings with black women and men, and his counterparts in African American secret societies in Live Oak were doing the same thing.[88] At least 408 men and 256 women registered by the end of the registration period.[89] Suwannee County resident J. L. Brundridge told Warren Harding that Democrats were slandering black political aims by "going thru the South making speeches to the effect that if the Republican Party is elected the Negro will be permisible to marry & intermingle with the whites which of course is not so and it is not what the Southern Negro wants. We only want justus & we know when we get it."[90] The threat of political violence hovered over African Americans in Suwannee. Brundridge concluded his letter to Harding with the plea: "I am a Poor Southern Negro. Please don't expose my note."

WOMEN AND THE BALLOT

When African American women became eligible to vote, the Florida voter registration movement gained new life. To say that African American women played a momentous role in the movement would be an understatement. From the time that four black women in Gainesville registered to vote on September 1, 1920, to the day of the election, black women *were* the movement.[91] The *Southwestern Christian Advocate* asserted that African American women in Florida accounted for a remarkable 40 percent of total women's voter registration in the state. "Remembering that Negroes constitute only 41 percent of Florida's total population, the *Advocate* noted, "it appears that Negro women are doing well and giving good account of their use of the franchise right."[92] While African American women had played important roles in black political organizations all along, the ratification of the Nineteenth Amendment and the coming of suffrage gave a new impetus to women's organizing efforts. Black women evaluated the political parties at least partially on the basis of their respective stances on women's suffrage. In Florida, U.S. senator Duncan U. Fletcher and Rep. Clark were identified with the antisuffrage wing of the Democratic Party. Clark equated the prospect of black women voting with "feminism, socialism and negroism," predicting that the passage of suffrage would usher in a race war in the South.[93] African American women in Florida applauded candidate Warren Harding's early statements in support of civil rights and women's suffrage.[94] Mary McLeod Bethune sent a telegram to Harding conveying to him "sincere thanks for Liberal suffrage statements."[95] After the ratification of expanded suffrage, Eartha White promised Harding "that you may depend upon us; and . . . you will find us to be one hundred per cent american republican citizens."[96]

The State Federation of Colored Women's Clubs continued its support for the Florida movement by encouraging African American women to form autonomous Republican clubs. Female activists in Fort Pierce created their own organization and filled all of its leadership positions with women.[97] In other cases federation women engaged in activist work with their husbands. For example, Mrs. Emma J. Colyer of Orlando, chair of the state federation's executive board, was married to J. A. Colyer, a delegate from Orange County to the Negro Uplift Association. Mrs. Colyer also served as the state grand worthy counselor of the Courts of Calanthe.[98] Colyer, along with her Orange County Calanthean sisters, attended the Pythian Grand Lodge where the KOP's membership passed their historic resolution. Her sisters in the state federation expressed complete confidence in her leadership abilities.[99]

Mary McLeod Bethune was president of the State Federation of Colored Women's Clubs. During the war, Mrs. Bethune had actively promoted a vision of expansive democracy honoring the elders while celebrating the contributions of African American women, men, and children alike to the war effort. Bethune brought this egalitarian perspective to the voter registration campaign. She spoke about the need for a "reconstruction movement" after the war.[100] Taking part in a spirited discussion that attempted to define the term "reconstruction," at the 1920 National Association of Colored Women's convention, Mrs. Bethune's focus group "stated that it involved the special interests of our people concerning the best consideration along all lines, such as jim-crow cars, lynchings, industrial affairs, etc."[101] Back in Florida, Mrs. Bethune organized a "reconstruction conference," composed of representatives from the NAACP, the NUA, and Miami's Colored Board of Trade to further coalition-building work among men and women.[102]

Eartha White, the federation's secretary, was also present at the reconstruction meeting. While Mary McLeod Bethune operated on a statewide level to bring Florida's civil rights organizations together, Miss White worked most intensively on the local level and helped to organize the Duval County women's division of the Harding-Coolidge Club. The first meeting of the women's Harding-Coolidge Club in Jacksonville was held at Bethel Baptist Institutional Church, an organizing center of the 1905 streetcar boycott. Every seat in the large church was filled. The women appointed female block captains to canvass each of the city's eleven wards to talk with black women about registering to vote. According to the African American press, "Spirited addresses were delivered by a number of speakers, and the big crowd of women expressed themselves as being ready to register, many of whom having already done so." Jacksonville women opened their own political education office.[103] Capturing the spirit of the movement, Sallie B. Smith, who identified herself as a "tailoress," composed a song for Warren G. Harding.[104]

Soon after African American women organized their Harding-Coolidge Club, black women in Jacksonville began marching down in groups to the registrars' offices to register. (In this first season of suffrage, they were not required to pay a poll tax.) A reporter marveled: "In the Seventh ward they began to arrive at 8 o'clock, and many of them sat down on the curbing to rest, so many hours were they in line." An eyewitness testified: "Some went with babies in their arms, and others took their lunches so that they would not have to fast while waiting to be registered at 7 o'clock last night when the books closed, [and] there were many still in line at the Seventh ward."[105] The numbers of newly registered voters climbed as female activists with the Harding-Coolidge Club canvassed and re-canvassed black neighborhoods. The spirits of Jacksonville's Democratic bosses plummeted as African American women's registration climbed: approximately two thousand black women qualified in the first week of expanded suffrage. White registrars harassed and insulted African American female registrants. Election officials tried to trick the women into giving incorrect age and personal information, thus making themselves liable to criminal prosecution.[106] Nevertheless, three thousand black women had registered by the end of the third week of September.

Sensing an impending catastrophe, the attorney general of Florida came to Jacksonville to rally Democratic men and women to defend white supremacy "in this city and county."[107] Four thousand black women made themselves eligible to vote by the end of September.[108] White women were given special guidance by Democratic officials in registering and were exempted from answering "embarrassing" personal questions such as their ages.[109] African American women received no such assistance, but five thousand of them were qualified voters by the middle of the first week of October. In that same week, a group of white Republicans published a broadside in the Jacksonville media pledging their support for white supremacy and an all-white Republican Party. By the end of that week, six thousand African American women had registered to vote.[110]

On October 12, the Duval County Sheriff's Department stated that it would be issuing five hundred arrest warrants for "hundreds of negro women in Duval County" said to have violated the election laws. "Indications are that the county jail will be filled by the end of the present week."[111] Two days before the registration books closed, Congressman Frank Clark gave a speech in Jacksonville promising "Anglo-Saxon" violence if African Americans "tried to govern this country."[112] Even as Clark uttered his threat, female activists were conducting their final canvassing sweeps through Jacksonville's black residential neighborhoods. On the morning of October 17, the city awoke to astonishing news: more than seven thousand African American women in Jacksonville—over half the female black population in the city—had become qualified voters. Their enthusiasm was infectious: over one thousand black men registered during the same period.[113] Black women had endured vicious harassment as well as threats of arrest and violence to make Jacksonville the leading edge of the Florida movement. Black citizens of the Gateway City had shown African Americans throughout the state that superior organization could defeat official corruption.

Similar organizing feats were being accomplished on a smaller scale in over two dozen Florida counties. African American women added an incredible momentum to the Florida movement. A. G. Samuels, writing on behalf of the "Colored Voters of Cocoa-Brevard County," in October 1920, joyously informed Warren G. Harding that "since the Colored Women has begun to Register it has caused the Colored men voters to take on new life in Politics all over the state, as they has never before."[114] Six hundred and thirty-nine African Americans—over 40 percent of the adult black population—added their names to the list of eligible voters in Brevard County.[115] On the first day of expanded suffrage in Alachua County, four African American women registered. Four days later that number had increased to forty-one.[116] In Gainesville proper, black registration was particularly strong in the neighborhood north of University Avenue, or Precinct 7.[117] During the first week of October, black women expanded their efforts. The *Gainesville Daily Sun* reported on Tuesday, October 5, that "Negro women poured into the offices yesterday in large numbers."[118] The Gainesville movement was aided by the active Knights of Pythias lodges that played a vital role in Alachua County.[119] The following week, Congressman Frank Clark and Governor-elect Cary A. Hardee came to Alachua to reinvigorate the white women's registration campaign. The core of Hardee's speech involved "scorning the negro affiliation with the Republican party [and], warning women and men alike to qualify to drown out the negro Republican vote."[120]

White registrars across Florida borrowed tactics developed by their counterparts in Jacksonville to intimidate black women with deception and threats. Officials tried to trap African American women into giving false testimony regarding birth dates and residence, thus opening the women to criminal prosecution. Walter White reported:

> In Orange and Osceola counties, a colored woman would attempt to register; on being asked her age, for example, she would say "twenty-four." She would then be asked the year in which she was born. Many of them being illiterate, would not know. The register would then probably say, "If you are twenty-four, you were born in 1892, weren't you?" The applicant, seeking to get the ordeal over, would reply in the affirmative. Before she had been away from the place very long a warrant for perjury had been sworn out against her and she had been arrested. I found many cases equally as flagrant where Negro women had been imprisoned for such "offenses" as these.[121]

Despite these obstacles, African American women in Orlando approached local registrars en masse. African American men and women in Orange County worked through their flourishing secret societies to register members of the black community.[122] Local officials reported that a week after the advent of women's suffrage, 363 people had registered. Three percent of this total were men; the rest were women and, of these,

African American women led their white counterparts by a margin of *fifteen to one*.[123]

Ancient City Democrats were bewildered to discover that black women were out-registering white women in their town. Mrs. N. S. Freeland, assistant secretary of the St. Augustine NAACP, credited the Colored Republican Club, based in the black precinct of Lincolnville, with being a primary force behind the St. Augustine movement.[124] Democrats fumed that an "unseen hand" was guiding the St. Augustine movement, and they blamed the campaign on "Bolshevistic carpet baggers who are using the ignorant element . . . as tools" in order to achieve the "furtherance of world wide Bolshevism."[125] Black St. Augustine had real grievances that could not be so easily explained away. When Alfred Twining, a noted travel writer, attended a segregated public event in St. Augustine that featured black entertainers, he commented on one woman's efforts to challenge Jim Crow:

> I saw a policeman go to the seated negro woman and tell her she could not sit there. She must move at once. I did not hear all of the argument, but the woman protested vehemently and refused to budge for a time; the officer grew more determined and seeing that a scene was inevitable if she did not get up and leave, the negress yielded. She went over to a crowd of negroes who had witnessed the episode and of course there was sympathy expressed as the woman gave vent to her anger at the indignity offered her.[126]

The Palatka movement was forged through a mix of the old and new tactics. For decades, African Americans had held together a Republican Club that maintained its legitimacy by regularly helping to elect black councilmen from Precinct 24. By 1918, however, black voter turnout had collapsed, and a mere seventeen voters bothered to vote for the black councilman L. L. Trapp.[127] Organizers in the Gem City had to make a concerted effort to boost these numbers in order to challenge a central premise of white supremacy: that black people entrusted politics to their "white friends" in the Democratic Party. The Putnam County Republican Club especially urged younger African Americans to register.[128] In addition, the newly-organized branch of the NAACP played an important role in the Palatka movement.[129] As with its Jacksonville counterpart, the initial group of NAACP members tended to be middle-aged residents drawn from the town's black professional class. Three charter members were current or former city councilmen: L. L. Trapp (merchant), Albert L. Browning (insurance salesman), and William Bell (retired minister). Mr. Bell, born in 1824, had served as a city councilman in Palatka during Reconstruction.[130] At least twenty-one charter members in the civil rights organization registered to vote.

The Palatka movement—like the Florida movement in general—was intergenerational. H. F. Fields worked as a wood yard laborer, and his wife Dinah toiled as a cook for a private family. They rented their home, which they shared with their daughter Jessie, who also cooked for a living. Jessie celebrated her twenty-first year by registering to vote with her grandmother, Lincie Dean, who had come to live with the family when her husband died. Mrs. Dean was seventy-seven years old and served as a midwife in her community. The oldest married couple listed as registered voters were John and Martha Brown. Mr. Brown, eighty-three, was retired. The Browns owned their own residence, but this did not free Martha Brown from the necessity of wage work. At age seventy-two she was employed as a laundry worker. On the other end of the age spectrum, at least ten black registrants had just come of voting age in 1920. The median age of the 233 listed black registrants of Precinct 24 was forty. The majority of African American women were domestic workers; the majority of the men were laborers.[131] One hundred ninety-six of these black voter registrants were married, thirty-one widowed, and fourteen single. One hundred and thirty-six registrants owned their homes while one hundred and five did not. Organizers in Palatka built a movement that reached across lines of age, sex, and class.[132]

African Americans in rural Putnam County added strength to the movement. From Interlachen, a report came that "at Mr. Wylie's office the women of this precinct, both white and colored, are gradually making known their decision to be qualified voters, and still to some who have waited long for this opportunity its realization seems 'too good to be true.' "[133] So many African Americans were qualifying to vote in early October that the local registrar claimed that black women were attempting to register illegally, thus holding the threat of arrest over them.[134]

African Americans in Volusia County also built on earlier efforts to organize a strong insurgency. In De Land, where the black Republican Club had played an important role in earlier elections, African American voters had already participated in the February 1920 municipal election, helping a dissident Democratic candidate defeat an opponent from the "White Citizens' ticket."[135] When women's suffrage came to De Land,

African American women made the most of it. Two weeks after the books had been opened to them, 65 black women, compared with 56 white women, had registered.[136] By the end of the registration period, 205 black women managed to register successfully in the town.[137] While African Americans did not constitute a majority of De Land voters, they nonetheless threatened to exercise a swing vote in municipal politics, and state officials advised local whites not to tolerate this "enemy from within." Florida state attorney general Van C. Swearingen brought local Democrats to their feet when he exclaimed that whites who entered into coalitions with black voters were "blacker than the blackest 'nigger' and should be run out of the town, the county and the state."[138]

Mary McLeod Bethune spearheaded the Daytona movement. Early on, Bethune convened a secret meeting of black ministers and activists on the campus of her school and proceeded to map out the campaign. Rackham Holt, one of Bethune's early biographers, captured the tone of the meeting:

> In telling language she set forth the issues and what difficulties might be encountered; and how necessary it was to face them. "Use your minds," she advised, "but keep your lips closed. Eat your bread without butter, but pay your poll tax! Nobody ever told me to pay my poll tax. My dollar is always there on time! Do not be afraid of the Klan. Quit running. Hold your head up high. Look every man straight in the eye and make no apology to anyone because of race or color. When you see a burning cross remember the Son of God who bore the heaviest.[139]

Bethune planned to use the ballot to address the lack of resources allocated to black education and the crumbling physical infrastructure of African American neighborhoods. The reform candidate for mayor promised to improve black educational facilities in Daytona "and also advocate[d] better streets and lights and sewage in the Negro district." His opponent advocated lower taxes and was supported by the Ku Klux Klan.[140] Mrs. Bethune's astute organizing work paid off. Daytona city precinct witnessed a record turnout: at least 453 African American women—well over half of the adult black female population—and 167 black men registered to vote, giving African Americans a strong voting presence in Daytona and Volusia County.[141]

West Palm Beach was a citadel of the Negro Uplift Association.[142] Fraternal lodges and churches emerged from the Great War stronger than ever and sought to reinforce the connection between black wartime service and equal citizenship.[143] In Palm Beach County, at least 722 African American men and 545 women registered to vote.[144] Election officials vowed to place "Democratic challengers" at the polls to catch illegal (black) voters, and Sheriff R. C. Baker promised to "have several deputy sheriffs at the polls prepared to arrest black violators of the election laws as fast as they appear and ask for ballots."[145] Congressman Clark came to the city to rally Democratic forces. Clark "attacked the negro problem with vigor and emphasis. It might, he said, be a good thing for Florida if it contained two parties of equal strength, but not until the Republican party got rid of the negro."[146]

With African American women in Florida organizing to vote, white employers repeated the old charge that an enfranchised black working class posed a grave threat to the state's prosperity and development. The specter of gender, race, and class warfare was stoked by Governor-elect Hardee's Democratic machine, which begged white women across the state to flock to the polls in order to save Florida from Negro domination. Hardee "urged the [white] women to vote the Democratic ticket in order that the white race might remain supreme in the country." John E. Matthews, who shared the speakers' platform with Governor Hardee, warned ominously "that all of these negro women were going to vote the Republican ticket and if the white women would not register, they would be ruled by their cooks and wash women."[147] A white man in Fort Pierce echoed the statewide Democratic cry: "Surely no white man nor white woman wants to occupy a lower sphere in our political life than a negro washerwoman—refuse to register and vote, and you so place yourself, you cannot get away from that fact."[148]

J. N. Andrews alerted his fellow employers in Pensacola that "some of the newly enfranchised colored women are organizing clubs to enforce the registration and voting of all their women where they find any that do not wish to do so. They are threatening them with what will happen to them. They threaten them also if they shall be seen carrying a bundle of clothes." In the course of his letter, Mr. Andrews exposed his real fear: if black female workers began to vote, they might refuse to wash white folks' dirty laundry. Andrews warned: "I hereby give notice that I do not intend for these clubs to interfere or intimidate any one satisfied to serve us. . . . I have always wanted the colored people to have everything that was their right. . . . But I do not recognize their right to meddle with other people who are quietly attending to their business. And if they force the issue we will take steps to rid our town of such pests."[149] Andrews wanted black Pensacolans—male and female—to understand that white Floridians were prepared to employ violence to preserve order in white households.

African Americans in Pensacola immediately responded to Andrews's statement. "It is true that we have various clubs and organizations among our people just like other people have," Aaron Brown wrote, "but the object of all is lawful and our purpose is to advise our people how to proceed in all matters pertaining to our citizenship and concerning the welfare of our city."[150] In response to Andrews's desire to see all African American women continue to work for low wages, Brown countered: "Even a poor, humble colored washerwoman might decide to change jobs for better wages." W. H. Campbell asserted that African American female workers had the right to live their own lives outside of their employer's household. He stated that if white employers such as Andrews were having trouble retaining domestic workers, they should look to the wages that they were paying: "The most independent creature among workers," Campbell wryly noted, "is a good colored laundress. Independent of advice or orders from her more idle sisters and independent of 'cheap Johns' who want her to do a bale of 'washing' for a pre-war price."[151]

African American responses to J. N. Andrews revealed a glimpse of the egalitarian perspective that African Americans were nurturing in their voter registration movement. Black Floridians envisioned a republic where democracy meant economic justice, equal pay, and dignity, as well as equal citizenship—not merely the right to vote for one or more candidates. The explosion of black working-class activism during the war years encouraged the public reemergence of a nineteenth-century African American philosophy that politics should be undergirded with a "jealous regard for the rights of labor." In turn, workers' struggles had a ubiquitous impact on black thought. In a review of W. E. B. Du Bois's book *Darkwater*, the Pensacola *Colored Citizen* argued:

Most people think that the Negro problem is one thing, and the problem of work or wages or education or government is another thing. But that is just what Dr. Du Bois does not believe. He proves that if you solve the problem of work and wages and education and government in the right way, you will solve the Negro problem at the same time.[152]

Negro Uplift Association leader Rev. S. H. Betts exhorted African Americans in the Panhandle to register to vote. After the NUA's 1919 state conference, Betts began a speaking tour in western Florida urging his audiences to "settle down, save their money, buy land, qualify and vote, just as all other races do, before they count for much."[153] Betts told African Americans to "quit supporting false leaders, men who will not stand by a righteous cause, but will sell their birthrights for a mess of pottage." He praised African American endeavors in land ownership: "Why," he pointed out, "in our little state of Florida, we own nearly half the land which we are now cultivating. Oh yes, its best for us to go to the country."

Like Booker T. Washington, Betts advocated the "casting down of buckets" in the southern countryside, but he also engaged in a vigorous crusade to ensure that African Americans could live with dignity in the rural South; not as disfranchised common laborers for white bosses, but as politically empowered citizens. Rev. Betts was a proponent of what historian E. P. Thompson called "rebellious traditional culture."[154] Betts framed the voter registration struggle squarely within the time-honored AME tradition of promoting collective racial autonomy, landownership, and protest. Indeed, he infused the Florida movement with an ideology that had been forged by the Florida AME in its "Industrial and Political" platform during Reconstruction.[155]

In fact, during the Jim Crow period, African Americans in Florida achieved an impressive level of farm ownership: over 40 percent of the black farm operators in the state owned a farm.[156] This did not mean that they escaped the necessity of laboring on white farms; they did not. African American farm owners in Florida often toiled as seasonal farm workers. A high rate of farm ownership also did not translate into the making of a rural "black bourgeoisie." Indeed, in terms of land values, implements, work mules, and dairy cows owned, black farm owners lagged severely behind their white counterparts.[157]

Still, landownership gave some African Americans a kind of buffer against white control in rural Florida. But ownership was only one of several different important variables that influenced African Americans' decisions on whether or not to register. Other important factors included marital status, age, and occupation. In rural Marion County for example, it is possible to compare partially reconstructed black voter registration figures with census data.[158] While these figures are not complete, they point out some important trends. In the small farming community of Citra, it is possible to identify at least 77 African Americans who registered to vote. Of these, 57 were landowners, 33 were farmers, and 14 were listed as farm laborers. Marital status was even more important an indicator for registering than landownership: 60 out of 77 black registered voters in Citra were married. Often, black couples like Richard and Mary Jenkins (owners) as well as Charles and Isabella Burner (renters) were both registered. The sex ratio for the registrants was roughly equal: 40 women and 37 men. The median age of the African Americans who registered to vote in Citra was forty-six. The oldest registrant was Nellie Mosely, age ninety, who lived with her daughter Marie Hearst, who also registered to vote. African Americans who registered to vote in nearby McIntosh shared similar characteristics. The median age of African American voter registrants in McIntosh was forty-five. The oldest voter registrant was Austin Ross, age seventy-five, a truck farmer who was married to Winny Ross—age sixty-five—who also registered to vote.[159]

B. J. and D. J. Jones, leaders of the Knights of Pythias and Negro Uplift Association delegates, were quietly conducting voter education work in rural Columbia County. The brothers were insurance salesmen for the Afro-American Insurance Company, a successful black-owned firm based in Jacksonville.[160] The Joneses' occupation afforded them a certain level of independence from white surveillance, while connecting them to other Afro-American agents and officials across the state—people such as Eartha White and company founder A. L. Lewis in Jacksonville—who were encouraging black political activists. These types of networks were facilitated by church, lodge, business, or union affiliations that belie the image of isolated African American rural communities. The Jones brothers worked to ensure that black citizens in Lake City and the surrounding countryside received instruction in voter registration.[161]

Ties of kinship and gender were important factors in the rural Columbia County movement. Female farmers in the area registered enthusiastically, including the women in the Tunsil family, beginning with Estele Tunsil, age twenty-one, married and working on a farm with her husband.[162] Estele's sister Eliza, employed nearby as a farm laborer, likewise registered. Maria Tunsil, twenty-four, also lived close by and worked as a farm laborer. Synthia Tunsil, the female elder of the Tunsil family at sixty-seven, worked on a farm that she owned with her husband. The Tunsil women lived on adjacent tracts, thus reinforcing the ties between community, kinship, and politics. Mrs. Minnie Niblack, age forty-two and one of six women of her family who registered to vote, was another notable registrant. Mrs. Niblack was the secretary of the newly organized Colored Teachers Association of Columbia County, an organization that joined scores of other black associations across the state to agitate for better schools.[163] According to extant records, the oldest married couple in Columbia County who registered were Jack and Florence Parker, ages seventy-four and sixty. They rented the farm that they worked on. The Parkers' granddaughter, Laura Johnson, lived with the couple. Laura, twenty-two, also registered to vote. Incomplete registration figures from Columbia listed 136 African American voter registrants in the county.[164] Ninety percent were either farmers or farm laborers. One hundred and seven were married. Eighty-nine hailed from farm-owning households.

REINVENTING THE REPUBLICAN PARTY

In the countryside and in the cities, African Americans were transforming the old Republican Party into a new, democratic vehicle that would destroy one-party rule and white supremacy. In August 1920, the Jacksonville Harding-Coolidge Club met and drafted a resolution that they sent to the Republican National Committee calling for the dismissal of Florida's top Republican official, Daniel Gerow, because

> the said Gerow does not desire to establish and maintain an active and efficient Republican party in Florida, but on the contrary has actively aided or acquiesced in the suppression of the Republican vote in this state and has endeavored to maintain a pretense of a party organization in the interest of a few individuals alone instead of building up the party's strength.[165]

The movement had generated a sense of self-confidence among its participants. "Politics" was no longer an activity restricted to powerful white folks or a few elite black leaders. It was something that ordinary people engaged in. The fifteen hundred members of the Harding-Coolidge club called for the dismissal of the head of the Florida Republican Party because he had failed to build a powerful, grassroots-based political party. Black Republicans in Jacksonville hoped to use a rejuvenated party to smash disfranchisement and white supremacy in Florida.[166] N. K. McGill, president of the Harding-Coolidge Club, informed Warren G. Harding: "We propose to extend this Club and its works all over the entire State of Florida and have begun now sending representatives all over the State."[167] The ultimate goal of the Florida movement was nothing less than the destruction of one-party rule in the South.

Southern Florida teetered on the brink of a new race war in the months leading up to the presidential election of 1920 as whites tried to strike terror into the heart of the state's black communities. Miami became a virtual battleground as African Americans began to more assertively challenge residential segregation even as they worked to become newly qualified voters. White vigilantes waged a campaign to keep blacks from moving too close to Highland Park, a white neighborhood. The Colored Board of Trade reported: "white residents (presumably) of Highland Park masked themselves and at an unearthly hour of the night visited colored homes at Waddell and K and ordered the owners to move by midnight the following Tuesday night." When an African American woman demanded compensation for relocation, the masked men riddled her house with bullets as a warning to the other black residents.[168]

On Tuesday evening, June 29, two powerful explosions rocked a black housing development on the edge of Highland Park. The *Miami Herald* reported: "It is said that white men driving an automobile through Avenue K threw two dynamite bombs into an unoccupied house on the west side of the avenue. The bombs exploded, tearing into the beams and flooring and wreaking havoc. A house about ten feet to the north was occupied and a negro named Aaron Adderly, claims he narrowly escaped destruction."[169]

Within minutes of the bombing, black residents armed themselves and took to the streets. Nearly three thousand black residents assembled at the intersection of Waddell and Avenue K where the bombing occurred and prepared for the worst. In response, Mayor William Smith called out the police and the American Legion. Carloads of white Legionnaires, special deputies, and police poured into the outskirts of Colored Town. Disaster loomed. A federal agent reported:

> At the time of the dynamiting, the negroes appeared to have a large
> supply of arms, as all were on the streets with a various assortment of
> weapons. They dispersed upon the command of the Chief of Police
> without disorder. If one side or the other had fired a shot, there is no
> doubt there would have been a serious disorder. As the matter now
> stands there is a tense feeling among the white and colored inhabitants
> of the district involved which might be precipitated by some overt act of
> a white or colored man.[170]

Immediately after the bombing, the Colored Board of Trade submitted an open letter to the mayor. The Florida movement had raised people's expectations about what they should expect from political leaders, and the middle-class members of the board understood that if they did not pose an assertive stance toward Miami's white power structure they would lose their credibility. "But let us remind you, friends," the Board began, "that this vicious attack on the part of murderous cowards has exerted itself twice within the past two months and up to this time not a single arrest has been made, no, not even on suspicion. The dynamiting escapade on the Odd Fellows hall some three years ago is still fresh in our memories and for that, no arrests have been made."[171] In turn, they warned Mayor Smith that times had changed:

> The rough element among us is very impatient. And we confess to you, friends, that Tuesday night's experiences have thoroughly convinced us that we are losing our grasp on the rowdy element of colored town. They have listened to us on numerous occasions and the results have not come. They are possessed with the idea that a better way is theirs and seem anxious to pursue it. We have been answered with such remarks as this: "They sent us three thousand miles away from home to make the world safe for democracy and it's up to us now to make Miami safe for our families."[172]

Just as the dynamite war died down in Miami, a new explosion rocked the city. Herbert Brooks, a young Bahamian worker, was accused of attacking an "aged white woman" on July 30, 1920. The white media transformed Brooks from an "assailant" to a "negro rapist" tried and convicted by white opinion.[173] On Sunday, August 1, Sheriff D. W. Moran took Brooks from his Dade County jail cell to transport the man to Jacksonville for safe-keeping from a mob said to be composed of the "respectable citizens of Miami."[174] Despite being "heavily handcuffed," Brooks allegedly jumped from the train near Daytona, "striking his head on a cross tie and mashing his brains, death occurring instantly."[175] A quick autopsy confirmed the official story, and Brooks's mutilated body was brought back to Dade County for burial.

Bahamian immigrants believed that Brooks had been murdered. Hundreds of Bahamians met the train that carried their countryman's corpse, possibly to prevent it from being mutilated even further at the hands of whites. "The arrival of his body here," a correspondent to *The Afro-American* noted, "was the signal for the rise of the colored population, who met his body at the station, attended the funeral in great crowds and buried it with ceremony. Several whites were chased by angry persons from the colored section."[176] The *Afro-American* asserted, "Only the arrival of the State militia prevented a pitched battle."[177] While the white press claimed that military force had "quieted" the Bahamians, the grievances of black Miamians remained stronger than ever.[178] Among Bahamians, the "Overseas Club" was one of the most popular organizations. "Some of the tenets of this organization appear to be radical in the extreme," an undercover federal agent warned, "as they consider the district they occupy to be a part of England, and amenable only to English laws."[179]

The Miami debacle was a reminder that something had to be done about Florida's rotten justice system. County sheriffs placed in power by the system of one-party rule made little pretense of enforcing laws fairly. White-on-black crime went unpunished while sheriffs used their authority to block African Americans from organizing unions or voting. Robert H. Shackelford, running for sheriff in Columbia County, promised to wield the whip hand for employers by stating in campaign literature that "the State Vagrancy Law of Florida is not being properly enforced and if elected Sheriff, I will see to it that the idle class get to work, and if not able to find employment will interest myself in their behalf."[180]

Black Floridians planned to use their votes to support county sheriffs who would enforce the laws equally—a revolutionary proposition in Florida. In Daytona, African Americans put their support behind the candidate for sheriff who was opposed by the Ku Klux Klan. Insurgent black voters in Holmes County supported the Independent candidate while African Americans in Pinellas County planned to support M. M. Whitehurst (Independent) for the position of sheriff over both the Democratic *and* Republican candidates because Whitehurst openly opposed lynching.[181] Whitehurst's Democrat opponent, Louis A. Allen, countered with the language of naked racial power: "There is no question where the democratic party stands on the negro question, and if you want to continue white supremacy in this county, you can do so by electing democrats. All red-blooded white citizens are urged to vote for LOUIS A. ALLEN, democratic candidate for sheriff."[182] Allen's "red-blooded" white people saw African American interest in these sheriffs' elections as the most dangerous challenge to white supremacy imaginable.

The Baltimore *Afro-American* exulted: "Florida is getting to be something else besides a Land of Flowers, It is becoming a state of the far South where colored people are registering and preparing to vote in unprecedented numbers."[183] Judge Kelsey Blanton from Polk County replied:

Is this to remain a white man's country? Is the white man to maintain his supremacy? If so, how much supremacy? Is his claim to supremacy a debatable question? If the negro has the right to assert political rights he has the right to triumph if he can, and the assertion of such right is essentially a challenge to the white man's position.[184]

A. J. Kershaw of Miami asked Judge Blanton and his allies to see reason:

May I suggest that inasmuch as the negroes of Florida constitute one-third of the population, form the very backbone of labor, and inasmuch as they have been here for decades—and will be here for all time to come—has it occurred to the white man that the best thing to do is to encourage the negro to measure up to the standards of good citizen-ship—not only to measure up to it but exercise it?[185]

The Pensacola *Colored Citizen* also tried to convince white Floridians that African American political involvement would benefit all: "In the matter of schools, there should be a large registration in order that he might vote to carry the bond issue, so that the schools of the city can be put on a first class basis—for the white man cannot improve his schools without improving the Negroes—now is the chance if he ever had one." The *Colored Citizen* noted that African American children did not have playgrounds, that black school teachers were paid substandard wages, and that voting was a way to attain a better future: "These things do not drop from Heaven. Why should he not have a word to say about who shall rule him—does he not have the law to obey?" For the most part, white Florid-ians were not listening. In their project to build a one-party state they had developed a set of political ethics that framed the world solely in terms of black or white, good or evil. In this context, interracial organizing was painfully difficult to achieve. Accept white domination or become an enemy of civilization: this was the ethic of the Anglo-Saxon nation.[186]

All across Florida, African Americans clenched their poll tax receipts, and gathered to discuss the road ahead of them on Election Day. In Gadsden County, African Americans knew that they would have to resort to armed self-defense in order to vote. J. T. Smith reported that Gadsden shopkeep-ers "ceased selling we Colored peoples any [ammunition] four weeks ago, although some of us are determined to go the pole that day regardless to the consequence."[187] A black woman from Lake Butler, who kept her identity anonymous due to fear of white retaliation, told Walter White,

"There is a cowardly element here that don't care any more to kill a negro, any more than a big rattler. Our negros was good enough to go to France and fight for us, but when it comes to laws they are on the books. But not enforced."[188]

The Florida movement succeeded in recruiting thousands of people because it was rooted in the organizations that cemented ties of mutuality and trust in black Florida. African Americans were divided on many issues. However, they shared a broad consensus on the most serious problems of their time, and they used their mutual aid institutions as organizing centers because these institutions helped them cope with the trauma of Jim Crow. The movement's success was not based on personal heroism, daring leadership, or moral certitude. Certainly, African American men and women displayed these attributes during the course of the struggle. Nevertheless, what really drove the statewide insurgency was the growing realization that disciplined organization was producing results. C. L. R. James observed that successful movement building involves people having "experience, experience of organization and of action. . . . It is only by independent organization and independent action that people discover their needs, discover their capacities."[189] African Americans in Florida were convinced that they held the keys to the abolition of one-party rule in the South. A black man from Jacksonville testified: "On the eve of one of the most important elections since the civil war, the electorate is aroused as never before."[190]

⊰ 9 ⊱

ELECTION DAY, 1920

The suffrage victory, according to Miss [Alice] Paul is "won but not paid for." We should worry! But we do. The struggle for white supremacy in the South now confronts us.[1]

ORLANDO REPORTER-STAR

THE FLORIDA MOVEMENT STOOD POISED at the brink of a great victory against one-party rule in the South. African Americans planned to use the ballot to challenge the fundamental elements of racial oppression: poverty wages, debt peonage, failing schools, racial violence, and corrupt law enforcement. The movement was so successful that the NAACP used Florida as the primary vehicle in its crusade to end disfranchisement in the South. While James Weldon Johnson and Walter White worked nationally to defend the movement, Mary McLeod Bethune, Eartha White, and local organizers across the state prepared African Americans for Election Day. White Floridians invested in the status quo battled to keep African Americans from voting. The events that transpired on November 2 shocked the nation and ultimately received a hearing before one of the most powerful committees of the United States Congress.

The signs posted by the Miami KKK signaled the trouble to come: "Beware! The Ku Klux Klan is again alive! And every Negro who approaches a polling place next Tuesday will be a marked man. This is a white man's country, boys, save your own life next Tuesday."[2] The Klan's actions followed a brutal police sweep of "Colored Town," where black

Miamians were arrested, "disturbed and humiliated."[3] Meanwhile, Dade County Democrats issued a call to arms:

WHITE VOTERS, REMEMBER!
WHITE SUPREMACY
IS BEING ASSAULTED IN OUR MIDST, AND THE MOST
SACRED
INSTITUTIONS OF THE SOUTH
ARE BEING UNDERMINED BY THE ENEMY FROM WITHIN.[4]

African Americans in Miami convened an emergency meeting to discuss what they were going to do on Election Day. They met in the Colored Odd Fellows Hall, a building that had been recently dynamited by white vigilantes.[5] As the men and women filed into the hall, they reflected with pride on the distance they had traveled in a few short years. In 1914 they had initiated a boycott of white businesses operating in the Negro section because these firms refused to hire black clerks and managers.[6] Only a few months had passed since many of the audience members filled the streets in defense of their homes after the latest wave of bombing attacks against their community. All of them were mercilessly penned into a ghetto whose boundaries shrank and expanded at the whim of the local white power structure.[7]

Once powerless, now organized, the individuals who came to the Odd Fellows Hall on this evening of crisis were people who toiled as domestics, common laborers, beauticians, carpenters, railway men, porters, teachers, hack drivers, seasonal farm laborers, shopkeepers, and janitors. Many were first-generation Bahamian immigrants. They were all the backbone of the voter registration campaign in southern Florida.[8] After the meeting was gaveled to order, the assembled cleared their throats and sang the stanzas of a song that was birthed in the soil of their state:

Stony the road we trod,
Bitter the chast'ning rod,
Felt in the days when hope unborn had died;
Yet with a steady beat,
Have not our weary feet
Come to the place for which our fathers sighed?

R. E. S. Toomey rose to address the tense assembly. Testing the waters, the Spanish-American War veteran called upon the audience members to remember their history.[9] Recounting the unfulfilled promises of

Reconstruction, Lieutenant Toomey brought his listeners up to the present, linking citizenship rights to black war service and civilian loyalty during World War I. He blasted "the business and moneyed men of the republican party" and stated that African Americans "did not like everything the republican party had done in Dade county but when it came to voting, in making a choice of two evils, [we] must take the lesser and vote the republican ticket."

After Toomey concluded his remarks, the people responded. One participant stood up and said he was tired of being "preached and prayed to death," and that African Americans needed to "stick together and that each must do something for himself." One person shouted "that he had been rocked in a republican cradle and there could not be any democratic negro and that the negro had the God-given right to social life in the world, that the present time was a crisis and the negro needed a new declaration and that there was coming into being a new negro." Another speaker "said that the colored man must now lay the foundations for the future, for without it he could do nothing."[10] Each person offered reasons why black Floridians should take the final step to the polls. In using a public forum to urge each other to vote, black Miamians had elevated an individual activity to a collective responsibility and lifted each other's spirits. Now they were prepared for Election Day.

So too, however, was the state Ku Klux Klan. The KKK reorganized in the summer of 1920 to crush the Florida movement. Indeed, new Klan chapters formed in counties and towns where African Americans were registering to vote: Gadsden, Orange, Duval, Palatka, Palm Beach, Daytona, Bartow, Miami, Lakeland, and others. A contemporary observer noted that the organization had one aim: "The Ku Klux Klan in each section of Florida carried on systematic terrorization of colored voters."[11] Fortified by the determination to defend white supremacy in its gravest hour yet, the KKK in Florida became the most formidable paramilitary force in the United States.

The NAACP hoped to use the U.S. Constitution and the threat of congressional inquiry to blunt the Klan's power and to destroy one-party rule in the South. The presidential election of 1920 was the first in two decades to coincide with the national census. Florida officials, like their counterparts in other states, were hopeful that an increase in population would allow the state to add another member to its congressional delegation.[12] The NAACP pointed out, however, that Section Two of the Fourteenth Amendment empowered Congress to *reduce* congressional representation in a state if that state's officials denied voting rights to eligible citizens.[13] The NAACP promised to put teeth into the Fourteenth Amendment by lobbying for a *reduction* of congressional representation in states that violated black voting rights. James Weldon Johnson stated: "Let a Republican Congress put the South to a test, and see if it is willing to lose a part of its representation rather than give the Negro the common right to a ballot."[14] The NAACP allied itself with Rep. George Tinkham of Massachusetts who announced plans to introduce a bill in the wake of the 1920 general elections that would reduce congressional representation in states that barred African Americans from voting.[15] Black Floridians concurred that reapportionment was the Achilles' heel of the Jim Crow South.[16]

Florida's Democrats quickly grasped the potential danger. Eli Futch, National Democratic Committee member from Florida, warned his party that the chair of the Census Committee, Rep. Isaac Siegel, was on record as stating that if "negro votes were being denied in the South, it was more than likely that the [Census] committee . . . would report a bill to Congress which, by authority and mandate of the Fourteenth Amendment to the Constitution, cut down the representation of the Southern States to Congress by at least half."[17]

Such a threat was meaningless unless African Americans in the South actively sought to exercise their voting rights and had those rights violated. In this case, the NAACP would submit evidence of election violations to the House of Representatives Census Committee when it convened in January. The Florida movement became the NAACP's major test case in the making, and some black Floridians held out at least a slim hope that federal vigilance might mitigate white political violence.[18] In supporting the threat of reducing "Southern representation because of disenfranchisement," Rev. John Hurst, the AME bishop of Florida, told NAACP officials, "If the Republicans will exert the power necessary to curb this spirit I say let them go ahead, and let the Negro leaders, far and near, back them up as far as they can."[19]

Democratic officials responded to the Florida movement with a three-pronged strategy. First, they urged white women to register. One top-ranking Democrat noted: "It used to be part of every demagogue aspiring to office in the South to dwell upon the negro issue, long after that issue was supposed to have been settled. It was settled until lately, and let us hope the good white women will settle it again. The women of the country have been drafted, and it is now their duty to go on the firing-line with their bullets of ballot."[20] White women hardly needed to be prodded.

Many saw the Florida movement as an attempt to place their "cooks and wash women" in charge of the society. A white woman from St. Petersburg proudly stated: "I have registered and shall vote because that is the most feasible means by which I can combat and overcome an ignorant vote."[21] Middle-class white women transformed their business and professional groups into political education organizations.[22] The *Okaloosa News* advised white men: "Mr. Voter, don't forget to carry your suffragette with you to the polls. . . . You should feel proud that you have a wife, mother, sister or daughter who can and will vote. It may be their vote that saves your state from going Republican [and] putting some negro into office."[23]

Second, Democratic officials engaged in outright intimidation in order to convince black Floridians to stay away from county registrars or voting booths on Election Day. In Jacksonville, the *Times-Union* crowed: "The work of arresting hundreds of negro women in Duval county who have violated the law in swearing falsely as to their qualifications to become electors, has already commenced. Indications are that the county jail will be filled by the end of the present week."[24] Janie Lowder, an African American woman in Jacksonville, wrote that "by publishing these statements of arresting these Poor Colored women it is just to frighten them from the Polls on Election Day and I have talked with a Great many and they say they are afraid to go & Cast their votes."[25] Meanwhile, election officials and sheriffs' departments across the state announced that armed deputies would be waiting to arrest African American "illegal voters" at the polls on November 2.

Third, local bureaucrats employed innovative strategies to suppress voter turnout. Jacksonville officials purged hundreds of African American names from the voter registration list.[26] Daytona election commissioners stated that "hundreds" of prospective voters would be turned away from voting booths on Election Day due to a shortage of election inspectors.[27] The Hamilton Board of County Officials announced that they would be omitting the names of Republican candidates on their election ballot. The board further declared the most recent GOP county convention to be null and void because the party had failed to poll 5 percent of the total vote in the last general election.[28] Simply put, the Republicans would have no one to vote for on Election Day. Fearing federal scrutiny, the state attorney general criticized Hamilton's way of running its election but did nothing to overturn it.[29] The would-be Republican candidate for county commissioner insisted that he would have been elected given "a free ballot & a fair count" in Hamilton.[30] County officials made certain that no such thing occurred in their bailiwick.

With a few notable exceptions, white Republicans turned their backs on black Republicans. Most white transplants in Florida were determined to continue transforming the Party of Lincoln into the Party of Business. When the Dade County GOP held its nominating convention, African Americans were excluded. Nor were black Miamians welcome at the party's public events. When local Democrats allegedly discovered a GOP pamphlet inviting African Americans to a rally, the Republican campaign committee offered a reward of fifty dollars to anyone who could uncover the identity of the person or persons guilty of printing the heinous flyer. The GOP's nominee for attorney general declared himself to be a true "southern man" and a staunch advocate of white supremacy. The president of the Republican Club crowed:

> There never has been a negro voice in the counsels of our party, nor shall [there] be so long as I have a word to say about it. . . . We have a white Republican party. We Republicans have wives and children. We are just as anxious as the Democrats that they shall be protected from any encroachment by the black race, and we will fight as quickly as any to prevent any such encroachment.[31]

At a St. Petersburg open-air rally on October 8, Mrs. Nellie R. Loehr, a leader of the local League of Women Voters and a Republican booster, noted that "the Republican white women had been asked by the negro women to attend their meeting and instruct them in the ways of a voter. She emphatically declared that this invitation had been refused."[32] In Palm Beach County, the Republican County Executive Committee reminded voters that "the candidates of the Republican Party in Palm Beach County were nominated in a convention composed of white men entirely and no pledges or promises of any kind have been made to the negro voters in consideration of their support, except that the laws will be administered fairly and justly."[33] Calvin Campbell, a transplanted northerner who aspired to become the county's tax collector on the GOP ticket, bragged: "In the town where he lived in Ohio, the home of McKinley, a negro was not permitted to remain over night even if he was arrested during the stay and locked in jail."[34] The central goals of the Organized White Republicans of Florida were to destroy African American influence in politics and to promote economic development.[35] Lily White candidates catered to "business interests" and "Democrats of the highest prominence."[36]

A CAMPAIGN OF TERROR

In the final days leading up to November 2, white supremacists planned a sustained campaign to sabotage the election in Florida. Gadsden County was a proving ground for Florida's newest disciples of violence. County officials banned African American public meetings. The KKK enforced the law. A. I. Dixie remembered that Klansmen were "burning crosses, where folks had their own little homes and a lot of them never returned, because they burn a cross and they know that that cross meant trouble."[37] "They ran some of the blacks out . . . they never did come back," recalled Inez Stevens-Jones. "They didn't want them having meetings. They wanted to keep them scattered."[38] Walter White reported that at Quincy: "A large branch of the Ku Klux Klan exists at this place and there was much intimidation of the Negro voters by the Klans. Dr. W. S. Stevens, the leading colored man of the town, was ordered to leave town because he called a meeting of the Courts of Calanthe, a fraternal order connected with the Knights of Pythias."[39] N. B. Young reported that the Ku Klux Klan wielded another powerful weapon: control of the public mail. The KKK disrupted the flow of communication between black organizations in rural Florida: "It is an open secret that one of the policies of the Ku Klux Klan is to open all mail of their suspects," noted Dr. Young, "not only in Quincy but all Post Offices where they are."[40]

John A. Simms, editor of the *Florida Sentinel,* told the NAACP, "Several prominent men were forced to leave town [Quincy] under threats of death for urging colored people to qualify, register and vote."[41] T. L. Sweet, the leader of the Harding-Coolidge Club in River Junction, became one of the political refugees from Gadsden. Late one evening, he was approached by A. L. Wilson and a local deputy sheriff "and told . . . that I was accused of being the leader of the colored people in the effort to have the colored women register and vote." Sweet was subsequently threatened by the county sheriff and a delegation of white business owners, who told him "that as there had never been a lynching in that part they thought it well that I should leave at once to be sure of my life." Sweet fled to Jacksonville.[42]

J. E. Foley, a farmer and a charter member of the local Greensboro NAACP, wasn't as lucky. On October 29, Mr. Foley was kidnapped by a mob of armed white men. According to a local correspondent, "The mob shot through the head of the bed where his wife was sleeping, presumably in an attempt to kill her."[43] Mr. Foley was taken from Greensboro to the nearby woods to be tortured and shot. Foley's tormentors tied his hands "behind his back by a necktie, while a sack of sand was fastened around his neck," and threw him into the Ocklockonee River, where his lifeless body was discovered in Leon County shortly after Election Day. The coroner could not determine "whether or not the gun shot wound proved fatal."[44] According to Greensboro NAACP branch president J. T. Smith, whites were infuriated that Mr. Foley had been trying to buy shotgun cartridges to defend his community from the KKK.[45]

The Colored Knights of Pythias in Gadsden convened an emergency lodge meeting. The besieged Knights violated the ban on public meetings in order to discuss the oath that members of the lodge had taken to pay their poll taxes and register to vote.[46] Now it was time to consider the final step: what would lodge members do on Election Day when local whites were already hatching plans to seize control of the polls by force of arms?[47]

The Pythians knew their lives were in grave danger, and they carried pistols and Winchester rifles on this late October evening in Chattahoochie to defend themselves if necessary. Once inside their lodge building, the Pythians assessed the grim situation they faced. Every debate circled back to the sacred oath that the KOP had made to engage in politics, an oath that rested on nearly half a century of black fraternalism. Weighing these facts, the Knights of Pythias made a difficult decision. They would honor the pledge they had made. The men would try to vote on Election Day.[48]

Suddenly, the lodge was hit by a deafening fusillade of shotgun blasts. Armed posses of the KKK had surrounded the building, and a pitched battle between the Knights and their attackers began.[49] As gunfire echoed through the skies of the Panhandle, a blaze ignited on the second floor of the embattled lodge. As the building collapsed, the Pythians had no choice but to escape as best as they could. Klansmen captured Rev. Phillyaw and beat him severely. An unknown number of Pythians were slaughtered. In a matter of days, white terrorists burned down four Pythian lodges in Gadsden and Liberty Counties and killed more KOP members.[50]

After wiping out Pythian lodges in Sumatra and Bristol, white terrorists destroyed the lodge in River Junction. This lodge housed a school for African American students at the Junction.[51] The headmaster of the school, A. F. House, was also a charter member of the Greensboro NAACP.[52] Mr. House was seized by a white mob and fatally beaten.[53]

N. B. Young wrote that there was a "Reign of Terror in Gadsden and Liberty Counties especially."[54] "If Congress will constitute a committee to investigate the recent campaign and election proceedings in Gadsden and Liberty counties, Florida," the *National Republican* noted, "enough material will be collected to shock not only the American people, but the entire civilized world."[55]

George F. Taylor of Mandarin had received several threats to cease his voter registration work among African American women. Mr. Taylor was "shot in the back as he sat at his dinner table by white men who objected to him teaching women of his Race to use the ballot."[56] Another black man in Duval County grew tired of hearing how Democratic registrars and deputy sheriffs were going to challenge the right of African American women to vote on Election Day. He publicly stated that he would himself challenge the votes of white women. Assassins came to his home a week before the election and shot him to death. They subsequently dumped his body on the St. John's County line.[57] White men kidnapped Reese Redding, a young black man, near Fort Myers. After being subjected to a "forced interview," Redding issued a terse statement: "The colored man has not reached the point where for him registering is his best need, and I know the women are no better able to vote and register than the men."[58] An anonymous "Colored Citizen" wrote to James Weldon Johnson: "A band of Ku Klux went to the home of Mr. Brunson of Sanford on the night of the 18th inst., and demanded him to sell his home and move from where he had lived for thirty years. Upon his refusal to do so he was given a severe beating by the mob and ordered to leave the home or they would return and kill him."[59]

In Columbia County, brothers B. J. and D. J. Jones had played integral roles in their community of Lake City for many years as Colored Pythians, businessmen, and, during the Great War, Liberty Loan drive boosters. With one week remaining in the registration period, white citizens kidnapped B. J. Jones. After beating him and placing a noose around his neck in the nearby woods, they allowed him to escape.[60] D. J. Jones was kidnapped by the KKK and beaten so badly that he had to be taken to Jacksonville, where several weeks after the election Walter White wrote that he lay "at the point of death from a stroke of paralysis brought on by the beating."[61] According to the *New York Times,* Jones's chief offense was organizing "meetings to instruct Negro women how to vote."[62]

County officials and other "unknown parties" engaged in a two-pronged campaign to preserve one-party rule in Suwannee County. On October

17, longtime African American activist T. S. Harris received a notice to leave Live Oak or face the consequences. At exactly the same time, the local sheriff began arresting African American women who had allegedly registered to vote under false pretenses. Subsequently, Harris's home was demolished by a bomb.[63] Frank Weiss, a white resident of Live Oak, was visited by "well known and prominent white citizens," who "came to me and threatened me with my life; they also said that my house would be raided and that they would take me out and do away with me if I affiliated with the Colored Republicans in Live Oak, Florida, stating that I had been too active in urging registration and qualification of the Colored people to vote in the general election on November 2nd, 1920." Weiss stayed in Live Oak, but lived "in dire fear, as each step of mine is watched; that I have a wife and children." Stating that his mail was being opened when "they suspect I am in correspondence with Republicans in other cities," Weiss warned that "said white citizens told me that on 'Election Day we are going to kill "nigger" women and men who dare to vote the Republican ticket at the polls.' "[64]

Frustrated by the persistence of African American political activism in central Florida, the Ku Klux Klan laid down the gauntlet in Orange County. Three weeks before Election Day, the KKK began warning the African American community at Ocoee that "not a single Negro would be permitted to vote."[65] Local Democrats in Ocoee hissed that the black voter registration campaign had made African Americans too assertive in their interactions with whites. When Ronnie Petsey, a young black man, allegedly ran an older white man off the road, he was shot down but successfully escaped and found sanctuary in the house of July Perry, a leader of local registration efforts.[66]

The Grand Master of the Florida Ku Klux Klan sent an ominous letter to two prominent white Republicans in Orlando, W. R. O'Neal, secretary of the Republican campaign committee, and Judge John Cheney. The Klan's master accused O'Neal of "going out among the negroes of Orlando and delivering lectures, explaining to them just how to become citizens, and how to assert their rights." Such activity would not be tolerated. The warning continued:

> If you are familiar with the history of the days of reconstruction . . . you
> will recall that the "Scalawags" of the north, and the Republicans of the
> south proceeded very much the same as you are proceeding, to instill into
> the negro the ideal of social equality. You will also remember that these

things forced the loyal citizens of the south to organize clans of determined men, who pledge themselves to maintain white supremacy and to safe guard our women and children.

And now if you are a scholar, you know that history repeats itself, and that he who resorts to your kind of a game is handling edged tools. We shall always enjoy WHITE SUPREMACY in this country and he who interferes must face the consequences.[67]

Vowing to maintain white supremacy forever and to stop African Americans from voting, the Ku Klux Klan marched in full regalia through the streets of Jacksonville, Daytona, and Orlando a few days prior to the election.[68] To a large extent however, the KKK's tactics in urban Florida backfired. While the NAACP in New York pleaded with federal and local authorities to ban the Klan's marches, a black activist in Jacksonville told the association to save its energy:

You folks up there seemed more alarmed than the Negroes here. Really, they know this is only to try to intimidate some. . . . The majority of the Negroes ridicule the [KKK] and are really ready to *start something* whenever the [Klan] is ready. The [Klan] is fully aware of it. Thousands of negroes went down looking for the parade and were in no way intimidated.[69]

In Daytona, the Klan was aided by a mysterious power outage that coincided perfectly with its march schedule. The *Daytona Daily News* claimed that this blackout was coincidental. However, Mary McLeod Bethune was certain that city fathers had orchestrated it to strike fear into the heart of the black community.[70] The *Daily News* boasted that the KKK's march was undertaken "to demonstrate the fact that the white race still maintains supremacy in this city and county, as well as in the South, and that fostering of the negro element in matters political will not be tolerated." Yet the paper had to admit that black neighborhoods in Daytona had organized themselves in preparation for the KKK, and "Every man in that locality was brought out, and made ready to resist the rumored attack."[71] The Klan thus wisely decided to avoid the black residential district. Instead, they marched over to Mary McLeod Bethune's school for young ladies and began encircling the campus dormitories. Even here, the Klan's magic did not have the desired effect. Without warning, 150 female students broke out singing "Be Not Dismayed Whate'er Betide, God Will Take Care of

You" from their dormitory rooms.[72] Humiliated, the Daytona Klan retreated back to safer haunts.

Why did so many black women, men, and young people in Florida seem to lose their fear of the KKK? Armed self-defense was part of a long tradition of black resistance in Florida. Equally important, African Americans in Jacksonville, Orlando, Daytona, and elsewhere had gained an enormous amount of self-confidence by organizing and participating in a statewide insurgency. The Florida movement created among African Americans a new sense of possibility that was grafted on to the survival strategies that had carried them through forty bitter years of disfranchisement.[73] This is a key to understanding why African Americans would fight against such prohibitive odds. The people who were willing to risk their lives in the Florida election of 1920 did not do so for an idea; they risked their lives for each other. The Florida Ku Klux Klan believed that if they terrorized African Americans prior to Election Day, the Florida movement would crumble. The Klan underestimated the power of a political movement based on relationships of trust. The Klan was no longer powerful enough to rule the state by itself. African Americans across the state locked arms and prepared to vote.

Election Day started on a positive note. On the morning of November 2, a group of seventy-five African American men and women from Gifford set out to cast their ballots at the Precinct 8 polling station in nearby Quay. Black people in Gifford had built one of the strongest Negro Uplift chapters in 1919, and now they were traveling the final footsteps of a journey toward freedom that had been paved with decades of aspiration, shattered hopes, and a renewed determination to break through the barrier of white supremacy. The very way that they approached the polls reflected the lessons that they had learned about democratic action: they walked in a large group, both to bolster each other's resolve and to reinforce the shared sacrifices that added momentum to their political efforts.

While African Americans in Manatee County were determined to vote, local Democrats were equally determined to crush them.[74] On the night before the election, a group of armed white men broke into a Knights of Pythias meeting place in Palmetto and warned the African American women and men present to stay away from the polls in Manatee County.[75]

Now twenty carloads of heavily armed white men patrolled the approaches to the polling places in the county. African Americans from Gifford had no choice but to turn back. They quickly petitioned W. E. B. Du Bois to demand a Department of Justice investigation into the incident: "The colored voters of Precinct number Eight (8) wish to inform the public through you, that between seventy-five and eighty men and women, were flatly told by an armed mob, who met and halted them on the way to the polls, that no negroes could vote at Quay, Florida."[76]

Another group of black citizens broke through to the courthouse at Palmetto. They were led by a twenty-two-year-old farm worker, Dan Thomas, and W. S. McGill, an AME minister.[77] As Thomas climbed the steps of the County Courthouse, a white man shot him in the back. Mr. Thomas fell, mortally wounded. A melee ensued, and a mob of white men descended on the black voters. African American women were kicked away from the polls, and Rev. McGill was driven from the county. Dan Thomas died the next day, leaving behind a wife and two young children. "The Colored people can't talk for fear of their lives," wrote a group of African Americans in Palmetto who begged the NAACP to help them. "They say they will kill anybody that makes it known and Mr. Asa Lamb (white) registration officer had to close the Poll at 11 O'clock a.m. the morning of the Election."[78] The local press transformed Dan Thomas into a "bad negro" who deserved to die.[79]

White Democrats used other strategies to undermine black voting. In addition to appointing armed deputies to stand menacingly at the polls, Democratic officials adopted a strategy of setting up segregated voting booths in the larger cities.[80] White voters' lines moved much more quickly than black ones, and it fell to African American organizers to convince black voters to stay in line and risk reprisal. In Daytona, this task was led by the indomitable Mary McLeod Bethune, who "walked up and down the uneasy, fearful line, instilling confidence—and the line held. They were not giving in."[81] In Jacksonville, where hundreds of African Americans waited to vote in a line that also barely moved, Eartha White served lemonade and tried to keep spirits high.[82]

Large groups of stationary black men and women were perfect targets for white terrorists. Dr. A. P. Holly told W. E. B. Du Bois that in Miami African Americans were allowed to vote only after their white counterparts had left the polling places. While a few black Miamians did vote at Precincts 8 and 9, Holly reported: "towards the closing hours, those still patiently waiting, were driven from one of the polling places by a crowd of democrats. They fled in all directions. One man ran & left his wife. Another one had tobacco juice spat in his face. Several hundred votes were thereby lost."[83] An anonymous female writer noted that as African American women and men fled from the polls, their tormentors cried:

" 'Git back nigger. Go back to Nigger town.' "[84] The same writer reported, "The people at Homestead 30 miles south of here were not allowed to vote at all." Charles S. Thompson, a black real estate agent, estimated that approximately one thousand black Miamians had been driven from the polls.[85] The *Miami Herald* bluntly admitted that the election was rigged:

> At two precincts, 8 and 9[,] negroes were kept standing in line for hours before being permitted to vote, first one subterfuge and then another being used to prevent voting, but they stuck to their posts and stood in the hot sun three to four hours during the forenoon and beyond the noon hour. . . . Later the negroes were driven off by a crowd of 25 or 30 whites.[86]

As Election Day in Florida progressed, a grim reality began to emerge. African American voting had been crushed in Dade, St. Lucie, and Manatee Counties. The line of prospective black voters held firm in Daytona, but showed signs of wavering in Jacksonville as armed deputies glared on. In Tallahassee, African Americans decided to approach the polls en masse and "the two city precincts were swamped with voters at the opening of the polls, colored men and women at first predominating."[87] In a clear breakthrough, the rural black district of Archer in Alachua County was turning out a Republican majority that repudiated James Cox as well as Frank Clark.[88] African Americans also voted in large numbers in St. Augustine, owing to a prearranged truce between black and white leaders and a nonsegregated voting line.[89] On the other hand, African American voting strength in Suwanee and Putnam Counties had been decimated by arrests and purges of the registration rolls before Election Day. Bradford, Perry, and Taylor Counties were lost entirely. In Lafayette County, one black person voted.[90] African Americans valiantly approached the polls in Lakeland, but many were seized and arrested.[91]

As defeats steadily mounted, the importance of middle Florida, centering on Gadsden County where local NAACP president J. T. Smith stated that "some of us are determined to vote," loomed large. In Quincy proper, Dr. W. S. Stevens led a group of African Americans to the county courthouse early in the day but was stopped and surrounded by a gang of white men. One of the men spat tobacco juice into Dr. Stevens's face, "And that first group," his daughter recalled, "they wouldn't let them in that courthouse. They didn't let them in to vote. No. They told him, 'you don't come in here.' "[92] N. B. Young wrote that Dr. Stevens "was maltreated, and all the Negroes of that county terrorized. The ballot box at Quincy was guarded to keep Negroes away. Practically the same condition existed at Madison, Florida."[93]

Terror raged in rural Gadsden and Liberty Counties. NAACP president Smith reported that roving bands of "2 and three hundred in auto with white caps over they faces and rifles furbid Negroes to vote in these two Co."[94] Several gunfights broke out throughout this region on Election Day. Joe Ragster, a black farmer, was arrested after battling a group of white "acting deputies" at Greensboro. Mr. Ragster's house was burned to the ground.[95] The black press reported, "At Sumatra, William Jackson a negro was killed on the day of the election for political activity."[96] The agony in J. T. Smith's letter to the NAACP is palpable: "I want to say that did not 9 Negro vote in my Co which is Gadsden or either Liberty."[97] Young reported that "the polls were guarded with armed men to keep Negroes from voting."[98] White supremacists had erected a firewall of repression that stretched across middle Florida. "We dare not write all that we would because in some places like Quincy, Fla. Negroes' mail has been opened, since last spring, and is handed to them from the post office opened," wrote an anonymous black writer from northern Florida to James Weldon Johnson. "The victims in that town have been told that they cannot leave, and are forced to say what they are told to say."[99] The Panhandle was lost.[100]

As late afternoon approached, African Americans in Jacksonville held their breath. Their voting lines had stalled in the second, sixth, seventh and eighth ward polling places, but this did not dissuade hundreds from bravely waiting their turn to vote.[101] Even though Jacksonville officials threatened to arrest black voters on the eve of the election, "colored women paid no attention to these stories, but formed lines two and three blocks long, some standing in line all day."[102] Jacksonville police seized a black photographer who was trying to document the election, destroyed his film, and held him on a $500 bond.[103]

White polling officials in Jacksonville had received their instructions in advance. Captain J. W. Floyd, a black political leader present at one of the precincts, noted:

In the wards where large numbers of the colored people lived, they placed the most ignorant election officials that they could find. These officials did everything in their power to prevent Negroes from voting, telling colored voters who had with them certificates certifying that they had qualified and registered, that their names were not on the registration books. In many cases colored people were told that they would have to go to the office of Frank M. Ironmonger, Supervisor of Registration for Duval County and secure a letter certifying that they had registered.[104]

By the end of the day, Floyd, Eartha White, and other black activists estimated that three to four thousand African Americans in Jacksonville had been turned away from the polls. One witness testified: "My own mother, a very active woman . . . stood at the polls from 8:15 until they closed about 5:30 P.M. My father did likewise and neither was permitted to cast their ballot [like] others in the 2, 6 and 7th wards."[105] "I was active in securing the registration of colored men and women because we all realized the value of the ballot," Eartha White told the NAACP. "We have already in hand more than 3,000 names, addresses and registration certificate numbers of qualified electors who stood in line . . . from 8 A.M. to 5:40 P.M." Miss White and her fellow organizers immediately went to work gathering evidence that the NAACP could place before the U.S. Congress when it convened in January. Eartha White emphasized, however, that local black citizens were concerned about their safety should they be called upon to testify about their experiences: "Many of these must be assured of some protection for if it was known that they gave such testimony, their lives would be in danger."[106]

BLOODY ORANGE COUNTY

Election officials in Ocoee planned a system of fraud that paralleled the Jacksonville strategy: poll workers would challenge black voters, who in turn would be forced to appear before the local notary public, R. C. Biegelow, and swear that they were registered voters. Whites in Ocoee later admitted that Biegelow was sent on a fishing trips which made it impossible for prospective voters to find him.[107] But African Americans at Ocoee still tried to vote. Zora Neale Hurston wrote that African Americans were "pushed and shoved at the polls. Then they were ordered away, but some of them persisted."[108] One of those who persisted was Mose Norman, who was accused by whites of bringing a shotgun to the polls. Whites also accused Norman of taking testimony from African Americans who had been denied the right to vote.[109] According to Hurston, a group of white men chased Norman from the polls. "Then the white mobs began to parade up and down the streets and grew more disorderly and unmanage-able." Someone suggested that the white crowd should pay Mose Norman a visit to bring him to his senses. It was believed that Norman had taken refuge at the house of July Perry, which was plainly visible across a small lake from the Ocoee court house. A mob began to march around the lake to Mr. Perry's house. Hurston believed that the white people of neighboring Winter Garden, "citing the evils of Reconstruction," came to Ocoee looking for trouble. However, Ocoee whites like Colonel Sam Salisbury proudly confessed to having participated in the ensuing events.[110] Salisbury was a native New Yorker and had formerly served as the chief of police in Orlando.

Arriving at July Perry's house, the mob, numbering around one hundred men, demanded that Perry and Norman surrender themselves. Receiving no answer, they tried to break down the front door. Perry had been warned in advance and was ready for this incursion. John Cheney was clear about the chain of events: "They broke down the door of Perry's home and the Negroes fired in self-defense."[111] Sam Salisbury was the first white casualty. The mob quickly regrouped and called for reinforcements from Orlando and Orange County.[112] Alerted by an electronic sign board that was being used for the first time to broadcast election returns, fifty carloads of white men from Orlando raced to the scene. Thus augmented, white paramilitary forces surrounded the northern Ocoee black community and laid siege to it.[113] They destroyed the local fraternal lodge building, set fire to the black churches, and engaged in an evening-long gun battle with African American residents. Fighting a bitter house-to-house campaign, whites torched African American residences as late as 4:45 in the morning.[114] July Perry was captured and lynched. Mose Norman disappeared and was never found. Hurston wrote that "Langmaid, a Negro carpenter [was] beaten and castrated."[115] White gunmen steadily drove African Americans into a nearby swamp, and the morning of November 3 witnessed "intermittent firing from blacks at bay as they are being pressed farther into the woods by the encircling whites."[116]

Hattie Smith of Youngstown, Ohio, had arrived in Ocoee in October to help care for her sister-in-law during the final days of her pregnancy.[117] On the evening of Election Day, Smith heard about the gunfight at July Perry's home, but since that was some distance from Smith's brother's home, it was thought that residents there would be safe from violence. Around midnight, however, Mrs. Smith and the rest of the household were awak-ened "by shots and screaming of women and children." Seeking to flee from their house, "we were met with a fusillade of revolver shots fired by a band of white men. With shots and curses they drove us back into the house."[118] Next the white mob set the house on fire. Mrs. Smith fled out the back door, but her brother was wounded, and his family decided to wait for help.

But help never came, not for Mrs. Smith's family or for any other African Americans in Ocoee. "My poor sister-in-law, her husband and child had perished in the flames along with probably twenty others, who were either burned or shot to death by the mob."[119] Local Afro-American Insurance agents confirmed Mrs. Smith's report, telling their home office in Jacksonville that "several women and children were among those burned to death in the election riots in that place."[120] While it was stated that "negro women were true shots with their guns," African Americans could not withstand a sustained assault by hundreds of armed white men who poured into the town from all directions. Driven from their homes, African Americans in Ocoee desperately fled from the area. The *Times-Union* reported that "many negroes have been seen walking along highways many miles from Ocoee."[121]

The Rev. R. B. Brooks, presiding AME elder in St. Augustine, stated, "The total number [of dead] will probably never be known because the bones of the murdered Negroes who were burned to death, were taken away as souvenirs by members of the mob."[122] Alexander Akerman concurred with Rev. Brooks's grim assessment. Akerman told U.S. senator William C. Kenyon: "I do not believe it will ever be known how many Negroes were killed. Every Negro schoolhouse, church and lodge room in that vicinity was burned, in some instances with women and children occupying the house, and thus burned to death."[123] The *Miami Herald* reported, "All negroes in that section have taken flight and it is not expected that the disturbance will spread."[124]

When Walter White arrived undercover in Orange County a few days later, he found that whites were still giddy with victory.[125] The United Confederate Veterans changed the timing of their convention in Orlando so that they could visit Ocoee and witness firsthand this latest victory for white supremacy.[126] Light-skinned enough to pass for a white man, White posed as a northerner interested in buying orange grove property in Orange County in order to find out what had happened in Ocoee and other black communities.[127] The real estate agent and taxi cab driver who took White to Ocoee told the assistant secretary of the NAACP that fifty-six African Americans had been killed in the massacre. White was also told that the massacre had been precipitated by white jealousy of black farmers like July Perry and Mose Norman, who were judged as being "too prosperous—'for a nigger.' " White was struck by the attitude of white residents of Orange County, who felt "that nothing unusual had taken place—that the white people had acquitted themselves rather meritoriously in checking unholy and presumptuous ambitions of Negroes in attempting to vote."[128] White landowners used the Ocoee Massacre as a pretext to drive the few remaining African Americans out of the town and to seize their property. Mrs. J. H. Hamiter, who lived in the southern branch of the Ocoee black community, which had not been directly assaulted on Election Day, wrote to a friend a few weeks later:

> The people on the south of town are being threatened that they must sell out and leave or they will be shot and burned as the others have been. I don't know the first step to take. Every where near here is crowded with people and I haven't been able to sell out as yet. It seemed to have been a pre-arranged affair to kill and drive the colored people from their homes as they were more prosperous than the white folks, so they are hoping to get their homes for nothing.[129]

In the end, white paramilitaries drove nearly five hundred African Americans out of Ocoee, and the town became Florida's newest white homeland. Walter White provided a chilling epilogue:

> At the time that I visited Ocoee, the last colored family of Ocoee was leaving with their goods piled high on a motor truck with six colored children on top. White children stood around and jeered the Negroes who were leaving, threatened them with burning if they did not hurry up and get away. These children thought it a huge joke that some Negroes had been burned alive.[130]

The NAACP cautiously estimated that between thirty and sixty black Floridians were murdered on Election Day.[131] Scores had been wounded, and hundreds more became political refugees in their own country. Whites had destroyed black fraternal lodges in three counties. African Americans now expected the nation to intervene in what was ultimately the bloodiest presidential election in the history of twentieth-century America. William Sutton had witnessed armed whites guarding the polling places in Liberty County in order to deter African American voters. Sutton placed his hope for justice outside of the state: "I am glad to read of so many who are in sympathy with the colored men and women who were not allowed to vote. I pray the day will come when all citizens regardless of color, will be able to cast their votes for whom they please, and think will lead our people to victory in political and civil rights in our country of America."[132]

BEFORE THE U.S. CONGRESS

In the aftermath of the election, the National Association for the Advancement of Colored People prepared to bring Florida to trial before the entire nation. The courtroom would be the powerful House Committee on the Census, scheduled to hold hearings during the final week of December 1920. This committee was charged with the matter of apportioning congressional representation based upon population gains or losses as calculated by the chief statistician for the Bureau of the Census. The U.S. Congress was also bound to observe provisions on representation and apportionment spelled out in the U.S. Constitution which forbade discrimination in the matter of voting.[133] This is where the smoking gun of southern disenfranchisement lay. The NAACP believed that it could prove that southern election officials had violated the Fourteenth and Fifteenth Amendments by creating one set of standards for white registration and another for black, and then by discriminating against African Americans trying to exercise their voting rights.[134] The Association's counsel James Cobb argued that weaving these pivotal amendments together would bind Congress to reduce representation in the states where discrimination had occurred.[135]

James Weldon Johnson, Walter White, and William Pickens delivered the proof of voting discrimination to the Census Committee. The NAACP's evidence included affidavits, statistics, photographs, and personal testimony, and the bulk of it came from Florida. Additional testimony from shattered voter registration efforts in Georgia, Virginia, and North Carolina was also presented.[136] The NAACP wanted at bare minimum a major congressional investigation that would blow the lid off one-party rule in the South. If successful, the NAACP, which had broken the grandfather clause in 1915, would be able to pry open another vital space for democracy in the South.

But James Weldon Johnson and the NAACP first had to reckon with the Census Committee. Its chair, Isaac Siegel (R., New York), was sympathetic to the NAACP's arguments and invited the civil rights organization to testify before the committee.[137] His colleagues were another story. James

Aswell (Louisiana), William W. Larsen (Georgia), and Carlos Bee (Texas) were, as events were to prove, prepared to combat any effort to show that African Americans were denied the right to vote in the South. Jacob Milligan (Missouri) reveled in using the term "nigger" whenever possible.[138] With the exception of Siegel, only Horace Towner of Iowa would play a mediating influence on the committee's antiblack bias. For the most part, the other northern congressmen kept their own counsel during the proceedings.

The pattern of the hearings was set early on. Reps. Bee, Larsen, and Aswell rudely interrupted NAACP witnesses, using personal anecdotes to make light of the claim that African Americans in the South were disfranchised. "Take Will May—that I happen to remember," Rep. Larsen recalled. "He voted. He is a nigger, a pretty good nigger." When James Weldon Johnson suggested that Congress had an obligation to enforce the U.S. Constitution, Rep. Aswell responded: "To my mind, this whole thing opens up an interminable investigation."[139]

NAACP informants fought an uphill battle to invest the hearings with gravity. When Walter White tried to present documentary evidence on disfranchisement from Florida, Congressman Larsen impatiently asked: "What do you think this committee has to do with all this stuff?" When White introduced the affidavits of 941 African Americans in Jacksonville who swore that they had been denied the right to vote, Rep. Aswell used the occasion to grill White on the fund-raising activities of the NAACP.[140]

On the third day of the hearings, James Weldon Johnson appeared before the committee. By now, Johnson was a seasoned veteran of the Jim Crow wars. He had been nearly beaten on a Jacksonville street because members of the white militia thought that his light-skinned female escort was a white woman. Johnson presented census figures for the populations of each southern state, showing the numbers of potential eligible voters and juxtaposed these with the actual voting population of each state to show that voter turnout in the South was being willfully suppressed. These figures proved to be so damning that Rep. Aswell finally cried out: "This Congress is very strong on economy, and I think the other witnesses will have the same set of figures. We ought not to print all of this. It is extravagant."[141]

Johnson drove home the point that the suppression of black ballots in the South undermined democracy throughout the nation. "This is not merely a question of the Negro, by any means," he said. "It is a question of Republican Government and of the fundamentals of American democracy.

We may as well face the question as to how long this situation is allowed to go on. It can not go on indefinitely." Johnson pointed with pride to the record of African Americans during the Great War, the advances that the race had made, and concluded his speech with a warning and a prophecy:

> We put the matter before you. Some of the Members have thought it was an irrelevant matter, but I say it is fundamental; it is the very root of republican government, and it is a question which is either going to come to this Congress or to some other Congress in the future, and with increasing force every time it comes up, and it seems to me it is better to pass on the question fairly and squarely and justly to-day and not wait until some unknown tomorrow.[142]

When Florida's congressmen appeared before the committee to testify, the tenor of the hearings changed entirely. When Florida Rep. William J. Sears expressed his commitment to maintain white supremacy, Rep. Carlos Bee blustered: "I will join hands with you." Congressman Frank Clark explained that Florida had the fairest election laws in the nation. He produced a telegram from J. Seth Hills in which the latter supposedly claimed that African Americans in Jacksonville voted without obstacles. Dr. Hills stated that this telegram was a forgery.[143] Clark submitted affidavits alleging election fairness from white officials such as Sheriff Gregory in Gadsden County. Gregory had helped to drive the president of the Harding-Coolidge Club out of the county before the election.[144] Finally, as Bishop John Hurst noted, Rep. Clark relied on coerced testimony from African Americans such as W. S. Stevens in Gadsden who was brought before a group of twenty white men in Quincy and told to sign statements "to the effect that colored people had never been prevented from voting in Gadsden county but rather have had free access to the ballot always."[145] Congressman Clark charged that the election in Florida had been administered fairly. However, Clark himself had run on a platform of white supremacy. He was most certainly aware that he was perjuring himself before a committee of the United States Congress.

Clark even denied that black Floridians had been politically active, saying: "The Negro is really a very docile and peaceable sort of fellow and is easily led." He concluded his testimony by reminding his colleagues that he spoke "from the American white man's standpoint. I want to see white political parties, and I want white men to run this country, which is a white man's country and should remain so."[146] After insulting the

NAACP's representatives, Census Committee members treated Clark's testimony with the profoundest respect. Florida's election received a clean bill of health from Congress.

The willingness of the U.S. Congress to set aside the Fourteenth and Fifteenth Amendments to the Constitution spelled the final doom of the Florida movement. The Ku Klux Klan had waged a brutally effective campaign of terror, but it was still not able to stop thousands of African Americans from trying to vote. State and municipal officials resorted to a broad array of measures including arrest, segregated voting lines, and threats of violence to depress voter turnout. Even this did not completely squelch African American activism. In the end, the Florida movement was defeated by a combination of municipal, state, *and* federal authorities who colluded to undermine the legitimacy of the presidential election of 1920. President-elect Warren G. Harding put his stamp of approval on the debased contest by taking a pre-inaugural vacation in Florida and refusing NAACP requests to investigate the claims of the people who had sacrificed everything they had to support the Republican Party.[147]

A new reign of terror stalked Florida in the weeks after the election. A writer told James Weldon Johnson that "freedom of speech is prohibited. . . . If facts could be secured from other localities, there would be sufficient ground to cut down the representation from the south, but they dare not speak facts."[148] In some areas, white officials banned public meetings of the NAACP.[149] In Miami, an African American woman informed Johnson, "There has been a lynching since the election and on or near the spot two whites were killed the next day."[150]

In Gadsden County, the violence continued. "This place was considerably stirred some time since when the store of Jeff Lamar, a well known colored man, was blown up by a charge of dynamite which had been placed under the floor by unknown persons," reported the *Daily Democrat*.[151] Whites in Gadsden were warned late one evening "that an armed force of negroes were headed toward River Junction from Hardaway," to lay siege to white settlements. In light of what had happened in Gadsden on Election Day, white people took this warning seriously, and "within a short time practically every family in River Junction and Chattahoochee had been aroused and told to arm themselves."[152] The fact that this rumor turned out to be a false alarm did not allay white fears of black retribution for election violence.

For most African Americans, however, the possibility of replying to the violence they had suffered on Election Day was out of the question.

White supremacists were secure in the knowledge that their activities would be safe from any consequences. Ruth Crowd Wilkerson wrote to James Weldon Johnson to say that her father, an ailing business owner, had been ordered to leave Jacksonville: "I do not know the cause of the trouble as my father is a law abiding citizen," wrote Mrs. Wilkerson. "I attribute the trouble to the fact that he just bought a home in a neighborhood where only a few colored people live. Will you please help him in some way [?]"[153] Mrs. Wilkerson's father was the founder of the illustrious Globe Theater in Jacksonville. Now he was a hunted man.[154] One anonymous writer from the state told the NAACP, "When the law gives us protection, it will not be necessary for us to write unsigned letters."[155]

The messages of democratic striving that African Americans had delivered to Warren Harding and the NAACP before the election were now transformed into notes of despair: "Just a line to say to you that the Negroes of Florida feel grateful for the good work your association is doing," wrote one woman to the NAACP a few days after the New Year had dawned. Earlier she might have used this occasion to communicate her ideas on democracy. Now she was moved to say: "We are powerless here to express ourselves publicly, but our prayers are for you and with you. We know that you are doing for us what we *cannot* do for ourselves."[156] It was a terribly painful admission of defeat.

LEGACIES OF
THE FLORIDA MOVEMENT

AMERICAN HISTORY has completely erased the martyrs of 1920. It is possible to walk through Tallahassee, the state capital of Florida, and have absolutely no inkling that one of the greatest democratic struggles of the nation's life occurred here. No streets are named for the activists who fought to regain the right to vote. No markers are dedicated to honor Floridians who died to secure freedom on this soil. Critics complain that civics and American history are no longer taught in the schools. Yet there has been no effort to learn from the experiences of Americans in twenty-eight Florida counties who braved terrorism in an effort to assume the rights and responsibilities of U.S. citizenship. It may be that the story of thousands of people rising up to demand justice, dignity, and equality in a one-party state is compelling only if it occurs in someone else's one-party state. Whatever the case, the task of commemorating the efforts of individuals who fought to save democracy remains undone. The Florida movement awaits its monuments.

The gap of understanding and experience that separates the participants of the Florida movement from our own time is substantial. Voter turnout is in steep decline, and increasing numbers of Americans feel disconnected from their nation's political process.[1] Columnist John Dean writes, "Of the 153 democracies in the world, the United States ranks near the bottom for voter involvement."[2] It is difficult—yet, arguably, a necessity—to try and imagine exactly what led people in another place and time to risk their lives to secure the right to vote. How and why did black Floridians reenergize the concept of democratic citizenship, and what lessons might this organizing achievement hold today?

At first glance, black Floridians' political activism appears to correspond to what Colin A. Palmer has called "the Generation of 1917," "a new generation of blacks [who] emerged who were more insistent in their demand for justice and . . . from then on, the style of protest in black America was more vigorous, sustained, and multifaceted."[3] Palmer echoes Alain Locke's thesis in *The New Negro*. Locke held that owing to African American migration, urbanization, and the democratic ethos of World War I, "a transformed and transforming psychology permeates the [black] masses."[4] More recently, historian Beth Tompkins Bates has argued that this ultimately created a "new-crowd protest politics" among African Americans.[5]

African American insurgencies after 1917, however, were firmly linked to earlier protests, and there was really nothing "new" at all about these open battles. A careful analysis of the record between 1865 and 1917 shows more continuity than discontinuity in black struggles. Black Floridians waged numerous campaigns against one-party rule and white supremacy. Male and female activists ensured that black Floridians held on to the ballot throughout most of the 1880s using mass action tactics. Dock and warehouse workers waged major strikes in the Gilded Age. The unemployed demanded municipal work relief programs. African American communities in Jacksonville and Pensacola even turned back the tide of segregation after successful streetcar boycotts. People in timber towns, rural areas, and cities repeatedly took up arms to prevent lynching. There was no need to call upon the New Negro after World War I because African American men and women had been dynamically fighting Jim Crow since its very inception.

This rich and multifaceted legacy of struggle explains how voter registration activists were able to link voting rights, economic justice, and the fight against racial oppression. The Florida movement's holistic approach to politics served as an effective tool of recruitment. African Americans discussed the most pressing social crises of the day and planned to use their votes to confront them. Black Floridians vanquished the forces of demobilization which, in more recent times, have led to declining voter turnout, especially among the nation's poor.[6]

The first public exhortations to register and vote were issued in the midst of Emancipation Day services in January 1919. Black Floridians had transformed this event into a day of remembrance when they reminded each other where they had come from, how they had earned freedom, and what they expected from the state in return for their service. This synthesis of the cultural and the political gained importance over time. When America entered World War I, an older generation of activists framed the sacrifices that younger black troops were making in France within a longer history of African American service to the republic. Cultural workers choreographed marches, stage productions, and memorial services where elderly ex-slaves, Civil War veterans, Red Cross nurses, and children all had a place of honor. These public performances bolstered African Americans' claims to equal citizenship. African Americans looked to the past to formulate many of their demands for the future.

Social movements cannot be orchestrated from above. They are not set into motion by manifestos or charismatic leaders. Black Floridians registered to vote because the women and men who asked them to take this risk were deeply rooted in their communities and in the institutions that had buffered them from white supremacy. Lodges, women's clubs, labor unions, and churches became organizing centers because they had proven to be reliable sites for promoting mutual aid, dignity, and survival. African Americans built on preexisting relationships of trust to forge a social movement. The oath that fifteen thousand members of the Knights of Pythias lodge took binding each of them to register to vote is a reminder that the Florida movement was driven by mutuality, not militancy.

The advent of women's suffrage provided a critical boost to the Florida movement. However, it is important to understand that in Florida—as in other parts of the South—African American women were not entering the political arena for the first time.[7] Indeed, black women in Florida could trace their political lineage back to Reconstruction, when women had rallied their communities to hold firm against Democratic fraud and coercion. White conservatives blamed female activists for enforcing black political solidarity in the 1880s. African American men credited women for playing leading roles in winning the streetcar boycotts in 1901 and 1905. In 1916, African American women's clubs in Jacksonville urged black men to pay their poll taxes. Three years later many of the same women were sponsoring voter registration workshops for the men. When expanded suffrage came in 1920, African American women were ready to make history—again.

The role of male and female workers in the making of the Florida movement is a reminder that the agency of lower-income individuals is decisive in the endeavor to revive political participation in the broader society. The extraordinarily diverse struggles that African American workers waged between 1916 and 1919 placed economic issues at the center of a revived political platform. Black workers' search for justice led them to pioneer a Great Migration out of Florida. During World War I, female domestic workers resisted "work or fight" statutes while railway men drafted petitions to the federal government demanding access to the nation's labor laws. At war's end, African American workers launched strikes throughout the state.

African American laborers, through their actions and demands, broke down the blatantly undemocratic nature of politics in the Jim Crow South. "Representative Negroes" who had urged African Americans to stay in the South, trust white elites, and cross picket lines were swept out of leadership. Working-class self-activity created a heightened level of accountability in politics. The stage was set for political insurgency. It wasn't that an entirely new generation of leaders was pushed to the fore. The example of Joseph Lee is instructive. This icon of Reconstruction-era politics was publicly repudiated by black trade unionists in 1916 for becoming a mouthpiece for the Jacksonville Chamber of Commerce. Four years later, African Americans welcomed Lee—shorn of his chamber baggage—back to the fray as a political organizer. All of this is to say that leadership in a social movement is not as important as the creativity, the self-confidence, and determined activism that the movement's followers promote.[8]

The white counterassault against the Florida movement was lethal and grounded in the history of the state. White conservatives had ushered in one-party rule with fraud and violence; they maintained their rule with routine doses of mayhem against black citizens. Racial violence in Florida was frequently genocidal in scope and scale. Whites destroyed African American settlements, drove black workers out of parts of the state, and used lynching and rape as weapons of social control. The flames of Ocoee augured the massacres in Perry and Rosewood a few years later. Indeed, the Florida terror should be judged in tandem with the race riots of East St. Louis, Chicago, Elaine, Tulsa, and other places. African Americans were organizing increasingly effective movements for justice, and their adversaries deployed violence to crush them. Mass murder is the bedfellow of white supremacy, and C. L. R. James was surely correct to note: "this barbarism exists only because nothing else can suppress the readiness for sacrifice, the democratic instincts and creative power of the great masses of the people."[9]

It would be a mistake to say that the Florida movement was destroyed entirely by forces within the state. Segregation did not originate in Florida, and the state's white supremacists did not invent one-party rule in the South. Racial oppression was enforced by an interlocking system of power with transmission lines radiating from northern firms, the U.S. Supreme Court, Congress, and other federal agencies. At the turn of the century, *Plessy v. Ferguson* cleared the way for Florida and other states to refine segregation. In later years, the federal government intervened to bolster the power of the southern elite. When Florida's employers complained that the U.S. Department of Labor was interfering with the maintenance of cheap labor after World War I, the federal government shut down the Division of Negro Economics in Florida. Federal authorities changed immigration law to benefit growers and left workers to fend for themselves. The U.S. Congress's refusal to enforce the Fourteenth and Fifteenth Amendments to the Constitution spelled democracy's doom in Florida. Indeed, the federal government's betrayal of African Americans in Florida saved Jim Crow from the most serious threat it would face for another generation.

The bloody aftermath of the Florida movement generated a variety of legacies. Some black Floridians justified a withdrawal from politics by pointing to Republican betrayals and Election Day violence in 1920. E. J. and Mattie Marshall, farmers from Plant City, told a WPA interviewer in the 1930s that they kept up with current affairs by subscribing to the *Pittsburgh Courier,* but that they did not try to vote. Mr. Marshall stated: "I ain't voted tall in the last few years. I quit foolin with it, I got disgusted. I always voted republican. . . . that lily white mess disgusted me."[10] For Rich Gray, a turpentine worker, disenfranchisement was reinforced by federal collusion with state authorities: "As fer votin, that's another thing I haint up to neither. No man! I don't do not votin. . . . Uncle Sam knowed what everybody is a-doin, and if you stick your finger in the fire, yor shore to git burned."[11] Zora Neale Hurston interviewed a turpentine worker near Cross City who told her: "I voted once in Georgia. . . . The colored folks don't vote around here. . . . I did used to hear my father talk about Republicans. It seemed like they used to do the people the most good, but look like they don't do that now."[12] African Americans grew disgusted with a Republican Party that accepted their votes only to betray them.

In the aftermath of the election of 1920, open political organizing efforts ground to a halt in sections of Florida—sometimes for an entire generation. When Charles S. Thompson, an African American member of the NAACP in Miami, was asked about black voting in 1931, he answered succinctly: "We have not had trouble here about voting since the Harding election, when more than 1,000 Negroes were driven from the polls[;] the reason is that very few of us vote."[13]

On the other hand, the Florida movement provided activists and tactics that would reemerge to form the foundation of a new civil rights movement a generation later. African Americans in Pensacola reorganized their NAACP chapter during the 1920s and boasted some 1,500 voters by the end of the decade.[14] African Americans in one movement county, Brevard, organized a vibrant NAACP chapter in 1934. The lead organizer of the chapter had been a high school student in Live Oak at the height of the voter registration movement. His name was Harry T. Moore, and in the following decade he would help the NAACP spearhead another statewide voter registration movement in Florida.[15]

Mary McLeod Bethune's activism in the movement as well as in the State Federation of Colored Women's Clubs prepared her to take a leadership position in Franklin D. Roosevelt's Black Cabinet during the New Deal years.[16] Eartha M. M. White never gave up her advocacy for the poor and was a legendary social activist well into the 1960s in Jacksonville.[17]

In Gadsden County, J. T. Smith and the NAACP chapter he had helped build survived by going underground. Smith patiently recruited a new generation of NAACP members by approaching them in secret.[18] In 1923, Smith told James Weldon Johnson: "our Branch has been in a very bad condition since 1920 douring the Genrial Election. They [white people] did so much develment here it got our peeples afred to take hold of the N.A.A.C.P. and the bigest Morgorty of our members quit altho they is a few real men yet holding on and we shall indever to try an keep it alive."[19] A. I. Dixie, who hailed from a sharecropping family in Gadsden, fondly remembered Smith as the organizer who had quietly introduced him to the NAACP one day in Greensboro by cautiously inviting him to a secret branch meeting in the 1940s.

Smith and the NAACP held on in Greensboro for four decades. He lived to see a new generation of Congress of Racial Equality (CORE) activists—some of whom hailed from Gadsden itself—initiate a voter registration movement in the county in 1964.[20] Two of these young activists were the children of A. I. Dixie. In 1964, A. I.'s son Jewell became the first African American to run for sheriff in nearly a century of Gadsden politics. Smith, however, finally had to leave the county because of threats on his life.

In the short term, the defeat of the Florida movement was a historic victory for white supremacy. If African Americans had been able to breach the wall of one-party rule in Florida, the larger edifice of Jim Crow might have crumbled decades earlier. Instead, the disease of political corruption deepened in Florida and throughout the nation over another four decades. A white man who wrote his Ph.D. dissertation on Live Oak recalled that when he moved to Suwannee County, "I first went to see the Sheriff. He took me right over to register to vote, backdating the entry because I had only been in the area a few days. Well, when he found out I made my living lending money to niggers, he made me a deputy sheriff. That way, he said, 'If you ever have to kill one, it'll be legal.'"[21] Stealing elections, brutalizing African Americans, and monkey-wrenching the democratic process continued to be a way of life in Florida and in America writ large.

It is now easier to understand the 2000 election debacle in Florida. Underneath the media circus of hanging chads, Republican mobs, and sore Democratic losers is the fact that thousands of African Americans—as well as significant numbers of Latinos and Haitian Americans—were wrongly purged from the rolls and prevented from voting. To be sure, there were important differences between the election days of 1920 and 2000. Open violence gave way to surreptitious voter roll purges. The final results of both elections, however, were strikingly similar: the nation lost control of its most sacred political institution because it could not deal forthrightly with its oldest and deepest social problem: racial oppression.

James Weldon Johnson explained to the United States Congress in 1920 that racism undermined democracy. The most virulent strains of political corruption in America originated in the effort to dehumanize and disfranchise African Americans. Until racism is eradicated, the nation stands on the brink of peril. W. E. B. Du Bois put it succinctly: "The price of repression is greater than the cost of liberty. The degradation of men costs something both to the degraded and those who degrade."[22]

The Florida movement teaches that hitherto powerless individuals may come together to formulate the boldest social justice agendas—but they must organize first. The movement gave its participants the confidence to think large and plan boldly to address the gravest social problems of their time. African Americans drew on personal ties of mutuality to create a politics that embraced the needs of ordinary people. This is the true genius of the Florida movement of 1919–1920. Black Floridians assumed that all people deserved dignity, and because of this their definition of democracy grew to become an expansive and sophisticated statement of human possibility. The only way to honor their prodigious sacrifices is to carry on the struggle.

NOTES

PREFACE: ELECTION DAY IN FLORIDA

1. Malachia Andrews interviewed by author, August 9, 1994, Behind the Veil: Documenting African American Life in the Jim Crow South, John Hope Franklin Research Center for African and African American Documentation, Duke University; hereafter cited as Behind the Veil Collection.

2. U.S. Commission on Civil Rights, *Voting Irregularities in Florida during the 2000 Presidential Election* (Washington, DC: Government Printing Office, 2001), 1.

3. "The Commission's findings make one thing clear: widespread voter disenfranchisement—not the dead-heat contest—was the extraordinary feature in the Florida election" (ibid., xi). For additional documentation see the appendices in ibid. See also "Contesting the Vote: Black Voters; Arriving at Florida Voting Places, Some Blacks Found Frustration," *New York Times*, November 30, 2000; "Irregularities Cited in Fla. Voting; Blacks Say Faulty Machines, Poll Mistakes Cost Them Their Ballots," *Washington Post*, December 12, 2000; Gregory Palast, *The Best Money Democracy Can Buy: An Investigative Reporter Exposes the Truth about Globalization, Corporate Cons, and High Finance Fraudsters* (London: Pluto Press, 2002), 6–43; and Vincent Bugliosi, *The Betrayal of America: How the Supreme Court Undermined the Constitution and Chose Our President* (New York: Thunders Mouth Press/Nation Books, 2001). For an analysis of the erosion of voting rights in the past two decades, see J. Morgan Kousser, *Colorblind Injustice: Minority Voting Rights and the Undoing of the Second Reconstruction* (Chapel Hill: University of North Carolina Press, 1999).

4. U.S. Commission on Civil Rights, *Voting Irregularities in Florida*, iv.

5. Charles Thompson to Warren G. Harding, September 20, 1920, roll 36, frames 957–959, Warren G. Harding Papers, Ohio Historical Society (microfilm edition), Manuscript Division, Library of Congress, hereafter cited as Harding Papers.

6. Nan Elizabeth Woodruff, *American Congo: The African American Freedom Struggle in the Delta* (Cambridge: Harvard University Press, 2003); Earl Lewis, *In Their Own Interests: Race, Class, and Power in Twentieth-Century Norfolk, Virginia* (Berkeley and Los Angeles: University of California Press, 1990); Brian Kelly, *Race, Class, and Power in the Alabama Coalfields, 1908–1921*

(Urbana: University of Illinois Press, 2001); Steven A. Reich, "Soldiers of Democracy: Black Texans and the Fight for Citizenship, 1917–1921," *Journal of American History* 92 (March 1996), 1478–1504; Glenda Gilmore, *Gender and Jim Crow: Women and the Politics of White Supremacy in North Carolina, 1896–1920* (Chapel Hill: University of North Carolina Press, 1996); Tera W. Hunter, *To 'Joy My Freedom: Southern Black Women's Lives and Labors after the Civil War* (Cambridge: Harvard University Press, 1997).

7. These interviews appear in William Chafe et al., eds., *Remembering Jim Crow: African Americans Tell about Life in the Segregated South* (New York: New Press, 2001).

8. Stewart E. Tolnay and E. M. Beck, *A Festival of Violence: An Analysis of Southern Lynchings, 1882–1930* (Chicago: University of Illinois Press, 1995), 37–38.

9. Alexander Keyssar, *The Right to Vote: The Contested History of Democracy in the United States* (New York: Basic Books, 2000), 117–171.

10. This literature includes Elsa Barkley Brown, "To Catch the Vision of Freedom: Reconstructing Southern Black Women's Political History, 1865–1880," in Ann D. Gordon, ed., *African American Women and the Vote, 1837–1965* (Amherst: University of Massachusetts Press, 1997), 66–99; Darlene Clark Hine, *Black Women in White: Racial Conflict in the Nursing Profession, 1890–1950* (Bloomington: Indiana University Press, 1989); Deborah Gray White, *Too Heavy a Load: Black Women in Defense of Themselves, 1894–1994* (New York: W. W. Norton, 1999); Nell Irvin Painter, *Exodusters: Black Migration to Kansas after Reconstruction* (New York: Alfred A. Knopf, 1976); Evelyn Brooks Higginbotham, *Righteous Discontent: The Women's Movement in the Black Baptist Church, 1880–1920* (Cambridge: Harvard University Press, 1993); Peter Rachleff, *Black Labor in Richmond, 1865–1890.* (Urbana: University of Illinois Press, 1989); Robin D. G. Kelley, *Hammer and Hoe: Alabama Communists during the Great Depression* (Chapel Hill: University of North Carolina Press, 1990); Robin D. G. Kelley, *Race Rebels: Culture, Politics, and the Black Working Class* (New York: Free Press, 1994); Joe Trotter, *Coal, Class, and Color: Blacks in Southern West Virginia, 1915–32* (Urbana: University of Illinois Press, 1990); Cynthia Neverdon-Morton, *Afro-American Women of the South and the Advancement of the Race, 1895–1925* (Knoxville: University of Tennessee Press, 1989); Neil R. McMillen, *Dark Journey: Black Mississippians in the Age of Jim Crow* (Urbana: University of Illinois Press, 1989); Leon Litwack, *Trouble in Mind: Black Southerners in the Age of Jim Crow* (New York: Alfred A. Knopf, 1998); Kevin K. Gaines, *Uplifting the Race: Black Leadership, Politics, and Culture in the Twentieth Century* (Chapel Hill: University of North Carolina Press, 1996); Hazel V. Carby, *Reconstructing Womanhood: The Emergence of the Afro-American Woman Novelist* (New York: Oxford University Press, 1987); Grace Elizabeth Hale, *Making Whiteness: The Culture of Segregation in the South,*

1890–1940 (New York: Vintage Books, 1998); George C. Wright, *Racial Violence in Kentucky, 1865–1940* (Baton Rouge: Louisiana State University Press, 1990); Jacqueline Jones, *American Work: Four Centuries of Black and White Labor* (New York: W. W. Norton, 1998); Greta de Jong, *A Different Day: African American Struggles for Justice in Rural Louisiana, 1900–1970* (Chapel Hill: University of North Carolina Press, 2002); and Kelly, *Race, Class, and Power in the Alabama Coalfields.*

11. Brown, "To Catch the Vision of Freedom"; Rachleff, *Black Labor in Richmond;* Lewis, *In Their Own Interests.*

12. Hunter, *To 'Joy My Freedom;* Kelley, *Race Rebels* and *Hammer and Hoe.*

13. Gilmore, *Gender and Jim Crow;* Higginbotham, *Righteous Discontent.*

14. Richard Kluger, *Simple Justice: The History of Brown v. Board of Education and Black America's Struggle for Equality* (New York: Vintage Books, 1977), 136.

15. Charles M. Payne, *I've Got the Light of Freedom : The Organizing Tradition and the Mississippi Freedom Struggle* (Berkeley and Los Angeles: University of California Press, 1995).

16. "The Afro-American League," *New York Freeman,* August 6, 1887.

17. Zora Neale Hurston, *Dust Tracks on a Road* (1942; reprint, New York: HarperCollins, 1996), 190.

18. C. L. R. James argued that racial oppression and labor repression intersected. "The Negro must be kept in his place," James noted. "As worker, as tenant-farmer, as sharecropper, he is at the mercy of his employer and he must be terrorized into acceptance of whatever conditions of life are offered to him." James, *History of Negro Revolt* (London: *Fact* Monograph No. 18, 1938), 64–65. Also see Oliver Cox, *Caste, Class, and Race: A Study in Social Dynamics* (New York: Doubleday, 1948; reprint, London: Modern Reader Paperbacks, 1970); and Jeffrey B. Perry, ed., *A Hubert Harrison Reader* (Middletown: Wesleyan University Press, 2001), 55–57. As Darlene Clark Hine has recently stated: "The white supremacists' major goal, after all, was to maintain a pliable, exploitable labor force that would remain permanently in a subordinate place." Clark Hine, "Black Professionals and Race Consciousness: Origins of the Civil Rights Movement, 1890–1950," *Journal of American History* 89, no. 4 (March 2003), 1280.

19. Nancy A. Hewitt, *Southern Discomfort: Women's Activism in Tampa, Florida, 1880s-1920s* (Urbana: University of Illinois Press, 2001); Winston James, *Holding Aloft the Banner of Ethiopia: Caribbean Radicalism in Early Twentieth-Century America* (London: Verso, 1998), 232–257.

20. V. O. Key, Jr., *Southern Politics in Race and Nation* (1949; Knoxville: University of Tennessee Press, 1984), 83,85.

21. Audrey Thomas McCluskey, "Ringing Up a School: Mary McLeod Bethune's Impact on Daytona," *Florida Historical Quarterly* 73 (October 1994), 202.

1. "The Van Buren," *Pensacola Gazette,* December 27, 1834.

2. This narrative is adapted from Howard Thurman, *Jesus and the Disinherited* (1949; Boston: Beacon Press, 1996), 30–31.

3. Howard Thurman, *The Luminous Darkness: A Personal Interpretation of the Anatomy of Segregation and the Ground of Hope* (New York: Harper and Row, 1965; Richmond, IN: Friends United Press, 1999), x. See also Howard Thurman, *With Head and Heart: The Autobiography of Howard Thurman* (New York: Harcourt Brace, 1979), 20–21.

4. Thurman, *The Luminous Darkness,* 101–102.

5. Walter Earl Fluker and Catherine Tumber, eds., *A Strange Freedom: The Best of Howard Thurman on Religious Experience and Public Life* (Boston: Beacon Press, 1998), 6.

6. See Susie King Taylor, *A Black Woman's Civil War Memoirs,* ed. Patricia W. Romero and Willie Lee Rose (1902; Princeton: Markus Wiener, 1997), 25–34; Chafe et al., *Remembering Jim Crow,* 56–88; and Kathleen Clark, "Celebrating Freedom: Emancipation Day Celebrations and African American Memory in the Early Reconstruction South," in W. Fitzhugh Brundage, ed., *Where These Memories Grow: History, Memory, and Southern Identity* (Chapel Hill: University of North Carolina Press, 2000), 107–132. For other examples of Florida survival stories passed down by elders to younger folk, see Martha Harvey Farmer interview by author, August 21, 1997, Behind the Veil Collection.

7. Zora Neale Hurston, *Every Tongue Got to Confess: Negro Folk-Tales from the Gulf South* (New York: HarperCollins, 2001).

8. Malachia Andrews interviewed by author, Behind the Veil Collection.

9. Jane Landers, "Gracia Real de Santa Teresa de Mose: A Free Black Town in Spanish Colonial Florida," *American Historical Review* 95 (February 1990), 9–30.

10. Ibid., 30.

11. Peter H. Wood, *Black Majority: Negroes in Colonial South Carolina from 1670 through the Stono Rebellion* (New York: Alfred A. Knopf, 1974), 23. David Robertson, *Denmark Vesey* (New York: Alfred A. Knopf, 1999), 23.

12. Benjamin Quarles, *The Negro in the American Revolution* (Chapel Hill: University of North Carolina Press, 1961, 1996), 173; Claudio Saunt, *A New Order of Things: Property, Power, and the Transformation of the Creek Indians, 1733–1816* (London: Cambridge University Press, 1999), 273–290; Ira Berlin, *Many Thousands Gone: The First Two Centuries of Slavery in North America* (Cambridge: Harvard University Press, 1998), 326–328.

13. Larry Eugene Rivers, *Slavery in Florida: Territorial Days to Emancipation* (Gainesville: University Press of Florida, 2000), 189–209; John K. Mahon and

Brent R. Weisman, "Florida's Seminole and Miccosukee Peoples," in Michael Gannon, ed., *The New History of Florida* (Gainesville: University Press of Florida, 1996), 183–206.

14. Claudio Saunt, "'The English Has Now a Mind to Make Slaves of Them All': Creeks, Seminoles, and the Problem of Slavery," *American Indian Quarterly* 22 (winter–spring 1998), 157.

15. For the war, see Joel W. Martin, *Sacred Revolt: The Muskogees' Struggle for a New World* (Boston: Beacon Press, 1991).

16. Alexis de Tocqueville, *Democracy in America,* ed. Daniel J. Boorstin (New York: Vintage, 1990), 1: 347. The French observer was stunned at the "rapacity" of the white settlers who had already pounded the Muskogees to a "half-decimated" state. 1: 351.

17. Kenneth Wiggins Porter, *The Black Seminoles: History of a Freedom-Seeking People,* ed. Alcione M. Amos and Thomas P. Senter (Gainesville: University Press of Florida, 1996), 6. Historian George Klos argues, "A Seminole was more of a patron than a master; the Seminole slave system was akin to tenant farming." Klos, "Blacks and the Seminole Removal Debate, 1821–1835," in David R. Colburn and Jane L. Landers, eds., *The African American Heritage of Florida* (Gainesville: University Press of Florida, 1995), 130.

18. Mary Frances Berry, *Black Resistance, White Law: A History of Constitutional Racism in America* (1971; New York: Penguin Books, 1994), 31–52. Saunt, *A New Order of Things,* 237. See also Kevin Mulroy, *Freedom on the Border: The Seminole Maroons in Florida, the Indian Territory, Coahuila, and Texas* (Lubbock: Texas Tech University Press, 1993), 4; Minnie Moore-Nelson, *The Seminoles of Florida* (Philadelphia: American Printing House, 1896), 9; Kenneth Wiggins Porter, "The Episode of Osceola's Wife: Fact or Fiction?" *Florida Historical Quarterly* 26 (July 1947), 93; George A. McCall, *Letters from the Frontiers: Written During a Period of Thirty Years' Service in the Army of the United States* (Philadelphia: J. B. Lippincott, 1868); Paul E. Hoffman, *Florida's Frontiers* (Bloomington: Indiana University Press, 2002), 274–281, 303–306; Wiggins, *The Black Seminoles;* and David S. Heidler and Jeane T. Heidler, *Old Hickory's War: Andrew Jackson and the Quest for Empire* (Mechanicsburg, PA: Stackpole Books, 1996), 3.

19. Berry, *Black Resistance, White Law,* 31–32; Laurence Foster, "Negro-Indian Relationships in the Southeast" (M.A. thesis, University of Pennsylvania, 1935), 22–23.

20. "Speech of Mr. Giddings," *Colored American,* March 13, 1841; W. E. B. Du Bois, *Black Reconstruction in America: An Essay toward a History of the Part Which Black Folk Played in the Attempt to Reconstruct Democracy in America, 1860–1880* (1935; reprint, New York: Free Press, 1965), 511; Berry, *Black Resistance, White Law,* 27–52.

21. William S. Coker and Susan R. Parker, "The Second Spanish Period in the Two Floridas," in Gannon, *The New History of Florida*, 163–164.

22. Woodburne Potter, *The War in Florida*, (Baltimore: Lewis and Coleman, 1836), 45.

23. Rivers, *Slavery in Florida*, 219; Canter Brown, Jr., "Race Relations in Territorial Florida, 1821–1845," *Florida Historical Quarterly* 73 (1995), 287–307.

24. Wiggins, *The Black Seminoles*, 66; Mulroy, *Freedom on the Border*, 29.

25. Charles Bingham Reynolds, *Old Saint Augustine: A Story of Three Centuries* (St. Augustine: E. H. Reynolds, 1888), 113.

26. For narrative accounts of slave resistance in antebellum Florida see Jonathan Walker, *Trial and Imprisonment of Jonathan Walker at Pensacola, Florida* (Boston: Anti-Slavery Office, 1850); and Franklin Y. Fitch, *The Life, Travels and Adventures of an American Wanderer* (New York: John W. Lovell Company, 1883), 38–41. For a broader discussion of slave resistance, see Raymond Bauer and Alice Bauer, "Day to Day Resistance to Slavery," *Journal of Negro History* 27 (October 1942), 388–419. African Americans used diverse methods of surviving and resisting racial oppression. Peter Wood (*Black Majority*, 285) argues that historians should carefully examine each act of resistance and avoid blanket statements. "To separate their reactions into docility on the one hand and rebellion on the other, as has occasionally been done, is to underestimate the complex nature of the contradictions each Negro felt in the face of new provocations and new penalties. It is more realistic to think in terms of a spectrum of response, ranging from complete submission to total resistance, along which any given individual could be located at a given time."

27. Ira Berlin, Marc Favreau, and Steven F. Miller, eds., *Remembering Slavery: African Americans Talk about Their Personal Experiences of Slavery and Emancipation* (New York: New Press, 1998), xxiv.

28. *Floridian and Advocate*, October 6, 1829, typescript copy in Red Hills of Florida Collection, Special Collections Library, Florida State University.

29. "Runaways," quoted in the *Floridian*, June 8, 1833, Red Hills of Florida Collection.

30. "Negro History, Pensacola," Box A879, Folder, "Florida Historical Material, 1936–1939," Federal Writers' Project, Works Progress Administration Papers, Manuscript Division, Library of Congress; hereafter cited as WPA Papers, Library of Congress. For the range of punishments inflicted on rebellious slaves in a Pensacola jail, see Walker, *Trial and Imprisonment*, 24–33.

31. For announcements of these ordinances, see *Apalachicola Gazette*, March 1, 1838, and April 18, 1840; *Apalachicola Commercial Advertiser*, December 28, 1844, and March 1, 1845; and *Apalachicola Courier*, November 12, 1839. These clippings appear in Mrs. Patrick Jeremiah Lovett, *Excerpts and*

Articles Pertaining to Apalachicola and Area (Birmingham, AL: 1962). For a broader discussion of social control ordinances aimed at free blacks in antebellum Florida, see "Code of Florida," *Colored American,* October 13, 1838.

32. Diary of A. M. Reed, typescript copy, Special Collections Library, Duke University (hereafter cited as A. M. Reed Diary); Daniel L. Schafer, "Freedom Was as Close as the River," in Colburn and Landers, *The African American Heritage of Florida,* 157.

33. U.S. House of Representatives, *Official Records of the Union and Confederate Navies in the War of the Rebellion,* 56th Congress, 2nd Session (Washington, DC: Government Printing Office, 1901), 572, 575.

34. Ibid., 584.

35. Benjamin Quarles, *The Negro in the Civil War* (1953; reprint, New York: Da Capo Press, 1989), 54, 62, 70. Schafer, "Freedom Was as Close as the River." "A Good Letter From a Soldier," *Christian Recorder,* December 10, 1864.

36. Noah Andre Trudeau, *Like Men of War: Black Troops in the Civil War, 1862–1865* (Boston: Little, Brown, 1998), 151; David J. Coles, " 'They Fought Like Devils': Black Troops in Florida during the Civil War," in Mark I. Greenberg, William Warren Rogers, and Canter Brown, Jr., eds., *Florida's Heritage of Diversity: Essays in Honor of Samuel Proctor* (Tallahassee Sentry Press, 1997), 38–39.

37. *Chelsea Telegraph and Pioneer,* March 5, 1865, cited in: Olustee Battlefield Historic Site Web Page, http://128.227.218.85/Olustee.

38. Rivers, *Slavery in Florida,* 245.

39. Catherine C. Hopley (pseud. Sarah E. Jones), *Life in the South; From the Commencement of the War, By a Blockaded British Subject* (London: Chapman and Hall, 1863), 282. For a larger discussion of women's resistance during the Civil War, see Tracy J. Revels, "Grander in Her Daughters: Florida's Women during the Civil War," *Florida Historical Quarterly* 77 (Winter 1999), 261–282.

40. Hopley, *Life in the South,* 282.

41. "Letter From 3rd U.S.C.T. July 27th, 1865," *Christian Recorder,* August 12, 1865.

42. Whitelaw Reid, *After the War: A Southern Tour* (1866; reprint, New York: Harper Torchbooks, 1965), 162; Susan Bradford Eppes, *Through Some Eventful Years* (Macon, GA: J. W. Burke Press, 1926), 279.

43. The following narrative is based on Reid, *After the War,* 182–193. Reid was so struck by this story that he returned a second time to corroborate the details with Cornish and his wife. For additional information on Sandy Cornish, see Mitch Kachun, *Festivals of Freedom: Memory and Meaning in African American Emancipation Celebrations, 1808–1915* (Boston: University of Massachusetts Press, 2003), 106–107.

44. Reid, *After the War,* 189.

45. Literature on comparative post-emancipation societies includes Frederick Cooper, Thomas C. Holt, and Rebecca J. Scott, *Beyond Slavery: Explorations of Race, Labor, and Citizenship in Postemancipation Societies* (Chapel Hill: University of North Carolina Press, 2000); Thomas C. Holt, *The Problem of Freedom: Race, Labor, and Politics in Jamaica and Britain, 1832–1938* (Baltimore: Johns Hopkins University Press, 1992); Ada Ferrer, *Insurgent Cuba: Race, Nation, and Revolution, 1868–1898* (Chapel Hill: University of North Carolina Press, 1999); Ron Ramdin, *From Chattel Slave to Wage Earner: A History of Trade Unionism in Trinidad and Tobago* (London: Martin Brian & O'Keeffe, 1982); and Frederick Cooper, *From Slaves to Squatters: Plantation Labor and Agriculture in Zanzibar and Coastal Kenya, 1890–1925* (New Haven: Yale University Press, 1980).

1. THE PROMISE OF RECONSTRUCTION

1. Du Bois, *Black Reconstruction in America*, 670. The definitive work on Reconstruction in Florida is Jerrell H. Shofner, *Nor Is It Over Yet: Florida in the Era of Reconstruction, 1863–1877* (Gainesville: University Presses of Florida, 1974). Professor Shofner's work superseded that of William Watson Davis, a disciple of Columbia historian William Dunning. See Davis, *The Civil War and Reconstruction in Florida* (New York: Columbia University Press, 1913). The earliest comprehensive study of Florida's Reconstruction is John Wallace, *Carpetbag Rule in Florida: The Inside Workings of the Reconstruction of Civil Government in Florida After the Close of the Civil War* (Jacksonville: Da Costa Printing and Publishing House, 1888). Also see Joe M. Richardson, *The Negro in the Reconstruction of Florida, 1865–1877* (Tallahassee: Florida State University, 1965).

2. "Letter from Jax," *Christian Recorder*, September 28, 1867. The *Recorder* was the national organ of the African Methodist Episcopal Church and enjoyed a wide circulation among African Americans in the southern states.

3. Jacob A. Remly to S. S. McHenry, Feb 28, 1867, roll 15, frame 484, Records of the Assistant Commissioner and Subordinate Field Offices for the State of Florida, Bureau of Refugees, Freedmen, and Abandoned Lands, 1865–1872, Department of Special Collections, P. K. Yonge Library of Florida History, University of Florida, and National Archives and Records Administration, Washington, DC, 2002; hereafter cited as Freedmen's Bureau Papers. For the work of the bureau in Florida, see Richardson, *The Negro in the Reconstruction of Florida.*

4. Jacob A. Remly to S. S. McHenry, April 30, 1867, roll 15, frames 490–491; Remly to McHenry, July 31, 1867, roll 15, frames 499–504, Freedmen's Bureau Papers.

5. Jacob A. Remly Report, September 10, 1868, roll 15, frame 688; Remly Report, October 31, 1868, roll 15, frame 544, Freedmen's Bureau Papers.

6. Larry Rivers and Canter Brown, Jr., *Laborers in the Vineyard of the Lord: The Beginnings of the AME Church in Florida, 1865* (Gainesville: University Press of Florida, 2001), 31–32.

7. "Suffrage," *Christian Recorder*, February 17, 1866. Around the same time, Rev. J. C. Gibbs was an active participant in the Colored People's Convention of South Carolina, a convention that sent a petition to Congress calling for black suffrage. Gibbs later served as secretary of state in Florida (1868–1873) as well as the superintendent of public instruction (1873–1874). See Philip S. Foner and George E. Walker, vol. 2 of *Proceedings of the Black State Conventions, 1840–1865* (Philadelphia: Temple University Press, 1980), 284–303.

8. John Hope Franklin and Alfred A. Moss, Jr., *From Slavery to Freedom: A History of Negro Americans*, 6th ed. (New York: McGraw-Hill, 1988), 208.

9. "Letter from 3rd U.S.C.T. July 27th, 1865," *Christian Recorder*, August 12, 1865.

10. "The Italy of America," *Fort Myers Press*, October 31, 1885. Another writer exulted: "what Southern France or Italy are to Europeans, Florida is to Americans." "A Card, William Hewitt," *Florida Dispatch,* November 28, 1877. Edward King, *The Great South: A Record of Journeys* (Hartford, CT: American Publishing Co., 1875).

11. Dennis Eagan, *Sixth Annual Report of the Commissioner of Lands and Immigration of the State of Florida for the Year Ending December 31, 1874* (Tallahassee: Charles H. Walton, 1874), 47.

12. "Florida vs. California," *Florida Times-Union,* June 5, 1887

13. The literature on African Americans in Reconstruction has grown considerably in the last few decades. See Willie Lee Rose, *Rehearsal for Reconstruction: The Port Royal Experiment* (1964; New York: Oxford University Press, 1976); Thomas Holt, *Black over White: Negro Political Leadership in South Carolina during Reconstruction* (Urbana: University of Illinois Press, 1977); Gerald Jaynes, *Branches without Roots: Genesis of the Black Working Class in the American South, 1862–1882* (New York: Oxford University Press, 1986); Julie Saville, *The Work of Reconstruction: From Slave To Wage Laborer in South Carolina, 1860–1870* (New York: Cambridge University Press, 1994); Eric Foner, *Reconstruction: America's Unfinished Revolution, 1863–1877* (New York: Harper & Row, 1988); Laura Edwards, *Gendered Strife and Confusion: The Politics of Reconstruction* (Urbana: University of Illinois Press, 1997); Michael L. Lanza, *Agrarianism and Reconstruction Politics: The Southern Homestead Act* (Baton Rouge: Louisiana State University Press, 1990); Rachleff, *Black Labor in Richmond;* David Montgomery, *Beyond Equality: Labor and the Radical Republicans, 1865–1872* (1967; Urbana: University of Illinois Press, 1972); and Ira Berlin et al., eds., *Freedom: A Documentary History of Emancipation, 1861–1867*, Series 1, vol. 3, *The Wartime Genesis of Free Labor: The Lower South* (New York: Cambridge University Press, 1990).

14. Richard Nelson Current, *Those Terrible Carpetbaggers: A Reinterpretation* (New York: Oxford University Press, 1988), 85.

15. "Description of Leon County, Florida," *Semi-Tropical* (July, 1876), 403. Florida native T. Thomas Fortune pointedly observed: "Gov Reed never did anything well in his life." *New York Globe*, May 12, 1883.

16. Harrison Reed to David Yulee, Feb. 16, 1868, Box 7, folder "Correspondence, Business & Legal paper, 1862–1866," David L. Yulee Papers, P. K. Yonge Library of Florida History, University of Florida; hereafter cited as Yulee Papers

17. For collusion between northern and southern wings of the political parties, see Shofner, *Nor Is It Over Yet*, 194. See also Lawrence N. Powell, *New Masters: Northern Planters during the Civil War and Reconstruction* (New Haven: Yale University Press, 1980), 139; Joseph A. Fry, *Henry S. Sanford: Diplomacy and Business in Nineteenth-Century America* (Reno: University of Nevada Press, 1982), 88; Edward C. Williamson, *Florida Politics in the Gilded Age, 1877–1893* (Gainesville: University Presses of Florida, 1976), 185; and Frederic Bancroft, ed., *Speeches, Correspondence and Political Papers of Carl Schurz*, vol. 1 (New York: G. P. Putnam's Sons, 1913), 333–334, 342.

18. Paul M. Gaston observes: "Southerners were told by *DeBow's Review* that the region must industrialize, diversify its staple-crop agriculture system, seek immigrants and capital from the North and from Europe, and infuse the region with a new spirit of business enterprise." Gaston, *The New South Creed: A Study in Southern Mythmaking* (Baton Rouge: Louisiana State University Press, 1970), 25. For agricultural diversification in Florida, see *A Graphic Review of Florida Agriculture* (Tallahassee: Florida Department of Agriculture, 1938).

19. I hold that the particular kind of economic development that occurred in Florida was not inevitable; nor was it a function of abstract "market forces." The work of Africanists has been especially important in developing this point. Frederick Cooper warns scholars to avoid falling into the trap of rationalizing economic oppression: "One frequently finds the same tendency to mistake particular structures for universal laws of behavior, to confuse 'the economy' or 'the society' with the interests of particular classes taken within specific structures as part of a self-propelled movement toward development or modernity." Cooper, *From Slaves to Squatters: Plantation Labor and Agriculture in Zanzibar and Coastal Kenya, 1890–1925* (New Haven: Yale University Press, 1980), 6. Walter Rodney urged students to study the concept of "development" in all of its political, environmental, and social dimensions. Rodney notes, "Development in the past has always meant the increase in the ability to guard the independence of the social group and indeed to infringe upon the freedom of others— something that often came about irrespective of the will of the persons within the societies involved." Rodney, *How Europe Underdeveloped Africa* (Washington, DC: Howard University Press, 1982), 105, 4.

20. Harriet Beecher Stowe, *Palmetto Leaves* (1873; reprint, Gainesville: University of Florida Press, 1968), x. For a later overview of Stowe's Florida plantation experiences, see, Stowe, "Our Florida Plantation," *Atlantic Monthly* (May 1879), 641–649. Also see John T. Foster and Sarah Whitmer Foster, *Beechers, Stowes, and Yankee Strangers: The Transformation of Florida* (Gainesville: University Press of Florida, 1999), 46–58.

21. Stowe to Duchess of Argyll, February 19, 1866, in Charles Edward Stowe, *Life of Harriet Beecher Stowe: Compiled from Her Letters and Journals* (Boston: Houghton Mifflin, 1891), 397. Eric Foner writes, "For even those Republicans most active in efforts to extend the legal rights of free Negroes insisted that black men must prove themselves capable of economic advancement before they could expect full recognition of their equality." Foner, *Free Soil, Free Labor, Free Men: The Ideology of the Republican Party before the Civil War* (New York: Oxford, 1970), 298.

22. Stowe to Charles Beecher, May 29, 1867, in Charles Edward Stowe, *Life of Harriet Beecher Stowe,* 402.

23. "Rev. Scull's Report" (1866), *Protestant Episcopal Church in the USA, Journal of the Convention of the Diocese of Florida* (Microfilm, 10 reels, Atlanta: SOLINET, 1992), reel 1, frames, 23–24.

24. Stowe, *Palmetto Leaves,* 279.

25. Observing black longshoremen laboring in Fernandina on a blistering summer day, Stowe marveled: "A gang of negroes, great, brawny, muscular fellows, seemed to make a perfect frolic of this job, which, under such a sun, would have threatened sunstroke to any white man." Ibid., 282.

26. Ibid., 287. Stowe held ideas similar to those of Quaker "free labor" advocates in post-emancipation British East Africa. See Cooper, *From Slaves to Squatters,* 44–45.

27. Stowe, *Palmetto Leaves,* 309–310.

28. Ibid., 298. One employer in Cedar Key wrote in 1867: "The prospects of our section of the State is gloomy as the negroes won't work and when they engage to do so are not to be relied upon." Unsigned Letter, n.d., File 5, Washington J. Lutterloh Papers, Southern Historical Collection, University of North Carolina, Chapel Hill.

29. Stowe, *Palmetto Leaves,* 307–308.

30. Ibid., 314.

31. Mary B. Graff, *Mandarin on the St. Johns* (Gainesville: University of Florida Press, 1963), 82–83.

32. "Land and Labor," *Christian Recorder,* May 31, 1877.

33. Another visitor to Florida, Abbie M. Brooks, complained that African American women workers preferred going into business for themselves to avoid "working and ironing" for white people. Diary entry, May 31, 1873, Abbie M.

Brooks Diary, Special Collections Library, Duke University; hereafter cited as Abbie M. Brooks Diary.

34. Thomas C. Holt (*The Problem of Freedom*, xxiii) notes that in the British West Indies a similar political drama was unfolding in post-emancipation Jamaica: "While planters preferred coercion, and policymakers voluntary wage labor, neither accepted the right of the freed people to choose an alternate path." In noting the multiple ways that courts enforced employers' coercive control over the labor process in the early republic, Christopher Tomlins writes, "On close inspection, the vista of freedom celebrated as the early republic's mark of modernity dissolves to reveal a less-elevated landscape." Tomlins, *Law, Labor, and Ideology in the Early American Republic* (Cambridge: Cambridge University Press, 1993), 390. David Montgomery notes that by mid-century, liberal reformers in the North adopted increasingly harsh laws known as "vagrancy" or "tramp laws" to compel workers to work. These laws became a staple of the Gilded Age South. Montgomery, *Citizen Worker: The Experience of Workers in the United States with Democracy and the Free Market during the Nineteenth Century* (Cambridge: Cambridge University Press, 1993), 83–88. This recent scholarship suggests that scholars may have to readjust their thinking on the level of faith that nineteenth-century reformers who came south after the Civil War placed in "free labor." For an earlier formulation of this ideology, see Foner, *Reconstruction*, 166–167. For a study of vagrancy statutes in colonial America, see Richard B. Morris, *Government and Labor in Early America* (New York: Columbia University Press, 1946), 3–16. For this racial ideology in French West Africa, see Frederick Cooper, *Decolonization and African Society: The Labor Question in French and British Africa* (Cambridge: Cambridge University Press, 1996), 151.

35. Du Bois, *Black Reconstruction*, 384. For labor conflicts during Reconstruction and the way that class interacted with race, see Barbara Fields, "Ideology and Race in American History," in J. Morgan Kousser and James M. McPherson, eds., *Region, Race, and Reconstruction: Essays in Honor of C. Vann Woodward* (New York: Oxford University Press, 1982), 165.

36. Du Bois, *Black Reconstruction*, 139. Florida's Black Code was a direct carryover from antebellum efforts to dominate and control free blacks. See "Code of Florida," *Colored American*, October 13, 1838; For discussions of Florida's Black Codes, see Shofner, *Nor Is It Over Yet*, 52; William Cohen, *At Freedom's Edge: Black Mobility and the Southern White Quest for Racial Control, 1861–1915* (Baton Rouge: Louisiana State University Press, 1991), 30; Foner, *Reconstruction*, 200; Stetson Kennedy, *Palmetto Country* (New York: Duell, Sloan & Pearce, 1942), 90–91; and Wali Rashash Kharif, "Refinement of Racial Segregation in Florida" (diss., Florida State University, 1983), 28–33.

37. Cohen, *At Freedom's Edge*, 228.

38. Letter to the Editor, *New York Tribune*, February 17, 1877.

39. Stowe, *Palmetto Leaves*, 315.

40. "An Ex-Milwaukeean in Florida," *Sunland Tribune* (Tampa), July 3, 1879.

41. James Woods Davidson, *The Florida of Today: A Guide For Tourists and Settlers* (New York: D. Appleton and Co., 1889), 113–114.

42. William A. Edwards, M.D., *Southern Florida: A Winter Sanitarium* (Philadelphia: Philadelphia Medical Times, 1886).

43. *Edinburgh Courant*, October 11, 1883, cited in *Florida Land and Mortgage Company (Limited)*, n.d., 21.

44. Eagan, *Sixth Annual Report*, 179. See also "Florida and Italy Compared and Contrasted," *Semi-Tropical*, July 1876.

45. "On the Labor Problem," *New York Globe*, April 28, 1883. For examples, see Iza Duffus Hardy, *Between Two Oceans: Or, Sketches of American Travel* (London: Hurst and Blacket, 1884), 333; and J. H. Beale, *Picturesque Sketches of American Progress* (New York: The Empire Co-Operative Association, 1889), 142.

46. Dr. W. B. Shoemaker, *Florida As It Is: It Tells All About the Industries of the State, Its Climate and Resources* (Newville, PA: Times Steam Print, 1887).

47. Cooper, *From Slaves to Squatters*, 2–3.

48. *The New York and Mobile Turpentine Manufacturing Company* (New York: E. A. Kingsland & Co., 1866), 8, Perkins Library Pamphlet Collection, Perkins Library, Duke University. There was a crude logic to this firm's political rhetoric. The company's directors expected it to begin garnering a net profit of $27,090 after only one year of operation and precariously low operating expenses ($24,030). The estimated wages of the turpentine workers would not have strained the company's plans.

49. Oliver Martin Crosby, *Florida Facts Both Bright and Blue: A Guidebook* (New York: 1887), 125.

50. Ibid., 21.

51. Ibid., 23. A major guide book that celebrated black disfranchisement as a boon to growth was "Dedicated to the Businessmen of the North." Hilary A. Herbert et al., *Why the Solid South? Or, Reconstruction and Its Results* (Baltimore: R. H. Woodward, 1890). For similar views, see James McQuade, *The Cruise of the Montauk: To Bermuda, The West Indies and Florida* (New York: Thomas R. Knox, 1885), 206, 217.

52. Jerrell H. Shofner, "The Labor League of Jacksonville: A Negro Union and White Strikebreakers," *Florida Historical Quarterly* 50 (January 1972), 278–282; Shofner, "Militant Negro Laborers in Reconstruction Florida," *Journal of Southern History* 39, no. 3 (August 1973), 397–408.

53. "What Will the Democrats Do?" *Florida Patriot*, October 23, 1880, in folder 107, L'Engle Papers, Southern Historical Collection, University of North Carolina, Chapel Hill. Canter Brown, Jr. offers invaluable portraits of Wallace

and other African American politicians in *Florida's Black Public Officials, 1867–1924* (Tuscaloosa: University of Alabama Press, 1998). Wallace's viewpoint jibed with that of D. Augustus Straker, a black political leader who left South Carolina after the end of Reconstruction. "The poor laborer's political will is yet manacled by his employer, the capitalist," Straker argued, "and he is asked to bow or starve. . . . This belittling condition is the result of the oppression of capital against labor." D. Augustus Straker, *The New South Investigated* (Detroit: Ferguson Company, 1888), 89–90.

54. U.S. Congress, *Testimony Taken by the Joint Select Committee to Inquire into the Condition of Affairs in the Late Insurrectionary States: Miscellaneous and Florida* (Washington, DC: Government Printing Office, 1872), 168; hereafter cited as *Florida Ku Klux Klan Hearings*.

55. *New York Globe*, June 30, 1883.

56. Wallace, *Carpetbag Rule in Florida*, 155.

57. "From the Land of Flowers," *Christian Recorder*, December 28, 1872.

58. "Another Church Gone," *Christian Recorder*, August 4, 1876.

59. *Great Southern Railway: A Trunk Line, Between the North and the Tropics, To Within Ninety Miles of Havana, Connecting at the Nearest possible Point With the West Indies, Central and South America* (New York: W. P. Hickock, 1878), 87.

60. "Notes of Travel Through the South," *Christian Recorder*, April 15, 1875. See also Eagan, *Sixth Annual Report*, 14–15.

61. "A Few Moments with the Leading Colored Men of Florida," *Christian Recorder*, October 21, 1871. For a report on black migrants to Marion County, see *Florida Dispatch*, February 6, 1878.

62. "Church and Things in Florida," *Christian Recorder*, May 31, 1877.

63. "Land and Labor," *Christian Recorder*, November 19, 1870.

64. Ibid.

65. "Experience with Farm Labor in Louisiana and Florida," *Florida Times-Union*, July 26, 1905. William D. Kelley, *The Old South and the New: A Series of Letters* (New York: G. P. Putnam's Sons, 1888), 16–33. See also Major Jones, *The Emigrants' Friend; Containing Information and Advice for Persons Intending to Emigrate to the United States* (London: Hamilton, Adams, 1880).

66. Eppes, *Through Some Eventful Years*, 356–357.

67. "Notes by the Way," *Christian Recorder*, March 29, 1883.

68. "The A.M.E. Conference," *Christian Recorder*, January 22, 1870. For the critical role played by the AME Church in Florida, see Rivers and Brown, *Laborers in the Vineyard of the Lord*.

69. *Florida Ku Klux Klan Hearings*, 171.

70. "Get Homes," *Christian Recorder*, July 26, 1877.

71. Ledyard Bill, *A Winter in Florida* (New York: Wood and Holbrook, 1870), 229.

72. Historian Charlton Tebeau writes: "Timber was the real prize at stake in many land deals during the Reconstruction era. The beneficiaries were not homesteaders, black or white, but influential men of all parties in the corrupt state government." Tebeau, *A History of Florida* (Coral Gables: University of Miami Press, 1972), 267. The end of Reconstruction in Florida would usher in an era of unprecedented state land giveaways to railroads and land companies at the expense of small farmers. See C. Vann Woodward, *Origins of the New South, 1877–1913* (Baton Rouge: Louisiana State University Press, 1951), 19–20.

73. Lanza, *Agrarianism and Reconstruction Politics,* 74. See also Bill, *A Winter in Florida,* 229.

74. "Lake City, Florida," *Christian Recorder,* July 20, 1882.

75. J. L. Miller, *A Guide into the South: An Open Gate to the Laborer, Large Returns to the Investor, An Index for the Traveler, A Great Welcome to the Deserving* (Atlanta: The Index Printing Co., 1910), 300–309. Another guidebook that elided the African American presence in rural Florida in order to promote white migration was A. A. Robinson, *Florida: A Pamphlet Descriptive of its History, Topography, Climate, Soil, Resources and Natural Advantages* (Tallahassee: Floridian Book and Job Office, 1882), 143.

76. Eagan, *Sixth Annual Report,* 145. Conversely, white Floridians were praised for staking out such homesteads.

77. *New York Evening Post,* April 3, 1873, cited in "Mr. Bryant in Florida," *Florida Historical Quarterly* 14, no. 4 (April 1936), 265. See also George M. Barbour, *Florida for Tourists, Invalids, and Settlers* (New York: D. Appleton, 1883), 234–240; "Education," *Florida Dispatch;* July 11, 1877; *Christian Recorder,* April 5, 1877; "Lake City," *Freeman* (Indianapolis), March 1, 1902.

78. "Letter from Tallahassee," *Christian Recorder,* June 10, 1871.

79. "Letter from Florida," *Christian Recorder,* November 14, 1868.

80. *Florida Ku Klux Klan Hearings,* 95–96.

81. "The Negro Problem," *Bartow Courier Informant,* May 10, 1893.

82. Historian Rowland Rerick stated that when the Democrats took control of Florida they "crippled the schools by decreasing the maximum county levy one-half." Rerick, *Memoirs of Florida,* ed. Francis P. Fleming, 2 vols. (Atlanta: The Southern Historical Association, 1902) 1: 341. Also see W. M. Sheats, "Twenty-Fifth and Twenty-Sixth Annual Reports of the Department of Public Instruction of Florida," in *Florida Message and Documents* (Tallahassee, 1895), 9–59.

83. For the low percentages of black Floridians who voted Democratic (11% in 1892), see J. Morgan Kousser, *The Shaping of Southern Politics: Suffrage Restriction and the Establishment of the One-Party South, 1880–1910* (New Haven: Yale University Press, 1974), 42.

84. Stewart Simkins to James Ormond, August 26, 1870, Box 1, folder, "Correspondence 1869, 1870," Ormond Family Papers. See also Charles

Dougherty to ?, July 21, 1878, Charles Dougherty Papers; both in P. K. Yonge Library of Florida History, University of Florida.

85. Brown, "To Catch the Vision of Freedom," 69. See also: Robert Cassanello, "The Great Migration, Migrants and Identity in the Making of New South Jacksonville, Florida, 1865–1920" (diss., Florida State University, 2000), 40–41.

86. For African American women's political activism see U.S. House of Representatives, *Bisbee v. Hull Contested Election,* 46th Congress, 1st Session, Misc. Doc. No. 26, 1879, 392–395, 427–431. See also *Florida Ku Klux Klan Hearings,* 236.

87. U.S. House of Representatives, *Bisbee v. Hull,* 431.

88. "Moorhead's Duel," *Florida Times-Union,* January 26, 1883.

89. "Facts for the Future," *Weekly Tallahasseean,* November 6, 1888.

90. King, *The Great South,* 414.

91. Barbour, *Florida for Tourists,* 238.

92. This cheap-labor ideology was promoted in the majority of Florida guidebooks of the nineteenth century, even when race was not explicitly mentioned. For example, a guidebook published under federal auspices asserted: "If the capitalist would desire to farm on a large scale, no better field than here. There are hundreds of large plantations in Middle Florida, lying contiguous, which can be bought low, and a farm of 100 to 10,000 acres can be made, and planted in cotton, cane, corn, rice, tobacco, and other corps, Labor is plenty and cheap, crops sure and good, always in demand, and fair prices rule." See James H. Foss, *Florida: Its Climate, Soil, Productions, and Agricultural Capabilities* (Washington, DC: Government Printing Office, 1882), 79.

93. Ralph L. Peek, "Aftermath of Military Reconstruction, 1868–1869," *Florida Historical Quarterly* 43 (October 1964), 123–141, and Peek, "Lawlessness in Florida, 1868–1871," *Florida Historical Quarterly* 40 (October 1961), 184. Peek's assessment of the Klan is: "The evidence shows that the violence was executed by the 'better sort' of white people, i.e., as distinguished from the 'cracker' class, or poorer element." "Lawlessness in Florida," 184. Michael Newton's recent history of the Klan in Florida concurs with this assessment. See Newton, *The Invisible Empire: The Ku Klux Klan in Florida* (Gainesville: University of Florida Press, 2001), 28–29.

94. Professor Emory Q. Hawk credited the KKK with paving the way for "economic progress in the South after 1880." Hawk acknowledged the demise of the Klan. "However, the Klan," he argued, "while in the hands of responsible leaders, was a powerful disintegrating force, operating in the very midst of the 'carpetbag' organization." Hawk, *Economic History of the South* (New York: Prentice-Hall, 1934), 443–445.

95. *Florida Ku Klux Klan Hearings,* 83. Palatka postmaster J. Andrew Shelley stated in 1938 that his father was the founder of the Reconstruction KKK in

Palatka while also serving as "sheriff of Putnam County, tax assessor and tax collector." Brian E. Michaels, *The River Flows North: A History of Putnam County, Florida* (Palatka: The Putnam County Archives and History Commission, 1976), 373.

96. *Florida Ku Klux Klan Hearings*, 107.

97. Ibid., 107, 114.

98. Ibid., 175.

99. Anna Robeson Burr, *Alice James: Her Brothers, Her Journal* (New York: Cornwall Press, 1934), 45–48.

100. *Florida Ku Klux Klan Hearings*, 222.

101. Ibid., 94.

102. "The Color Line," *Palatka Daily News*, April 8, 1887. Laura Edwards discusses this yearning by employers to re-create the coercive power over their employees that they enjoyed in slavery in "Captives of Wilmington: The Riot and Historical Memories of Political Conflict, 1865–1898," in David S. Cecelski and Timothy B. Tyson, eds., *Democracy Betrayed: The Wilmington Race Riot of 1898 and Its Legacy* (Chapel Hill: University of North Carolina Press, 1998), 126.

103. "The Color Line in Florida," *New York Tribune*, January 20, 1877.

104. "Ku Klux in Florida," *Christian Recorder*, November 27, 1873.

105. "Hints for the Consideration of White Men," n.d., Dr. F. A. Byrd Collection, Special Collections Library, Florida State University. This document was incorrectly processed in 1968 as a slavery-era document.

106. Ibid. (emphasis in original).

107. Franklin and Moss, *From Slavery to Freedom*, 228–230.

108. U.S. Senate, *Report of the Senate Committee on Privileges and Elections With the Testimony and Documentary on the Election in the State of Florida in 1876*, 44th Congress, 2nd Session (Washington, DC: Government Printing Office, 1877), 277, 336–337; hereafter cited as *Report of the Senate Committee on Privileges and Elections*.

109. Ibid., 46 (emphasis in original).

110. Ibid., 17.

111. U.S. House of Representatives, *Finley v. Bisbee Contested Election*, 45th Congress, 3rd Session, 1878–1879, Misc. Doc. No. 10, 408–415. For other examples of employer coercion in Jacksonville, see ibid., 553–558.

112. *Report of the Senate Committee on Privileges and Elections*, 431. Yulee's viewpoint was widely shared by industrial boosters throughout the South. See A. K. McClure, *The South: Its Industrial, Financial, and Political Condition* (Philadelphia: J. B. Lippincott, 1886), 218. In a subsequent election, where the Democratic Party took control of Palatka, a local correspondent celebrated the "Redemption" of his town and believed that it would bring an era of low taxes. See "City Election in Palatka," *Weekly Floridian*, April 8, 1884.

113. U.S. House of Representatives, *Finley v. Bisbee*, 414.

114. "Washington's Letter," *Florida Times-Union*, June 23, 1899

115. *Report of the Senate Committee on Privileges and Elections*, 346–347.

116. Ibid., 25.

117. Ibid., 27.

118. Evidence of coercion in the election found in ibid., 341, 94–96, 139–140; Shofner, *Nor Is It Over Yet*, 310–311; and Ralph L. Peek, "Election of 1870 and the End of Reconstruction in Florida," *Florida Historical Quarterly* 45 (April 1967), 352–368.

119. *Report of the Senate Committee on Privileges and Elections*, 325.

120. Shofner, *Nor Is It Over Yet*, 313–327; C. Vann Woodward, *Reunion and Reaction: The Compromise of 1877 and the End of Reconstruction* (1951; New York: Oxford University Press, 1991); Foner, *Reconstruction*, 575–582.

121. "A Talk With Gov. Drew," *New York Daily Tribune*, May 25, 1877.

122. Ibid.

123. William T. Cash, *History of the Democratic Party in Florida* (Tallahassee: Democratic Historical Foundation, 1936), 70.

124. J. Randall Stanley, *History of Gadsden County* (Quincy: Gadsden County Historical Commission, 1948), v. As another southern economic guidebook noted, "it is the assurance and confidence which the business world has that the whites of the South will continue through the Democratic Party to maintain their political supremacy, which causes it to retain hundreds of millions of dollars of investments which its capitalists already have here; and it is the confidence in the continuance of that rule which will cause them to continue to eagerly seek here other investments. On the other hand, let it be known to the business world that, by political revolution, white supremacy as represented in the Democratic party has been overthrown in Georgia, and that the Republican party, with its black cohorts, had grasped the reins of power in the State, and capital and investment would as promptly flee our borders as darkness follows the disappearance of the sun." Miller, *A Guide into the South*, 273.

125. Eppes, *Through Some Eventful Years*, 371.

126. "Shooting Affray in Hernando," *Sunland Tribune*, June 9, 1877; "More Murder," *Christian Recorder*, August 9, 1877; *Sunland Tribune*, July 21, 1877; "Statement of Mary R. Tanner," *Key West Dispatch*, reprinted in *Sunland Tribune*, September 1, 1877; "Another Act of Lawlessness in Hernando," *Sunland Tribune*, October 6, 1877; "More Murders in Hernando," *Sunland Tribune*, January 11, 1879.

127. Letter to the Editor, *Christian Recorder*, May 10, 1877. See also "Visiting Behind the Curtain," *Christian Recorder*, April 5, 1877; and "Presentation at Lake City, Fla.," *Christian Recorder*, June 28, 1877.

128. "Where to Live in Florida," *New York Tribune*, February 3, 1877.

129. Letter to the Editor, *New York Tribune*, February 17, 1877. Emphasis mine.

130. Woodward, *Reunion and Reaction,* 210–217.

131. "Harriet Beecher Stowe Indignant," *Florida Times-Union*, June 16, 1887.

132. F. W. Loring and C. F. Atkinson, *Cotton Culture and the South: Considered with Reference to Emigration* (Boston: Office of Loring & Atkinson, 1869), 78.

133. "The Republican Rally," *Florida Times-Union*, August 6, 1888.

134. The Florida Railway and Navigation Company, *The Key Line* (1884), 11.

135. *Report of the Senate Committee on Privileges and Elections,* 431.

136. Florida Railway and Navigation Company, *Key Line,* 6.

137. John Hope Franklin has captured the origins of this myth-making trend on a national level: "The critical period is the period following the war, at which time the South was licking its wounds and involved very much in nostalgia related to the war and the antebellum period. They were very firm on what they felt the position of the country should be in respect to race. And the North was interested primarily in the South's resources. It was the perfect trade-off: we'll let you take this race thing and run with it as long as you let us invest and exploit the South's resources. That was the gospel of the New South, and all the new legislation and Jim Crow stuff came when the Northerners were coming down in larger numbers investing in the South." Franklin, "Keeping Tabs on Jim Crow," *New York Times Magazine,* April 23, 1995, 35. For the northern-based roots of the myths of Reconstruction, see Kenneth M. Stampp, *The Era of Reconstruction* (New York, 1966), 13, 16; and Patrick Gerster and Nicholas Cords, "The Northern Origins of Southern Mythology," *Journal of Southern History* 43, no. 4 (November 1977), 567–582.

138. Caroline Mays Brevard, *A History of Florida: From the Treaty of 1763 to Our Own Times* (De Land: Florida State Historical Society, 1925), 128; H. E. Bennett, *A History of Florida: With Questions, Supplementary Chapters and an Outline of Florida Civil Government* (New York: American Book Company, 1904), 188; Davidson, *The Florida of Today,* 113.

139. "Florida Under the Democracy Reviewed," *Weekly Floridian*, May 6, 1884.

140. T. Thomas Fortune, *Black and White: Land, Labor, and Politics in the South,* (New York: Fords, Howard, & Hulbert, 1884), 173. Fortune wrote passionately on issues pertaining to African Americans and white workers in the Deep South and Florida throughout the late nineteenth century. His book *Black and White* is a forgotten classic in political economics that drew heavily on his experiences in Florida as well as on the ideas of Henry George and other labor reformers. The literature on the corrosive impact of financial power on the

nation's democratic institutions during the Gilded Age is vast. In 1871, former abolitionist Wendell Phillips stated, "The great question of the future is money against legislation. My friends, you and I shall be in our graves long before that battle is ended; and, unless our children have more patience and courage than saved this country from slavery, republican institutions will go down before moneyed corporations." Quoted in Carlos Martyn, *Wendell Phillips: The Agitator* (New York: Funk & Wagnall, 1890), 388. For other examples, see Henry Demarest Lloyd, *Wealth Against Commonwealth* (New York: Harper & Brothers, 1894); Mark Twain and Charles Dudley Warner, *The Gilded Age: A Tale of Today* (1873; reprint, New York: Penguin Books, 2001); Matthew Josephson, *The Robber Barons: The Great American Capitalists, 1861–1901* (1934; reprint, New York: Harcourt Brace Jovanovich, 1962); and Jonathan M. Wiener, *Social Origins of the New South: Alabama, 1860–1885* (Baton Rouge: Louisiana State University Press, 1978), 35–73.

2. THE STRUGGLE TO SAVE DEMOCRACY

1. "Real Estate and Politics," *New York Age*, March 30, 1889.

2. "Francis Phillip Fleming," *Florida Times Union*, September 29, 1888.

3. U.S. House of Representatives, *Bisbee v. Finley Contested Election*, 47th Congress, 1st Session, 1881–1882, 414–415.

4. Du Bois, *Black Reconstruction*, 526–579; Jaynes, *Branches without Roots*, 280–300. For the broader trend toward disfranchisement in the South, see Heather Richard Cox, *The Death of Reconstruction: Race, Labor, and Politics in the Post–Civil War North, 1865–1901* (Cambridge: Harvard University Press, 2001); Michael Perman, *Struggle for Mastery: Disfranchisement in the South, 1888–1908* (Chapel Hill: University of North Carolina Press, 2001); John W. Cell, *The Highest State of White Supremacy: The Origins of Segregation in South Africa and the American South* (Cambridge: Cambridge University Press, 1982); and Joel Williamson, *The Crucible of Race: Black-White Relations in the American South since Emancipation* (New York: Oxford University Press, 1986).

5. "The Florida Conference," *New York Globe*, March 15, 1884.

6. Literature on similar Independent movements in the South includes: Rachleff, *Black Labor in Richmond;* Jane Dailey, *Before Jim Crow: The Politics of Race in Postemancipation Virginia* (Chapel Hill: University of North Carolina Press, 2000); and Stephen Kantrowitz, *Ben Tillman and the Reconstruction of White Supremacy* (Chapel Hill: University of North Carolina Press, 2000), 98–109.

7. *Florida Sentinel*, January 26, 1900.

8. For an expansive discussion of African American women, resistance, and domestic labor, see Hunter, *To 'Joy My Freedom;* and Tera W. Hunter,

"Domination and Resistance: The Politics of Wage Household Labor in New South Atlanta," *Labor History* 34 (spring–summer 1993), 205–220.

9. Clifton Johnson observed: "One of the few times in the South when I heard a black person called 'colored' was at a private house where I lodged in Florida. A little girl came in and said to her grandmother, 'There's a colored lady out on the porch wants to speak to you.' 'Colored lady!' commented the grandmother, derisively. 'Colored lady! Say "that nigger"!' " Johnson, *Highways and Byways of the South* (New York: Macmillan, 1904), 331.

10. Helen Harcourt, *Home Life in Florida* (Louisville: John P. Morton, 1889), 346. See also Max O'Rell [pseudonym], *Jonathan and His Continent: Rambles through American Society*, trans. Paul Blouet (New York: Cassell, 1889), 281, and Johnson, *Highways and Byways of the South,* 334.

11. Harcourt, *Home Life in Florida,* 348. For other complaints about African American domestic workers' struggles for autonomy, see "The Domestic Servant Question," *Florida Mirror* (Fernandina), October 21, 1890; "The Servant Girl Problem," *Florida Metropolis,* January 11, 1906; and "A Northern Man," *Florida Metropolis,* February 25, 1907.

12. Iza Duffus Hardy, *Oranges and Alligators: Sketches of South Florida Life* (London: Ward and Downey, 1886), 108–110.

13. "Ladies Union," *Florida Metropolis,* January 3, 1903.

14. Shoemaker, *Florida As It Is,* 156. African American women took the viewpoint that employers were ganging up to keep wages down. A traveler in Florida observed in speaking with a black laundry worker, "She was disposed to be critical of her wages, and mentioned doing a wash for a white family of eight persons for twenty-five cents a week." Johnson, *Highways and Byways of the South,* 37. See also T. C. Bridges, *Florida to Fleet Street* (London: Hutchinson, 1926), 41.

15. Barbara Agresti, "Household and Family in the Postbellum South: Walton County, Florida, 1870–1885" (diss., University of Florida, 1976), 197. This tradition of resistance continued into the twentieth century. In the wake of the 1901 Jacksonville fire, African American women laundry and domestic workers demanded higher wages to cope with spiraling inflation. Employers blustered: "The suburbs yesterday showed hundreds of ladies hunting for wash women, and in many instances colored women declined to do this kind of service, although they had been accustomed to it in the past. One lady, the wife of a prominent business man, in speaking of the difficulty to secure help, said: 'I have had a colored woman who had done my washing for many years, and she is an excellent one, too, but she told me to-day that she would not do it, because there would soon be plenty of money in the city. I offered her extra inducements, and she positively refused. Many others complain in the same way.' " "Hunting Wash Women," *Florida Metropolis,* May 7, 1901.

16. A. M. Reed Diary, entry for November 10, 1877.

17. "Status of the Race," *New York Globe,* September 22, 1883. See also Jerrell H. Shofner, *History of Jefferson County* (Tallahassee: Sentry Press, 1976), 323–326.

18. Faye Perry Melton of Ocala remembered: "There was also a commissary or store nearby where the hands could trade wages for food, tobacco or other necessities. Most of the time, the black people owed more to the commissary than they made in wages each week. This caused them to be constantly in debt, so they very seldom received money for wages." *Memories of Fort McCoy* (Ocala, FL, 1987).

19. Johnson, *Highways and Byways of the South,* 341.

20. "Emigration of Labor," *Jasper News,* April 25, 1890; "Cotton Picking Becomes High," *Gainesville Daily News,* September 24, 1904. "On the Move," *Pensacola News,* January 8, 1890; "Disheartened Cotton Planters," *Bradford Times,* January 22, 1892; "What Shall We Do?" *Jasper News,* April 25, 1890. See also Shofner, *History of Jefferson County,* 323–326.

21. "Negroes Leaving For Alabama," *Atlanta Constitution,* July 4, 1895.

22. *Florida Dispatch,* October 10, 1877.

23. "More Advice," *Florida Dispatch,* December 5, 1877.

24. Joseph Tucker to Henry Sanford, July 18, 1870; Lyman Phelps to Henry Sanford, July 11, 1882, Henry Shelton Sanford Papers (Microfilm), University of Florida. Sanford's overseers experimented with Swedes, Germans, and African Americans—all of whom eventually struck or demanded higher pay. See also Joseph A. Fry, *Henry S. Sanford: Diplomacy and Business in Nineteenth-Century America* (Reno: University of Nevada Press, 1982).

25. "The Housekeepers Were Deeply Interested," *Florida Metropolis,* July 21, 1905; "Mammy," *Florida Metropolis,* January 23, 1906.

26. *Prospectus of the Florida and North Carolina Phosphate Lands of Mr. C. M. Hawkins, Raleigh, N.C.* (n.d.), Perkins Library Pamphlet Collection, Duke University. Oliver Cox argued that in the United States, "race relations are basically an aspect of labor relations." Cox, *Capitalism and American Leadership* (New York: Philosophical Library, 1962), 227. More recently, Paul Gilroy writes: "Discussion of racial domination cannot therefore be falsely separated from wider considerations of social sovereignty such as the conflict between men and women, the antagonism between capital and labor, or the manner in which modes of production develop and combine." Gilroy, "One Nation under a Groove: The Cultural Politics of 'Race' and Racism in Britain," in David Theo Goldberg, ed., *Anatomy of Racism* (Minneapolis: University of Minnesota Press, 1990), 264.

27. J. Lester Dinkins writes, "By the turn of the century, wages paid for common labor had risen to $1.10 for a ten hour work shift, with white employees generally receiving about 75 cents more than Negroes for the same amount of work." Dinkins, *Dunnellon, Boomtown of the 1890s: The Story of Rainbow*

Springs and Dunnellon (St. Petersburg: Great Outdoors Publishing, 1969); For additional evidence of differential wage scales based on race see "The Florida Season," *New York Age*, February 2, 1889.

28. Lady Duffus Hardy, *Down South* (London: Chapman and Hall, 1883). For a sketch of Hardy, see Helen C. Black, *Notable Women Authors of the Day* (London: MacLaren, 1906), 198–204.

29. Hardy, *Down South*, 224. Another northern visitor approvingly quoted the insights of "an Irish lady of cultivation" in Fernandina: "She seemed to be very sensible upon the subject of the negro. Said that they were much better off in slavery than when in the wilds of Africa killing each other and taking a delight in new methods of torture such as their savage minds and wicked hands could invent and perpetrate." Abbie M. Brooks Diary, April 26, 1872.

30. *Florida Metropolis* (Jacksonville), July 21, 1905; Barbour, *Florida for Tourists*, 238.

31. *Florida Times-Union*, March 17, 1904.

32. T. W. Osborn to William Chandler, November 12, 1880, vol. 50, William E. Chandler Papers, Manuscript Division, Library of Congress; hereafter cited as Chandler Papers. Senator Chandler had been involved in Florida politics since Reconstruction. He came to Florida in 1877 as part of the congressional delegation charged with investigating the state's contested 1876 presidential election returns. Subsequently, Chandler refereed political patronage appointments in Florida. He carried on a regular correspondence with African American Republicans in the late nineteenth century. The "Mississippi Plan" referred to the strategy of terrorism and fraud used to drive African Americans out of politics during Reconstruction. See Du Bois, *Black Reconstruction*, 412. The tissue ballot was a thin piece of paper that allowed the voter to stash several marked ballots into the ballot box at once.

33. "Florida," *Florida Times-Union*, November 7, 1888.

34. "Political Murder in Florida," *Washington Bee*, October 26, 1889. For other examples of black residents being waylaid after giving testimony see Malachi Martin to William Chandler, February 14, 1881, vol. 50, Chandler Papers; Ellen F. Wetherell, *Facts from Florida* (Lynn, Mass., 1897), 15–18; Edward C. Williamson, "Black-Belt Political Crisis: The Savage-James Lynching, 1882," *Florida Historical Quarterly* 45 (April 1967), 402–409; and U.S. House of Representatives, *Bisbee v. Finley*, 893–896.

35. M. M. Moore to Joseph Lee, August 26, 1881, Joseph E. Lee Papers, Ike Williams III Collection; hereafter cited as Lee Papers.

36. H. C. Bailey to F. P. Fleming, November 5, 1889, Box 10, folder 5, Governor Francis P. Fleming Papers, Florida State Archives.

37. Joseph Lee to Horatio Bisbee, July 23, 1882, Lee Papers.

38. "Situation in Florida," *Christian Recorder* (Philadelphia), March 3, 1881; "Mob Violence in Florida," *New York Daily Tribune*, February 11, 1881.

39. *Report of the Adjutant General, for the Years 1881 and 1882* (Tallahassee: Tallahasseean Book & Job Office, 1882).

40. "What Crosby Says," *Florida Journal,* July 24, 1884.

41. Malachia Martin to William Chandler, November 8, 1880, vol. 50, Chandler Papers.

42. Ibid.

43. "Deserting the Republicans," *Weekly Floridian* (Tallahassee), November 7, 1882.

44. " 'A Free Ballot and a Fair Count,' " *Weekly Floridian,* November 14, 1882.

45. "The State Vote," *Weekly Floridian,* December 5, 1882. For statistics on African American voting in Florida, see Kousser, *The Shaping of Southern Politics,* 15, 28, 68.

46. For the expansion of these markets, see C. B. Rogers to W. J. Lutterloh, January 5, 1870, file #5, Washington J. Lutterloh Papers, Southern Historical Collection, Wilson Library, University of North Carolina, Chapel Hill. See also James, *Holding Aloft the Banner of Ethiopia,* 232–257; and Hewitt, *Southern Discomfort.*

47. "Peculiarities of Key West," *New York Age,* November 3, 1888.

48. Melton McLaurin, *The Knights of Labor in the South* (Westport, CT: Greenwood Press, 1984), 81–82; Canter Brown, Jr., "Prelude to the Poll Tax: Black Republicans and the Knights of Labor in 1880s Florida," in Greenberg, Rogers, and Brown, *Florida's Heritage of Diversity,* 69–81. Also see Leon Fink, *Workingman's Democracy: The Knights of Labor and American Politics* (Urbana: University of Illinois Press, 1983); Edwards, *Gendered Strife and Confusion,* 218–254; and Philip S. Foner and Ronald L. Lewis, eds., *Black Workers: A Documentary History from Colonial Times to the Present* (Philadelphia: Temple University Press, 1989), 209–235.

49. J. W. Menard to Joseph E. Lee, January 24, 1880, Lee Papers. In contrast, when campaigning Democrats came to Key West, they limited their efforts to "Conch Town" or the white area of the Key. See William Artrell to Joseph Lee, July 27, 1880, Lee Papers.

50. "Peculiarities of Key West," *Christian Recorder,* November 3, 1888. White visitors saw the multiracial character of Key West in a more negative light. See "Our Key West Trip," *Fort Myers Press,* December 18, 1886. White residents of nearby Fort Myers used the multiracial composition of Key West as a reason for seceding from Monroe County and carving out a new county on the mainland. See "Lee County," *Fort Myers Press,* March 10, 1887.

51. Prior to the election of 1888 a white candidate for the county judgeship stepped aside in favor of James Dean. This sharply contrasts with white Republicans' behavior elsewhere in the state.

52. "Freest Town in the South," *New York Age,* December 1, 1888.

53. For the Ten Years War and African American involvement, see Lisa Brock and Digna Castañeda Fuertes, *Between Race and Empire: African-Americans and Cubans before the Cuban Revolution* (Philadelphia: Temple University Press, 1998), 8–9.

54. For stresses in the Republican coalition in Key West, see William Artrell to Joseph E. Lee, October 4, 1881, Lee Papers.

55. Josiah Walls to Joseph Lee, August 28, 1882, Lee Papers. For a biographical portrait of Walls, see Peter D. Klingman, *Josiah Walls, Florida's Black Congressman of Reconstruction* (Gainesville: University of Florida Press, 1976).

56. *The Proceedings of the State Conference of the Colored Men of Florida* (Washington, DC, 1884), Frederick Douglass Papers, Manuscript Division, Library of Congress. See also M. M. Lewey, "The Florida Conference," *New York Globe,* March 15, 1884.

57. "'Pope Repudiated,'" *Florida Journal,* July 21, 1884.

58. U.S. House of Representatives, *Bisbee v. Finley,* 738.

59. Ibid., 750–761, 408–409.

60. "Florida Politics," *New York Globe,* August 9, 1884.

61. Woodward, *Origins of the New South,* 19–20.

62. "Congressman Bisbee," *New York Globe,* January 26, 1884. For the Readjusters in Virginia, see Rachleff, *Black Labor in Richmond*; and Dailey, *Before Jim Crow.*

63. *The Proceedings of the State Conference of the Colored Men of Florida.* For information on Dean, see Brown, *Florida's Black Public Officials,* 84.

64. "Alachua to the Front," *Florida Journal;* Jackson, "Republicans and Florida Elections," 203. For an analysis of the Independent movement, see Williamson, *Florida Politics in the Gilded Age.* The *Key West News* argued: "The Colored people of this State can never get their full rights until the whites are about equally and permanently divided politically. This will bring about a division of the colored voters also, and then we shall have reached a healthy condition of things." Quoted in *New York Globe,* August 9, 1884.

65. "Gen Walls on Fusion," *New York Globe,* February 9, 1884. See also "Anti-Bourbonism in Florida," *New York Globe,* April 21, 1883; "Why There is Dissatisfaction Among Colored Voters," *New York Globe,* August 18, 1883; and "Florida Politics," *New York Globe,* August 9, 1884.

66. "A Jailers Barbarity," *Florida Journal,* July 17, 1884; "Pope and Greeley," *Florida Journal,* July 28, 1884.

67. "A Solid Platform," *Florida Journal,* June 30, 1884.

68. Ibid.

69. "Columbia Heard From," *Florida Journal,* June 30, 1884.

70. "A Republican Rebellion," *Florida Times-Union,* July 1, 1884.

71. *New York Globe,* April 21, 1883. Menard was the first African American to be elected to Congress; in 1869, he had won election in Louisiana. However,

Congress refused to seat him. He then moved to Florida in 1871 and embarked on a career as editor and political leader. John Willis Menard, *Lays in Summer Lands,* ed. Larry Eugene Rivers, Richard Mathews, and Canter Brown, Jr. (Tampa: University of Tampa Press, 2002).

72. John Wallace to Joseph E. Lee, May 2, 1882, Lee Papers. For white dissent, see "Pointed Letter from Stalwart," *Jacksonville Journal,* July 31, 1884; and "No Perry For Him," *Jacksonville Journal,* July 31, 1884.

73. "Grand Rally at Live Oak," *Weekly Floridian,* August 12, 1884; "Businessmen for Perry," *Weekly Floridian,* September 16, 1884; "Letter from Manatee County," *Weekly Floridian,* September 2, 1884.

74. "The Independent Pow-Wow," *Weekly Floridian,* August 12, 1884.

75. "A Campaign of Falsehood," *Weekly Floridian,* July 22, 1884. Florida historian Rowland Rerick (*Memoirs of Florida,* 341) stated that when the Democratic Redeemers took control of Florida they "crippled the schools by decreasing the maximum county levy one-half."

76. "Florida Under the Democracy Reviewed," *Weekly Floridian,* May 6, 1884; "A New Florida," *Weekly Floridian,* April 17, 1883.

77. "Qualified Suffrage," *Weekly Floridian,* May 13, 1884.

78. "The Race Issue," *Florida Journal,* August 7, 1884. This analysis of Long's speech is taken from "Democratic Doctrine," *New York Globe,* September 20, 1884. Also see "General Perry's Party at Manatee," *Weekly Floridian,* August 19, 1884; "Deeds Versus Words," *Weekly Floridian,* September 23, 1884; and "Goodrich Warmed Up," *Florida Times-Union,* October 24, 1889.

79. "The Race Issue," *Florida Journal,* August 7, 1884. For Long's role as a Florida booster, see Robinson, *Florida: A Pamphlet,* 141–143.

80. The *Florida Times-Union* similarly complained: "The white people of the South are rapidly becoming disgusted with the business of taking upon themselves the heaviest burdens of taxation for the benefit of those who vote solidly and stolidly against every measure they propose for the common welfare—simply because they propose it." "Negro Education," *Times-Union.* November 5, 1889.

81. The intersection between race, gender, and violence has been brilliantly explored by Jacqueline Dowd Hall in *Revolt against Chivalry: Jessie Daniel Ames and the Women's Campaign against Lynching* (New York: Columbia University Press, 1979, 1993). For recent insightful works, see Gilmore, *Gender and Jim Crow;* and Hale, *Making Whiteness,* 232–235.

82. "Florida's Vote for Governor," "Official Vote of Leon County," and "Mr. Pope Interviewed," *Weekly Floridian,* November 11, 1884; Jackson, "Republicans and Florida Elections," 268–272. In the 1886 elections, African Americans in some portions of the state attempted to organize Independent tickets. See "Pensacola Letter," *New York Freeman,* October 16, 1886. R. C. Long was later

forced to resign his leadership position. See *New York Globe*, September 27, 1884.

83. "Sir," *Weekly Floridian*, December 2, 1884.

84. For the impact of the poll tax see Kousser, *The Shaping of Southern Politics*, 210–211, 213–214.

85. For the bonding legislation pertaining to county offices, see Kathryn Trimmer Abby, *Florida: A Land of Change* (Chapel Hill: University of North Carolina Press, 1941), 330–331. A black correspondent from Pensacola complained, "Granting that the rich white Republicans should have the big offices that require a bond that the colored man cannot give . . ." "Florida Politics," *New York Age*, August 25, 1888. An example of how the bonding system shifted power upwards in Florida politics—for federal as opposed to state office—can be found in the correspondence between a Republican who was trying to raise the necessary $12,000 bond to assume the office of postmaster in Madison. This gentleman wrote to Joseph E. Lee: "I am now at work trying to give the Bond which is $12,000 thousand dollars. I have found four gentlemen who will sign from $1000 to 1,500 each. I shall not be able to get up the whole amount here. The present incumbent has all the abler men on his Bond and they will certainly stick to their friends." E. G. Alexander to Joseph Lee, March 21, 1882, Box 2, Lee Papers.

86. Widespread fraud and violence were uncovered by a congressional committee that investigated the 1888 elections in Florida. For example: "Madison district, No. 1.—At this district an election was duly held, as provided by law, and 615 votes were cast. After the close of the polls, the Democratic inspectors delayed for some two hours the counting of the vote, and then proceeded very slowly, occupying two hours more in counting some seventy votes. When they had proceeded thus far, an armed body of white Democrats appeared at the polls, and forcibly carried off the ballot box. Consequently no return was made of this vote." *Contested Election Case of Goodrich v. Bullock from the Second Congressional District of Florida*, 51st Congress, 1st Session, (Washington, DC: Government Printing Office, 1890), 10. Confederate veteran M. H. Waring testified to massive violence against those individuals—white and black—who opposed the Bourbon Democracy. Ibid., 225–227. See also "Political Crimes of the South," *New York Age*, February 9, 1889; and "Florida Goes Democratic," *New York Daily Tribune*, October 5, 1892.

87. "The Registration Law," *Florida Journal*, August 25, 1884. For the implementation of voter restriction measures in Florida, see Kousser, *The Shaping of Southern Politics*, 92–103.

88. "The Elections," *Quincy Herald*, November 8, 1890.

89. J. Morgan Kousser (*The Shaping of Southern Politics*, 91–92) writes: "Markedly democratic during the 1880s, Florida became solidly Democratic by the 1890s. The registration, poll tax, eight-box, and secret ballot laws simply

exterminated the opposition." For more information on disenfranchisement in Florida see ibid., 91–103; Paul Lewinson, *Race, Class and Party: A History of Negro Suffrage and White Politics in the South* (New York: Oxford University Press, 1932), 119; and Walter Dean Burnham, *Critical Elections and the Mainsprings of American Politics* (New York: W. W. Norton, 1970), 78.

90. "The Republican Irruption," *Florida Times-Union*, August 3, 1888.

91. African American longshoremen were periodically able to forge alliances with white workers in other states of the Jim Crow South. See Daniel Rosenberg, *New Orleans Dockworkers: Race, Labor, and Unionism, 1892–1923* (Albany: SUNY Press, 1988); Eric Arnesen, *Waterfront Workers of New Orleans: Race, Class, and Politics* (Urbana: University of Illinois Press, 1994); and Bruce Nelson, *Divided We Stand: American Workers and the Struggle for Black Equality*, (Princeton: Princeton University Press, 2001).

92. "The Pensacola Trouble," *Atlanta Constitution*, February 4, 1887.

93. McLaurin, *The Knights of Labor in the South*, 60–61.

94. *New York Freeman*, February 12, 1887.

95. Ibid. Also see "A Riot At Pensacola," *Atlanta Constitution*, February 1, 1887.

96. "To the Officers and Members of the Stevedores' Associations 1 and 2," quoted in "Trouble in the Bay," *Pensacola Commercial*, February 2, 1887.

97. *New York Freeman*, February 19, 1887.

98. Ibid.

99. Governor Perry to Sheriff Ellerman, August 31, 1888, Governors' Letterbooks, Florida State Archives (hereafter cited as Governors' Letterbooks); William Mizell, Jr., *The Vanished Town of Kings Ferry Located on the South Banks of the St. Mary's River Nassau County, Florida* (1965).

100. "Big Riot By Longshoremen," *Florida Times-Union*, September 8, 1888; "Fernandina Is Indignant," *Florida Times-Union*, September 9, 1888.

101. Perry to J. A. Ellerman, September 3, 1888, Governors' Letterbooks.

102. Perry to Captain W. D. Ballintine, September 7, 1888. "Adjutant General's Report," *Florida Senate Journal* (1888), 14–15; "The Sheriff's Head Cut Off," *Florida Times-Union*, September 12, 1888.

103. "Riotous Blacks," *Daily News* (Pensacola), January 22, 1890.

104. *Florida Times-Union*, January 24, 1890.

105. "At Apalachicola," *Daily News*, January 23, 1890.

106. Governor Fleming to E. M. Montgomery, January 22, 1890, Governors' Letterbooks; "Report of the Adjutant General for the Biennial Period Ending December 31, 1890," in *Florida House of Representative Reports* (1891), 23; Rerick, *Memoirs of Florida*, 377.

107. "At Apalachicola, One Man Shot Yesterday," *Daily News*, January 24, 1890.

108. "The 'Straights' Got There," *Florida Times-Union*, November 7, 1888.

109. McLaurin, *The Knights of Labor in the South*, 94–95.

110. "A Lesson of the Times," *Florida Times-Union*, November 20, 1888.

111. "Relief By Labor," *Florida Times-Union*, November 20, 1888; "Epidemic Mobs," *Pensacola Commercial*, December 10, 1888.

112. "Laborers' Meeting," *Florida Times-Union*, November 23, 1888.

113. "A Lesson of the Times," *Florida Times-Union*, November 20, 1888; "All Is Harmony Now," *Florida Times-Union*, November 24, 1888.

114. "Executive Committee Work," *Florida Times-Union*, November 23, 1888.

115. "The Labor Question Settled," *Florida Times-Union*, November 24, 1888.

116. "Moody is Mum," *Florida Times-Union*, January 25, 1889.

117. "Everyone Favors the Bill," *Florida Times-Union*, April 9, 1889.

118. Editorial, *Florida Times-Union*, April 13, 1889.

119. Ibid. Also see "The Negro Can't Be Assimilated," *Pensacola Commercial*, October 5, 1888.

120. "Justice At the South: Moving Towards Legal Disfranchisement," *New York Age*, June 1, 1889.

121. Brown, *Florida's Black Public Officials*, 54–63; "Judge Dean's Removal," *Florida Sentinel*, quoted in *New York Age*, August 17, 1889; Brown, "Prelude to the Poll Tax," 80.

122. "Proclamation By the Governor," *Pensacolian*, February 7, 1885; "Onward! Upward!" *Pensacola Commercial*, March 15, 1885.

123. "The Collection of City Taxes," *Pensacola Commercial*, March 25, 1885.

124. "Pensacola Free," *Pensacola Commercial*, March 15, 1885.

125. For continued African American labor organizing see "Mill Hands Out on a Strike," *Pensacola Daily News*, September 18, 1899; "Pensacola," *Florida Times-Union and Citizen*, September 6, 1899; and McLaurin, *The Knights of Labor in the South*, 178–180.

126. "Peace for Capital and Labor," *Florida Times-Union*, May 25, 1901.

127. W. E. B. Du Bois brilliantly analyzed white workers' tendency to undermine solidarity in *Black Reconstruction*, 17–30. Also see David Roediger, *The Wages of Whiteness: Race and the Making of the American Working Class* (New York: Verso, 1991); and Nelson, *American Workers and the Struggle for Black Equality*.

128. Here I concur with Alex Lichtenstein, who argues that many of the "racialist" institutions that arose in the New South such as segregation or convict labor were important components of the region's path of modernization. Lichtenstein, *Twice the Work of Free Labor: The Political Economy of Convict Labor in the New South* (London: Verso, 1996). Also see Cell, *The Highest State of White Supremacy*.

129. For anti-enticement and "after dark" laws, see *Acts and Resolutions Adopted by the Legislature of Florida at Its First Session Under the Constitution of A.D. 1885* (Tallahassee: N. M. Bowen, 1887), 149, 156; and "Let it be done here too," *Florida Metropolis,* January 27, 1906. Also see "New Vagrancy Law Should Be Enforced," *Florida Metropolis,* July 1, 1907.

130. "The Labor Question," *Gainesville Sun,* November 25, 1904; "Cotton Picking Becomes High," *Gainesville Sun,* September 24, 1904; "In Justice Court," *Gainesville Sun,* September 1, 1904; "Granger Made Arrests," *Gainesville Sun,* December 24, 1904; "Violate the Labor Law," *Florida Metropolis,* November 15, 1901. For an excellent analysis of the political significance of the new systems of forced labor see Jaynes, *Branches without Roots,* 301–316.

131. A. I. Dixie interview with author, August 22, 1997, Behind the Veil Collection. For a sample of municipal vagrancy statutes, see *Code of Ordinances of the City of Quincy, Florida* (Quincy: Quincy Publishing Co., 1939), 11, 83; *Charter and Ordinances of the City of Daytona, Florida* (De Land: E. O. Painter Printing Co., 1921), 73; and *Charter and Ordinances of the City of Tallahassee, Florida* (Tallahassee: T. J. Appleyard, 1924), 137–138.

132. "An Original Sheriff," *Palatka Daily News,* April 17, 1920. For labor coercion practiced by sheriffs on behalf of employers, also see A. I. Dixie interview with author, Behind the Veil Collection.

133. "Florida," *New York Tribune,* April 29, 1891.

134. "Under our laws as they now stand the poorer class must pay their debts if it takes their shirts from their backs but the well-to-do, and those owning homes can cheat, swindle and defraud their creditors to their heart's content by taking the benefit of the homestead." "An Unjust Law," *Jasper News,* July 7, 1893.

135. David M. Oshinsky, *"Worse than Slavery": Parchman Farm and the Ordeal of Jim Crow Justice* (New York: Free Press, 1996), 70–76. For the centrality of convict labor in the development of Florida, see J. C. Powell, *The American Siberia: Or, Fourteen Years' Experience in a Southern Convict Camp* (1891; reprint, Montclair, NJ: Patterson Smith, 1970). "On Charge of Peonage," *Fernandina News,* September 13, 1906; Jeffrey A. Drobney, "Where Palm and Pine Are Blowing: Convict Labor in the North Florida Turpentine Industry, 1877–1923," *Florida Historical Quarterly* 72 (April 1994), 411–434; and Jerrell H. Shofner, "Mary Grace Quackenbos, a Visitor Florida Did Not Want," *Florida Historical Quarterly* 58 (January 1980), 273–290.

136. "Why Scarce," *Florida Metropolis,* January 11, 1906.

137. "Report of the State's Prison," *House Journal, 1889 Legislature of Florida.* Also see "Punishing Criminals," *Florida Metropolis,* January 9, 1906, and *Journal of the Florida Senate, 1901* (Tallahassee: State Printer, 1901), 76.

138. "Allan Rodgers on Good Roads," *Florida Metropolis*, March 1, 1907. Also see "Dade County Roads Built By Convicts," *Florida Metropolis*, March 8, 1907; and "Convicts & Road Work," *Florida Metropolis*, March 23, 1907.

139. Powell, *The American Siberia;* "They Show the Cruel Scars: Brutal Treatment of Convicts in Hillsboro," *Florida Metropolis*, April 15, 1901; "Four Convicts and Guard Met Horrible Death: Fire Destroys Stockade—Men Are Chained And Could Not Escape," *Florida Metropolis*, October 16, 1905; Jan H. Johannes, Sr., *Yesterday's Reflections: Nassau County, Florida* (Callahan: Florida Sun Printing, 1976), 13; Richard Barry, "Slavery in the South Today," *Cosmopolitan Magazine* 42 (March 1907), 481–491; "A New Labor Scheme," *Chicago Defender*, October 16, 1915; N. Gordon Carper, "Martin Tarbert, Martyr of an Era," *Florida Historical Quarterly* 52 (October 1973), 115–131.

140. *Christian Recorder*, August 5, 1886.

141. Department of Commerce, Bureau of the Census, *Prisoners and Juvenile Delinquents in the United States: 1910* (Washington, DC: Government Printing Office, 1918), 27.

142. Kharif, "Refinement of Racial Segregation in Florida."

143. "A Florida Court Room," *New York Freeman*, September 24, 1887; "County Politics in Pensacola," *New York Age*, June 2, 1888; "The United States Court," *Florida Times-Union*, November 6, 1889.

144. "Pensacola Letter," *New York Freeman*, February 5, 1887; *New York Freeman*, March 26, 1887; "Florida Politics," *New York Freeman*, April 9, 1887; "Florida Topics," *New York Freeman*, April 30, 1887; "Palatka (Fla.) Pencilings," *New York Age*, June 23, 1888.

145. *New York Globe*, March 31, 1883. See the following report for a confirmation of railroad segregation in the same year: "Editorial Correspondence," *South Florida Journal*, January 11, 1883. See also "Sunday Excursions," *New York Age*, June 2, 1888; "A Trip over the Transit Railroad," *Weekly Floridian*, May 15, 1883; and O'Rell, *Jonathan and His Continent*, 260–261.

146. "Florida Lawyers," *New York Freeman*, March 12, 1887.

147. "Pensacola People," *New York Age*, February 4, 1888.

148. "New Laws Enacted," *Florida Times-Union*, May 23, 1887; "The Color Line in Cars," *Florida Times-Union*, May 23, 1887.

149. "Florida Topics," *New York Freeman*, June 11, 1887. See also "Anglo Saxon Supremacy," *New York Age*, August 3, 1890, and Williamson, *Florida Politics in the Gilded Age*, 185. For a British traveler's support of Jim Crow laws in Florida, see George Aflalo, *Sunshine and Sport in Florida and the West Indies* (Philadelphia: George W. Jacobs, 1907), 71.

150. "Florida Topics," *New York Freeman*, April 30, 1887.

151. "Meets with Approval," *New York Freeman*, July 9, 1887; *New York Freeman*, July 23, 1887.

152. Letter to the Editor, *New York Freeman*, July 23, 1887.

153. "Bishop Daniel Alexander Payne's Reply," *Christian Recorder*, August 10, 1882.

154. David Leon Chandler, *Henry Flagler: The Astonishing Life and Times of the Visionary Robber Baron Who Founded Florida* (New York: Macmillan, 1986). For a more balanced assessment of Flagler, see Edward N. Akin, *Flagler: Rockefeller Partner and Florida Baron* (Kent, OH: Kent State University Press, 1988).

155. Pete Daniel, *The Shadow of Slavery: Peonage in the South, 1901–1969* (New York: Oxford University Press, 1972), 96, 101.

156. "Flagler Tells of His Great Work," *Florida Metropolis*, October 19, 1905.

157. For the East Coast Railway's convict lease contract, see *Journal of the Florida House of Representatives* (1886). Pete Daniel (*The Shadow of Slavery*, 95–101) discusses Flagler's subsequent use of debt peons in Florida.

158. Daniel, *The Shadow of Slavery*, 198. Field, like many of his elite northern contemporaries, felt that *neither* African Americans *nor* new European immigrants should vote: "What is wise at the North is wise at the South. The negro stands on the same ground as the foreign emigrant, both utterly unfitted to be entrusted with the ballot." Henry M. Field, *Bright Skies and Dark Shadows* (New York: Charles Scribner's Sons, 1890), 175.

159. Field, *Bright Skies and Dark Shadows*, 199.

160. Rayford W. Logan, *The Betrayal of the Negro: From Rutherford B. Hayes to Woodrow Wilson* (1965; reprint, New York: Da Capo Press, 1997), 68.

161. Lyman Phelps to William Chandler, March 13, 1890, vol. 80, Chandler Papers.

162. J. N. Stripling to William Chandler, April 6, 1894, vol. 93, Chandler Papers.

163. Peter D. Klingman writes perceptively on this group. See Klingman, *Neither Dies nor Surrenders: A History of the Republican Party in Florida, 1867–1970* (Gainesville: University Presses of Florida, 1984), 108–111. See also D. J. Daniels to Joseph Lee, May 29, 1882, Lee Papers.

164. Harrison Reed to Henry Sanford, May 5, 1884, Henry Shelton Sanford Papers. For similar sentiments in Orlando, see "Orlando's Election," *Florida Times-Union*, December 18, 1888.

165. "The County Republican Convention," *Ocala Banner*, August 15, 1890.

166. "Joe Lee's Job Is In Jeopardy," *Florida Metropolis*, April 8, 1909. For Black and Tan Republicanism in Mississippi, see McMillen, *Dark Journey*, 58–69.

167. *Contested Election Case of Goodrich v. Bullock*, 565.

168. *Daily Sun* (Gainesville), November 9, 1904.

169. "The Lincoln League," *Florida Metropolis*, April 30, 1901. For national GOP and racial politics, see Paul D. Casdorph, *Republicans, Negroes, and*

Progressives in the South, 1912–1916 (Tuscaloosa: University of Alabama Press, 1981).

170. Samuel Pasco to W. H. Gleason, June 30, 1894, Box 2, folder: "Correspondence 1894 April–September," William H. Gleason Papers, P. K. Yonge Library of Florida History, University of Florida. For Gleason, see Jonathan Daniels, *Prince of Carpetbaggers* (New York: J. B. Lippincott, 1958), 270.

171. Napoleon Broward to W. H. Gleason, May 30, 1908, Box 9, folder, "Politics," Gleason Papers. For a discussion of Broward's resolution, see Samuel Proctor, *Napoleon Bonaparte Broward: Florida's Fighting Democrat* (Gainesville: University of Florida Press, 1950), 252. Historian Rayford Logan's assessment of the GOP's betrayal of black southerners (*The Betrayal of the Negro,* 66) rings doubly true in Florida: "The tariff had taken the place of federal subsidy to railroads in promoting peace and harmony at the expense of the constitutional rights of the freedmen."

172. "Why Roosevelt is Coming South," *Florida Times-Union,* September 28, 1905.

173. "How the Cars Will Be Divided," *Florida Metropolis,* October 20, 1905.

174. "Hoping for Something New," *Florida Times-Union,* October 19, 1905.

175. "Business Men of Jacksonville Who Talked with the President Today," *Florida Metropolis,* October 21, 1905. On Roosevelt's views on white "race suicide," see Alan Dawley, *Struggles for Justice: Social Responsibility and the Liberal State* (Cambridge: Harvard University Press, 1991), 107.

176. "The President at the College," News of the Colored People Section, *Florida Metropolis,* October 23, 1905. Located in the rear section of the *Florida Metropolis,* editor W. I. Lewis's column, "News of the Colored People," was a single sheet of local and statewide reporting on African American life in Florida. The page was based on correspondence received from black informants from across the state. Items cited from this page will be distinguished from other *Metropolis* items by the abbreviation "NCP."

177. "Duties Precede Rights," *New York Age,* October 26, 1905.

178. "The President at the College," NCP, *Florida Metropolis,* October 23, 1905.

179. For the GOP's abandonment of African Americans, see Richard B. Sherman, *The Republican Party and Black America: From McKinley to Hoover, 1896–1933* (Charlottesville: University Press of Virginia, 1973).

180. "Talked Like a Democrat," *Florida Metropolis,* October 24, 1905. Also see G. N. Green, "Republicans, Bull Moose, and Negroes in Florida, 1912," *Florida Historical Quarterly* 43 (October 1964), 153–164.

181. "Reasons For Defeat," *Evening Telegram,* November 15, 1892.

182. "Invitation to Republicans: Provided They Are White Electors," *Florida Metropolis,* April 26, 1907.

183. Andrew Carnegie believed he was only being pragmatic in saying: "In the South, the ignorant are the immense majority. To give suffrage without restriction to the blacks would mean that the intelligent whites were powerless, overwhelmed. Government would be in the hands of men steeped in ignorance of political responsibilities to a degree impossible for Northern people to imagine. Only residence among them can give a true impression." "Mr. Carnegie on the Negro," *Florida Times-Union,* March 2, 1904.

184. *Pensacola Daily Commercial,* September 6, 1888. For broader discussions of railroads and political corruption, see Woodward, *Origins of the New South,* 19–20; and Richard White, "Information, Markets, and Corruption: Transcontinental Railroads in the Gilded Age," *Journal of American History* 90, no. 1 (June 2003), 19–43.

185. A. H. Steagull to William S. Jennings, March 28, 1901, Box 9, folder "1901: January," Governor William Jennings Papers, P. K. Yonge Library of Florida History, University of Florida. For Democratic corruption in Clay County see F. M. Simonton to William Jennings, November 22, 1900, Jennings Papers. For Democratic corruption in Coconut Grove see F. M. Long to William Jennings, May 16, 1901, Jennings Papers.

186. Affidavit, April 15, 1905, Box 6, folder 1: "Complaints & Investigations, Nassau, Orange and Volusia, 1905–6," and U. M. Bennett to Napoleon Bonaparte Broward, April 14, 1905, Governors' Papers, Florida State Archives; "Ballot Box Robbed; Entire Gubernatorial Vote in Baker County Precinct is Missing," *Florida Times-Union,* August 19, 1916.

187. Cindy Hahamovitch, *The Fruits of Their Labor: Atlantic Coast Farmworkers and the Making of Migrant Poverty, 1870–1945* (Chapel Hill: University of North Carolina Press, 1997); Paul Ortiz, "Farm Worker Organizing in America: From Slavery to Cesar Chavez and Beyond," in Charles D. Thompson and Melinda Wiggins, eds., *The Human Cost of Food: Farmworker Lives, Labor, and Advocacy* (Austin: University of Texas Press, 2002), 249–275.

3. WE ARE IN THE HANDS OF THE DEVIL: FIGHTING RACIAL TERRORISM

1. "More Murder," *Christian Recorder,* August 9, 1877.

2. "Vote Democratic," *Okaloosa News Journal,* October 29, 1920.

3. Between 1882 and 1930 the per capita lynching rate in Florida per 100,000 African Americans was 79.8. For Georgia during the same period, the figure was 41.8; Louisiana, 43.7; Mississippi, 52.8. For lynching rates in Florida, see Tolnay and Beck, *A Festival of Violence,* 37–38; Works on lynching include Jacqueline Jones Royster, ed., *Southern Horrors and Other Writings: The Anti-Lynching Campaign of Ida B. Wells, 1892–1900* (Boston: Bedford Books, 1997). For other studies of racial violence during the period under discussion,

see White, *The Rope and the Faggot;* Arthur F. Raper, *The Tragedy of Lynching* (1933; reprint, New York: Dover, 1970). Kennedy, *Palmetto Country;* and W. Fitzhugh Brundage, *Lynching in the New South: Georgia and Virginia, 1880–1930* (Urbana: University of Illinois Press, 1993).

4. Michael D'Orso, *Like Judgment Day: The Ruin and Redemption of a Town Called Rosewood* (New York: Boulevard Books, 1996); Maxine D. Jones et al., "A Documented History of the Incident Which Occurred at Rosewood, Florida in January 1923," Submitted to the Florida Board of Regents, December 22, 1923 (Tallahassee: Board of Regents, 1993).

5. "Florida Topics," *New York Freeman,* June 25, 1887.

6. In Florida, a suspected criminal's skin color was his or her most precious asset—or liability. For examples of unprosecuted white-on-black murder, see E. W. Carswell, *Washington: Florida's Twelfth County* (Chipley: E. W. Carswell, 1991); Michaels, *The River Flows North,* 372–373; Ralph Bellwood, *Tales of West Pasco* (Hudson, FL: Albert J. Makovec, 1962), 14–16; "A Negro Killed; Shot by John G. Chaires," *Weekly Tallahasseean,* September 5, 1901; "Verdict in Chaires Case," *Weekly Tallahasseean,* September 19, 1901; and "Uncomplimentary," *Fort Myers Press,* March 28, 1885. As white-on-white crime escalated, the state's reformers acknowledged that Jim Crow had ruined the state's jury system. See "Hanging Needed in Duval: A Low Villain Using His Pistol Because He thinks a White Man Can't Be Hanged in Duval county—Life in Danger," *Florida Times Union,* August 7, 1887; and "Curious Inconsistency of Jury Verdicts," *Pensacola Journal,* January 28, 1906. The class of the alleged criminal also mattered. In one of its more candid moments (May 13, 1897), the *Tampa Weekly Tribune* admitted, "A Negro or poor white man who steals a loaf of bread will be sentenced to prison; while rich white man, who has money and social standing can steal thousands of dollars; and is able to laugh at law and remain free."

7. "Pensacola People," *New York Age,* June 23, 1888. African American women in Florida fell prey to white violence—including sexual violence—on many occasions. See Testimony of Hannah Tutson, *Florida Ku Klux Klan Hearings,* 59–64; "Ku Klux in Florida," *Christian Recorder,* November 27, 1873; "Southern White Gentleman Rapes Little Race Child," *Chicago Defender,* March 18, 1916. Much more research is needed in this area, and historian Elsa Barkley Brown criticizes historians who have glossed over violence against black women. See Brown, "Negotiating and Transforming the Public Sphere: African American Political Life in the Transition from Slavery to Freedom," in Jane Dailey, Glenda Gilmore, and Bryant Simon, eds., *Jumpin' Jim Crow: Southern Politics from Civil War to Civil Rights* (Princeton: Princeton University Press, 2000), 28–66; and Darlene Clark Hine, "Rape and the Inner Lives of Black Women in the Middle West: Preliminary Thoughts on the Culture of Dissemblance," *Signs* 14 (summer 1989), 912–920.

8. See "Burned at the Stake," *Courier-Informant* (Bartow), June 5, 1901; and "Negro Burned at Stake," *St. Petersburg Times,* June 8, 1901.

9. "That Reward," *Courier Informant,* June 5, 1901.

10. "Negro Killed By Police Officer," *Florida-Times Union,* April 9, 1904.

11. "A Shockingly Brutal Murder Committed in Bay County," *Apalachicola Times,* May 22, 1920.

12. "Court House Notes," *Panama City Pilot,* November 25, 1920.

13. John Porter to William Chandler, October 2, 1890, vol. 82, Chandler Papers.

14. The literature on African American armed resistance includes Timothy Tyson, *Radio Free Dixie: Robert F. Williams and the Roots of Black Power* (Chapel Hill: University of North Carolina Press, 1999); Quarles, *The Negro in the American Revolution;* Kenneth Wiggins Porter, "Florida Slaves and Free Negroes in the Seminole War, 1835–1842," *Journal of Negro History* 28 (October 1943), 390–421; Gwendolyn Midlo Hall, *Africans in Colonial Louisiana: The Development of an Afro-Creole Culture in the Eighteenth Century* (Baton Rouge: Louisiana State University Press, 1992), 97–118; Akinyele K. Umoja, "Eye for an Eye: The Role of Armed Resistance in the Mississippi Freedom Movement" (diss., Emory University, 1996); Sundiata Keita Cha-Jua, "'A Warlike Demonstration': Legalism, Armed Resistance, and Black Political Mobilization in Decatur, Illinois, 1894–1898," *Journal of Negro History* 83 (winter 1998); Vincent Harding, *There Is a River: The Black Struggle for Freedom* (New York: Vintage Books, 1981); and George C. Wright, *Racial Violence in Kentucky, 1865–1940: Lynchings, Mob Rule, and "Legal Lynchings"* (Baton Rouge: Louisiana State University Press, 1990).

15. Thurman, *The Luminous Darkness,* 6.

16. S. D. Jackson, "Pensacola Letter," *Christian Recorder,* October 27, 1887.

17. For examples, see "Negro Riot at Apalachicola," *Quincy Herald,* September 3, 1887; "Cole Incident," *Florida Times-Union,* July 29, 1888; "The Gadsden County Tragedy," *New York Age,* March 1, 1890; "Murders at Micanopy," *Evening Telegram,* January 12, 1892; "The Titusville Riot," *Indian River Advocate,* October 28, 1892; "War Wages At Wildwood," *Florida Times-Union,* December 26, 1893; "Negro Riot in Florida," *New York Tribune,* December 27, 1893; "Bullets for Blacks: Shot Negroes by the Scores," *Florida Times-Union,* December 27, 1893; "Lynched by White Men," *Richmond Planet,* August 10, 1895; "Butchery of Colored Men," *Richmond Planet,* October 31, 1896; "A Residence Dynamited in East Jacksonville," *Florida Metropolis,* September 6, 1904; "Tragedy at Monticello," *Gainesville Sun,* December 29, 1904; "Bloody Scenes in Baker County," *Florida Metropolis,* September 13, 1904; and Wetherell, *Facts from Florida.*

18. "Ku Klux in Florida," *Christian Recorder,* November 27, 1873; "More Murder," *Christian Recorder,* August 9, 1877; "Shooting Affray in Hernando,"

Sunland Tribune, June 9, 1877; "Jacksonville, Fla. District," *Christian Recorder,* July 2, 1891; "Negro Preacher Whipped," *Gainesville Daily Sun,* September 7, 1904; Johnson, *Highways and Byways of the South,* 356–357.

19. "Driven from home," *Richmond Planet,* November 6, 1897.

20. "Lawlessness in Florida," *South Florida Journal,* June 21, 1883.

21. *New York Freeman,* October 8, 1887; "Pensacola," *Florida Times-Union and Citizen,* October 23, 1899. For the Knights of Labor in west Florida, see McLaurin, *The Knights of Labor in the South,* 180.

22. Anonymous interview with author, July 1998. In author's possession. Some of my informants were very reticent about incidents of racial violence going back several decades because of a fear of retaliation by white citizens.

23. "A Negro Made Way With Near Bellvile," *Florida Times-Union,* April 7, 1904.

24. "Situation in Florida," *Christian Recorder,* March 3, 1881.

25. "Father and Son Killed Aged Negro for a $5 Debt," and "Another Account of Tragedy," both in *Florida Metropolis,* January 23, 1913.

26. F. G. Humphreys to William Chandler, February 15, 1890, vol. 80, Chandler Papers.

27. Hardy, *Oranges and Alligators,* 53–54.

28. See "Cornelius Brown is Badly Shot," *Florida Times-Union,* April 13, 1904.

29. "A Colored Man Brutally Murdered," *Richmond Planet,* February 15, 1896; "White Kills Mitchell," *Florida Times-Union,* February 8, 1896; "White Found Not Guilty," *Florida Times-Union,* May 15, 1896. African American hack drivers occupied a strategic place in the Jim Crow economy and deserve their own study.

30. "Drew The Color Line," *Pensacola Daily News,* August 25, 1903.

31. "The Jacksonville Times-Union Endorses Lynching," Box C343, folder: Clippings 1918 June, Papers of the National Association for the Advancement of Colored People, Manuscript Division, Library of Congress; hereafter cited as NAACP Papers. For media justification of lynching in Florida also see "After Four Year's [*sic*] Absence," *New York Age,* February 16, 1889. The literature on lynching, its causes, and its impact on American society is vast. Ida Barnett Wells's investigative work remains the starting point. For a collection of Wells's essays, see Royster, *Southern Horrors.* For lynching in Florida, see Kennedy, *Palmetto Country;* and D'Orso, *Like Judgment Day.* Important theoretical and historical works include Hall, *Revolt against Chivalry;* LeeAnn Whites, "Love, Hate, Rape, Lynching: Rebecca Latimer Felton and the Gender Politics of Racial Violence," in Cecelski and Tyson, *Democracy Betrayed,* 143–162; and W. Fitzhugh Brundage, ed., *Under Sentence of Death: Lynching in the South* (Chapel Hill: University of North Carolina Press, 1997).

32. "Skinned Alive," *Richmond Planet,* May 25, 1895.

33. O'Rell, *Jonathan and His Continent,* 187–188.

34. "Awful Brutality," *Richmond Planet,* September 10, 1904; "Wash Bradley Meets Fate of Lynchers' Vengeance at Levyville," *Gainesville Daily Sun,* September 7, 1904.

35. "Negro Preacher Whipped," *Gainesville Daily Sun,* September 7, 1904. Leon Litwack (*Trouble in Mind,* 13) notes that lynching and acts of racial terror, "seemed designed not only to punish the alleged offenders but also to send a message to the entire community." Jacquelyn Dowd Hall (*Revolt against Chivalry,* 141) argues: "lynching functioned as a mode of repression because it was arbitrary and exemplary, aimed not at one individual but at blacks as a group."

36. "Farmer Boy" to William Bloxham, May 22, 1898, Box 12, folder 2, Governor William Bloxham Papers, Florida State Archives.

37. Nell Irvin Painter has explored the complex intersections between sex, economics, and racial violence in "'Social Equality,' Miscegenation, Labor, and Power," in Numan V. Bartley, ed., *The Evolution of Southern Culture* (Athens: University of Georgia Press, 1988), 47–67. See also Nancy MacLean, "The Leo Frank Case Reconsidered: Gender and Sexual Politics in the Making of Reactionary Populism," in Dailey, Gilmore, and Simon, *Jumpin' Jim Crow,* 183–218; Hall, *Revolt against Chivalry;* and Whites, "Love, Hate, Rape, Lynching."

38. O. L. Williams to William Bloxham, October 31, 1898, Governor William Bloxham Papers.

39. Oliver Cox, *Caste Class and Race: A Study in Social Dynamics* (1948; reprint, New York: Monthly Review Press 1970), 555.

40. "The Color Line that Belts the Earth," *Florida Times-Union,* March 20, 1904. For a critique of the increasingly apolitical bent of the literature on racial violence see J. Morgan Kousser et al., "Revisiting a Festival of Violence (Lynchings in the American South)," *Historical Methods* 31 (fall 1998), 171–175. Nell Irvin Painter's *Exodusters* offers a convincing argument about the overlap between politics and racial violence. See also the impressive essays on the Wilmington Massacre of 1898 in Cecelski and Tyson, *Democracy Betrayed.*

41. Hannah Arendt, *The Origins of Totalitarianism* (New York: Harcourt Brace, 1951), 465. Arendt pioneered the concept of "the banality of evil," meaning situations where atrocities become so commonplace that they lose "the quality of temptation." See Arendt, *Eichmann in Jerusalem: A Report on the Banality of Evil* (New York: Viking, 1963), 150.

42. J. Randall Stanley, *History of Jackson County* (Marianna: Jackson County Historical Society, 1950), 205 (emphasis added). For writings that explained the rationale for white violence, see Brevard, *A History of Florida,* 168–178;

William T. Cash, *History of the Democratic Party in Florida: Including Biographical Sketches of Prominent Florida Democrats* (Live Oak: Florida Democratic Historical Foundation, 1936), 68; John McKinnon, *History of Walton County* (Atlanta: Byrd Printing Co., 1911), 342; and Margaret Fairlie, *History of Florida* (Kingsport, TN: Kingsport Press, 1935), 257.

43. The extent to which this was so can be partially gauged in an incident involving Duval County circuit court judge Daniel A. Simmons in 1918. Lecturing a grand jury, Simmons made a brief negative reference to Ku Klux Klan violence in Florida during Reconstruction. The very next day, a chastened Simmons apologized to the jury and the white public: "As you know, I spoke purely extemporaneously; I used no notes of any kind. I didn't note at the time I began talking to you gentlemen that I would even refer to the Ku Klux Klan, but I did not intend to say, and I am sure you did not understand me to say that the Ku Klux Klan which I said was organized for the purposes of freeing the South of Negro domination and carpet bag rule and which did free the South of Negro domination and carpet bag rule, was a bunch of rowdies and bandits from the beginning. Such was not the case. Every unbiased student of history knows that such was not the case, and that the real manhood of the South, the real Anglo-Saxon people of the United States, was organized into that noble clan to free our beloved Southland of the Black pall that had settled down upon it as a result of the misguided judgment of our friends of the North." "The Judge Apologizes," *New York Age,* June 8, 1918.

44. "The Best Will Prevail," *Miami Herald,* October 30, 1920.

45. L. Allen, Nellie B. Ramsdell, and Russell L. Fuller, "History of Sumter County," typescript for the Federal Writers' Project, 1936, American Guide, Sumter, Florida, P. K. Yonge Library of Florida History, University of Florida, 11.

46. C. M. Hooper to William Chandler, December 16, 1890, vol. 82, Chandler Papers.

47. Nor were white women immune from this kind of humiliation. The widow of W. C. Crum received a threatening letter from the self-described "WHITE CAPS" of Tampa who threatened to beat her son and run him out of town. Years earlier, Mrs. Crum's now-deceased husband appointed a black man as an assistant postmaster. Both were severely beaten, and the black postal official was driven out of Tampa. Some area whites seemed to believe in the biblical homily that the sins of the father should be visited upon the son, and warned Mrs. Crum accordingly. See "Whitecappers Write a Letter," *Florida Times-Union,* March 4, 1904.

48. F. G. Humphreys to William Chandler, February 15, 1890, vol. 80, Chandler Papers.

49. For the assassination of Saunders and its bitter aftermath, see "Waylaid and Murdered: A United States Officer Assassinated in Florida," "The 'Florida

Troubles,'" and "The Saunders Murder," *New York Daily Tribune*, February 15, 17, and 18, 1890.

50. Humphreys to Chandler, February 15, 1890.

51. Hernandos XIII Regulators to W. S. Jennings, n.d., Box 8, folder: "correspondence 1900: November," Governor William Sherman Jennings Papers, P. K. Yonge Library of Florida History, University of Florida. For a similar case see F. P. Cone to Governor N. B. Broward, January 26, 1907, Box 5, folder, "January 1907," Governor Napoleon Bonaparte Broward Papers, P. K. Yonge Library of Florida History.

52. "Phosphate in Demand: Florida Product Wanted Over in Europe," *Florida Metropolis*, May 6, 1905; "A Prosperous Year for Phosphate Producers," *Florida Metropolis*, July 20, 1905; "Larger Profits in Turpentining," *Florida Times-Union*, July 1, 1903; "Another Big Naval Stores Company Formed," *Florida Metropolis*, June 22, 1905.

53. "The Combine Among the Naval Stores Exporters," *Florida Metropolis*, February 13, 1907.

54. "Naval Stores Industry," *Panama City Pilot*, January 23, 1908.

55. "Turpentine Men to Meet," *Fernandina News*, September 13, 1906. For an overview of the Florida turpentine industry, see Drobney, "Where Palm and Pine Are Blowing."

56. "The Turpentine Man and the Trade," *Florida Times-Union*, March 3, 1904.

57. "Turpentine Men Meet in Bartow," *Florida Times-Union*, November 2, 1903.

58. "The Passing Throng," *Atlanta Journal-Constitution*, July 21, 1905.

59. "Who Constitute the Vagrants," *Florida Metropolis*, January 26, 1906.

60. "Why Scarce," *Florida Metropolis*, January 11, 1906.

61. "An Answer to 'Logger,'" *Florida Metropolis*, January 12, 1905.

62. For the operation of one turpentine company store, see "Report, 1923," Box, "1920–1923," file, "Johnston-McNeill & Company," William C. Powell Papers, Special Collections Library, Duke University.

63. P. Smith to Governor Bloxham, June 19, 1883, Box 5, Florida Governors' Papers, Florida State Archives; "Red Records of Blood," *Evening Telegram*, January 11, 1892.

64. "Duel at Sanderson Results in two Deaths," *Florida Metropolis*, July 31, 1905. See also "Bloody Scenes in Baker County," *Florida Metropolis*, September 16, 1904.

65. "Instantly Killed in Pasco County: Negro Laborer Made Trouble and Was Shot," *Florida Times-Union*, July 24, 1903.

66. "A Double Killing," *Florida Metropolis*, June 27, 1905.

67. "Six Killed and Eight Wounded," *New York Tribune*, July 27, 1896; "A Horrible Tragedy," *Jasper News*, July 31, 1896.

68. "Two Men Killed in Race Riot," *Pensacola Daily News,* December 31, 1902.

69. Ibid.

70. "Delenda Est Carthago," *Bartow Courier Informant,* August 9, 1893. See also "The Negro Can't Be Assimilated," *Pensacola Daily Commercial,* September 28, 1888; "The Whites are Getting There," *Ocala Banner,* February 27, 1891; "The True Policy for the Black Belt of Florida," *Pensacola Daily Journal,* January 5, 1887; "Not Wanted in Wauchula," *Florida Metropolis,* October 9, 1909.

71. "Slaves," *New York Daily Tribune,* November 22, 1891.

72. Harry A. Peeples, *Twenty-Four Years: In the Woods, On the Waters and In the Cities of Florida* (Tampa: Tribune Printing Company, 1906), 12–13.

73. "The Tie Cutters Shot Into," *Ocala Banner,* November 22, 1895. Also see "Outrage at Fort Meade," *Weekly Floridian* (Tallahassee), April 22, 1884.

74. Pasco County residents remembered the massacre in great detail: "It was a dark night. All the shanties where the 'niggers' slept were in a row facing the mill yard. One of our crowd took a jug of coal oil and poured it on the pine-tags just in front of the shanties. We were lined up in good shooting distance in front of each shanty, and then several men lit the coal-oil on fire and stepped back in line. You could see the front of the shanties as clear as day, and the niggers, awakened by the first shot came boiling out the doors. That was the only way they could get out. Just as fast as one came in sight he was cut down, until the last one was dead." Bellwood, *Tales of West Pasco,* 14–16.

75. "Are Establishing a Modern Colony," *Pensacola Daily News,* April 2, 1903.

76. "Florida's New Christian Colony," *New York Age,* November 5, 1914, in *Tuskegee Institute News Clipping File,* ed. John W. Kitchens (Microfilm, 252 reels, Tuskegee Institute, 1978), reel 3, frame 403.

77. "Village in Florida Is Without Negroes," *Schenectady Gazette,* July 13, 1919, in *Tuskegee Institute News File,* reel 11, frame 41. See also Samuel E. Mays, *Genealogical Notes on the Family of Mays and Reminiscences of the War between the States* (Plant City: Plant City Enterprise, 1927), 194–195.

78. "The Afro-American League," *New York Freeman,* August 6, 1887.

79. For background on the league, see Emma Lou Thornbrough, "The National Afro-American League, 1887–1908," in David M. Reimers, ed., *The Black Man in America since Reconstruction* (New York: Thomas Y. Crowell, 1970), 94–109.

80. "Looking Westward," *Southern Leader,* quoted in *New York Age,* January 5, 1889.

81. "The Southern Problem," *New York Age,* February 18, 1888. T. L. McCoy was an African American Republican Party leader in Putnam County who eventually advocated black political independence from the GOP. See

"A Reply: Palatka," *Florida Journal* (Jacksonville), August 28, 1884, and "A Letter from McCoy," *Palatka Daily News,* April 30, 1885.

82. "African Emigration," *Christian Recorder,* July 25, 1878.

83. "Negroes Return to Africa," *Sunland Tribune* (Tampa), May 11, 1878.

84. *Daily News* (Pensacola), January 26, 1895.

85. Quoted in *New York Globe,* November 17, 1883.

86. "How Lynchings Can Be Stopped," *Christian Recorder,* May 4, 1892.

87. "Pensacola Letter," *Christian Recorder,* January 28, 1886.

88. "Anti-lynching Resolutions," *Christian Recorder,* May 13, 1897.

89. Albert N. Doyle, who served as city marshal in Palatka from 1870 to 1884, wrote a graphic account of police violence: "A Jailer's Barbarity," *Florida Journal,* July 17, 1884.

90. "A Lynching Prevented," *New York Age,* August 18, 1888.

91. For Fowler as a GOP candidate see "The Election Yesterday," *Palatka Daily News,* May 6, 1885; and "The Republican Slate," *Palatka Daily News,* March 25, 1887.

92. "A Lynching Prevented," *New York Age,* August 18, 1888.

93. The Grand Army of the Republic was the Union veterans' fraternal organization. See "Emancipation Celebration," *Florida Times-Union,* December 23, 1890; and "J. B. Armstrong, Lake City," *Christian Recorder,* May 14, 1873. See also chapter 4 for a discussion of African Americans' historical memories of slavery, the Civil War, and Reconstruction.

94. For records of the black militia companies, see Adjutant General Papers, Official Correspondence, Record Group 172, Florida State Archives. For a broader discussion of the black militia, see Otis A. Singletary, *The Negro Militia and Reconstruction* (New York: McGraw-Hill, 1963); and Stephen Kantrowitz, "One Man's Mob Is Another Man's Militia: Violence, Manhood, and Authority in Reconstruction South Carolina," in Dailey, Gilmore, and Simon, *Jumpin' Jim Crow,* 67–87.

95. "Negroes of Tampa Celebrate Emancipation," *Florida Peninsular,* January 5, 1870; "Military," *Florida Peninsular,* January 4, 1871.

96. "Emancipation Day," *Evening Telegram,* January 1, 1892.

97. "We have one military company, the Jacksonville Guards, uniformed and equipped, numbering about 60 men and commanded by Captain Franklin, an old soldier": "Florida's Progress," *New York Globe,* August 18, 1883.

98. "Annual Return of the Militia of the state of Florida, for the year ending December 31, 1891," Adjutant General Papers, Official Correspondence, Record Group 172. It is important to note that black militias, where they did exist, were not called during "emergencies" such as labor conflicts as their white counterparts were. This is an area that begs for more research. Black newspaper editor W. I. Lewis believed that the last remnant of the black militia in Florida

was dissolved in 1893. Lewis's observation on black militias was found in NCP, *Florida Metropolis*, March 12, 1903.

99. W. I. Lewis to William E. Chandler, April 27, 1896, vol. 102, Chandler Papers.

100. "Soldiers and Negroes Clash," *St. Augustine Evening Record*, September 7, 1904.

101. "Wholesale Burglaries," *St. Augustine Evening Record*, September 8, 1904.

102. James Weldon Johnson, *Along This Way: The Autobiography of James Weldon Johnson* (New York: Viking, 1933), 165–170. See also "Camp Hand Shot by Militiaman," *Florida Metropolis*, June 14, 1909; "The Tampa Rifles," *Morning Tribune* (Tampa), May 27, 1897; and "Florida Politics," *New York Age*, August 25, 1888.

103. "Fired With Fatal Result," *Semi-Weekly Times Union* (Jacksonville), April 17, 1896.

104. "Killed Him," *Florida Sentinel*, quoted in *Richmond Planet*, April 25, 1896.

105. C. C. Ellis to William D. Bloxham, April 12, 1897, Carton 11, folder, "General County Correspondence: Alachua–Clay, 1897–1900," Governor William Bloxham Papers.

106. "Crushed His Skull," *Florida Times-Union*, July 5, 1892.

107. Ibid. See also "From Jacksonville," *Palatka Weekly Times*, July 7, 1892.

108. The Jacksonville chief of police was suspended by Mayor Robinson for failing to take action to keep the peace. See "His Honor, The Mayor," *Florida Times-Union*, July 7, 1892. State officials were also critical of Jacksonville authorities for allowing the situation to get out of hand. See "Report of the Adjutant General," *Florida Message & Documents* (1893), 18–19.

109. "Fired Upon by Negroes," and "The Jacksonville Riot," *Atlanta Constitution*, July 7 and 8, 1892.

110. "Crushed His Skull," *Florida Times-Union*, July 5, 1892.

111. "Were All Under Arms," *Florida Times-Union*, July 6, 1892.

112. "The Law is Triumphant," *Florida Times-Union*, July 8, 1892.

113. "The Soldiers Are Gone," *Florida Times-Union*, July 9, 1892.

114. For the belated mobilization of the militia, see "Report of the Adjutant General" (1893). Also C. A. Finley to N. B. Broward, July 5, 1898, vol. 25, Governor Francis P. Fleming's Letterbooks, Florida State Archives; C. A. Finley to Fleming, July 6, 1892, ibid.

115. "The Law is Triumphant," *Florida Times-Union*, July 8, 1892.

116. Royster, *Southern Horrors*, 70. For the Paducah case, see Wright, *Racial Violence in Kentucky*, 169.

117. William Bloxham to F. W. Knights, June 25, 1897, vol. 48, Governor Bloxham's Letterbooks, Florida State Archives. "Negro Brute's Deed Calls Out

Lynchers," *Florida Times-Union,* June 25, 1897; "The Key West Trouble," *Florida Times-Union,* June 26, 1897; "Desperate Darkeys," *Tampa Morning Tribune,* June 27, 1897; *New York Tribune,* June 26, 1897. "All Quiet At Key West," *Fort Myers Press,* July 1, 1897. See also "Can't Lynching be Stopped?" *Afro American Sentinel* (Omaha), July 3, 1897, quoted in Herbert Aptheker, ed., *A Documentary History of the Negro People in the United States* (1951; New York: Citadel Press, 1990), 2: 796.

118. William Bloxham to William McKinley, June 26, 1897, vol. 48, Governor Bloxham's Letterbooks.

119. "William Gardiner Killed at Key West," *Florida Times-Union,* June 26, 1897; "Island City Incidents," *Tampa Morning Tribune,* June 29, 1897.

120. William Bloxham to William McKinley, June 25, 1897, vol. 48, Governor Bloxham's Letterbooks.

121. "Local Militia Ready to Go," *Florida Times Union,* June 26, 1897; "Quiet at Key West," *Florida Times-Union,* June 27, 1897.

122. "Key West Kickers," *Morning Tribune* (Tampa), August 12, 1897; "Johnson Justly Judged," *Morning Tribune* (Tampa), August 13, 1897.

123. "Anti Mob and Lynch Club Organized by Negroes at Dunnellon," *Tampa Weekly Tribune,* October 26, 1899. J. Lester Dinkins, a local historian of the region, traced the origins of the miners' organization to 1895. See Dinkins, *Dunnellon,* 147–148.

124. Ellis C. May, *'Gaters, Skeeters and Malary: Recollections of a Pioneer Florida Judge: Volume One* (New York: Vantage Press, 1952), 117.

125. "Lynching at Dunnellon," *Florida Times-Union,* June 13, 1899.

126. "The Dunnellon Trouble," *Ocala Banner,* June 16, 1899. For one account of the escalating violence in Dunnellon, see Ellis C. May, *From Dawn to Sunset: Recollections of a Pioneer Florida Judge: Volume 2* (New York: Vantage Press, 1955), 148, 150.

127. "Only One Lynched," *Florida Times-Union and Citizen,* June 16, 1899; "Everything Reported Quiet at Dunnellon," *Florida Times-Union and Citizen,* June 14, 1899.

128. "That Lynching in Florida," *Richmond Planet,* July 22, 1899.

129. "On the Move," *Daily News* (Pensacola), January 8, 1890; "Among the Phosphate Kings," *Florida Times-Union,* February 5, 1890.

130. For an overview of the phosphate industry in Florida see Ortiz, "Like Water Covered the Sea," 121–125.

131. For the miners' ethos of self-defense, see "Lawless Negroes," *Ocala Banner,* January 16, 1891.

132. "Dunnellon," *Florida Times-Union and Citizen,* October 17, 1899.

133. Dinkins, *Dunnellon,* 147.

134. Based on interviews done with local residents in the 1960s, J. Lester Dinkins believed that the Anti-Mob and Lynch Club members sought the

confrontation with the Stephens clan, whom they blamed for the majority of racial violence in the town. See ibid., 146–148.

135. "He Killed Them," *Richmond Planet*, May 23, 1896; "Race War in Florida," *New York Tribune*, May 18, 1896; "Four Men Fell," *Florida Times-Union*, May 13, 1896. For an armed self-defense case with some similarities to the Trice affair, see Johnson, *Highways and Byways of the South*, 351.

136. "The Negroes Terrorized: An Ugly State of Affairs in Manatee County," *Florida Times-Union*, May 17, 1896.

137. "The Race War in the Newspapers," *Manatee River Journal*, May 21, 1896.

138. Several years later, whites and African Americans in Manatee County were still at each other's throats. After a black man had been shot and killed by a white storekeeper in 1900, the local black population was said to be on the verge of insurrection. See "Will Watson, Negro," *Tampa Weekly Tribune*, July 12, 1900; and "Negroes Threaten War vs. Whites at Palmetto in the Death of Watson," *Tampa Weekly Tribune*, July 19, 1900.

139. Black Floridians in Pensacola, Jacksonville, Apalachicola, Tampa, Gainesville and other cities volunteered to raise citizens' militias. For a sample of these letters, see Governor William Bloxham to C. F. Call, June 13, 1898; Bloxham to M. M. Lewey, June 9, 1898; Bloxham to General Josiah T. Walls, July 2, 1898, all in: Governor Bloxham's Letterbooks, vol. 51.

140. "J. J. Hendry Advised that Negroes in Tampa Willing to Serve in War," *Tampa Weekly Tribune*, April 7, 1898.

141. Willard B. Gatewood, Jr., *"Smoked Yankees" and the Struggle for Empire: Letters from Negro Soldiers* (Urbana: University of Illinois Press, 1971); Willard B. Gatewood, Jr., "Negro Troops in Florida, 1898," *Florida Historical Quarterly* 49 (July 1970), 1–15.

142. For commentaries on African American armed resistance in Florida see "Kept His Word: A Colored Man's Bravery," *Richmond Planet*, January 25, 1896; and "A Brave Defender," *Richmond Planet*, May 23, 1896. Black Floridians were ardent subscribers to the *Planet* and other black newspapers that advocated armed self-reliance. In 1896, the *Planet* ran an endorsement in an African American newspaper in Orlando stating: "John Mitchell, the great apostle of justice, has his heart and mind in his work." See "Was a Beauty," *Richmond Planet*, January 25, 1896.

143. "The 'Winchester' Negro," *Florida Times-Union*, July 13, 1890; *Quincy Herald*, July 19, 1890.

144. Astute legislators recognized on second thought that open rejection of the U.S. Constitution might invite federal intervention into the state's politics. House members politely voted Beard's bill down. See "Beard's Proposition Is Killed in the House," *Florida Metropolis*, May 9, 1907.

145. Governor Broward's address is taken from a typewritten proof found in his personal papers. See Box 5, folder, "January 1907," Governor Broward Papers. For reaction to Broward's address, see "Message of the Governor," *Florida Metropolis,* April 11, 1907.

146. "Lynching," *Panama City Pilot,* April 30, 1908.

147. For examples of this assumption, see Judith Stein, *The World of Marcus Garvey: Race and Class in Modern Society* (Baton Rouge: Louisiana State University Press, 1988), 42; Lee E. Williams and Lee E. Williams II, *Anatomy of Four Race Riots: Racial Conflict in Knoxville, Elaine (Arkansas), Tulsa, and Chicago, 1919–1921* (Hattiesburg: University and College Press of Mississippi, 1972), 8–9; and Arthur I. Waskow, *From Race Riot to Sit-In, 1919 and the 1960s: A Study in the Connections between Conflict and Violence* (New York: Doubleday, 1966), 10.

4. TO GAIN THESE FRUITS THAT HAVE BEEN EARNED: EMANCIPATION DAY

1. This historical battle over the meaning of the past was an integral part of racial conflict during the Jim Crow era. It is in this context that Ira Berlin notes: "The struggle over slavery's memory has been almost as intense as the struggle over slavery itself. For many, the memory of slavery in the United States was too important to be left to the black men and women who experienced it directly." Berlin, Favreau, and Miller, *Remembering Slavery,* xiii. The literature on historical memory in the South is extraordinarily rich. For examples, see W. Fitzhugh Brundage, "White Women and the Politics of Historical Memory in the New South, 1880–1920," in Dailey, Gilmore, and Simon, *Jumpin' Jim Crow,* 115–139; David W. Blight, *Race and Reunion: The Civil War in American Memory* (Cambridge: Harvard University Press, 2001); W. Fitzhugh Brundage, ed., *Where These Memories Grow: History, Memory, and Southern Identity* (Chapel Hill: University of North Carolina Press, 2000); Chafe et al., *Remembering Jim Crow;* and Edward L. Ayers, *The Promise of the New South: Life after Reconstruction* (New York: Oxford University Press, 1993).

2. *Dallas Morning News,* April 10, 1911.

3. Du Bois, *Black Reconstruction,* 711–729; Litwack, *Trouble in Mind,* 71–77; John David Smith, *An Old Creed for the New South: Proslavery Ideology and Historiography, 1865–1918* (Westport, CT: Greenwood Press, 1985).

4. C. L. R. James observed: "There are and always will be some who, ashamed of the behaviour of their ancestors, try to prove that slavery was not so bad after all, that its evils and its cruelty were the exaggerations of propagandists and not the habitual lot of the slaves. Men will say (and accept) anything in order to foster national pride or soothe a troubled conscience." *The Black*

Jacobins: Toussaint L'Ouverture and the San Domingo Revolution (1938; New York: Vintage Books, 1989), 13.

5. Carl L. Crippen to William Chandler, March 1, 1890, vol. 80, Chandler Papers. For memorials honoring Jefferson Davis, see "Memorial Services," and "Jefferson Davis," *Florida Mirror* (Fernandina), December 10 and 12, 1889. For a dedication of a Confederate monument see "A Memorable Day at Quincy," *Weekly Floridian*, May 20, 1884. For Confederate Memorial Day ceremonies, see "The Graves to Be Decorated," and "Dead Heroes are Honored," *Florida Metropolis*, April 25 and 27, 1901; and "Tribute Paid to Confederate Dead," *Florida Times-Union*, April 27, 1904. For commemorations of Robert E. Lee, see "January Nineteenth," *Weekly Tallahasseean*, January 24, 1901; "The South to Honor Him," *Florida Metropolis*, January 18, 1907; and "Mayor Asks All To Honor Memory of Gen. R. E. Lee," *Florida Metropolis*, January 16, 1913. Also see "Confederate Veterans," *Ocala Banner*, February 28, 1896; "Heroes of Lost Cause," *St. Petersburg Times*, November 22, 1902; and "Southern Women," *Florida Metropolis*, April 6, 1909. For the functions that these monuments play, see Benedict Anderson, *Imagined Communities, Reflections on the Origin and Spread of Nationalism* (London: Verso, 1983), 6.

6. "Florida Paying Veterans Better Than Any Other State in the South," *Florida Metropolis*, May 3, 1919.

7. Fairlie, *History of Florida*, 254. See also Caroline Mays Brevard, *A History of Florida: With Questions, Supplementary Chapters and an Outline of Florida Civil Government* (New York: American Book Company, 1919), 188. Carter G. Woodson observed: "The thought of the inferiority of the Negro is drilled into him in almost every class he enters and in almost every book he studies." Woodson, *The Mis-Education of the Negro* (1933; reprint, Nashville: Winston-Derek, 1990), 1.

8. Litwack, *Trouble in Mind*, 71.

9. "Another Professor Talks," *Florida Times-Union*, July 9, 1910. Edward Said notes that the impetus for constructing such a history on the part of a dominant group represents "the clear need to project their power backward in time, giving it a history and legitimacy that only tradition and longevity could impart." Said, *Culture and Imperialism* (New York: Vintage Books, 1994), 16.

10. An effort by black Floridians to "erect a monument in honor of the Negro soldiers who died in Cuba during the late war" failed. "Editorial," *Southwestern Christian Advocate*, March 23, 1899.

11. Beth Tompkins Bates, *Pullman Porters and the Rise of Protest Politics in Black America, 1925–1945* (Chapel Hill: University of North Carolina Press, 2001), 35.

12. Joyce A. Hanson, *Mary McLeod Bethune and Black Women's Political Activism* (Columbia: University of Missouri Press, 2003), 25–28.

13. For the critical role of historical memory in black freedom struggles, see W. E. B. Du Bois, *The Souls of Black Folk* (1903; reprint, New York: Vintage Books, 1990), 16–35; Wilson Jeremiah Moses, *Afrotopia: The Roots of African American Popular History* (Cambridge: Cambridge University Press, 1998); Blight, *Race and Reunion,* 300–380; Thavolia Glymph, "'Liberty Dearly Bought,': The Making of Civil War Memory in Afro-American Communities in the South," in Charles M. Payne and Adam Green, eds., *Time Longer Than Rope: A Century of African American Activism, 1850–1950* (New York: New York University Press, 2003); and Kathleen Clark, "Celebrating Freedom: Emancipation Day Celebrations and African American Memory in the Early Reconstruction South," in Brundage, *Where These Memories Grow,* 107–132. For historical memory and other political struggles, see Lawrence Goodwyn, *Breaking the Barrier: The Rise of Solidarity in Poland* (New York: Oxford University Press, 1991), 128; and Jeffrey Gould, *To Lead as Equals: Rural Protest and Political Consciousness in Chinandega, Nicaragua, 1912–1979* (Chapel Hill: University of North Carolina Press, 1990), 172–174.

14. S. W. Anderson to Joseph Lee, November 20, 1882, Lee Papers,.

15. "Negro History," Box A879, folder, "Florida Historical Material, 1936–1939," WPA Papers, Library of Congress.

16. Rawick, *Florida Narratives,* 182. Also see "Dade County, Florida Ex-Slave Stories," Box 4, Florida Negro Papers, University of South Florida (the Florida Negro Papers, hereafter so cited, consist of WPA materials collected in Florida by Zora Neale Hurston and other WPA field workers). Wallace, *Carpetbag Rule in Florida,* 25.

17. Rawick, *Florida Narratives,* 55–56. For an overview of the period, see John Hope Franklin, *The Militant South, 1800–1861* (Cambridge: Harvard University Press, 1956).

18. Martha Harvey Farmer interview with author, Behind the Veil Collection.

19. Malachia Andrews interview with author, Behind the Veil Collection.

20. Wetherell, *Facts from Florida,* 21.

21. Ibid., 21–22. E. C. F. Sanchez, a Democratic official in Gainesville, validated this observation. See "Section IV," typed manuscript, n.d., folder, "Civil War, Gainesville," E. C. F. Sanchez Papers, P. K. Yonge Library of Florida History, University of Florida. Susan Bradford Eppes, one of Florida's staunchest supporters of the antebellum way of life, confirmed her family's slaves' joy at Emancipation. See "The Negro of the Old South: A Bit of Period History," manuscript, n.d., page 82, Box 368, Pine Hill Plantation Papers, Special Collections Library, Florida State University. Eppes's book was published in 1925 under the same title.

22. "Information Wanted," *Christian Recorder,* June 14, 1900. For examples of other Florida notices, see also "Notice to Louisiana Ministers," *Christian*

Recorder, August 26, 1880; "Information Wanted," *Christian Recorder,* December 21, 1893; "Information Wanted," *Christian Recorder,* May 10, 1894; and "Information Wanted of My Aunt," *Christian Recorder,* July 25, 1900.

23. *The Proceedings of the State Conference of the Colored Men of Florida.*

24. Ibid.

25. For the belief in the justice of slave pensions, see "The Colored Department," *New Enterprise* (Madison), March 5, 1903, and NCP, *Florida Metropolis,* February 24, 1903.

26. Johnson, *Highways and Byways of the South,* 361.

27. "Ex Slave Club," Box 4, folder, "Dade County, Florida Ex-Slave Stories," Florida Negro Papers.

28. Capitalizing on formerly enslaved African Americans' beliefs in slavery compensation, various "ex-slave pension agents" preyed on aging black citizens with fraudulent pension schemes. See "Was a Bogus pension Agent," *Florida Metropolis,* November 25, 1901; and "Swindled Ex-Slaves," *New York Age,* November 2, 1905.

29. Kachun, *Festivals of Freedom,* 106–107.

30. "An Uncalled for Attack on Ministers," *Christian Recorder,* June 13, 1889. For descriptions of Emancipation Day events in Florida also see "Florida Facts," *New York Age,* June 2, 1888; "Celebrated Emancipation," *Florida Metropolis,* January 3, 1906; and "Daytona Will Celebrate New Year's Day," *Chicago Defender,* December 18, 1915.

31. "Major Wright, Speaker at Daytona Emancipation Day Celebration," NCP, *Florida Metropolis,* January 12, 1920.

32. "Emancipation Day Was Celebrated Here," *Pensacola Journal,* January 21, 1906.

33. F. A. Pappy to Joseph E. Lee, December 14, 1880, Lee Papers. See also "Pensacola People," *New York Age,* April 27, 1889. Joseph E. Lee to Emancipation Association of Valdosta, November 28, 1914, Box 2, folder, "Law Practice; Personal Correspondence, 1914, Sept.-Dec," Joseph E. Lee Papers, Florida State Archives. One young man who witnessed several Emancipation Day events in Valdosta was Louis Lomax. He later recalled: "The public rendering of Negro history occurred on January first of each year. That was Emancipation Day and a cause for great speaking and celebration. The Emancipation Day services were mammoth things." Lomax, *The Negro Revolt* (New York: Harper & Row, 1962), 61.

34. "Emancipation Day," *Ocala Banner,* January 9, 1891.

35. "Emancipation Day," *Evening Telegram* (Jacksonville), January 1, 1892.

36. "Emancipation Day," *Ocala Banner,* January 3, 1896.

37. "Emancipation Celebration at Ocala Conspicuous For Women Speakers," Newspaper clipping, January 6, 1923, Box 3, folder, "Miscellaneous:

Newspaper clippings, 1913–1939," Armwood Family Papers, Special Collections Library, University of South Florida.

38. "Negro Customs," Box 1, folder, "Customs—No Date," Florida Negro Papers.

39. Ibid.

40. Viola B. Muse, "Celebrations and Amusements Among Negroes of Florida," January 19, 1937, Florida Negro Papers.

41. Ibid.

42. "A colored excursion party arrived here," *Quincy Herald,* May 24, 1889.

43. "The Celebration," *South Florida Argus* (Sanford), May 22, 1886.

44. "Milton," *Florida Times Union,* May 24, 1899.

45. "MacClenny News," NCP, *Florida Metropolis,* May 24, 1915.

46. "Memorial Day Exercises," NCP, *Florida Metropolis,* May 31, 1905.

47. *New York Age,* June 9, 1888. David W. Blight writes about the origins of Decoration Day in *Race and Reunion,* 64–97.

48. "A Florida Grand Army Post," *New York Age,* May 4, 1889.

49. "Memorial Day Exercises," NCP, *Florida Metropolis,* May 31, 1905. For the African American GAR in St. Augustine, see "Hotel Life in Florida," *New York Age,* January 26, 1889.

50. "Memorial Day Observed," NCP, *Florida Metropolis,* June 1, 1915.

51. Ibid.

52. "Decoration Day," NCP, *Florida Metropolis,* June 1, 1903.

53. Anonymous to Joseph E. Lee, n.d. [1879], Lee Papers, Ike Williams III Private Collection.

54. Higginbotham, *Righteous Discontent,* 43.

55. "Status of Afro-Americans," *New York Age,* June 30, 1888.

56. "Societies in the South," *New York Age,* July 28, 1888.

57. "The Land of Flowers," *New York Age,* July 14, 1888.

58. *New York Freeman,* July 2, 1887. Another disapproving observer in Pensacola complained: "The way most of our people worship the Lord in our churches, jumping upon the benches, jumping their dresses off great many times, the excessive clapping of the hands, and making such loud noises, is altogether uncalled for and far behind this intelligent age." *New York Freeman,* September 18, 1886.

59. Hezekiah Butterworth, *A Zig Zag Journey in the Sunny South or Wonder Tales of Early American History* (Boston: Estes and Lauriat, 1887), 243, 246.

60. "Church Services Among the Negroes," *Christian Recorder,* March 3, 1881.

61. Zora Neale Hurston, "The Sanctified Church," Box A878, WPA Papers, Library of Congress.

62. Sterling Stuckey argues, "The ring in which Africans danced and sang is the key to understanding the means by which they achieved oneness in

America." Stuckey, *Slave Culture: Nationalist Theory, and the Foundations of Black America* (New York: Oxford University Press, 1987), 12.

63. "Six Months in Florida," *Christian Recorder*, April 26, 1883. For another anti–ring shout column in the AME journal see "Preachers Wanted in Florida," *Christian Recorder*, October 12, 1882. Black leaders also attacked other religious practices in Florida that admitted of African influence. For a criticism of African burial practices in Florida see "Colored Graveyards," *New York Globe*, March 3, 1883.

64. William Artrell to Joseph Lee, October 26, 1881, Lee Papers, Ike Williams III Private Collection.

65. William Artrell to Joseph Lee, November 14, 1881, Lee Papers, ibid.

66. For a typical anti-Reconstruction speech delivered by one of the state's premier Democratic politicians, see "Speech Lakeland, Florida October 1928," Box 2, folder: "Speeches," Park Monroe Trammell Papers, P. K. Yonge Library of Florida History, University of Florida.

67. "Colored News," *Florida Mirror* (Fernandina), June 9, 1897.

68. "A Florida Rip Van Winkle," *New York Globe*, December 15, 1883; "Funeral for R. W. Butler," *Florida Metropolis*, May 4, 1911.

69. Rawick, *Florida Narratives*, 29.

70. *New York Freeman*, February 5, 1887.

71. Harriet Jefferson interviewed by Mausiki Stacey Scales and Tywanna Whorley, August 8, 1994, Behind the Veil Collection.

72. Item from the *Florida Sentinel*, quoted in *New York Age*, November 9, 1905. For the actual celebration see "Windjammers Ignored in Pensacola," *Florida Sentinel*, quoted in *New York Age*, December 14, 1905.

73. See "Quincy News," and "Freedman's Day Successful," *Florida Metropolis*, February 15 and 18, 1907.

74. For African American participation in the Revolution see Quarles, *The Negro in the American Revolution*; and Sylvia Frey, *Water from the Rock: Black Resistance in a Revolutionary Age* (Princeton: Princeton University Press, 1991).

75. NCP, *Florida Metropolis*, January 18, 1906.

76. A typical announcement read: "The colored citizens of Palatka are hereby officially called to meet at Central Academy School Building, on next Monday evening, November 4th, for the purpose of reorganizing to carry into effect the emancipation movement and make arrangements to celebrate that festival next January." "Palatka Dots," NCP, *Florida Metropolis*, November 1, 1912. See also "Emancipation Celebration," and "Crescent City Briefs," both NCP, *Florida Metropolis*, November 15 and 20, 1912.

77. "Sanford Notes," NCP, *Florida Metropolis*, January 14, 1913.

78. "Bartow News," NCP, *Florida Metropolis*, January 15, 1913.

79. "Daytona Items," NCP, *Florida Metropolis*, January 9, 1913.

80. "Gainesville Celebrates Emancipation Proclamation," NCP, *Florida Metropolis,* January 6, 1913.

81. "Fort Pierce News," and "Emancipation Day Celebration," both NCP, *Florida Metropolis,* January 9 and 3, 1913.

82. "Fifty Years," NCP, *Florida Metropolis,* January 3, 1913.

5. TO SEE THAT NONE SUFFER: MUTUAL AID AND RESISTANCE

1. Marcel Mauss, *The Gift: The Form and Reason for Exchange in Archaic Societies,* trans. W. D. Halls (New York: W. W. Norton, 2000), 82.

2. "Grand United Order of Odd Fellows Souvenir Program for the Annual Thanksgiving Services," Box 3, folder, "Miscellaneous Programs, 1903–1937," Armwood Family Papers.

3. Thurman, *The Luminous Darkness,* 5.

4. Sociologist Aldon D. Morris writes, "throughout time, for significant numbers of oppressed people, the groundwork for social protest has been laid by the insurgent ideas rooted within their churches, labor unions, voluntary associations, music, informal conversations, humor, and collective memories of those elders, who participated in earlier struggles." Morris, "Political Consciousness and Collective Action," in Morris and Carol McClurg Mueller, eds., *Frontiers in Social Movement Theory* (New Haven: Yale University Press, 1992), 370–371. For the importance of these institutions in African American life, see Franklin and Moss, *From Slavery to Freedom,* 94–95, 379–380; Elsa Barkley Brown, "Womanist Consciousness: Maggie Lena Walker and the Independent Order of Saint Luke," *Signs* 14 (spring 1989), 610–633; Hunter, *To Joy My Freedom,* 67–73; Rachleff, *Black Labor in Richmond,* 22; Lewis, *In Their Own Interests,* 72; Ira Berlin, *Slaves without Masters: The Free Negro in the Antebellum South* (New York: Pantheon, 1974), 313; Jacqueline Rouse, *Lugenia Burns Hope: Black Southern Reformer* (Atlanta: University of Georgia Press, 1989); Hewitt, *Southern Discomfort,* 125–129, 201–204; David T. Beito, *From Mutual Aid to the Welfare State: Fraternal Societies and Social Services, 1890–1967* (Chapel Hill: University of North Carolina Press, 2000); Loretta J. Williams, *Black Freemasonry and Middle-Class Realities* (Columbia: University of Missouri Press, 1980); and Melville J. Herskovits, *The Myth of the Negro Past* (1941; Boston: Beacon Press, 1990), 161.

5. Vincent Harding (*There Is a River,* 209) notes that black secret societies played vital roles in assisting fugitive slaves in the antebellum period. Ira Berlin (*Slaves without Masters,* 313) writes that during the era of slavery, African Americans "saw benevolent societies not only as a source of protection and fraternity, but also as an opportunity to pull the black community together and improve the condition of their people." See also Herskovits, *The Myth of the Negro Past,* 161.

6. *History and Manual of the Colored Knights of Pythias* (Nashville: National Baptist Publishing Board, 1917), 219–220.

7. NCP, *Florida Metropolis*, September 27, 1905.

8. "Independent Brotherhood," *Freeman* (Indianapolis), March 15, 1902.

9. Sutton E. Griggs, *Unfettered: A Novel* (Nashville: Orion, 1902), 242.

10. "The Universal Brotherhood," *Evening Telegram* (Jacksonville), January 9, 1892.

11. "Law of Self Preservation," *New York Age*, March 9, 1889.

12. "Colored Masons Meet," NCP, *Florida Metropolis*, January 16, 1906; "Masonic Grand Lodge," NCP, *Florida Metropolis*, February 27, 1907.

13. Franklin and Moss, *From Slavery to Freedom*, 339. Sterling D. Spero and Abram L. Harris, *The Black Worker: The Negro and the Labor Movement* (New York: Atheneum, 1969).

14. Montgomery, *Citizen Worker*.

15. "Coast Line Engine Crushes Colored Man," *Lakeland Star*, October 14, 1920.

16. "Colored Column," *St. Petersburg Times*, January 3, 1903. For other railroad accidents, see "Negro Switch Tender Meets a Horrible Death," *Florida Times-Union*, September 8, 1899; "Negro Workman Killed By Seaboard Air Line Train," *Florida Metropolis*, December 17, 1907; "Millville," *Panama City Pilot*, January 2, 1908; "A Negro Killed By Train," *Daily News* (Pensacola), April 9, 1890; "One Colored Train Hand Killed and Another Fatally Injured," *Florida Times-Union*, December 18, 1890; "A Train Hand, Colored . . . Was Killed," *Bradford Times*, February 5, 1892; and "A Negro Brakeman . . . Accidentally Run Over and Killed," *Bartow Courier-Informant*, October 18, 1893. It was also not uncommon for black workers to suffer crippling injuries on Florida's railroads. See "Lost His Leg," *Daily News* (Pensacola), January 26, 1895; and "Weley Cusby . . . Limping Around the Streets," *Palatka Daily News*, February 12, 1887.

17. *Quincy Herald*, June 20, 1891.

18. *Quincy Herald*, June 27, 1891.

19. See "General Church News," *Christian Recorder*, August 30, 1900; "Deaths and Burials," NCP, *Florida Metropolis*, November 12, 1912; "Charles Robinson Was Killed by Live Wire," *Florida Times-Union*, July 6, 1910; "Sam Crawley Drops Dead," *Bradford Telegraph*, August 23, 1889; "A Negro . . . Killed by a Falling Tree," *Jasper News*, December 1, 1893; "Fatal Accident At Mandarin," *Florida Times-Union*, February 16, 1883; "An Aged Negro Killed While Felling a Tree," *Daily News*, September 1, 1899; "The Colored Department," *Madison Enterprise*, February 25, 1904; and "A Negro Boy Drowned," *Jasper News*, July 14, 1893.

20. J. S. Adams, *Florida: Its Climate, Soil and Productions* (New York: Sisher & Field, 1870), 38.

21. "Drowned in the River," *Florida Metropolis,* April 7, 1905.

22. "Negro Seriously Hurt Today," *Daily News,* January 10, 1903. See also "Negro Dock Hand Falls Into River and Drowns," *Florida Times-Union,* July 1, 1910; "Unknown Negro Man Working at Clyde Terminals Drowned," *Florida Times-Union,* October 3, 1911; "Pensacola: Death of a Bayman While Unloading a Vessel," *Florida Times-Union,* October 24, 1899; "Bad Accident to A Negro," *Daily News,* December 26, 1902; "Deaths and Burials," NCP, *Florida Metropolis,* November 21, 1919; and "Negroes Drown in Apalachicola River," *Florida Metropolis,* November 26, 1919.

23. James H. Foss, *Florida: Its Climate, Soil, Productions, and Agricultural Capabilities* (Washington, DC: Government Printing Office, 1882), 79.

24. "Florida Facts," *New York Freeman,* September 10, 1887.

25. African American labor unions were especially concerned with honoring recently deceased members. For black workers, mutuality and unionism were intertwined. For an example of a burial service organized by members of the Laborers' Union, see NCP, *Florida Metropolis,* May 16, 1905. For a funeral overseen by the Cigar Makers' Union, see NCP, *Florida Metropolis,* June 27, 1905.

26. "An Important Question," *Daily News* (Pensacola), September 21, 1899.

27. "The Colored Department," *New Enterprise* (Madison), February 19, 1903.

28. "Pensacola," *New York Freeman,* September 18, 1886.

29. "Societies in the South," *New York Age,* July 28, 1888. The September 18, 1886, issue of *New York Freeman* reported that in Pensacola, the "A.M.E. Church Burial and Endowment Association celebrated its fourth anniversary at Kupfrian's Park on Monday. This is quite a good society, well officered and numerically large."

30. A. I. Dixie interview with author, August 10, 1994, Behind the Veil Collection.

31. Ibid. Historian David T. Beito (*From Mutual Aid to the Welfare State,* 57) notes, "The fraternal concept of reciprocity entailed mutual obligations between members and the organization to which they belonged."

32. See *Polk's Quincy and Gadsden County Directory, 1927* (Jacksonville: R. L. Polk & Co., 1927), 13–14.

33. "Live Oak Notes," NCP, *Florida Metropolis,* March 7, 1919.

34. "Palatka Dots," NCP, *Florida Metropolis,* November 20, 1912. See also "A Card of Thanks," NCP, *Florida Metropolis,* November 1, 1912.

35. Joel Buchanan interview with Louise Perry Haile, March 3, 1918, Fifth Avenue Blacks Oral History Project, Samuel Proctor Oral History Archives, University of Florida. For additional information on this mutual aid society, see Bruce Ergood, "The Female Protection and the Sun Light: Two Contemporary

Negro Mutual Aid Societies," *Florida Historical Quarterly* 50 (July 1971), 25–38.

36. "Drowned in the River," *Florida Metropolis,* April 12, 1901.

37. NCP, *Florida Metropolis,* April 16, 1901.

38. NCP, *Florida Metropolis,* April 13, 1901.

39. Jane Landers, *Black Society in Spanish Florida* (Urbana: University of Illinois Press, 1999), 130–132; Robert L. Hall, "African Religious Retentions in Florida," in Colburn and Landers, *The African American Heritage of Florida,* 42–70; Eugene D. Genovese, *Roll, Jordan, Roll: The World the Slaves Made* (New York: Pantheon, 1974), 194–202; David Barry Gaspar, *Bondmen and Rebels: A Study of Master-Slave Relations in Antigua* (Baltimore: John Hopkins University Press, 1985; reprint, Durham: Duke University Press, 1993), 144–145, 245; Lorena S. Walsh, *From Calabar to Carter's Grove: The History of a Virginia Slave Community* (Charlottesville: University Press of Virginia, 1997), 104–106; Michael Mullin, *Africa in America: Slave Acculturation and Resistance in the American South and the British Caribbean, 1736–1831* (Urbana: University of Illinois Press, 1992), 62–74; Herskovits, *The Myth of the Negro Past,* 198–206.

40. Entry dated April 7, 1872, in Abbie M. Brooks Diary. Historian Jane Landers (*Black Society in Spanish Florida,* 130) writes that enslaved African Americans on the northeastern Atlantic coast of Florida "often decorated graves with the last objects touched by the deceased, in the manner of the Congo."

41. Martin Richardson, "An Unusual Graveyard," March 18, 1937, Box 1, folder, "Cemeteries," Florida Negro Papers.

42. See Herskovits, *The Myth of the Negro Past,* 200–201.

43. Burial Notice, NCP, *Florida Metropolis,* November 21, 1905.

44. Paul Diggs, "Characteristic Traits in Regard to Negro Funerals," November 18, 1938, Florida Negro Papers.

45. "From the Land of Flowers," *New York Globe,* August 18, 1883.

46. "Grand Lodge of Masons," *Florida Metropolis,* May 12, 1911.

47. "Resolution of Respect," NCP, *Florida Metropolis,* March 2, 1907. The Carpenters also ensured decent funerals for members' spouses. See "Another feather in the Carpenter's Union Cap," *Evening Telegram,* November 21, 1892.

48. "Resolutions From Odd Fellows," NCP, *Florida Metropolis,* November 13, 1912. For another example of an Odd Fellows' burial service, see "Gainesville Briefs," NCP, *Florida Metropolis,* December 4 and 11, 1912. "Black Americans counted, the fraternal lodge's public presence announced time and again," notes historian Nick Salvatore, "regardless of white attitudes." Salvatore, *We All Got History: The Memory Books of Amos Webber* (New York: Random Books, 1996), 67.

49. "Mr. Floyd," NCP, *Florida Metropolis,* July 20, 1905.

50. NCP, *Florida Metropolis,* May 15, 1905. Also see "Mount Zion's Sick Members," NCP, *Florida Metropolis,* July 18, 1907.

51. NCP, *Florida Metropolis,* May 12, 1905.

52. "Strike to Involve All Trades Unions," *Florida Times-Union,* August 9, 1905.

53. Ibid.

54. *History and Manual of the Colored Knights of Pythias,* 492.

55. Ibid., 491. For an example of such a visit, organized by the members of the Syracuse Lodge in Jacksonville, see "Among the Colored People," *Florida Metropolis,* April 11, 1901.

56. "Orlando News Notes," NCP, *Florida Metropolis,* October 19, 1905. A black correspondent reported, "Orlando is well-stocked with secret and benevolent societies. There are two Masonic lodges, two Odd Fellow lodges, two Households of Ruth, one court of Calanthe, one Court of Heroines of Jericho and an association of the Knights of Pythias." "Orlando News Notes," NCP, *Florida Metropolis,* September 11, 1905.

57. "Gainesville Briefs," NCP, *Florida Metropolis,* December 2, 1912.

58. "Palatka Notes," NCP, *Florida Metropolis,* December 5, 1912.

59. See also "The Report of the Sick Members of the Mt. Zion A.M.E. Church," NCP, *Florida Metropolis,* April 9, 1909.

60. "Florida Odd Fellows," *New York Age,* June 30, 1888; Aquilina Howell interview with author, August 18, 1997, Behind the Veil Collection.

61. *Pensacola Daily Commercial,* September 3, 1888.

62. Salvatore, *We All Got History,* 261.

63. This despite the fact that the Pythians' building had burned down. See "Pythian Grand Officers," NCP, *Florida Metropolis,* May 21, 1901; and "Chivalry of Pythians," NCP, *Florida Metropolis,* May 24, 1901. The Odd Fellows were also active in raising funds for destitute members and their families. "The Odd Fellows," NCP, *Florida Metropolis,* May 27, 1901. For unions, see "Cigarmakers' Union No. 29," NCP, *Florida Metropolis,* May 31, 1901; and "The International Bricklayers' Union of America," NCP, *Florida Metropolis,* June 1, 1901.

64. "General laws of the Independent Afro-American Relief Union of Gadsden County, Florida" (1932), Special Collections Library, Duke University.

65. The Georgia Colored Knights of Pythias followed the same practice. See Knights of Pythias Medical Records Ledger, 1920–21, Special Collections Library, Duke University.

66. Smith, *An Old Creed for the New South;* Blight, *Race and Reunion,* 255–299.

67. "Negro Preacher Killed Near Alachua," *Florida Times-Union,* April 22, 1904.

68. "Shaw Not Guilty Said Grand Jury," *Daily Sun* (Gainesville), October 12, 1905.

69. "Fatal Shooting Ends Quarrel," *Florida Metropolis,* October 11, 1905.

70. "Coroner's Jury Acquits Taylor," *Florida Metropolis,* October 13, 1905.

71. Exposing the limits of black solidarity, some of the witnesses to the case, both during the coroner's inquisition and the subsequent trial, were African Americans who testified that Taylor had been acting in self-defense. See "Taylor Case Still on Trial," *Florida Metropolis,* December 13, 1905.

72. NCP, *Florida Metropolis,* October 13, 1905; "S. C. Taylor is Arrested," *Florida Metropolis,* October 17, 1905.

73. "S. C. Taylor is Arrested," *Florida Metropolis,* October 17, 1905.

74. "Taylor Verdict Is Not Guilty," *Florida Metropolis,* December 14, 1905.

75. "Ladies Union," NCP, *Florida Metropolis,* October 26, 1905.

76. NCP, *Florida Metropolis,* October 12, 1905. Miss Eartha M. M. White is an extraordinary figure in the annals of Florida history and deserving of a full-length biography. She was a tireless community organizer, an advocate of women's suffrage, and an ardent promoter of African American history.

77. "Lakeland News Notes," NCP, *Florida Metropolis,* January 28, 1913.

78. William Artrell to Joseph Lee, May 3, 1881, Box 2, Lee Papers, Ike Williams III Private Collection. Adolph Reed criticizes a tendency among some scholars to posit "a nostalgic image of organic solidarity in black communities under Jim Crow." Reed, *W. E. B. Du Bois and American Political Thought: Fabianism and the Color Line* (New York: Oxford University Press, 1997), 159.

79. "Mrs. Amy Henderson Dead," NCP, *Florida Metropolis,* November 5, 1901.

80. "Ocala News Notes," NCP, *Florida Metropolis,* December 11, 1912. For Ocala as a center of black fraternal culture, see "Masonry in Florida," *New York Globe,* April 15, 1884. For a list of fraternal organizations in Ocala, see *Ocala City Directory, 1908–9* (Ocala: L. J. Brumby, 1908), 24–25.

81. "Marianna News," NCP, *Florida Metropolis,* December 9, 1919. The bylaws of the Independent Afro-American Relief Union in Gadsden County were crystal clear: "All members must pay their endowment each month and any member failing to pay their endowment if death should occur, the beneficiary will receive no death benefit." "General laws of the Independent Afro-American Relief Union of Gadsden County, Florida" (1932), Special Collections Library, Duke University.

82. "Footless," *Florida Metropolis,* June 24, 1905; "Revolting Spectacle," *Florida Metropolis,* May 29, 1905.

83. "A Florida Society," *New York Age,* February 18, 1888.

84. "Wanted 'Blue Blood' Charter," *Pensacola Daily News,* January 19, 1903. Adolph Reed argues, "Black people are neither more or less capable of pettiness and class prejudice than anyone else. . . . Skin tone, family connections, and even more arbitrary considerations all created fissures in the phantom

unity of the pre–civil rights community just as they do today." Reed, "Dangerous Dreams: Black Boomers Wax Nostalgic for the Days of Jim Crow," *Village Voice*, April 16, 1996, 27.

85. Kelly, *Race, Class, and Power in the Alabama Coalfields*, 97–107; Kevin K. Gaines, *Uplifting the Race: Black Leadership, Politics, and Culture in the Twentieth Century* (Chapel Hill: University of North Carolina Press, 1996).

86. "Educational Meetings," *New York Freeman*, September 3, 1887. Also see Henry Williams and Orion Ellis interview with author, July 29, 1998, Behind the Veil Collection.

87. One controversy erupted in Gainesville when a black minister interrupted a wedding taking place in his church because he had not been informed in advance about the ceremony. According to a local report, "The deacons of the church met that night and immediately dismissed him from the church as pastor." "Notes from Gainesville," NCP, *Florida Metropolis*, July 8, 1907.

88. "What Mill Hands Say," *Florida Metropolis*, May 25, 1901; "Delegation of Carpenters Visits Ministers," NCP, *Florida Metropolis*, September 20, 1905.

89. "Notice to My Customers and Friends," *Florida Metropolis*, April 7, 1909.

90. "Knights of Pythias," folder: "Counties: Duval Clubs & Societies," Box A56, WPA Papers, Library of Congress.

91. *History and Manual of the Colored Knights of Pythias*, 110.

92. "The Odd Fellows' endowment bureau pays to the heirs of a deceased member $200. The total amount paid to date by this bureau is $19,275. The Odd Fellows are justly proud of this feature of their order." "Odd Fellows Anniversary," NCP, *Florida Metropolis*, May 15, 1905. And "Maj. J. E. Clark, past master at Eatonville of the Odd Fellows, spoke highly of the work of the bureau while he was in the city last week. He said $1,800 was paid out to widows on the 18th inst." NCP, *Florida Metropolis*, September 25, 1905.

93. *History and Manual of the Colored Knights of Pythias*, 480.

94. Ibid., 482. For an example of a contested election for high office in the Masons, see "De Land Notes," NCP, *Florida Metropolis*, December 20, 1907.

95. *History and Manual of the Colored Knights of Pythias*, 487.

96. Robin D. G. Kelley (*Race Rebels*, 38) emphasizes the ways that African American lodges provided living models of democracy in the era of one-party rule.

97. *Acts and Resolutions of the Legislature of Florida, Seventh Regular Session* (Tallahassee: Tallahasseean Book and Job Print, 1899), 261–262.

98. *History and Manual of the Colored Knights of Pythias*, 389.

99. "Florida Pythians Protest to Governor," *New York Age*, June 10, 1915.

100. For examples of mutuality in rural Florida, see Martha Harvey Farmer interview with author, August 21, 1997; Carrie Carr interview with author,

August 21, 1997; Daisy Young interviewed by Mausiki Stacey Scales and Tywanna Whorley, July 27, 1994, Behind the Veil Collection.

101. A. I. Dixie interview with author, August 10, 1994, Behind the Veil Collection. For a sampling of Pythian lodges through the state, see "Quincy Notes," NCP, *Florida Metropolis,* February 15, 1907; "Orlando Notes," NCP, *Florida Metropolis,* December 20, 1907; "Palatka News Notes," NCP, *Florida Metropolis,* December 23, 1907; "Daytona Notes," NCP, *Florida Metropolis,* January 4, 1907.

102. This calculation is based on a comparison of membership figures and census data. See "Pythian Grand Lodge," NCP, *Florida Metropolis,* May 24, 1919, and *Fourteenth Census of the United States,* Volume 3, *Population* (Washington, DC: GPO, 1923), 185–186.

103. For the road to *Plessy,* see Franklin and Moss, *From Slavery to Freedom,* 224–238.

104. August Meier and Elliot Rudwick, "The Boycott Movement against Jim Crow Streetcars in the South, 1900–1926," *Journal of American History* 55 (March 1969), 756–775; Blair Murphy, " 'A Gratuitous Insult to Every One with a Drop of Negro Blood': African American Citizenship, Identity, and the Protest over Jim Crow Transportation" (diss., Duke University, in progress).

105. "Street Car Bill Passed," *Florida Metropolis,* November 6, 1901.

106. "Fletcher Will Sign The Bill," *Florida Metropolis,* November 8, 1901.

107. "Important Mass Meeting," NCP, *Florida Metropolis,* November 20, 1905.

108. Newspaper clipping, "Nearly Ready to Begin," January 11, 1895, Bethel Baptist Institutional Church Archives, Jacksonville. I am indebted to the staff at Bethel Baptist for taking time out from their busy schedules to give me a tour of their church's sanctuary and archives in the summer of 1999.

109. See "Bethel Baptist," and "Bethel's Annual Outing," NCP, *Florida Metropolis,* July 8 and 18, 1905.

110. J. D. Wetmore to George Baldwin, June 7, 1905, Box 41, folder 1846, George Baldwin Papers, Southern Historical Collection, University of North Carolina, Chapel Hill.

111. "The Great Baptist Union," *Florida Metropolis,* May 22, 1905.

112. "New Street Car Law Operative Saturday," *Florida Metropolis,* June 29, 1905.

113. "Florida 'Jim Crow' Bagged," *New York Age,* August 3, 1905.

114. "Boycott On In Jacksonville," *New York Age,* July 20, 1905.

115. "Among the Exchanges," *Indianapolis Freeman,* March 22, 1902.

116. Elsa Barkley Brown ("Negotiating and Transforming the Public Sphere," 28–32) has reminded historians that much of the antiblack violence of this period was directed against African American women.

117. Quoted in "A Negro Street-Railway Company," *Literary Digest,* October 17, 1903.

118. "Boycott Street Cars," NCP, *Florida Metropolis,* November 8, 1901.

119. "Hackmen To Meet Committee," NCP, *Florida Metropolis,* December 2, 1902.

120. "Result of the Boycott," *Florida Metropolis,* November 11, 1901; "Negroes Fire on Streetcars," *Atlanta Constitution,* November 11, 1901.

121. "Tried to Wreck A Street Car," *Florida Metropolis,* November 15, 1901.

122. Ibid.; "Bill To Repeal The Ordinance," *Florida Metropolis,* November 20, 1901.

123. "Negroes Boycott Street Cars," *Freeman,* November 30, 1901

124. "Mr. Avery's Race Separation Bill," *Pensacola Journal,* April 25, 1905.

125. "Negros [*sic*] Have Filed Protest," *Pensacola Journal,* April 30, 1905.

126. "Avery's 'Jim Crow' Bill Enacted Into Law," *Florida Metropolis,* May 17, 1905; " 'Jim Crow' Bill Is Signed," *Florida Metropolis,* May 22, 1905; " 'Jim Crow' Bill Passed Both Houses Unanimously," *Pensacola Journal,* May 13, 1905.

127. John E. Hartridge to William H. Tucker, May 28, 1905, Box 41, folder 1845, George Baldwin Papers.

128. "Negroes Continue to Boycott Street Cars," *Pensacola Journal,* May 20, 1905.

129. *Pensacola Journal,* July 2, 1905.

130. "An Epidemic of Insanity," *Afro-American Ledger,* July 15, 1905; "Car Boycott in Jacksonville," *Pensacola Journal,* July 5, 1905.

131. "The Passing Throng," *Atlanta Constitution,* July 24, 1905.

132. H. H. Hunt to George Baldwin, August 1, 1905, Box 41, folder 1857, George Baldwin Papers.

133. "Afro-American Good For Something," *New York Age,* July 27, 1905. For additional evidence of the boycott's success see George Baldwin to Stone & Webster, July 12, 1905, Box 41, folder 1851, George Baldwin Papers.

134. Many African American leaders supported a strictly legal strategy to counter the new Jim Crow law. See "Nolan Jacksonville's Mayor," *New York Age,* June 29, 1905.

135. For efforts to bribe black newspaper editors and subvert the boycott, see J. Wetmore to George Baldwin, June 8 and June 7, 1905, Box 41, folder 1846, George Baldwin Papers. For the elaborate—and unsuccessful—attempt to bribe Joseph Lee and other black leaders, see additional company correspondence in folder 1854, George Baldwin Papers.

136. "Nolan Jacksonville's Mayor," *New York Age,* June 29, 1905. For the boycott circular, see "Minister's Alliance Meeting," NCP, *Florida Metropolis,* June 7, 1905.

137. An eminent AME divine, Rev. R. B. Brooks, was forced to make a public statement announcing his support for the boycott, after suspicions that he opposed it. See "Mt. Zion's Quarterly Meeting," NCP, *Florida Metropolis*, July 10, 1905. See also "Ministerial Alliance Meeting," and "A.M.E. Ministers Stand Pat," both NCP, *The Florida Metropolis*, July 18 and 14, 1905.

138. "Will Test The Jim Crow Law," and "Colored People Will Fight Avery Law," *Pensacola Journal*, July 11 and 25, 1905. Purcel was based in Pensacola and Wetmore in Jacksonville.

139. "Ordinance to Separate Races," *Pensacola Journal*, August 3, 1905.

140. "Jim Crow Law Gets a Black Eye," *Afro-American Ledger*, July 29, 1905; "Avery Law Is Unconstitutional," and "Negroes Are Again Riding," *Pensacola Journal*, July 27 and August 1, 1905.

141. "Negroes Are Again Riding," *Pensacola Journal*, August 1, 1905.

142. "Ordinance to Separate Races," *Pensacola Journal*, August 3, 1905; "Race Separation Is Declared Valid," *Florida Times-Union*, 1906.

143. "Negro Woman Creates Disturbance on Street Car," *Florida Metropolis*, June 5, 1907.

144. "Rumpus on Street Car Cost Negro Woman $40," *Florida Metropolis*, June 6, 1907. African Americans also continued to file lawsuits against segregation on Florida's railroads. See "Business of Two Courts," *Florida Metropolis*, January 17, 1906.

145. "Amazons Make Trouble on Street Car Yesterday," *Florida Metropolis*, January 21, 1907.

146. "Pulled From Street Car; Negress Got Awfully Mad," *Florida Times-Union*, November 14, 1911.

147. This story is taken from "Told Story of an Assault," *Daily News* (Pensacola), March 31, 1903.

148. For an in-depth discussion of gender and resistance, see Glenda Gilmore, "Murder, Memory, and the Flight of the Incubus," in Cecelski and Tyson, *Democracy Betrayed*, 82–83.

149. "Fourteen Arrested," *Weekly Tallahasseean*, November 6, 1903.

150. "Whites and Blacks Have Trouble in Miccosukee Saturday Night," *Florida Times-Union*, November 4, 1903.

151. Ibid. (emphasis added).

152. "The Jack Johnson Buttons," *Indianapolis Freeman*, May 14, 1910.

153. "Result of Reno Affair Starts Mob Violence in the City," *Florida Times-Union*, July 5, 1910.

154. "Quiet in Pensacola After Riots of Fourth," *Florida Times-Union*, July 6, 1910. For examples of race riots in other cities in the wake of the fight, see "Race Riots Follow Johnson's Victory in Jeffries Fight," *Florida Times-Union*, July 5, 1910.

155. "Segregation Made to Pay," *Afro-American*, April 4, 1914, in *Tuskegee Institute News Clipping File*, reel 3, frame 452.

156. "Oppose 'The Nation,'" *Chicago Defender*, June 17, 1916.

157. "No Birth of A Nation for Palatka," *Palatka Advocate*, November 29, 1916, in *Tuskegee Institute News Clipping File*, reel 4, frame 545.

158. "Better Schools," *Palatka Advocate*, n.d., 1916, in *Tuskegee Institute News Clipping File*, reel 5, frame 162.

159. "Palatka," NCP, *Florida Metropolis*, August 15, 1919.

6. LOOKING FOR A FREE STATE TO LIVE IN

1. Gertrude Williams interviewed by Mausiki Scales, August 11, 1994, Behind the Veil Collection.

2. John Hope Franklin and Alfred A. Moss (*From Slavery to Freedom*, 472) write that in 1916, "the Pennsylvania Railroad brought 12,000 to work in its yards and tracks; all but 2,000 came from Florida and Georgia." James Weldon Johnson paid tribute to the pioneering role played by African American workers in Florida, telling Charles S. Johnson, "I think the first point from which the movement started was Northeastern Florida and the first concerns to bring these people North were the railroads, especially the Pennsylvania." James Weldon Johnson to Charles S. Johnson, National Urban League Records, Series 6, Box 86, folder, "Migration Study Correspondence, 1918–1924," Manuscript Division, Library of Congress (hereafter cited as National Urban League Records). For newspaper articles charting the dimensions of the black labor exodus from Florida see "Florida Losing Its Negroes," *Journal* (Providence, RI), November 9, 1916; "10,000 Workers Leave Florida For the North" (newspaper name illegible), October 10, 1916, both in *Tuskegee Institute News Clippings File*, reel 5, frame 482.

3. General treatments of the Great Migration include Carter G. Woodson, *A Century of Negro Migration* (Washington, DC: 1918; reprint, New York: AMS Press, 1970); James R. Grossman, *Land of Hope: Chicago, Black Southerners, and the Great Migration* (Chicago: University of Chicago Press, 1989); Emmett J. Scott, *Negro Migration during the War* (New York: Oxford University Press, 1920); Florette Henri, *Black Migration: Movement North, 1900–1920* (Garden City, NY: Anchor Press, 1975); and Peter Gottlieb, *Making Their Own Way: Southern Blacks' Migration to Pittsburgh, 1916–1930* (Urbana: University of Illinois Press, 1987).

4. "Colored Labor For Connecticut," *Guardian*, March 25, 1916, in *Tuskegee Institute News Clipping File*, reel 5, frame 445.

5. "Negro Laborers Going North," *Daily Democrat* (Tallahassee), July 16, 1916; Unpublished manuscript, Box 86, folder, "Miscellany," National Urban League Records.

6. American Sumatra was the product of a 1907 merger of twelve tobacco firms. See Miles Kenan Womack, Jr., *Gadsden: A Florida County in Word and Picture* (Dallas: Taylor, 1976), 105–106; Stanley, *History of Gadsden County*, 158–159.

7. A. I. and Samuel Dixie interviewed by author, August 10, 1994, Behind the Veil Collection.

8. A. I. Dixie interviewed by author, August 22, 1997, Behind the Veil Collection.

9. Malachia Andrews interviewed by author, August 9, 1994, Behind the Veil Collection.

10. Interview with A. I. Dixie, 1997.

11. Alvin and Mary Butler interviewed by author, July 24, 1998, Behind the Veil Collection.

12. See Janie F. Roberts interviewed by Joel Buchanan, July 10, 1984, Fifth Avenue Black Oral History Project, Oral History Program, University of Florida.

13. "Fearful Frenzy of Florida Farmers," *Afro-American*, August 26, 1916.

14. This account is taken from the *Florida-Times Union*, August 19 and 20, 1916; see also "Two Women Lynched," *Richmond Planet*, August 26, 1916. For an equally brutal incident in Jackson County, see "Logan Brothers Acquitted of the Murder of Negroes," *Montgomery Advertiser*, March 3, 1916, in *Tuskegee Institute News Clipping File*, reel 5, frame 364.

15. Labor shortages in the Hartford Valley tobacco crop during that summer caught the attention of African Americans throughout the South. The National Urban League worked with the Connecticut Leaf Tobacco Association to recruit black workers for the harvest. See National Urban League Records, Series 1, Box 1, folder: "Connecticut Leaf Tobacco Assoc. 1916, 1918, 1921." In the South, black newspapers publicized the labor shortage. See "25 More Boys Leave for North," *Savannah Tribune*, July 22, 1916, in *Tuskegee Institute News Clipping File*, reel 5, frame 445.

16. "Many Want to Come North," *New York Age*, February 22, 1917, *Tuskegee Institute News Clipping File*, reel 6, frame 594.

17. W. E. B. Du Bois, "The Migration of Negroes," *Crisis*, June 1917, 63–66.

18. For comparative regional wage rates, see T. J. Woofter, "Migration of Negroes from Georgia, 1916–1917," in U.S. Department of Labor, *Negro Migration in 1916–1917* (Washington, DC: Division of Negro Economics, U.S. Department of Labor, 1919), 85; U.S. Department of Labor, *The Negro at Work during the World War and during Reconstruction: Statistics, Problems, and Policies Relating to the Greater Inclusion of Negro Wage Earners in American Industry and Agriculture* (Washington, DC: Government Printing Office, 1921), 10.

19. *Daily Democrat* (Tallahassee), July 2, 1916.

20. *Daily Democrat,* August 5, 1916.

21. "Negro Laborers Going North," *Daily Democrat,* July 16, 1916.

22. *Daily Democrat,* August 2, 1916.

23. A. I. and Samuel Dixie interview, 1994.

24. *Daily Democrat,* August 2, 1916. For American Sumatra's presence in Connecticut, see the National Urban League's Connecticut Leaf Tobacco Association file cited above.

25. *Daily Democrat,* August 2, 1916.

26. "Negro Labor in the North," *New York Age,* July 27, 1916, in *Tuskegee Institute News Clipping File,* reel 5, frame 486.

27. "500 Negro Laborers Keenly Disappointed," *Florida Times-Union,* August 3, 1916.

28. "Southerners Plan to Stop Exodus," *Chicago Defender,* August 12, 1916.

29. Emmett J. Scott, comp., "Letters of Negro Migrants of 1916–1918," *Journal of Negro History* 4 (July 1919), 292.

30. "Workmen Kept from Leaving," *Afro-American,* August 19, 1916. Mayor Bowden issued this order in the final week of July 1916. While he did not disclose what he meant when he spoke of "demoralized" conditions, he may have been referring to the rape of a six-year-old black girl by a white Jacksonville teenager in late February. The alleged rapist's father, who was reportedly very wealthy, was quickly able to get the charge of rape reduced to a lesser charge. It appears that the case was thrown out of court in mid-March. African Americans in Jacksonville were enraged, and called mass meetings at the Knights of Pythias hall in an effort to salvage the case—all to no avail. See "Southern White Gentleman Rapes Little Race Child," *Chicago Defender,* March 18, 1916.

31. *Florida Times-Union,* August 3, 1916.

32. *Afro-American,* August 19, 1916.

33. Undated manuscript, Box 86, folder, "Migration Study—Negro Migrants, Letters," National Urban League Records, Series 6: "Early Surveys." See also Scott, *Negro Migration during the War,* 73.

34. *Chicago Defender,* August 19, 1916.

35. "Many Negroes Were Again Disappointed," *Florida Times-Union,* August 7, 1916.

36. *Florida Times-Union,* August 10, 1916.

37. *Artisan* (Jacksonville), July 29, 1916. By 1916, the *Artisan* spoke almost exclusively for white labor. Its stance toward African Americans ranged from pity to vigorous hostility. Little thought was given to forming coalitions with black union workers to break the stranglehold of the city's business elite on civic power. For the possibilities and limitations of interracial solidarity in the later Jim Crow era, see Kelley, *Hammer and Hoe;* and Michael Honey, *Southern*

Labor and Black Civil Rights: Organizing Memphis Workers (Urbana: University of Illinois Press, 1993).

38. *Afro-American,* August 19, 1916.

39. C. W. Johnston, *The Sunny South and Its People* (Chicago: Press of Rand McNally, 1918), 248.

40. "Colored Labor Growing Scarce," *Gazette News* (Daytona), September 6, 1918, in *Tuskegee Institute News Clippings File,* reel 8, frame 25.

41. "Minister Asserts Brutality Drove Negroes North," *New York Tribune,* July 2, 1917, in *Tuskegee Institute News Clippings File,* reel 6, frame 475.

42. NCP, *Florida Metropolis,* January 8, 1919.

43. *Fort Myers Messenger* quoted in "Negro Press on Migration North," *New York Age,* March 15, 1917, in *Tuskegee Institute News Clippings File,* reel 6, frame 534.

44. "Labor Recruiters for Muscle Shoals Plant Arrested," *Montgomery Advertiser,* March 15, 1917, in *Tuskegee Institute News Clippings File,* reel 8, frame 275.

45. Scott, "Letters of Negro Migrants of 1916–1918," 324. Scott, who had formerly served as Booker T. Washington's secretary, and Carter G. Woodson, editor and founder of the *Journal of Negro History,* documented the Great Migration via the letters of the migrants themselves. Scott compiled two sets of letters that potential migrants wrote to the *Chicago Defender* and other black newspapers between 1916 and 1918 in the "Documents" section of the *Journal of Negro History* in 1919. These letters are poignant documents of African American aspirations and also provide the historian with important insights into how black workers viewed segregation in Florida. The greatest number of letters are from Pensacola and Jacksonville, but letters also arrived from De Land, Live Oak, Sanford, Warrington, Miami, and other towns.

46. Emmett J. Scott, comp., "Additional Letters of Negro Migrants of 1916–1918," *Journal of Negro History* 4 (October 1919), 439. The U.S. Department of Labor's first major report on black migration in this period noted that African Americans in Florida wrote letters "desiring to leave the South" at a higher rate than their counterparts in the Deep South. See Department of Labor, *Negro Migration in 1916–1917,* 28–29.

47. Unpublished manuscript, Box 86, folder, "Migration Study— Migration Meeting Report," National Urban League Records.

48. Scott, "Letters of Negro Migrants of 1916–1918," 334.

49. Ibid., 427. African American women wrote letters from Florida to northern black publications asking about available positions as cooks, domestic workers, laundresses, chambermaids, dish washers, and other occupations. See ibid., 315–318.

50. Ibid., 331.

51. "Letters on Migration," Box 86, folder: "Migration Study, Migrants Letters," National Urban League Records.

52. "Negro League Members Heard Governor Catts," in *Tuskegee Institute News Clipping File*, reel 6, frame 554. For Catts's life, see Wayne Flynt, *Cracker Messiah: Governor Sidney J. Catts of Florida* (Baton Rouge: Louisiana State University Press, 1977); and Flynt, *Duncan Upshaw Fletcher: Dixie's Reluctant Progressive* (Tallahassee: Florida State University Press, 1971), 23.

53. "Business Men May Employ Lawyer to Fight Labor Agents," *Florida Times-Union*, July 29, 1916.

54. "Labor Recruiters for Muscle Shoals Plant Arrested," *Montgomery Advertiser*, April 29, 1918, in *Tuskegee Institute News Clippings File*, reel 8, frame 275.

55. "To Stop Raiding the Farms," *Montgomery Advertiser*, May 11, 1918, in *Tuskegee Institute News Clippings File*, reel 8, frame 242.

56. Grossman, *Land of Hope*, 27.

57. "An Act Defining Who are Emigrant Agents, Prescribing a Tax Thereon, Also Providing a Penalty," Chapter 5192 [No. 87], *Laws of Florida*, 1903.

58. "An Act Requiring Emigrant Agents Doing Business in this State to Procure a County license . . . ," Chapter 7273 [No. 15], *Laws of Florida*, 1917.

59. "Labor Recruiting Matter is Taken Up by Floridians: Congressional Delegation in Capital Busy," *Florida Times-Union*, August 18, 1916.

60. Joseph Lee had served as a member of the Florida legislature during Reconstruction. He went on to hold a number of federal and municipal positions in Jacksonville. See Brown, *Florida's Black Public Officials*, 103–104. Peter D. Klingman briefly notes Lee's role in the Florida Republican Party in *Neither Dies nor Surrenders*, 48.

61. "Local Business Men Seeking a Solution of the Labor Problem," *Florida Times-Union*, July 30, 1916.

62. Ibid.

63. Ibid.

64. "We have appealed to the talented tenth for a remedy," lamented Carter Woodson (*The Mis-Education of the Negro*, 68), "but they have nothing to offer."

65. "Ministers Try to Help Whites Keep Laborers South," *Chicago Defender*, August 19, 1916.

66. William Chafe has uncovered this tension between black leaders and white businessmen in the Jim Crow South. Chafe writes: "To achieve a better life economically, politically, or educationally, blacks had to deal with 'the Man,' and use whatever wiles were necessary to pry loose the money or actions required to help their race." William H. Chafe, *Civilities and Civil Rights: Greensboro, North Carolina, and the Black Struggle for Freedom* (New York:

Oxford University Press, 1980), 17. See also J. Douglas Smith, *Managing White Supremacy: Race, Politics, and Citizenship in Jim Crow Virginia* (Chapel Hill: University of North Carolina Press, 2002).

67. "Mayor Orders Halt in Club Practice of Local Police," *Florida Times-Union*, August 3, 1916.

68. "New Note in Labor Problem; Representative Negroes Urge Their Race to Remain Here," *Florida Times-Union*, August 6, 1916.

69. The Jacksonville Chamber of Commerce claimed that black workers did not know how much they were being paid, and that their employers were actually paying high wages. "Misinformation as to prevailing day wages at some of the plants here, was taken up also at the meeting, it being shown that instead of $1.10 per day, from $1.25 to $1.75 is being received." *Florida Times-Union*, July 30, 1916.

70. "Officers of Negro Labor Unions," *Florida Times-Union*, August 14, 1916.

71. "Negro View of the Exodus," *Montgomery Advertiser*, September 26, 1916, in *Tuskegee Institute News Clippings File*, reel 5, frame 473.

72. W. T. B. Williams, "The Negro Exodus from the South" (1919), republished in Foner and Lewis, *Black Workers*, 306.

73. Johnson, *Along This Way*, 315.

74. For Johnson's role in the NAACP's decision to organize the South, see ibid.

75. George S. Chaires to N. B. Young, May 24, 1915, Box G42, File, "St. Augustine, Fla. 1915–1939," NAACP Papers. The Tallahassee branch had this same problem. In the Deep South, the NAACP could not take root as an interracial organization.

76. "St. Augustine Organizes for Advancement," *New York Age*, July 6, 1918; "St. Augustine Notes," NCP, *Florida Metropolis*, June 14, 1919; "Names of Branches," *Crisis*, August 1920.

77. James Weldon Johnson to Margaret Downs McCleary, January 10, 1917, Box G41, folder, "Jacksonville, Fla. 1915–1917," NAACP Papers; "Application for NAACP Charter," February 20, 1917, Box G41, file: "Jacksonville, Fl," NAACP Papers.

78. Brown, *Florida's Black Public Officials*, 109; NCP, *Florida Metropolis*, December 26, 1918.

7. ECHOES OF EMANCIPATION:
THE GREAT WAR IN FLORIDA

1. "The Negro in Wartime," *New York City American*, September 21, 1918, in *Tuskegee Institute News Clipping File*, reel 8, frame 806.

2. Ibid.

3. David Levering Lewis, *W. E. B. Du Bois: Biography of a Race, 1868–1919* (New York: Henry Holt, 1993), 578.

4. Franklin and Moss, *From Slavery to Freedom,* 310–323; Reich, "Soldiers of Democracy"; Nan Elizabeth Woodruff, *American Congo: The African American Freedom Struggle in the Delta* (Cambridge: Harvard University Press, 2003), 74–109; Kelly, *Race, Class, and Power in the Alabama Coalfields,* 132–161.

5. This is changing. See especially Hunter, *To 'Joy My Freedom,* 222–227; Gilmore, *Gender and Jim Crow,* 190–192; and Hanson, *Mary McLeod Bethune and Black Women's Political Activism,* 96–99.

6. "Colored Citizens of Quincy Pledge Loyalty to America," *Gadsden County Times,* April 19, 1917.

7. For African American participation in the American Revolution, see Quarles, *The Negro in the American Revolution;* and Frey, *Water from the Rock.* For the War of 1812, see Franklin and Moss, *From Slavery to Freedom,* 99–101; and Berlin, *Slaves without Masters,* 124–130. For the Civil War, see George W. Williams, *History of the Negro Race in America, from 1619 to 1880: Negroes as Slaves, as Soldiers and as Citizens,* 2 vols. (New York, 1883; reissue, 1969); and Susie King Taylor, *Reminiscences of My Life: A Black Woman's Civil War Memoirs,* ed., Patricia W. Romero and Willie Lee Rose (New York, 1902; reprint, New York: Markus Wiener, 1988).

8. "County Registration Showed Many Local Americans Active," *Palatka Advocate,* June 9, 1917, in *Tuskegee Institute News Clipping File,* reel 7, frame 359.

9. "Colored Registrants Leave for the Army Camp," *Times-Herald* (Palatka), April 5, 1918.

10. NCP, *Florida Metropolis,* October 1, 1918.

11. Emmett J. Scott, special assistant to the secretary of war, drew from the Mobilization Division of the Provost Marshal General's Office to estimate that 12,904 African Americans—compared with 12,769 whites—were drafted in Florida. Scott, *Scott's Official History of the American Negro in the World War* (Chicago: Homeward Press, 1919), 67–68. See "Sent Colored Citizens Instead," *Afro-American,* May 23, 1919. During World War I, John Hope Franklin estimates, "Approximately 31 per cent of the Negroes who registered [for the draft] were accepted, while 26 per cent of the whites who registered were accepted. This was due not to the superior physical and mental qualifications of Negroes, but to the inclination of some draft boards to discriminate against Negroes in the manner of exemptions." Franklin and Moss, *From Slavery to Freedom,* 457. Scott (*Official History,* 9) estimated that four hundred thousand African Americans eventually served in the military. For black soldiers' experiences in the war, see "Soldier's Experience Overseas," NCP, *Florida Metropolis,* April 4, 1919. Also see W. E. B. Du Bois, "Soldiers," *Crisis,* November 8, 1918.

12. NCP, *Florida Metropolis,* April 8, 1919.

13. Scott recorded the exploits of this unit's division in *Official History,* 130–189.

14. NCP, *Florida Metropolis,* March 11, 1919.

15. NCP, *Florida Metropolis,* July 24, 1918.

16. W. E. B. Du Bois, "Documents of the War," *Crisis,* May 1919, 18.

17. NCP, *Florida Metropolis,* October 9, 1918.

18. NCP, *Florida Metropolis,* November 9, 1918.

19. NCP, *Florida Metropolis,* October 11, 1918.

20. NCP, *Florida Metropolis,* October 14, 1918.

21. NCP, *Florida Metropolis,* January 22, 1919.

22. Edward Loring Miller, "Negro Life in Gainesville: A Sociological Study," (M.A. thesis, University of Florida, 1938), 120–121.

23. NCP, *Florida Metropolis,* October 19, 1918.

24. NCP, *Florida Metropolis,* October 9, 1918.

25. NCP, *Florida Metropolis,* May 19, 1919. For Liberty bond activism in Lake City, De Land, and Sanford, see "Patriotic Meeting of the Colored People," *Citizen-Reporter* (Lake City), May 3, 1918; NCP, *Florida Metropolis,* October 7, 1918; and *Florida Metropolis,* October 26, 1918.

26. For information on Bethune, see Maxine D. Jones, "No Longer Denied: Black Women in Florida, 1920–1950," in Colburn and Landers, *The African American Heritage of Florida;* Hanson, *Mary McLeod Bethune and Black Women's Political Activism;* and Rackham Holt, *Mary McLeod Bethune: A Biography* (Garden City, NY: Doubleday, 1964).

27. Wilhelmina W. Johnson interviewed by Joel Buchanan, May 27, 1981, Fifth Avenue Black Oral History Project, Oral History Program, University of Florida.

28. Frances R. Keyser, "Life of Mary McLeod Bethune, 1926" (photocopy), *Mary McLeod Bethune Papers: The Bethune Foundation Collection, Part 2: Correspondence Files, 1914–1955* (Bethesda, MD: University Publications of America, 1997; hereafter cited as *Bethune Papers*), reel 1, frame 672. Bethune was a regional Red Cross lecturer and gave talks on American Red Cross war work throughout the Deep South.

29. "Closing Exercises of the Daytona Normal and Industrial Institute," NCP, *Florida Metropolis,* May 19, 1919.

30. A good overview of Eartha White's prewar biography is given in "Few Years Well Spent By Miss Eartha Magdalina White," NCP, *Florida Metropolis,* January 15, 1919.

31. William J. Breen, "Black Women in the Great War: Mobilization and Reform in the South," *Journal of Southern History* 44 (August 1978), 436–439.

32. "Miss Eartha White's Report," NCP, *Florida Metropolis,* December 14, 1918.

33. "Doings at Bethel Baptist Church," NCP, *Florida Metropolis*, August 6, 1919.

34. Miss White was a charter member of the Jacksonville NAACP branch. See "Application for Charter of the Jacksonville Branch," Box G41, folder: "Jacksonville, Fla. 1915–1917," NAACP Papers.

35. "Fernandina Women Did Well in Drive," NCP, *Florida Metropolis*, November 26, 1918; also NCP, *Florida Metropolis*, October 5 and 26, 1918.

36. "Should White Soldiers Salute Colored Officers? We Should Say Not," *Leader* (Tarpon Springs), November 15, 1917, in *Tuskegee Institute News Clipping File*, reel 7, frame 408; "Loyal Patriotic Negroes Rallying to the Colors," *Times-Herald* (Palatka), April 26, 1918. Some white Floridians saw the war bringing a subtle shift in race relations. See C. D. Dennis to Albert Blanding, August 22, 1918, Box 1, folder, "Correspondence 1910, 1916–1918, 1924–1925," Albert Blanding Papers, P. K. Yonge Library of Florida History, University of Florida.

37. Black newspaper editor W. I. Lewis made this claim in a NCP column dated May 2, 1919. After searching several major Florida newspapers including the *Times-Herald* (Palatka), the *Citizen Reporter* (Lake City), the *Miami Herald*, the *Pensacola Journal*, and both major Jacksonville dailies, I found just one mention of black casualties during the war. See "Services Today Colored Soldier of Dade County," *Miami Herald*, August 1, 1920.

38. NCP, *Florida Metropolis*, October 24, 1918.

39. NCP, *Florida Metropolis*, July 12, 1919. African Americans also used the medium of film to highlight black war service. See *Florida Metropolis*, October 18, 1918; NCP, *Florida Metropolis*, December 13, 1919; and "Official Record of the Colored Soldiers," NCP, *Florida Metropolis*, December 21, 1918.

40. NCP, *Florida Metropolis*, December 23, 1919. See also NCP, *Florida Metropolis*, October 2, 1918.

41. For information on the Division, see Franklin and Moss, *From Slavery to Freedom*, 473.

42. James Weldon Johnson, "Response to a Governor," *New York Age*, July 28, 1918, *Tuskegee Institute News Clipping File*, reel 8, frame 28. "Bond is Welded Between Labor and Employers," *Florida Metropolis*, July 17, 1918.

43. "Colored People Will Gather in Immense Mass Meeting," *Florida Metropolis*, July 15, 1918.

44. "Will Work For Better Basis of Understanding For Labor and Employers in this City," *Florida Times-Union*, July 17, 1918.

45. Johnson, "Response to a Governor."

46. In 1905, W. I. Lewis wrote, "J. H. Blodgett is in the lead of all the men of his race here as a developer and owner of real estate, and there is but one man here of any race who has built more good houses in this city since it was

destroyed by fire in 1901." See Lewis, "Colored Men of Jacksonville," *Voice of the Negro* (July 1905), 475. For additional information on Blodgett, see NCP, *Florida Metropolis,* January 27, 1906.

47. Johnson, "Response to a Governor."

48. Flynt, *Cracker Messiah,* 86–87.

49. Johnson, "Response to a Governor."

50. George Haynes discussed this complaint of Florida's employers in the Department of Labor publication *The Negro at Work during the World War and during Reconstruction,* 65.

51. By 1920, African American women in the United States had organized at least ten domestic workers' unions that gained affiliation with the American Federation of Labor. See Elizabeth Ross Haynes, "Negroes in Domestic Service," *Journal of Negro History* 8 (1923), 435–436. African American women in Georgia also fought against work-or-fight ordinances during this era. See Hunter, *To 'Joy My Freedom,* 219–238.

52. Walter White, "Florida, 1918," *Papers of the National Association for the Advancement of Colored People, Part 10, Peonage, Labor and the New Deal, 1913–1939,* ed. August Meier and John Bracy, Jr. (Microfilm), reel 23, frame 283.

53. Ibid.

54. For the period of federal control, see Walker D. Hines, *War History of American Railroads* (New Haven: Yale University Press, 1928); United States Railroad Commission, *Report of the Railroad Wage Commission to the Director General of Railroads* (Washington, DC: Railroad Wage Commission, 1918), 83.

55. For a general treatment of black railroaders during the war years, see Eric Arnesen, *Brotherhoods of Color: Black Railroad Workers and the Struggle for Equality* (Cambridge: Harvard University Press, 2001), 42–83.

56. "Convention of Railroad Men Opens in Chicago," *Chicago Defender,* October 2, 1920. Philip S. Foner discusses the formation of independent black unions during the Great War in *History of the Labor Movement in the United States,* vol. 7, *Labor and World War I, 1914–1918* (New York: International Publishers, 1987), 242–243. The National Brotherhood's strategy was to "enter the unions side by side with their white brothers; but in the event of discrimination, we urge that the Negroes, in any place, shall organize their own unions to exact justice from both the employer and the white labor unions." Foner, *History of the Labor Movement in the United States,* vol. 8, *Postwar Struggles, 1918–1920* (New York: International Publishers, 1988), 197. For additional information on the Brotherhood see David Montgomery, *The Fall of the House of Labor: The Workplace, the State, and American Labor Activism, 1865–1925* (Cambridge: Cambridge University Press, 1987), 381.

57. For information about color bars in the railroad industry and unions, see Spero and Harris, *The Black Worker;* William Harris, *The Harder We Run: Black Workers since the Civil War* (New York: Oxford University Press, 1982), 45–48; William H. Harris, *Keeping the Faith: A. Philip Randolph, Milton P. Webster, and the Brotherhood of Sleeping Car Porters, 1925–37* (Chicago: University of Illinois Press, 1977); and Eric Arnesen, " 'Like Banquo's Ghost, It Will Not Down': The Race Question and the American Railroad Brotherhoods, 1880–1920," *American Historical Review* 99 (December 1994), 1601–1634. African American railroad firemen were hard-pressed to hold on to their jobs after turn-of-the-century technological improvements in engine design made the position more appealing to white workers. Black workers were all too aware that, as Jacqueline Jones notes, "modernization wore a white face." Jones, *American Work: Four Centuries of Black and White Labor* (New York: W. W. Norton, 1998), 329.

58. Philip S. Foner, *History of the Labor Movement in the United States,* vol. 6, *On the Eve of America's Entrance into World War I* (New York: International Publishers, 1982), 143–188.

59. Hines, *War History of American Railroads,* 164–166.

60. Petition of Florida East Coast Railway Firemen to W. G. McAdoo, October 28, 1918, in the microfilm collection *Black Workers in the Era of the Great Migration, 1916–1925,* ed. James Grossman (Frederick, MD: University Publications of America, 1985), reel 7, frame 462. See also Berry Tillman to W. S. Carter, November 11, 1919, in ibid., frame 466.

61. Hines, *War History of American Railroads,* 169. Spero and Harris (*The Black Worker,* 295) argue that General Order 27 was issued in response to pressure from Robert L. Mays, president of the Railway Men's International Benevolent Industrial Association.

62. Railroad firemen based in Miami sent in a similar petition to the U.S. Director General of Railroads, asking him to help them obtain a wage increase because they had pledged so much of their meager earnings to Thrift Stamp drives and Liberty loans. See "Florida East Coast Railway Firemen" to W. G. McAdoo, October 28, 1918, in *Black Workers in the Era of the Great Migration,* reel 7, frame 462.

63. "Petition to the United States Railroad Administration," August 19, 1919, ibid., reel 9, frames 870–871. Duval County railroad workers made similar arguments. See petition titled "In The Matter of Application for Compensation for Back Time Before the United States Railroad Administration," ibid., reel 10, frame 489.

64. Lyman Delano to H. P. Daugherty, August 18, 1919, in ibid., reel 9, frames 758–759.

65. John W. Taylor to Woodrow Wilson, August 4, 1919, in ibid., reel 9, frame 861.

66. John W. Taylor to H. P. Daugherty, Department of Labor, March 13, 1920, in ibid., reel 10, frame 20.

67. "Bahama Negroes to Work Florida Land," *Register* (Mobile), March 19, 1918, in *Tuskegee Institute News Clippings File,* reel 8, frame 20; "Asserts Bahama Negroes Best Farm Hands," *Florida Metropolis,* February 4, 1919; "The Bahama Negro," *Palm Beach Post,* September 2, 1920. The *Miami Herald* called for Chinese labor, asserting that the Chinese worker "makes an ideal house servant when he is properly trained." Quoted in "Chinese Farm Labor," *Panama City Pilot,* September 9, 1920.

68. Hahamovitch, *The Fruits of Their Labor,* 100–105.

69. See "Governor Catts Will Recommend Abolishing Negro Economics," *Florida Metropolis,* April 3, 1919. See U.S. Department of Labor, *The Negro at Work during the World War and during Reconstruction,* 65. For the events leading up to the closure of the Negro Division of Economics in Florida see George Haynes to William Wilson, March 22, 1919, in *Black Workers in the Era of the Great Migration,* reel 14, frame, 207; George Haynes to W. A. Armwood, April 16, 1919, Box 4, folder, "Correspondence: 1917–1947," Armwood Family Papers, Special Collections Library, University of South Florida; William B. Wilson, "Memorandum for the Director, Investigation and Inspection Service," in *Black Workers in the Era of the Great Migration,* reel 14, frame 211.

70. Sidney Catts to William B. Wilson, April 22, 1919, and Catts to Wilson, April 7, 1919, in *Black Workers in the Era of the Great Migration,* reel 14, frames 227 and 214.

71. George Haynes, "Antagonisms Met With," n.d., in ibid., reel 14, frames 2–3.

72. U. A. Smythe to Frankfurter, September 24, 1918, in ibid., reel 19, frame 653.

73. NCP, *Florida Metropolis,* January 4, 1919.

74. Rev. Baker's wife was a member of the Florida State Federation of Colored Women's Clubs and spoke at the National Association of Colored Women's 1920 convention in Alabama. See National Association of Colored Women, *Minutes of the Twelfth Biennial Convention* (published by the Association, 1920).

75. NCP, *Florida Metropolis,* January 4, 1919.

76. "South Florida Methodist Conference," NCP, *Florida Metropolis,* February 25, 1919.

77. "Tallahassee News Notes," NCP, *Florida Metropolis,* May 17, 1919.

78. "Application For Charter of Tallahassee, Florida Branch," Box G-42, folder, "Tallahassee, Fla. 1915–1939," NAACP Papers.

79. "St. Petersburg Celebrated Emancipation," NCP, *Florida Metropolis,* January 4, 1919.

80. "Live Oak to Honor Her Soldiers," NCP, *Florida Metropolis,* August 11, 1919.

81. Information on T. S. Harris's political activism is found in *Bradford County Telegraph*, November 12, 1920.

82. "Unique Celebration of the February Birthdays at the Community Meeting," NCP, *Florida Metropolis*, March 3, 1919.

83. "Presbyterian Honored Their Soldiers," NCP, *Florida Metropolis*, March 26, 1919. Biographical information on Matthew M. Lewey obtained from Brown, *Florida's Black Public Officials*, 104. The 55th Massachusetts was the sister regiment of the more famous 54th black infantry regiment.

84. *Indianapolis Freeman*, April 16, 1904.

85. Paul Laurence Dunbar, "The Colored Soldiers," in Henry Louis Gates, Jr. et al., eds., *The Norton Anthology of African American Literature* (New York: W. W. Norton, 1997), 889–890; "Many Heard Dr. Nance at Stanton," NCP, *Florida Metropolis*, April 29, 1919.

86. "Key West Notes," *Florida Metropolis*, May 29, 1919.

87. Historian Charles Payne (*I've Got the Light of Freedom*, 178) has noted the role that historical memory played in the modern civil rights movement.

88. David Levering Lewis splendidly describes the New York march and its larger context in *When Harlem Was in Vogue* (New York: Alfred A. Knopf, 1981), 1–5.

89. "Line of March for Welcome Home Parade Tonight," NCP, *Florida Metropolis*, May 1, 1919. I have reconstructed the line of march in Jacksonville from this article.

90. The following account of the Welcome Home Parade is taken from "Unbounded Enthusiasm To Welcome Soldiers," NCP, *Florida Metropolis*, May 2, 1919.

91. Brown, *Florida's Black Public Officials*, 114.

92. Gates et al., *Norton Anthology of African American Literature*, 766.

93. "Address By Dr. J. A. Gregg," NCP, *Florida Metropolis*, May 3, 1919.

94. "Soldier's Experience Overseas," NCP, *Florida Metropolis*, April 4, 1919. A short time later, a black correspondent from West Palm Beach joyfully reported that "Lee Murray, one of the boys who had been over sea helping to make the world safe for democracy is home again." NCP, *Florida Metropolis*, August 2, 1919. C. L. R. James cited the importance of returning African servicemen for the anticolonial struggle in postwar Ghana in *Nkrumah and the Ghana Revolution* (Westport, CT: Lawrence Hill, 1977), 42–43.

95. "Application for Charter of Greensboro Branch," Box C-40, folder, "Greensboro, Fla., 1920–1925," NAACP Papers.

96. Florida Republican Party Delegates, 1916, Box 3, folder, "Republican Party Roll of Delegates to Republican State Convention, 1916, Palatka," Joseph E. Lee Papers, Florida State Archives.

97. "The League for Democracy," *Florida Metropolis*, June 9, 1919.

98. *Jasper News* quoted in Flynt, *Cracker Messiah*, 269.

99. "Congressman Frank Clark," *Florida Times-Union* (Jacksonville), October 16, 1920.

100. "'Yellow-Faced Coon' Says Tampa Paper," *Afro-American* (Baltimore), June 6, 1919.

101. In Jacksonville, the Colored Labor Union's secretary reported: "At the meeting of the colored central labor union, held last Thursday night, all committees reported progress in their respective locals, and that organizing movements in the city are growing rapidly, and the central union is expecting to see the city well organized at an early date." See "Labor Meeting," NCP, *Florida Metropolis,* February 25, 1919. For a broader discussion of African American labor activism, see Wayne Flynt, "Florida Labor and Political 'Radicalism,' 1919–1920," *Labor History* 9 (winter 1968), 85–88.

102. An employer fumed: "I want to say that if all the loafing negroes between the ages of 18 to 35 years were rounded up and put to work, I do not think that there would be any [labor] shortage at all. It looks as though they are looking for big pay and little work. Quite a number of them are ex-soldiers." "Too Many Idlers," *Florida Metropolis,* May 27, 1919.

103. "Fight Among Unions," *Tampa Sunday Tribune,* September 11, 1919; "Negro Laborers Ask $3[,] Hold Up Big Job," *Tampa Morning Tribune,* June 7, 1919.

104. "Orange Pickers May Strike for More Pay," *Palatka Daily News,* November 15, 1919. A year later, the packinghouse owners were still fighting to keep the rate at eight cents.

105. Quoted in the *New York Age,* May 29, 1920.

106. "Growers and Shippers to Gather Wage Data," *Florida Grower,* December 25, 1920. A. P. Spencer, the vice-director of the Extension Division, College of Agriculture (now the University of Florida), wrote in 1920: "The farm labor is one of the perplexing problems that threaten to interfere with the 1920 crop. . . . Farm labor, like every other labor, is asking for shorter hours, which means less to be accomplished in a week or a day's time." "Handling the Farm Labor Situation," *Ocala Banner,* March 12, 1920. Historians should be very careful about accepting at face value statements made by employers and state agricultural agencies regarding the condition of labor markets. Historian Cindy Hahamovitch (*The Fruits of Their Labor,* 82) notes that during this period, "the buying and selling of labor was . . . intimately bound up with notions of race." She argues that southern employers judged that any decline in the pool of labor, no matter how small, added up to a "labor shortage" especially if it involved paying African American workers higher wages as a result.

107. For turpentine workers' struggles, see "In Retrospect," Box "1920–1923," folder, "Johnston, McNeill & Company," William C. Powell Papers, Manuscript Department, Perkins Library, Duke University; and *Apalachicola Times,* September 11, 1920.

108. "Skilled Labor in Jacksonville Exceeds Demand," *Florida Metropolis,* January 17, 1919. The rate of $3.50 per day is mentioned often during the 1919 and 1920 growing seasons. See *Florida Grower,* December 11, 1920. This rate was advertised as the "common labor" rate in various parts of the state, and where the rate was lower African American workers engaged in protests to raise it. See "Colored Janitors Co. Court House Demand More Pay," *Florida Metropolis,* April 8, 1920.

109. "Labor Should Have All the Profits," *Florida Grower,* November 13, 1920.

110. "To the White Republicans," *Jasper News,* October 1, 1920.

111. "Mt Zion's Anniversary and Reconstruction Meeting," NCP, *Florida Metropolis,* July 15, 1919. Historian Philip S. Foner notes that the twenty-three African American delegates to the AFL's 1919 Atlantic City convention urged their white counterparts " 'to loosen up and give the Black man of the South a chance to organize.' " Thanks to the work of Mr. Watson and the other black delegates, the full AFL convention endorsed the Committee on Organization's resolution to "call for special emphasis on organizing Black members within the AFL." Foner, *History of the Labor Movement in the United States,* vol. 8, *Postwar Struggles,* 201.

112. Flynt, *Cracker Messiah,* 220.

113. "Florida Daily Believes Negroes Should Have Unions of Their Own," *Herald* (Baltimore), July 19, 1919, in *Tuskegee Institute News Clipping File,* reel 9, frame 877.

114. "Florida State Federation of Labor Contradicts Itself," and "Florida Labor Weakens," *New York Age,* May 1, 1920.

115. "Open Shop Packing," and "Adopting Open Shop," *Palatka Daily News,* November 8, 1919. In Manatee County, employers formed the "Liberty Council" to put down labor insurgencies. See "Liberty Council Formed to Assist in Solving Economic And Labor Problems of the Day," *Manatee River Journal,* July 31, 1919. See also "Knight Refuses to Recognize Wage Award," *Florida Metropolis,* February 22, 1919.

116. "Truck Growers," *Florida Grower,* October 16, 1920; "Uniform Wage Scale," *Florida Grower,* November 6, 1920; "Citrus Market Conditions," *Florida Grower,* October 30, 1920.

117. Walter White, unpublished field report, *Papers of the National Association for the Advancement of Colored People, Part 10,* reel 23, frames 284–285.

118. "Labor in the Potato Section," *Palatka Morning Post,* April 12, 1920; "Labor Agitators Arrested by Hastings Officers," *Daily-Herald* (Palatka), April 16, 1920. See also "Catches Labor Agent," *Okaloosa News* (Crestview), June 6, 1919, and *Apalachicola Times,* May 8, 1920.

119. "Waiters' Strike Barely Averted," *Cleveland Advocate,* March 27, 1920.

120. For information on this campaign, see Flynt, "Florida Labor and Political 'Radicalism,' " 79–87.

121. D. C. Russell, testimony before the National War Labor Board, Tampa, in *Black Workers in the Era of the Great Migration*, reel 5, frames 63–66. See also Miners' Testimony before the National War Labor Board, Tampa, December 9, 1918, in ibid., reel 5, frame 394.

122. "Welfare of the Colored People," *Fort Meade Leader*, n.d., in ibid., reel 5, frame 106.

123. Ibid.

124. "Anniversary and Reconstruction Meeting," NCP, *Florida Metropolis*, July 15, 1919.

125. "K. of P. Foment Strike," *Afro-American* (Baltimore), July 4, 1919.

126. "To Colored Citizens," NCP, *Florida Metropolis*, February 5, 1919.

127. "To Colored Citizens of Florida," NCP, *Florida Metropolis*, March 11, 1919.

128. "Fort Pierce News," NCP, *Florida Metropolis*, March 18, 1919.

129. "Gifford News," NCP, *Florida Metropolis*, May 1, 1919.

130. "Gifford News," NCP, *Florida Metropolis*, April 4, 1919.

131. "Tallahassee News," NCP, *Florida Metropolis*, April 21, 1919.

132. "South Florida Methodist Conference," NCP, *Florida Metropolis*, February 25, 1919.

133. "He is a veteran of the Spanish-American war, and applied to enter the service again when his country entered the great war in Europe but was denied on account of his age." NCP, *Florida Metropolis*, April 3, 1919.

134. *Ocala City Directory: 1908–9* (Ocala: L. J. Brumby, 1908), 24.

135. "Dr. Betts Strongly Encouraged," NCP, *Florida Metropolis*, June 23, 1919.

136. "Protective Meeting Has Good Meeting," *Colored Citizen* (Pensacola), April 16, 1920.

137. Deborah Gray White (*Too Heavy a Load*, 116–120) notes the obstacles that African American women confronted during this era in asserting political leadership within black communities.

138. "Gifford News," NCP, *Florida Metropolis*, March 13, 1919.

139. "Tallahassee News," NCP, *Florida Metropolis*, April 21, 1919.

140. "Echoes from State Federation of Colored Women's Clubs," NCP, *Florida Metropolis*, June 21, 1919.

141. Young favored liberal arts education and sought to turn Florida A & M into a first-rate institution of higher learning. This set him on a collision course with the state legislature and northern educational foundations. See J. H. Brinson to Jackson Davis, August 11, 1921, reel 25, frame 201, Papers of the General Education Board, Florida A & M College, 1903–1952.

142. "Colored Citizens' State Convention Closed," NCP, *Florida Metropolis*, April 28, 1919.

143. NCP, *Florida Metropolis*, April 28, 1919.

144. NCP, *Florida Metropolis*, March 11, 1919. Information on H. Y. Tookes: "Thanksgiving at Monticello," NCP, *Florida Metropolis*, December 9, 1919.

145. "Florida Senate Refuses to Heed Race Complaints," *Cleveland Advocate*, May 24, 1919.

146. "Legislature Refuses to Hear Petition," *Afro-American*, May 19, 1919.

147. "Florida Senate Refuses to Heed Race Complaints," *Cleveland Advocate*, May 24, 1919.

148. Sidney Catts to John Shillady, March 18, 1919, Box C351, folder "Lynching Florida, 1919–1922," NAACP Papers.

149. Logan, *The Betrayal of the Negro*, 371–372.

8. WITH BABIES IN THEIR ARMS:
THE VOTER REGISTRATION MOVEMENT

1. John Hurst to John R. Shillady, January 14, 1919, Box C284, file, "Voting 1919," NAACP Papers.

2. NCP, *Florida Metropolis*, February 19, 1920.

3. "Fort Meade Negroes Started a Ruckus," *Fort Meade Leader*, quoted in the *De Land Daily News*, April 13, 1920.

4. *Apalachicola Times*, May 1, 1920.

5. P. O. Knight to Frank Burke, April 7, 1920, in *Federal Surveillance of Afro-Americans, 1917–1925: The First World War, the Red Scare, and the Garvey Movement*, ed. Theodore Kornweibel, Jr. (Frederick, MD: University Publications of America, 1986), reel 13, frame 470.

6. In common with their sisters throughout the South. See Gilmore, *Gender and Jim Crow*, 203–224; and Higginbotham, *Righteous Discontent*, 185–229.

7. Anonymous to Walter White, December 30, 1920, Box C312, folder, "KKK-Jan," NAACP Papers.

8. "Postal Clerks Meet," NCP, *Florida Metropolis*, May 31, 1919.

9. "National Convention of Railway Postal Clerks," NCP, *Florida Metropolis*, July 8, 1919. For information on the Alliance, see Spero and Harris, *The Black Worker*, 123–124; and Foner, *History of the Labor Movement in the United States*, vol. 7, *Labor and World War I*, 242.

10. "Postal Clerks Meet," NCP, *Florida Metropolis*, May 31, 1919.

11. William Greider writes: "Politics begins in personal relationships. Indeed, without that foundation, politics usually dissolves into empty manipulation by a remote few. People talking to one another—arguing and agreeing and developing trust among themselves—is what leads most reliably to their own political empowerment." Greider, *Who Will Tell The People: The Betrayal of American Democracy* (New York: Simon & Schuster, 1992), 223–224.

Sociologist William A. Gamson underscores the importance of "preexisting social relationships" in social movement recruiting. See Gamson, "The Social Psychology of Collective Action," in Morris and Mueller, *Frontiers in Social Movement Theory*, 61–62. See also Lawrence Goodwyn, *Democratic Promise: The Populist Movement in America* (New York: Oxford University Press, 1976); and Francesca Polletta, *Freedom Is an Endless Meeting: Democracy in American Social Movements* (Chicago: University of Chicago Press, 2002), 16–21.

12. Antonio Gramsci challenged the belief that members of one group habitually followed leaders within "their" group out of habits of deference. Gramsci believed that "leaders" in political parties or social movements frequently undermined their effectiveness by taking their "followers" for granted. Gramsci, *Selections from the Prison Notebooks,* ed. and trans. Quintin Hoare and Geoffrey Nowell Smith (1971; rpt. New York: International Publishers, 1995), 144–145.

13. Works that stress intergenerational linkages in the making of civil rights struggles include Aldon D. Morris, *The Origins of the Civil Rights Movement: Black Communities Organizing for Change* (New York: Free Press, 1984); Chafe, *Civilities and Civil Rights*; John Dittmer, *Local People: The Struggle for Civil Rights in Mississippi* (Urbana: University of Illinois Press, 1994); Gilmore, *Gender and Jim Crow;* and Payne, *I've Got the Light of Freedom.*

14. Social space here refers to self-generated places and moments created by African Americans to discuss politics and organizing outside of the gaze of white supremacy. Social movements rise or fall on their ability to generate such spaces, and this is especially true in movements that arise in repressive, one-party states. See Linda Fuller, *Where Was the Working Class? Revolution in Eastern Germany* (Chicago: University of Illinois Press, 1999), 164.

15. Louis J. Brinkman to Warren G. Harding, July 18, 1920, roll 36, frames 590–592, Harding Papers.

16. Walter F. White, "Election Day in Florida," in *Crisis,* January 20, 1921, 108.

17. E. J. W. Day to Warren G. Harding, October 28, 1920, roll 36, frame 648, Harding Papers.

18. "Why the Negro Should Register 3,000 Votes," *Colored Citizen,* April 30, 1920.

19. Letter to the Editor, *Pensacola Journal,* September 30, 1920.

20. For a brilliant formulation of the ways that African Americans accomplished this in the early years after the end of slavery, see Brown, "To Catch the Vision of Freedom."

21. I have been able to identify the names, ages, and occupations of over 1,500 African Americans who registered to vote for the 1920 presidential election. While this represents a fraction of those who registered, it does give a general idea of the scope of this campaign. These figures are taken from six counties:

Duval, Marion, Columbia, Putnam, Palm Beach, and Dade. Due to the paucity of election records in Florida, this sample is far from being complete. It does however, give a good cross-section of urban (Jacksonville), small-town (Palatka), and rural (Citra and McIntosh) communities. For further analysis of African American voter registration figures in 1919–1920, see Ortiz, " 'Like Water Covered the Sea,' " 393–475.

22. "Christian Citizenship Mass Meeting," NCP, *Florida Metropolis*, February 13, 1919.

23. African Americans employed religious idioms for two reasons. First, the church served for many as the primary institutional base of the movement. Equally important, black Floridians viewed the struggle they had joined as no less than a spiritual battle between good (equality) and evil (white supremacy). Charles Thompson, a house painter from Jacksonville, told Warren G. Harding, "i do no this god is on your side & i know that is a Plenty if god is With you the Devel just as Well go on Back Where he come from & stay there for he shoreley can not do you no harm." Charles Thompson to Warren G. Harding, September 20, 1920, roll 36, frame 956, Harding Papers.

24. "Brooklyn Citizens' Club," NCP, *Florida Metropolis*, August 6, 1919.

25. The Brooklyn club sponsored an Emancipation Day ceremony attended by over two hundred people that same year. Women's Club members drew clear connections between black history, democracy, and politics. NCP, *Florida Metropolis*, January 3, 1920.

26. State Federation of City Federation of Colored Women's Clubs, Program, June 28–30, 1916, folder: "National Association of Colored Women," Eartha M. M. White Collection, Thomas G. Carpenter Library, University of North Florida. For similar examples of African American women's leadership in North Carolina, see Gilmore, *Gender and Jim Crow*, 203.

27. "Pythian Grand Lodge," NCP, *Florida Metropolis*, May 24, 1919; NCP, *Florida Metropolis*, May 17, 1919.

28. "Grand Chancellor Andrews' Official Visits," *Florida Metropolis*, April 1, 1920.

29. *Afro-American*, July 4, 1919.

30. NCP, *Florida Metropolis*, June 10, 1919. Robin D. G. Kelley (*Race Rebels*, 38) insightfully notes, "The social links created through organizations such as the Knights of Pythias, the Odd Fellows, the Masons, the Elks, and the Independent Order of St. Luke occasionally translated into community and labor struggles." Other works that deal with aspects of black fraternal orders and politics include James, "A History of the Negro Revolt," 82–83, and *Nkrumah and the Ghana Revolution*, 54–55; and Brown, "Womanist Consciousness." Adam Fairclough discusses the important roles that African American fraternal organizations played in civil rights battles in Louisiana in

Race and Democracy: The Civil Rights Struggle in Louisiana (Athens: University of Georgia Press, 1995), 69–71.

31. "Lo! The Poor Democrat!" *Crisis,* June 1, 1920.

32. For a portrait of Lee as a federal office holder, see "Among the Colored People," *Evening Telegram* (Jacksonville), February 8, 1892.

33. Brown, *Florida's Black Public Officials,* 103; George B. Tindall, *The Emergence of the New South, 1913–1945* (Baton Rouge: Louisiana State University Press, 1967), 144.

34. "Reasons For Defeat," *Evening Telegram,* November 15, 1892.

35. "Strong Republican Organization," NCP, *Florida Metropolis,* March 25, 1919.

36. "Republican Club House Warming and Installation," NCP, *Florida Metropolis,* June 10, 1919.

37. "Republican Club Headquarters," NCP, *Florida Metropolis,* April 1, 1919.

38. N. B. Young's position at the state's black college constrained his ability to provide open support for the NAACP in the state. However, he was able to act as the national NAACP's "eyes and ears" in Florida, forwarding information to New York when needed.

39. For Lewey's service record, see "Memorial Day Observed," NCP, *Florida Metropolis,* June 1, 1915.

40. "Citizens' Meeting at Grant's Memorial Church," NCP, *Florida Metropolis,* October 25, 1919.

41. "Citizens' Meeting at St. Paul's Sunday Night," NCP, *Florida Metropolis,* September 30, 1919.

42. "Citizens' Meeting at St. Stephen," NCP, *Florida Metropolis,* November 18, 1919.

43. "Republican Club Home-Coming," NCP, *Florida Metropolis,* February 10, 1920.

44. For an insightful critique of patronage politics, see Adolph Reed, "Why Is There No Black Political Movement," in his *Class Notes: Posing as Politics and Other Thoughts on the American Scene* (New York: New Press, 2000), 3–9.

45. Within such spaces, black Floridians discussed what Charles Payne (*I've Got the Light of Freedom,* 74) terms the "big" ideas: "citizenship, democracy, the powers of elected officials." For the success of the Jacksonville movement, see "Organizing Electors for the General Election," *Florida Times-Union* (Jacksonville), July 5, 1920.

46. I have compiled this voting list by cross-referencing affidavits presented to the U.S. Congress with Jacksonville city directories. The main sources are: House of Representatives, Committee on the Census, Apportionment of Representatives, 66th Congress, 3rd Session, 1921 H.R. 14498, H.R. 15021,

H.R. 15158, and H.R. 15217 (Washington, DC: Government Printing Office, 1921); and R. L. Polk & Co.'s *Jacksonville's City Directory: 1920* and *1921*.

47. This list contains a bias toward the more residentially "stable" group of African Americans in Jacksonville, those who were listed as "householders" as opposed to the more transient "renter" group. A city directory, by its nature, makes it far easier to locate householders than renters. Furthermore, in terms of gender analysis, a dependence upon male-centered city directories, which list husbands' occupations but omit women's, is problematic. Just as problematic is the difficulty in counting boarders or lessees who do not have their own street address listing. For example, omitted in my sample is Lizzie Brown, who according to the NAACP's affidavit was living at 723 Jefferson. Brown, however, is not given her own listing in the directory. Listed instead at 723 Jefferson, as a householder, is Effie Bostick, a laundry worker. It is possible that Bostick was either Lizzie Brown's landlord or perhaps an extended family member. Similarly, Lillie Mae Blair, another person on the NAACP's congressional affidavit, is not listed in the city directory, but was living with Mrs. Hattie Laporch, a laundry worker and a widowed householder, at 731 W. State. In any case, I want to alert the reader that people such as Lizzie Brown and Lillie Mae Blair are underrepresented in my sample. So too is Claridia Mae Bentley, living with Susan Gardner (name misspelled in the directory). Mrs. Gardner was also a widowed householder and a laundry worker living at 1004 W. Union. Had I been able to piece together more bits of evidence, it is likely that this sample would reveal an even stronger base of working-class or nonprofessional voter registrants.

48. "Citizens' Meeting at St. Paul's Sunday Night," NCP, *Florida Metropolis,* September 30, 1919.

49. "Citizens' Meeting at St. Stephens," NCP, *Florida Metropolis,* November 18, 1919.

50. NCP, *Florida Metropolis,* March 29, 1920. See also Nassau County Republican Party resolution, March 28, 1920, Joseph E. Lee Papers, Florida State Archives.

51. Alexander Akerman to William C. Kenyon, November 6, 1920, Box C285, file, "Voting, Jacksonville, Florida, 1920," NAACP Papers; Williamson, *Florida Politics in the Gilded Age,* 160.

52. NCP, *Florida Metropolis,* July 22, 1919.

53. "St. Petersburg News," NCP, *Florida Metropolis,* July 7, 1919. Black Floridians had a long tradition of raising funds to improve their schools, and it makes sense that they would emphasize education as a primary goal of political action. For examples of school fundraising, see "St. Petersburg Notes," NCP, *Florida Metropolis,* November 27, 1912; "News Items from Fort Meade," NCP, *Florida Metropolis,* November 25, 1912; "Lake City News," *Florida Metropolis,* December 4, 1912.

54. Clara Blackman to William Wilson, June 26, 1919, in *Black Workers in the Era of the Great Migration*, reel 14, frames 359–362.

55. "Negroes Have Club," *St. Petersburg Daily Times*, September 24, 1920.

56. "Republicans and Color," and "Precinct Books on Registration," *St. Petersburg Daily Times*, October 10, 1920; "Ninety Per Cent of the Negro Voters in Pinellas County Have Registered," *Florida Times-Union*, October 4, 1920.

57. "Flourishing Pythian Lodge at Sanford," NCP, *Florida Metropolis*, April 12, 1919. The *Sanford Herald* reported that one hundred African American men, compared with fifty-four white men, had registered in Precincts 1 and 3. "Register is Now the Slogan," *Sanford Herald*, September 24, 1920.

58. For the new lodge see "Colored People Progressive," *Bradford County Telegraph*, September 3, 1920; for African American voter registrants in Starke see "Qualified Electors," *Bradford County Telegraph*, October 29, 1920.

59. "White Women Exceed Negroes," *Daily Democrat* (Tallahassee), October 22, 1920; "Urges Registration of White Women," *Daily Democrat*, September 29, 1920; "R. A. Gray Will Conduct the School for Voters," *Daily Democrat*, October 20, 1920.

60. A. I. Dixie interview with author, August 10, 1994, Behind the Veil Collection.

61. Inez Stevens-Jones interview with author, August 14, 1997, Behind the Veil Collection. Inez Stevens-Jones was Dr. Stevens's oldest living daughter. I am indebted to her for sharing what were intensely personal and very painful memories regarding her father's political activism. Stevens's medical skill is attested to in "Quincy Notes," NCP, *Florida Metropolis*, February 23, 1907. For a brief profile of Dr. Stevens, see "The Tallahassee Colored Column," *Daily Democrat*, August 15, 1916.

62. Samuel Dixie interview with author, August 16, 1997, Behind the Veil Collection.

63. Republican Party Convention Delegates List, 1916, Joseph E. Lee Papers, Florida State Archives.

64. "To Colored Citizens of Florida," NCP, *Florida Metropolis*, March 11, 1919.

65. Inez Stevens-Jones interview with author.

66. Ibid.; "Statement of Walter F. White," December 17, 1920, Box C312, file, "KKK 1920," NAACP Papers.

67. A. I. Dixie interview with author, August 10, 1994.

68. T. L. Sweet to Walter White, December 6, 1920, in Box C285, NAACP Papers.

69. This branch's members, who hailed from Greensboro, River Junction, and Juniper, held their organization meeting on September 20, 1919. See Box G40, folder, "Greensboro, Fla. 1920–25," NAACP Papers.

70. J. T. Smith to Walter White, October 23, 1920, Box G40, NAACP Papers.

71. "Quincy," *Pensacola Journal,* October 10, 1920.

72. "White Women Must Register," *Pensacola Journal,* September 29, 1920. In response, Gadsden Democrats created their own voter education centers for white women. See "Organize Instruction Schools For Democratic Women Voters," *Gadsden County Times,* September, 1920, Box C312, File, "KKK 1921-Jan," NAACP Papers.

73. W. N. Mitchell to Warren G. Harding, 10 July, 1920, roll 36, frame 836, Harding Papers.

74. "An Open Letter," *Miami Herald,* October 26, 1920. This letter also appeared in several other Florida newspapers around the same time. It ran in the Lakeland *Evening Telegram* on October 29, 1920.

75. A. L. Taylor to NAACP, July 5, 1920, Box C352, folder, "Lakeland, Fla. 1920," NAACP Papers.

76. "Lakeland News Notes," NCP, *Florida Metropolis,* January 4, 1913.

77. "Lakeland News," NCP, *Florida Metropolis,* June 11, 1914.

78. *Lakeland Star,* September 16, 1920.

79. "Negroes Out-Register White Women," *Lakeland Star,* September 16, 1920.

80. See "Tell Negroes to Register or Go to Jail," *Lakeland Star,* October 8, 1920.

81. "Interesting Program Arranged For Women," *Lakeland Star,* September 21, 1920.

82. "Lodge Members Being Forced to Register," *Lakeland Star,* October 14, 1920.

83. "Democratic Meeting," *Jasper News,* September 17, 1920.

84. "Negroes Hasten to Pay that Poll Tax," *Tampa Tribune,* March 5, 1920; "'Unseen Hand' Is Sending Negro Women Registrations Far Above That of Whites," *Florida Metropolis,* September 21, 1920. In a typical lament, Franklin County Democrats complained, "There was an unusual number of negroes registered and paid poll taxes, and there seemed to be an unusual activity among them." "Apalachicola Notes," *Florida Times-Union,* October 15, 1920. By the end of the registration period on October 15, at least 569 African Americans had registered to vote in Franklin County. "The County Registration," *Apalachicola Times,* October 23, 1920.

85. T. S. Harris to Joseph E. Lee, December 9, 1879, Lee Papers, Ike Williams III Private Collection.

86. Brown, *Florida's Black Public Officials,* 65.

87. Florida Republican Party Delegates, 1916, Box 3, folder, "Republican Party roll of Delegates to Republican State Convention, 1916, Palatka," Joseph E. Lee Papers, Florida State Archives.

88. *Apalachicola Times,* September 25, 1920. A teenager by the name of Harry T. Moore was attending school in Suwannee County at this time. Moore would go on to lead an enormously successful voter registration campaign in Florida in the late 1940s. He was assassinated along with his wife in 1951. See Ben Green, *Before His Time: The Untold Story of Harry T. Moore, America's First Civil Rights Martyr* (New York: Free Press, 1999).

89. "Suwannee County Registration Shows Up in Fine Shape," *Florida Times-Union,* October 16, 1920. Information on T. S. Harris's political activism is found in *Bradford County Telegraph,* November 12, 1920.

90. J. L. Brundridge to Warren G. Harding, August 7, 1920, roll 36, frames 599–600, Harding Papers.

91. "Three Percent of Women Registrants Signed Wednesday," *Gainesville Daily Sun,* September 2, 1920. The Nineteenth Amendment was ratified on August 26. A week later, Clay Crawford, Florida secretary of state, issued letters to the state's county supervisors of registration decreeing that women's suffrage was in effect. Generally, women in the state began registering to vote on or soon after Tuesday, September 7. Women in Suwannee, St. Lucie, Duval, Putnam, Columbia, and Okaloosa Counties began registering on the 7th. Women in Apalachicola were registering by the 11th. See "Women May Register and Vote in General Election," *Florida Times-Union,* September 5, 1920; "Miss Ada Roberson First to Register in Suwannee County," *Florida Times-Union,* September 8, 1920; "The Ladies Are Registering," *Apalachicola Times,* September 11, 1920; "The Registration of Women Commences To-Day," *Fort Pierce News-Tribune,* September 7, 1920; and "Women register at DeFuniak," *Okaloosa News,* September 10, 1920. For ratification in the South see Marjorie Spruill Wheeler, *New Women of the New South: The Leaders of the Woman Suffrage Movement in the Southern States* (New York: Oxford University Press, 1993).

92. "Negroes Lack Interest," *Southwestern Christian Advocate,* October 7, 1920.

93. "Clark Fears it Will Bring Race War," *Citizen-Reporter* (Lake City), March 15, 1918. Paula Giddings discusses white southern politicians' fear of African American women voters in *When and Where I Enter: The Impact of Black Women on Race and Sex in America* (New York: William Morrow, 1984). For African American women's struggle to gain the franchise, see Ann D. Gordon, ed., *African American Women and the Vote, 1837–1965* (Amherst: University of Massachusetts Press, 1997).

94. Newspaper clipping, n.d., Box 4, folder, "Politics: Miscellaneous-1919–1934," Armwood Family Papers, Special Collections Library, University of South Florida.

95. Mary McLeod Bethune to Warren G. Harding, August 28, 1920, roll 36, frame 561, Harding Papers.

96. Eartha White to Warren G. Harding, September 21, 1920, roll 36, frame 1007, Harding Papers.

97. Negro Women's Harding and Coolidge Club of Fort Pierce to Harding, September 22, 1920, roll 36, frame 782, Harding Papers. Across the peninsula, 175 African American women in Fort Myers also registered to vote. See "Over 700 Voters Have Registered," *Fort Myers Tropical News*, October 12, 1920.

98. "Pythian Grand Lodge," NCP, *Florida Metropolis*, May 24, 1919. J. A. Colyer had been active in the Odd Fellows for at least two decades. See "Orlando Notes," NCP, *Florida Metropolis*, January 1, 1907.

99. "State Federation of Colored Women's Clubs," NCP, *Florida Metropolis*, June 12, 1919.

100. Ibid.

101. National Association of Colored Women, *Twelfth Biennial Convention* (1920).

102. "Echoes from the State Federation of Colored Women's Clubs," NCP, *Florida Metropolis*, June 21, 1919.

103. "Political Mass Meeting of Duval County Women," newspaper clipping, n.d., roll 36, frame, 1008, Harding Papers.

104. Sallie B. Smith to Warren Harding, October 28, 1920, roll 36, frames 936–937, Harding Papers.

105. "7,502 Women Registered in the City," *Florida Times-Union* (Jacksonville), September 28, 1920.

106. "Negress Jailed, Charged Swearing Falsely When Attempting to Register," *Florida Times-Union*, October 9, 1920; "Jail For Those Who Violate The Law in Getting on Voting Books," *Florida Times-Union*, October 12, 1920; "Jail For Illegal Voters," *Florida Times-Union*, October 17, 1920.

107. "Appeal Is Made for White Supremacy," *Florida Times-Union*, September 25, 1920.

108. "Increase in Registration of Women Recorded," *Florida Times-Union*, September 30, 1920.

109. "White Women To Be Registered on Special Days," *Florida Times-Union*, September 29, 1920; "White Women Are Urged to Line Up With Democrats," *Florida Times-Union*, October 6, 1920; "Want to Register Without Giving Their Exact Ages," *Florida Times-Union*, September 21, 1920; "Giving Exact Age Not Now Required," *Florida Times-Union*, September 29, 1920. In Orlando, it was said that "the men seem somewhat troubled over being obliged to require the women to state their age, it being a time honored tradition that we are ashamed of our years." *Orlando Morning Sentinel*, September 10, 1920. Asking African American women about their ages and other intimate details such as their marital status did not seem to bother white registrars in Florida.

110. "To The White Voters of Florida," "Tabulation of Registration Figures," and "Negro Men and Women Are Crowding to Courthouse To Qualify For Election," *Florida Times-Union,* October 3, 5, and 9, 1920.

111. "Jail For Those Who Violate The Law in Getting on Voting Books," *Florida Times-Union,* October 12, 1920;

112. "Congressman Frank Clark," *Florida Times-Union,* October 16, 1920.

113. "Registration Books Closed," *Florida Times-Union,* October 17, 1920.

114. A. G. Samuels to Warren Harding, October, 1920, roll 36, frames 902–903, Harding Papers.

115. "White and Negro Voters in Brevard," *Star Advocate* (Brevard), October 29, 1920. Black voter registration was especially strong in Cocoa and Titusville city precincts.

116. "Woman Registrants to Date," *Gainesville Daily Sun,* September 5, 1920.

117. "Women Registrants Have Increased," *Gainesville Daily Sun,* September 12, 1920.

118. "Registration Books Close," *Gainesville Daily Sun,* October 5, 1920.

119. For Gainesville Pythian activities, see "Gainesville Briefs," NCP, *Florida Metropolis,* May 26, 1919.

120. "Many Hear Clark and Hardee Talk Present Politics," *Gainesville Daily Sun,* October 13, 1920.

121. Walter White, "Election Day in Florida," *Crisis,* January 20, 1921, 108.

122. "Negro Women are Registering in Orlando," *St. Augustine Evening-Record,* September 16, 1920.

123. "Negro Women Keen on Coming Election," *Orlando Morning Sentinel,* September 15, 1920.

124. N. S. Freeland to NAACP, November 8, 1920, Box C284, folder, "Voting Nov 1–9, 1920," NAACP Papers. For the development of the African American community in Lincolnville, see Geoffrey Mohlman, "Lincolnville: An Anthropological History of St. Augustine" (Senior B.A. thesis, University of South Florida, 1991).

125. "The 'Unseen Hand,' " *St. Augustine Evening-Record,* November 1, 1920. White middle-class women organized a voter education program through the Business and Professional Women's Forum and urged their sisters to save white supremacy. See "Business Women to Push Registration With All Vigor," *St. Augustine Evening-Record,* September 28, 1920; and "White Women Register," *St. Augustine Evening-Record,* October 9, 1920.

126. Amanda Twining and Alfred T. Cooke, eds., *Down in Dixie: A Memorial to Alfred Twining* (1925), 348–349.

127. "City Election," *Times-Herald* (Palatka), April 5, 1918.

128. "Palatka News," NCP, *Florida Metropolis,* September 26, 1919; "Palatka News," NCP, *Florida Metropolis,* November 28, 1919.

129. "Application for Charter, Palatka," July 1, 1919, Box G42, folder, "Palatka, Fla," NAACP Papers.

130. Brown, *Florida's Black Public Officials*, 74.

131. "Complete List Qualified Putnam County Voters," *Times-Herald* (Palatka), October 22, 1920. In compiling this sample, I cross-checked the 1920 unpublished federal census schedules for Precinct 24 with the list of voters referred to in the *Times-Herald*. Tabulated registration list in author's possession. This can only be considered a partial list of registered voters since the figures were published after city and county officials had purged "ineligible" voters from the rolls, likely striking two hundred names—a tactic aimed at disenfranchising African Americans. For an excellent discussion of various techniques used to prevent African Americans from voting, see Litwack, *Trouble in Mind*, 218–229.

132. "Record Registration in All County Precincts," *Times-Herald*, October 29, 1920.

133. *Times-Herald*, October 1, 1920.

134. "Negro Girls Said to Have Registered Illegally," *Florida Times-Union*, October 15, 1920.

135. "De Land Election Bielby Ticket Wins 200 Negro Votes," *De Land Daily News*, February 11, 1920. This was an interracial alliance that Rev. Howard Thurman discussed in later years.

136. "De Land Women Register," *Florida Times-Union*, September 22, 1920.

137. Out of a black adult female population of 599. "769 Women Register in De Land Precinct," *De Land Daily News*, October 18, 1920.

138. "State Candidates Have Hot Meeting," *De Land Daily News*, May 8, 1920.

139. This account is taken from Mrs. Bethune's manuscript copy of *Mary McLeod Bethune: A Biography*, written by Rackham Holt and eventually published in 1964. See "Biography," in *The Bethune Foundation Collection, Part 1*, ed. Elaine M. Smith, reel 1, frame 412.

140. *Bethune Foundation Collection, Part 1*, reel 1, frame 413.

141. "Many Hundreds of Daytona Voters Will Not Be Able to Cast Ballots on November 2," *Daytona Daily News*, October 15, 1920; "The Way They Do it Down in Florida," *National Republican*, November 6, 1920.

142. "To Celebrate the Fourth," NCP, *Florida Metropolis*, June 18, 1919.

143. "West Palm Beach Notes," NCP, *Florida Metropolis*, May 20, 1919.

144. "Fond Hopes of Republicans," *Palm Beach Post*, October 24, 1920; "White Women Will Outvote Negro Women," *Negro World*, October 16, 1920, in *Tuskegee Institute Clipping File*, reel 12, frame 180.

145. "Officers Will Arrest Negroes Who Try to Vote Illegally November 2," *Palm Beach Post*, October 30, 1920. The *Fort Pierce News-Tribune* of October

29, 1920, announced a similar strategy in Fort Pierce: "it is well known that some of the negroes who have registered are not citizens; they were born in the Bahaman Islands and have never been naturalized. . . . And any one who presents himself at the polls who is not fully fitted for the ballot will find himself in the hands of the law! Let all take warning!"

146. "Appeal to White Women by Frank Clark," *Palm Beach Post,* October 23, 1920.

147. "Cary A. Hardee Urges Women of County to Register and Vote to Keep White Race in Power," *Florida Times-Union,* September 23, 1920.

148. Letter to the Editor, *Fort Pierce News-Tribune,* September 21, 1920.

149. "Colored Clubs to Try to Coerce Voters," *Pensacola Journal,* September 29, 1920.

150. Letter to the Editor, *Pensacola Journal,* September 30, 1920. The Escambia County Republican Club met at the local Knights of Pythias hall on Coyle Street. See "Republican Club," *Colored Citizen,* March 19, 1920. The Knights of Pythias hall in Pensacola was a popular venue for a wide variety of cultural, social, and political events. See "Seen and Heard While Passing," *Colored Citizen,* February 11, 1916.

151. Letter to the Editor, *Pensacola Journal,* September 30, 1920.

152. "Dr. Du Bois Writes New Book," *Colored Citizen,* March 5, 1920.

153. For information on Betts's speaking tour, see "Campbellton News," NCP, *Florida Metropolis,* April 28, 1919; "Address by Dr. S. H. Betts," NCP, *Florida Metropolis,* November 4, 1919; "Dr. Betts Strongly Supported," NCP, *Florida Metropolis,* June 23, 1919; and "Dr. Betts Still Working," NCP, *Florida Metropolis,* April 12, 1919. The following direct quotes are culled from "Address by Dr. S. H. Betts."

154. I am modifying Thompson's concept somewhat. Thompson originally (*Customs in Common,* 9) used this term to mean that rural people referred back to "the paternalist regulations of a more authoritarian society" to help legitimize contemporary protest.

155. For this platform, see chapter 1.

156. For statistics on farm ownership, see Charles S. Johnson et al., *Statistical Atlas of Southern Counties* (Chapel Hill: University of North Carolina Press, 1941), 73.

157. U.S. Department of Commerce, Bureau of the Census, *Negro Population, 1790–1915* (Washington, DC : Government Printing Office, 1918), 478, 677.

158. In both McIntosh and Citra, I have compared two lists of registered voters that appeared in the *Ocala Banner* with census enumerators' schedules.

159. Unpublished Population Schedules, Citra and McIntosh, Florida, 1920, in U.S. Department of Commerce, Bureau of the Census, *Fourteenth Census of the United States;* "How Women Registered in Marion," *Ocala Banner,*

October 15, 1920; "Registered Qualified Electors Marion," *Ocala Banner,* October 22, 1920.

160. For information on the Jones brothers, see Edward F. Keuchel, *A History of Columbia County, Florida* (Tallahassee Sentry Press, 1981), 169.

161. *New York Times,* October 7, 1920.

162. The following is drawn from "List of Qualified Voters of Columbia Co.," *Lake City Reporter,* October 22, 1920, and Columbia County Precincts, Unpublished U.S. Census Population Schedules, 1920.

163. "Lake City Locals," NCP, *Florida Metropolis,* April 12, 1919.

164. The published registration records are incomplete because county officials purged the names of many African American registrants in Lake City, including B. J. and D. J. Jones, from the rolls.

165. "Resolution Received and Adopted at a Republican Mass Meeting Held in Jacksonville, Florida, August 30, 1920," roll 36, frames 791–793, Harding Papers.

166. A. G. Samuels to Warren Harding, October 13, 1920, roll 36, frames 902–903, Harding Papers.

167. "Resolution Received and Adopted at a Republican Mass Meeting," Harding Papers.

168. "Question Unionism Was Not Discussed," *Miami Herald,* May 14, 1920; *Miami Herald,* June 30, 1920.

169. *Miami Herald,* June 30, 1920.

170. Agent Leon F. Howe Field Report, July 2, 1920, in *Federal Surveillance of Afro-Americans,* reel 13, frame 553. African Americans in Key West were similarly charged with stockpiling weapons and ammunition. See "Race Men Evidently Planned an Arsenal," *Cleveland Advocate,* September 20, 1919.

171. "Colored Citizens Ask 'Even Break,'" *Miami Herald,* July 4, 1920. The hall had been dynamited by whites in retaliation for black challenges to residential segregation. For the bombing, see Howe Field Report, July 2, 1920, in *Federal Surveillance of Afro-Americans,* reel 13, frame 553.

172. "Colored Citizens Ask 'Even Break,'" *Miami Herald,* July 4, 1920.

173. For the evolution of this story see "Miami Mob Searches Jail in Vain for Negro Brute Who Assaulted Aged White Woman," *Palm Beach Post,* July 31, 1920; and "Dade County Courts Plan Swift Justice for Negro Rapist," *Palm Beach Post,* August 1, 1920.

174. W. A. Mosely fired off an angry letter to the *Herald* on July 31, stating: "Some of the taxpayers would like to know the names of the 'respectable citizens of Miami,' who attempted to force Deputy Sheriff Simpson to tell what became of the prisoner. That was a crime punishable by imprisonment." Mosely argued that had the "mob" not forced the sheriff to spirit Mr. Brooks out of Miami "he could have been tried Monday and hanged Friday." See "Respectable Citizens?" *Miami Herald,* August 2, 1920.

175. "Negro Rapist Leaps to Death From Train," *Palm Beach Post,* August 2, 1920.

176. "Would Wipe Out Miami, Fla.," *Afro-American,* August 6, 1920.

177. "Bahamians Quiet," *Palm Beach Post,* August 3, 1920.

178. "Brooks Positively Identified as Assaulter of White Woman," *Miami Herald,* August 3, 1920.

179. Agent Leon F. Howe, "Dynamiting of Negro Houses, July 7, 1920," in *Federal Surveillance of Afro-Americans,* reel 13, Frame 555. The following year, Marcus Garvey's Universal Negro Improvement Association boasted 1,000 members in Miami, many of them undoubtedly Bahamian residents. Raymond A. Mohl, "Race Relations in Miami since the 1920s," in Colburn and Landers, *The African American Heritage of Florida,* 342.

180. "Vote For Shackelford," *Lake City Reporter,* June 4, 1920.

181. Agent Leon F. Howe, "Dynamiting of Negro Houses," July 7, 1920; "Independent Candidate Out for Sheriff," *Holmes County Advertiser,* October 8, 1920; "To the Voters of Holmes County," and "Second Section," *Holmes County Advertiser,* October 29, 1920; "Whitehurst Calls For Fairness," *St. Petersburg Daily Times,* October 29, 1920.

182. "White People Take Warning," *Miami Herald,* October 27, 1920.

183. "Mysterious Body in Florida," *Afro-American* (Baltimore), April 2, 1920, in *Tuskegee Institute News Clipping File,* reel 11, frame 933. See also "Paying Poll Tax in Florida," *New York Age,* April 3, 1920.

184. "Negro in Politics is Menace to the Nation," *Tribune* (Tampa), October 25, 1920, in *Tuskegee Institute News Clipping File,* reel 12, frame 5.

185. "From the Negro's Side," *Miami Herald,* November 1, 1920.

186. "Why the Negro Should Register 3,000 Votes," *Colored Citizen,* April 30, 1920; "Tuesday Election Day: Vote Democratic," *Okaloosa News-Journal,* October 29, 1920.

187. J. T. Smith to Walter White, October 23, 1920, Box G40, NAACP Papers.

188. Anonymous to Walter White, December 30, 1920, Box C312, folder, "KKK-Jan," NAACP Papers.

189. C. L. R. James, *Party Politics in the West Indies* (Port of Spain: privately published, 1962), 126.

190. John K. Douglass to Warren G. Harding, September 21, 1920, roll 174, frames 656–657, Harding Papers.

9. ELECTION DAY, 1920

1. Quoted in *Florida Times-Union,* September 21, 1920.

2. "Ku Klux Warning," *Afro-American,* November 26, 1920, in *Tuskegee Institute News Clipping File,* reel 11, frame 632. For additional KKK activity in

Miami, see U.S. Congress, House, Committee on Rules, *The Ku-Klux Klan Hearings*, 67th Congress, 1st Session (Washington, DC: Government Printing Office, 1921), 51 (hereafter cited as *Ku-Klux Klan Hearings*).

3. "That Police Raid," *Miami Herald*, October 20, 1920.

4. "White Voters," *Miami Herald*, November 1, 1920.

5. For information about the bombing, see Howe Field Report, July 2, 1920, in *Federal Surveillance of Afro-Americans*, reel 13, frame 553.

6. "Segregation Made to Pay," *Afro-American*, April 4, 1914, in *Tuskegee Institute News Clipping File*, reel 3, frame 452.

7. "Makes Offer to City," *Miami Herald*, July 1, 1920; "Colored Citizens Ask 'Even Break,' " *Miami Herald*, July 4, 1920.

8. In piecing together a composite portrait of audience members, I am drawing on the voter registration and census records cited in the following: Miami Precincts 8 & 9, Unpublished U.S. Census Population Schedules, 1920, and "Registered Voters," *Miami Herald*, October 30, 1920. Tabulated voter registration list in author's possession.

9. The following account is based on "Colored People Stage Rally at I.O.I.F. Hall," and "Stick Together and Vote G.O.P.," *Miami Herald*, October 30 and 31, 1920.

10. Ibid.

11. Report of Walter White, Box C312, folder, "KKK 1920," NAACP Papers, 4; hereafter cited as White Report. White Floridians joined their counterparts in several southern states who also organized new KKK chapters in 1920. See "To Organize," *Jasper News*, August 6, 1920; "Ku Klux Klan to Invade Florida?" *Palm Beach Post*, August 7, 1920; "State News Items," *Jasper News*, August 13, 1920; "Ku-Klux Klan is resurrected in Nine States of the South," *New York World*, October 10, 1920 (*Tuskegee Institute News Clipping File*, reel 11, frame 649); and "Ku-Klux-Klan Is Robbing Negro of Vote," *New York Call*, November 1, 1920. A newspaper editor investigating Klan activity in the South told a congressional committee the Klan organizations in Florida and Texas—both states where African American movements were occurring—were the most lethal. See *Ku-Klux Klan Hearings*, 12. For an excellent discussion of the African American struggles in Texas during this era, see Reich, "Soldiers of Democracy." See also Michael Newton, *The Invisible Empire: The Ku Klux Klan in Florida* (Gainesville: University Press of Florida, 2001), 42–43.

12. "Florida Does Not Gain A Congressman," *St. Augustine Evening Record*, October 8, 1920.

13. The GOP's journal of record also gave support to this position. See "Making the South Safe for Democracy," *National Republican*, March 8, 1919. Amendment XIV, Section 2, reads as follows: "Representatives shall be appointed among the several States according to their respective numbers, counting the whole number of persons in each State, excluding Indians not

taxed. But when the right to vote at any election for the choice of Electors for President and Vice-President of the United States, Representatives in Congress, the executive and judicial officers of a State, or the members of the legislature thereof, is denied to any of the male inhabitants of such State, being twenty-one years of age and citizens of the United States, or in any way abridged, except for participation in rebellion, or other crime, the basis of representation therein shall be reduced in the proportion which the number of such male citizens shall bear to the whole number of male citizens twenty-one years of age in such State." This strategy had been debated by black leaders in years past.

14. "Reduction of Southern Representation," *New York Age*, August 14, 1920.

15. "Enfranchise the Negro," *National Republican*, July 19, 1919.

16. John K. Douglass to Warren G. Harding, September 21, 1920, roll 174, frames 656–657, Harding Papers.

17. Eli Futch, "To the Democratic Voters," n.d., James B. Hodges Papers, P. K. Yonge Library of Florida History, University of Florida. The Democrats were cognizant of this danger. See "The South Vitally Interested," *Holmes County Advertiser*, October 1, 1920.

18. "South's Representation May Be Cut Unless Race is Allowed the Ballot," *Cleveland Advocate*, October 30, 1920.

19. See John Hurst to John R. Shillady, January 14, 1919, Box C284, folder, "Voting, 1916, 1918," NAACP Papers.

20. Futch, "To the Democratic Voters."

21. "Why I have Registered and Shall Vote in November," *St. Petersburg Daily Times*, September 30, 1920.

22. "St. Augustine Women Active for Registration," *Florida Times-Union*, October 5, 1920.

23. *Okaloosa News*, October 29, 1920.

24. "Jail For Those Who Violate Law in Getting On Voting Books," *Florida Times-Union*, October 12, 1920.

25. Janie Lowder to NAACP, October 11, 1920, Box C285, folder, "Voting, Jacksonville, Florida, 1920," NAACP Papers.

26. "Illegal Registrations Among Negroes Pass 4,000 Mark," *Florida Metropolis*, October 16, 1920.

27. "Many Hundreds of Daytona Voters Will Not Be Able to Cast Ballots on November 2," *Daytona Daily-News*, October 15, 1920; "The Way They Do it Down in Florida," *National Republican*, November 6, 1920.

28. "Commissioners Proceedings," *Jasper News*, October 22, 1920. The area press also warned Republicans to cease their political activities because of heightened labor conflict. "To the White Republicans," *Jasper News*, October 1, 1920.

29. See *Report of the Attorney General of the State of Florida* (Tallahassee: T. J. Appleyard, 1921), 134. State Democratic officials were afraid that Hamilton County's technique of disenfranchisement would bring federal scrutiny to Florida. See *Apalachicola Times,* October 30, 1920.

30. J. B. Shiver to Warren G. Harding, February 12, 1921, roll 110, frame 200, Harding Papers.

31. "Republicans Search for Trickster," *Miami Herald,* October 2, 1920; "Republican Admits Negro Ballots Big Factor in Florida," *Miami Herald,* October 23, 1920; "A. W. Corbett Is A Participant in Hot Time At Miami," *St. Augustine Evening Record,* September 30, 1920.

32. "Negro Question is Imminent Issue," *St. Petersburg Daily Times,* October 9, 1920.

33. "Voters!" *Palm Beach Post,* October 31, 1920.

34. "Republicans Hold Rally In City Park," *Palm Beach Post,* October 31, 1920. Some new Republicans were former Democrats, disgruntled by Woodrow Wilson's stand on the League of Nations. See W. H. H. Gleason to Maj. J. T. Scott, October 11, 1919. Box 9, folder: "Republican Party, 1896–1927," Gleason Papers. Democrats noted with chagrin the desertions from their ranks to the GOP. See "Party Politics in Florida," *St. Petersburg Daily Times,* September 5, 1920. At Stuart, a town in Palm Beach County, a local correspondent reported that some members of the town's Republican Club "were formerly democrats who are democrats still in principles but who believe that change in party and policy is demanded for the best interests of the county." "Stuart," *Palm Beach Post,* October 5, 1920.

35. W. H. H. Gleason, a white Republican in Florida, blistered the national GOP for tacitly accepting the support of the Lily Whites. Gleason argued that the Lily Whites discredited the party and weakened its potential base of support. Gleason to J. T. Scott, October 1, 1920, Box 9, folder, "Republican Party, 1896–1927," Gleason Papers.

36. "Republicans Plan Active Campaign to Elect G. W. Allen," *Florida Times-Union,* August 30, 1916; *Florida Times-Union,* August 7, 1916.

37. A. I. Dixie interview with author, August 10, 1994, Behind the Veil Collection.

38. Inez Stevens-Jones interview with author, Behind the Veil Collection.

39. "Statement of Walter F. White," Box C312, file, "KKK1920," NAACP Papers, 5.

40. N. B. Young to Walter F. White, February 3, 1921, Box C312, file, "KKK 1921-Feb.," NAACP Papers.

41. White Report, 3.

42. T. L. Sweet to Walter White, December 6, 1920, Box C285, folder, "Voting, Jacksonville, Florida, 1920," NAACP Papers.

43. "That Election Day Orgy of Murder in Darkest Florida," *National Republican,* November 27, 1920.

44. "Body of Murdered Negro Found in the Ocklockonee River," *Gadsden County Times,* November 4, 1920, newspaper clipping in Box C312, folder, "KKK 1921-Jan," NAACP Papers.

45. J. T. Thomas to NAACP, January 19, 1920, Box C312, folder, "KKK 1921-Jan," NAACP Papers.

46. "Grand Chancellor Andrews' Official Visits," NCP, *Florida Metropolis,* April 1, 1920.

47. J. T. Smith to Walter White, October 23, 1920, Box G40, NAACP Papers.

48. Inez Stevens-Jones interview with author.

49. A. I. and Samuel Dixie interview with author, Behind the Veil Collection.

50. "Negro Lodges Are Burned to Ground," *Daily Democrat* (Tallahassee), October 23, 1920; N. B. Young to Walter White, January 10, 1921, Box C312, folder, "KKK 1921-Jan," NAACP Papers.

51. "Negro Lodges Are Burned to Ground," *Daily Democrat* (Tallahassee), October 23, 1920.

52. Greensboro Membership Charter, NAACP Papers.

53. "That Election Day Orgy of Murder in Darkest Florida," *National Republican,* November 27, 1920.

54. Young to White, January 10, 1921.

55. "That Election Day Orgy of Murder in Darkest Florida."

56. "Drive Women From Polls in South," *Chicago Defender,* October 30, 1920.

57. "Negro Assassinated," *St. Augustine Evening Record,* October 25, 1920.

58. "Outlaws Reign in Jacksonville," *Cleveland Advocate,* October 16, 1920.

59. Anonymous to James Weldon Johnson, August 25, 1920, Box C312, "KKK-July-Dec 1920," NAACP Papers.

60. "Try to Intimidate Negro Politician," *New York Times,* October 7, 1920.

61. White, "Election Day in Florida," 108; "Statement of Walter White," 4.

62. "Rapid Justice Is Handed Killers," *Lake City Reporter,* October 8, 1920; *Bradford County Telegraph,* October 15, 1920; *New York Times,* October 7, 1920.

63. *Bradford County Telegraph,* November 12, 1920.

64. "Here is Affidavit of Florida White Man," *Cleveland Advocate,* October 23, 1920.

65. Alexander Akerman to William C. Kenyon, November 6, 1920, C285, NAACP Papers; "Memorandum from National Association for the Advancement of Colored People," December 3, 1920, in Box C284, file, "Voting December 1920," NAACP Papers.

66. Lester J. Dabbs, "A Report of the Circumstances and Events of the Race Riot on November 2, 1920 in Ocoee, Florida" (M.A. thesis, Stetson University, 1969), 20; "Election Crookedness," *National Republican,* January 1, 1921.

67. Grand Master, KKK, to W. R. O'Neal, October 28, 1920, Box C285, folder, "Voting, Jacksonville, Florida, 1920," NAACP Papers; "Liberty Limited," *Survey,* December 4, 1920.

68. "'White Cavalcade' Marches Through Orlando Streets," *Orlando Morning Sentinel,* October 31, 1920; "Ku Klux Klan Demonstrates that White Supremacy Will Be Maintained in Volusia County," *Daytona Daily News,* November 2, 1920; "Silent Hosts of Ku Klux Klan Parade With Impressive Numbers," *Florida Times-Union,* October 31, 1920.

69. J. Seth Hill to James Weldon Johnson, October 31, 1920, Box C285, NAACP Papers. Hill's prophecy apparently came true. See "Negroes Joke Klans," *Times Plain Dealer,* December 15, 1920, in *Tuskegee Institute News Clipping File,* reel 11, frame 626.

70. Holt, *Mary McLeod Bethune,* 121.

71. "Ku Klux Klan Demonstrates that White Supremacy Will Be Maintained in Volusia County," *Daytona Daily News,* November 2, 1920.

72. Holt, *Mary McLeod Bethune,* 119–123; McCluskey, "Ringing Up a School," 204; Leonard R. Lempel, "The Mayor's 'Henchmen and Henchwomen, Both White and Colored': Edward H. Armstrong and the Politics of Race in Daytona Beach, 1900–1940," *Florida Historical Quarterly* 79 (winter 2001), 278–279.

73. "At bottom the popular movement had acquired an immense self-confidence. . . . the revolution had awakened them, had given them the possibility of achievement, confidence and pride. That psychological weakness, that feeling of inferiority with which the imperialists poison colonial peoples everywhere, these were gone." James, *Black Jacobins,* 244.

74. Franklin Verun to James Weldon Johnson, January 11, 1921, Box C312, folder, "KKK 1921-Jan," NAACP Papers.

75. Verun to Johnson, January 8, 1920, ibid.

76. Voters of Precinct 8, St. Lucie County, Florida to the *Crisis,* January 6, 1921, in Box C 312, folder, "KKK 1921-Jan," NAACP Papers. For the St. Lucie incident, also see "How Whites Stopped Negroes from Voting," *New York Age,* January 15, 1921.

77. Information on Dan Thomas appears in the 1920 U.S. Census.

78. J. E. Timothy, J. Isaac, A. V. Billings, Tobi Fairbanks, N. Bigott and J. C. Bigott to NAACP, December 31, 1920, Box C312, folder, "KKK 1921-Jan," NAACP Papers.

79. "Dan Thomas Shot," *Manatee River Journal,* November 4, 1920.

80. "Democrats are First on List," *Pensacola Journal,* November 2, 1920.

81. Holt, *Mary McLeod Bethune,* 122.

82. Jones, "No Longer Denied," 266.

83. A. P. Holly to W. E. B. Du Bois, January 13, 1921, Box C285, folder, "Voting 1921," NAACP Papers.

84. Anonymous to James Weldon Johnson, January 5, 1921, Box C312, folder, "KKK 1921-Jan," NAACP Papers.

85. Charles Thompson to NAACP, August 11, 1931, Box C85, folder, "Voting, Miami 1932," NAACP Papers.

86. "Overwhelming Majority Given Democratic Ticket," *Miami Herald,* November 3, 1920.

87. "A Very Heavy Vote Polled in County," *Daily Democrat* (Tallahassee), November 2, 1920.

88. "Proposed Bond Amendment Defeated by Large Majority," *Florida Times-Union,* November 4, 1920.

89. Mrs. N. S. Freeland to NAACP, November 8, 1920, Box C284, folder, "Voting, Nov 1–9, 1920," NAACP Papers.

90. "Scattering Returns from Election," *Florida Times-Union,* November 5, 1920.

91. "Voting Heavy in Lakeland," *Lakeland Star,* November 2, 1920. For the suppression of the ballot in Suwannee County, see "The House of T. S. Harris," *Bradford County Telegraph,* November 12, 1920.

92. Inez Stevens-Jones interview with author.

93. N. B. Young to Walter White, undated letter, Box C312, folder, "KKK 1921-Jan," NAACP Papers. Few African Americans in that county were able to vote. See "Harding Sweeps the Country," and "Further Election Returns," *Enterprise-Recorder* (Madison), November 5 and 12, 1920.

94. J. T. Smith to NAACP, January 19, 1920, Box C312, folder, "KKK 1921-Jan," NAACP Papers.

95. "Joe Ragsdale Shooting Affray at Hardaway," *Gadsden County Times,* November 4, 1920; "Election Day Orgy of Murder in Florida," *Atlanta Independent,* December 2, 1920. Whether by design or accident, white newspapers in Florida frequently misspelled the names of African Americans who were assassinated.

96. "Election Day Orgy of Murder in Florida," *Atlanta Independent,* December 2, 1920.

97. J. T. Smith to NAACP, January 19, 1920.

98. N. B. Young to Walter White, January 27, 1921, Box C312, folder, "KKK 1921-Jan," NAACP Papers.

99. Anonymous to James Weldon Johnson, January 11, 1920, Box C312, folder, "KKK 1921-Jan," NAACP Papers.

100. The published report from Gadsden election officials read: "Republican votes cast in the county were very few." See "Scattering Returns from State Election," *Florida Times-Union,* November 5, 1920.

101. "Something Worth Investigating," *National Republican,* November 20, 1920.

102. White Report.

103. James W. Floyd to James Weldon Johnson, November 12, 1920, Box C284, folder, "Voting, Nov 1–9, 1920," NAACP Papers.

104. Ibid.

105. Anonymous to James Weldon Johnson, January 7, 1921, Box C312, folder, "KKK1921-Jan," NAACP Papers.

106. White Report, 3–4.

107. Dabbs, "A Report of the Circumstances," 24.

108. Zora Neale Hurston, "The Ocoee Riot," Box 2, folder, "Atrocities Perpetrated Upon June 1938" (WPA Papers), Florida Negro Papers. See also "Notes Taken by Stetson Kennedy on Dialogue between Zora Neale Hurston and Dr. Carita Dogget Course," n.d., Box 1, folder 13, Stetson Kennedy Papers, Federal Writers' Project, WPA Papers, Southern Historical Collection, University of North Carolina, Chapel Hill.

109. Hurston, "The Ocoee Riot."

110. See "Ocoee Claims 2 White Victims," *Orlando Morning Sentinel,* November 3, 1920. Ironically, Salisbury's mansion is now the site of Ocoee's historical museum.

111. White Report, 4.

112. Hurston, "The Ocoee Riot."

113. "Race Riot in Orange County," *Florida Times-Union,* November 3, 1920; "Small Negro Boy Hid Under Store at Ocoee 48 Hours," *Florida Times-Union,* November 6, 1920.

114. "Ocoee Claims 2 White Victims," *Orlando Morning Sentinel,* November 3, 1920.

115. Hurston, "The Ocoee Riot."

116. "As Negro Houses Burned At Ocoee," *Orlando Morning Sentinel,* November 4, 1920; "An Open Letter to the Governor of the State of Florida," *National Republican,* November 13, 1920.

117. L. E. Williams to John E. Nail, December 31, 1920, Box C312, folder, "KKK 1921-Jan," NAACP Papers.

118. "Woman Escaped from Florida Mob But Rest of Family Died," *New York Age,* December 18, 1920.

119. Ibid.

120. White Report, 4.

121. "Negroes Leave Ocoee," *Florida Times-Union,* November 5, 1920. For another summary of the aftermath of the Battle of Ocoee, see "Small Negro Boy Hid Under Store at Ocoee 48 Hours," *Florida Times-Union,* November 6, 1920.

122. White Report, 2.

123. Alexander Akerman to Hon. William C. Kenyon, November 6, 1920, Box C285, folder, "Voting, Jacksonville, Florida 1920," NAACP Papers.

124. "Flames Sweep Black Belt," *Miami Herald,* November 4, 1920.

125. James Weldon Johnson to J. Seth Hills, November 4, 1920, Box C285, folder, "Voting, Jacksonville, Florida 1920," NAACP Papers.

126. "Reunion of Vets Came to Close After Notable Session," *Orlando Morning Sentinel,* November 13, 1920.

127. "Says 30 Negroes Were Slain in Florida On Election Day," *New York Post,* December 15, 1920, in *Tuskegee Institute News Clipping File,* reel 12, frame 480.

128. White Report, 8.

129. Mrs. J. H. Hamiter to Mrs. Huston, November 28, 1920, NAACP Papers.

130. White Report, 8.

131. "Between 30 and 60 Negroes Killed in Florida Election Day," *Baltimore Herald,* November 7, 1920, in *Tuskegee Institute News Clipping File,* reel 11, frame 651.

132. "Wilma, Fla.," *Atlanta Independent,* December 3, 1920.

133. House, Committee on the Census, *Hearings before the Committee on the Census,* 66th Congress, 3rd Session (Washington, DC: Government Printing Office, 1921); hereafter cited as *Hearings before the Committee on the Census.*

134. W. E. B. Du Bois, "The Election and Democracy," in *Disfranchisement of Colored Americans in the Presidential Election of 1920* (New York: NAACP, 1920), 5. Box C284, folder, "Voting October 21–31," NAACP Papers.

135. *Hearings before the Committee on the Census,* 80.

136. At the local level, Florida NAACP activists such as Dr. N. B. Young in Tallahassee, AME Bishop John Hurst, and Capt. James W. Floyd (both in Jacksonville) were active in compiling evidence on disfranchisement in the wake of the election. See James Floyd to James Weldon Johnson, November 12, 1920, Box C284, folder, "Voting Nov 1–9, 1920," NAACP Papers.

137. For Siegel's invitation see Walter White to J. W. Floyd, November 27, 1920, Box C285, folder, "Voting, Jacksonville, Florida, 1920," NAACP Papers.

138. *Hearings before the Committee on the Census,* 42.

139. Ibid., 39, 79.

140. Ibid., 46, 61.

141. Ibid., 73.

142. Ibid., 77.

143. Ibid., 205, 190. "Dr. J. Seth Hills Denies Having Sent Telegram to Representative Frank Clark," *Florida Sentinel,* January 7, 1921, in Box C312, folder, "KKK1921," NAACP Papers.

144. *Hearings before the Committee on the Census,* 187.

145. John Hurst to Walter White, February 5, 1921, Box C312, folder, "KKK 1921-Feb," NAACP Papers.

146. *Hearings before the Committee on the Census*, 197.

147. Richard B. Sherman notes, "There was little evidence that before taking office Harding gave any thought to the position of Blacks. . . . During one pre-inaugural discussion of racial problems in the South between Harding and Black leaders in Florida . . . it was embarrassingly clear that he thought his visitors were job-seeking politicians. During a long, rambling discourse it became plain that he had never heard of the Tuskegee Institute nor of its famous founder, Booker T. Washington. The meeting led one participant to remark, 'If you'd eliminate damn from that fellow's vocabulary he couldn't do anything but stutter.' " Richard B. Sherman, *The Republican Party and Black America: From McKinley to Hoover, 1896–1933* (Charlottesville: University Press of Virginia, 1973), 102–103.

148. Anonymous to James Weldon Johnson, January 7, 1921, Box C312, file, "KKK-1921," NAACP Papers.

149. For the continued suppression of black political organizations, see "Whites Oppose Meeting of N.A.A.C.P. in Florida," *Chicago Defender*, April 2, 1921.

150. Anonymous to James Weldon Johnson, January 15, 1921, Box C312, file, "KKK-1921," NAACP Papers.

151. *Daily Democrat* (Tallahassee), November 15, 1920.

152. "Some Little Excitement," *Apalachicola Times*, November 20, 1920.

153. Ruth Crowd Wilkerson to James Weldon Johnson, January 30, 1921, Box C312, folder, "KKK 1921-February," NAACP Papers.

154. Frank Crowd founded the Globe Theater (originally known as the "Bijou") on July 19, 1908. The artists who performed there over the years read like a "Who's Who" of outstanding musicianship. For an overview of the Globe and Mr. Crowd's role in the building of the institution, see "The Globe Theater at Jacksonville, Fla.," *Indianapolis Freeman*, May 21, 1910.

155. Anonymous to NAACP, January 10, 1921, Box C312, folder, "KKK 1921-Jan," NAACP Papers.

156. Anonymous to NAACP, January 11, 1921, Box C312, folder, "KKK 1921-Jan," NAACP Papers.

CONCLUSION: LEGACIES OF THE FLORIDA MOVEMENT

1. U.S. Census Bureau Public Information Office News Release, "African Americans Defy Trend of Plunging Voter Turnout, Census Bureau Reports," *United States Department of Commerce News*, July 19, 2000; Steven J. Rosenstone and John Mark Hansen, *Mobilization, Participation, and Democracy in America* (New York: Macmillan, 1993); Frances Fox Piven and Richard A.

Cloward, *Why Americans Still Don't Vote: and Why Politicians Want It That Way* (Boston: Beacon Press, 2000).

2. John Dean, "Why Americans Don't Vote—and How That Might Change," *CNN Com Law Center,* November 8, 2000.

3. Colin Palmer, *Passageways: An Interpretive History of Black America,* vol. 2, *1863–1965* (New York: Harcourt Brace, 1998), 107.

4. Alain Locke, ed., *The New Negro: An Interpretation* (1925; New York: Johnson Reprint Corporation, 1968).

5. Beth Tompkins Bates, "A New Crowd Challenges the Agenda of the Old Guard in the NAACP, 1933–1941," *American Historical Review* 102, no.2 (April 1997), 340–377; and Bates, *Pullman Porters and the Rise of Protest Politics.*

6. For a discussion of the forces of demobilization in modern American politics, see Adolph Reed, Jr., *Stirrings in the Jug: Black Politics in the Post-Segregation Era* (Minneapolis: University of Minnesota Press, 1999).

7. Brown, "Womanist Consciousness"; Gilmore, *Gender and Jim Crow;* White, *Too Heavy a Load.*

8. C. L. R. James, "Letters on Politics," in Anna Grimshaw, ed., *The C. L. R. James Reader* (Oxford: Blackwell, 1992), 271–276.

9. Grimshaw, *The C. L. R. James Reader,* 159.

10. Paul Diggs, "Overseer of Tenants," February 15, 1939, folder 112, Federal Writers' Project, WPA Papers, Southern Historical Collection, University of North Carolina, Chapel Hill.

11. Paul Diggs, "South Florida Turpentine Corporation," folder 113, WPA Papers, Southern Historical Collection, UNC.

12. Zora Neale Hurston, "Cross City: Turpentine Camp," August 1939, folder 13, WPA Papers, Southern Historical Collection, UNC.

13. Charles Thompson to NAACP, August 11, 1931, Box C285, folder, "Voting, Miami, Florida 1932," NAACP Papers.

14. *Colored Citizen,* June 22, 1928, clipping in reel 1, frame 640, *Part F: The Voting Rights Campaign,* NAACP Papers.

15. See Green, *Before His Time.*

16. Hanson, *Mary McLeod Bethune and Black Women's Political Activism.*

17. Jones, "No Longer Denied," 262–267.

18. A. I. Dixie interview with author, August 16, 1997, Behind the Veil Collection.

19. J. T. Smith to James Weldon Johnson, October 10, 1923, NAACP Papers.

20. See also Due and Due, *Freedom in the Family.*

21. Richard Wayne Sapp, "Suwannee River Town, Suwannee River Country: Political Moieties in a Southern County Community" (diss., University of Florida, 1976), 83.

22. W. E. B. Du Bois, *John Brown,* ed. David Roediger (1909; reprint, New York: Library of America, 2001), 4.

SELECTED BIBLIOGRAPHY

ARCHIVAL COLLECTIONS

P. K. Yonge Library of Florida History, University of Florida, Gainesville

PRIVATE PAPERS

Albert Hazen Blanding Papers
Napoleon Bonaparte Broward Papers
Charles Dougherty Papers, 1878–1888
William Henry Gleason Papers
James B. Hodges Papers
May Mann Jennings Papers
William Sherman Jennings Papers
Peter O. Knight Papers
Austin Shuey Mann Papers
Ormond Family Papers
E. C. F. Sanchez Papers
Henry Shelton Sanford Papers (microfilm)
Samuel Swann Papers
Park Monroe Trammell Papers, 1876–1936
David L. Yulee Papers

STATE PAPERS

Records of the Assistant Commissioner and Subordinate Field Offices for the State
of Florida, Bureau of Refugees, Freedmen, and Abandoned Lands, 1865–1872

Florida State Archives, Department of State, R. A. Gray Building, Tallahassee

FLORIDA GOVERNORS' PAPERS AND CORRESPONDENCE, RECORD GROUP 101

William D. Bloxham Papers
Napoleon Bonaparte Broward Papers

Sidney J. Catts Papers
Francis P. Fleming Papers
Florida Governors' Letterbooks
William S. Jennings Papers
Henry L. Mitchell Papers
Park Trammell Papers

PRIVATE PAPERS

Mary McLeod Bethune Collection
William Terrell Eddins Diaries
Stetson Kennedy Florida Folklife Collection
Joseph E. Lee Papers

COUNTY PAPERS

Gadsden County Soldiers and Sailors Discharge, 1918–1919 (microfilm)

University of North Florida, Jackonsville
Eartha M. M. White Papers

Edward Waters College, Jacksonville
Afro-American Life Insurance Company Collection

Florida Historical Society, University of South Florida, Tampa
Armwood Family Papers
The Florida Negro Papers
La Union Martí-Maceo Papers

Special Collections Library, Florida State University, Tallahassee
Bird and Ulmer Papers
Captain Hugh Black Papers
Brumby Family Papers
Dr. F. A. Byrd Papers
Susan Bradford Eppes Papers
Florida Promotional and Historical Materials Collection
Pine Hill Plantation Papers

Red Hills of Florida Collection
William S. Rosasco Papers

Manuscript Division, Library of Congress

Franz Boaz Papers (microfilm)
William E. Chandler Papers
Frederick Douglass Papers (microfilm)
John Patterson Green Papers
Warren G. Harding Papers (microfilm)
National Association for the Advancement of Colored People Papers
National Urban League Records
Republican Party Campaign Collection
Thaddeus Stevens Papers
Works Progress Administration Papers, Federal Writers' Project

Archive of Folk Culture, Library of Congress

Zora Neale Hurston Collection

Private Collection of Ike Williams III, Jacksonville

Joseph E. Lee Papers

Southern Historical Collection, Manuscript Department, University of North Carolina, Chapel Hill

George Baldwin Papers
E. M. L'Engle Papers
Federal Writers' Project, Works Progress Administration Papers
Stetson Kennedy Papers
Washington J. Lutterloh Papers

Special Collections Library, Duke University, Durham

Abbie M. Brooks Diary
Georgia Colored Knights of Pythias Medical Record Ledger, 1920–21
William Powell Papers
A. M. Reed Diary (typescript copy)
George E. Scott Papers

MICROFILM COLLECTIONS

Mary McLeod Bethune Papers: The Bethune Foundation Collection, Part 2. Bethesda, MD: University Publications of America, 1997.

Black Workers in the Era of the Great Migration, 1916–1925. Edited by James Grossman. Frederick, MD: University Publications of America, 1985.

Federal Surveillance of Afro-Americans 1917–1925: The First World War, the Red Scare, and the Garvey Movement. Edited by Theodore Kornweibel, Jr. Frederick, MD: University Publications of America, 1986.

General Education Board Archives, Series I, Appropriations, Early South Projects. New York: Rockefeller University; Wilmington, DE: Scholarly Resources, Inc., 1993.

League of Women Voters Papers, 1918–1974. Frederick, MD: University Publications of America, 1985–.

Papers of the National Association for the Advancement of Colored People. Edited by August Meier and John Bracy, Jr. Frederick, MD: University Publications of America, 1986–.

Protestant Episcopal Church in the USA. Atlanta: SOLINET, 1992.

Tuskegee Institute News Clipping File. Edited by John W. Kitchens. Tuskegee, AL: Division of Behavioral Science Research, Carver Research Foundation, Tuskegee Institute, 1976.

FEDERAL AND STATE DOCUMENTS

Journals of the Florida House of Representatives, 1886–1920.

Sixth Annual Report of the Commissioner of Lands and Immigration of the State of Florida For the Year Ending December 31, 1874. Tallahassee: Charles H. Walton, 1874.

U.S. Commission on Civil Rights. *Voting Irregularities in Florida during the 2000 Presidential Election.* Washington, DC: Government Printing Office, 2001.

U.S. Congress. *Testimony Taken by the Joint Select Committee to Inquire into the Condition of Affairs in The Late Insurrectionary States: Miscellaneous and Florida.* Report 22, vol. 13. 42nd Congress, 2nd Session. Washington, DC: Government Printing Office, 1872.

———. House. *Contested Election Case of Goodrich V. Bullock from the Second Congressional District of Florida.* 51st Congress, 1st Session. Washington, DC: Government Printing Office, 1890.

———. House. *Horatio Bisbee, Jr. v. Jessie J. Finley.* 47th Congress, 1st Session. 1881–1882.

———. *Bisbee v. Hull Contested Election.* 46th Congress, 1st Session, Misc. Doc. No. 26. 1879.

———. House. *Jessie J. Finley v. Horatio Bisbee, Jr., Contested Election with Minority Report.* 45th Congress, 3rd Session. H. rp. 95, 1878–1879.

———. House. *Official Records of the Union and Confederate Navies in the War of the Rebellion.* 56th Congress, 2nd Session. Washington, DC: Government Printing Office, 1901.

———. House. Committee on the Census, *Hearings before the Committee on the Census.* 66th Congress, 3rd Session. Washington, DC: Government Printing Office, 1921.

———. Senate. *Report of the Senate Committee on Privileges and Elections With the Testimony and Documentary on the Election in the State of Florida in 1876.* 44th Congress, 2d Session. Washington, DC: Government Printing Office, 1877.

U.S. Department of Commerce. Bulletin 141, *Mortality Statistics: 1918.* Washington, DC: Government Printing Office, 1920, 28–29.

———. Bureau of the Census. *Negro Population, 1790–1915.* Washington, DC: Government Printing Office, 1918.

———. *Fourteenth Census of the United States, Volume III: Population.* Washington, DC: Government Printing Office, 1923.

———. Unpublished Population Schedules, Florida, 1920: Citra; Columbia County; McIntosh; Miami; Palatka; West Palm Beach. *Fourteenth Census of the United States.* University of Florida (microfilm).

U.S. Department of Labor. *The Negro at Work during the World War and during Reconstruction: Statistics, Problems, and Policies Relating to the Greater Inclusion of Negro Wage Earners in American Industry and Agriculture.* Washington, DC: Government Printing Office, 1921.

———. *Negro Migration in 1916–1917.* Washington, DC: Division of Negro Economics, U.S. Department of Labor, 1919.

U.S. Railroad Commission. *Report of the Railroad Wage Commission to the Director General of Railroads.* Washington, DC: Railroad Wage Commission, 1918.

INTERVIEWS

Behind the Veil Collection, John Hope Franklin Research Center for African and African American Documentation, Duke University

Andrews, Malachia. Interview by Paul Ortiz, August 9, 1994.

Bowles, Pauline. Interview by Paul Ortiz, July 23, 1998.

Buchanan, Gussye. Interview by Paul Ortiz, July 26, 1998.

Butler, Alvin and Mary. Interview by Paul Ortiz, July 24, 1998.

Carr, Carrie. Interview by Paul Ortiz, August 21, 1997.

Clark, Oneida. Interview by Paul Ortiz, July 27, 1998.

Dixie A. I. Interview by Paul Ortiz, August 22, 1997.

Dixie, A. I. and Samuel. Interview by Paul Ortiz, August 10, 1994.

Dixie, Laura and Samuel. Interview by Paul Ortiz, August 5, 1994.

Dixie, Samuel. Interview by Paul Ortiz, August 16, 1997.

Farmer, Martha Harvey. Interview by Paul Ortiz, August 21, 1997.

Gainey, Otto. Interview by Paul Ortiz, July 29, 1998.

Hooten, Henry and Lillian. Interview by Paul Ortiz, July 11, 1994.

Howell, Aquilina. Interview by Paul Ortiz, August 18, 1997.

Jefferson, Harriet. Interview by Mausiki Scales and Tywanna Whorley, August, 1994.

Montgomery, Rosebud. Interview by Paul Ortiz, July 27, 1998.

Speed, Cornelius. Interview by Paul Ortiz, July 27 and August 3, 1994.

Stevens-Jones, Inez. Interview by Paul Ortiz, August 14, 1997.

Williams, Gertrude. Interview by Mausiki Scales, August 11, 1994.

Williams, Henry, and Orian Ellis. Interview by Paul Ortiz, July 29, 1998.

Wright, Thomas A. Interview by Paul Ortiz, July 31, 1998.

Young, Daisy. Interview by Mausiki Scales and Tywanna Whorley, July 27, 1994.

Fifth Avenue Black Oral History Project, Samuel Proctor Oral History Archives, University of Florida

Haile, Louise Perry. Interview by Joel Buchanan, March 3, 1983.

Johnson, Wilhelmina W. Interview by Joel Buchanan, May 27, 1981.

Roberts, Janie F. Interview by Joel Buchanan, July 10, 1984.

Preserving the Past for the Future: An African American Oral History Project. Oral History Project, Book 6. Jefferson County Public Library, Monticello, Florida.

Byrd, John. Interview by Kris Odahowski and Allen Walker, fall 1990.

NEWSPAPERS AND SERIALS

The Afro-American (Baltimore, MD)

The Apalachicola Times

The Artisan (Jacksonville)
The Bartow Courier-Informant
The Bradford County Telegraph
The Chicago Defender
The Christian Recorder
The Citizen-Reporter (Lake City)
The Clay County News
The Cocoa Tribune
The Colored Citizen (Pensacola)
The Crisis (New York)
The Daily Democrat (Tallahassee)
The Daytona Daily News
The De Land Daily News
The Enterprise Recorder (Madison)
The Evening Telegram (Jacksonville)
The Florida Advocate (Wauchula)
The Florida Dispatch
The Florida Grower
The Florida Metropolis (Jacksonville)
The Florida Mirror (Fernandina)
The Florida Peninsular (Tampa)
The Florida Times-Union (Jacksonville)
The Fort Myers Press
The Fort Pierce News-Tribune
The Gadsden County Times
The Gainesville Sun
The Hastings Herald
The Holmes County Advertiser
The Homestead Enterprise
The Indian River Advocate
The Indianapolis Freeman
The Jacksonville Journal
The Jasper News
The Kissimmee Valley Gazette
The Lakeland Star

The Lakeland Telegram

The Leesburg Commercial

The Live Oak Democrat

The Madison New Enterprise

The Manatee River Journal

The Miami Herald

The National Republican

The New York Age

The New York Freeman

The New York Globe

The New York Tribune

The Ocala Banner

The Okaloosa News (Crestview)

The Orlando Morning Sentinel

The Norfolk Journal and Guide (Norfolk, VA)

The Palatka Daily News

The Palatka Morning Post

The Palatka Weekly Times

The Palm Beach Post

The Panama City Pilot

The Pensacola Journal

The Pensacola News

The Pensacolian

The Polk County Record

The Quincy Journal

The Richmond Planet (Richmond, VA)

The Sanford Herald

The Semi-Tropical

The St. Augustine Evening Record

The St. Petersburg Daily Times

The Star Advocate (Brevard County)

The Sunland Tribune (Tampa)

The Tampa Morning Tribune

The Tampa Weekly Tribune

The Taylor County Herald

The Washington Bee
The Weekly Floridian (Tallahassee)
The Weekly Tallahassean

BOOKS AND ARTICLES

Abby, Kathryn Trimmer. *Florida: A Land of Change.* Chapel Hill: University of North Carolina Press, 1941.

Acuna, Rodolfo F. *Anything but Mexican: Chicanos in Contemporary Los Angeles.* London: Verso, 1996.

Agresti, Barbara. "Household and Family in the Postbellum South: Walton County, Florida, 1870–1885." Ph.D. dissertation, University of Florida, 1976.

Akin, Edward N. *Flagler: Rockefeller Partner and Florida Baron.* London: Kent State University Press, 1988.

Allen, Theodore W. *Racial Oppression and Social Control.* Vol. 2, *The Invention of the White Race.* London: Verso, 1994.

Anderson, Benedict. *Imagined Communities: Reflections on the Origin and Spread of Nationalism.* London: Verso, 1983.

Anderson, James D. *The Education of Blacks in the South, 1860–1935.* Chapel Hill: University of North Carolina Press, 1988.

Aptheker, Herbert, ed. *A Documentary History of the Negro People in the United States.* Volume 2. 1951; reprint, New York: Citadel Press, 1990.

Arendt, Hanna. *Eichmann in Jerusalem: A Report on the Banality of Evil.* New York: Viking, 1963.

———. *The Origins of Totalitarianism.* New York: Harcourt Brace, 1951.

Arnesen, Eric. *Brotherhoods of Color: Black Railroad Workers and the Struggle for Equality.* Cambridge: Harvard University Press, 2001.

———. *Waterfront Workers of New Orleans: Race, Class, and Politics.* Urbana: University of Illinois Press, 1994.

Arsenault, Raymond. *St. Petersburg and the Florida Dream, 1888–1950.* Gainesville: University Press of Florida, 1996.

Ayers, Edward L. *The Promise of the New South: Life after Reconstruction.* New York: Oxford University Press, 1993.

Barbour, George M. *Florida for Tourists, Invalids, and Settlers.* New York: D. Appleton, 1883.

Bauer, Raymond, and Alice Bauer. "Day to Day Resistance to Slavery." *Journal of Negro History* 27 (October 1942), 388–419.

Bellwood, Ralph. *Tales of West Pasco*. Hudson, FL: Albert J. Makovec, 1962.

Bennett, H. E. *A History of Florida: With Questions, Supplementary Chapters and an Outline of Florida Civil Government*. New York: American Book Company, 1904.

Berlin, Ira. *Slaves without Masters: The Free Negro in the Antebellum South*. New York: Pantheon, 1974.

Berlin, Ira, Marc Favreau, and Steven F. Miller, eds. *Remembering Slavery: African Americans Talk about Their Personal Experiences of Slavery and Emancipation*. Foreword by Robin D. G. Kelley. New York: New Press, 1998.

Bill, Ledyard. *A Winter in Florida*. New York: Wood and Holbrook, 1870.

Blackburn, Robin. *The Making of New World Slavery: From the Baroque to the Modern, 1492–1800*. London: Verso, 1997.

Breen, William J. "Black Women in the Great War: Mobilization and Reform in the South." *Journal of Southern History* 44 (August 1978), 436–439.

Brevard, Caroline Mays. *A History of Florida: From the Treaty of 1763 to Our Own Times*. De Land, FL: Florida State Historical Society, 1925.

Brock, Lisa, and Digna Castañeda Fuertes. *Between Race and Empire: African-Americans and Cubans before the Cuban Revolution*. Philadelphia: Temple University Press, 1998.

Brown, Canter, Jr. "The Florida Crisis of 1826–1827 and the Second Seminole War." *Florida Historical Quarterly* 73 (April 1995), 419–442.

———. *Florida's Black Public Officials, 1867–1924*. Tuscaloosa: University of Alabama Press, 1998.

———. "Race Relations in Territorial Florida, 1821–1845." *Florida Historical Quarterly* 73 (January 1995), 287–307.

———. " 'Where Are Now the Hopes I Cherished?' The Life and Times of Robert Meacham." *Florida Historical Quarterly* 69 (July 1990), 1–36.

Brown, Elsa Barkley. "To Catch the Vision of Freedom: Reconstructing Southern Black Women's Political History, 1865–1880." In Ann D. Gordon, ed., *African American Women and the Vote, 1837–1965*. Amherst: University of Massachusetts Press, 1997, 66–99.

———. "Womanist Consciousness: Maggie Lena Walker and the Independent Order of Saint Luke." *Signs* 14 (spring 1989), 610–633.

Brundage, Fitzhugh. *Lynching in the New South: Georgia and Virginia, 1880–1930*. Urbana: University of Illinois Press, 1993.

Burnham, Walter Dean. *Critical Elections and the Mainsprings of American Politics*. New York: W. W. Norton, 1970.

Butterworth, Hezekiah. *A Zig Zag Journey in the Sunny South or Wonder Tales of Early American History.* Boston: Estes and Lauriat, 1887.

Canova, Andrew P. *Life and Adventures in South Florida.* Palatka, FL: Southern Sun Publishing House, 1885.

Carby, Hazel V. *Reconstructing Womanhood: The Emergence of the Afro-American Woman Novelist.* New York: Oxford University Press, 1987.

Carper, N. Gordon. "Martin Tarbert, Martyr of an Era." *Florida Historical Quarterly* 52 (October 1973), 115–131.

Carswell, E. W. *Washington, D.C.: Florida's Twelfth County.* Chipley, FL: E. W. Carswell, 1991.

Carter, Dan. *Scottsboro: A Tragedy of the American South.* New York: Oxford University Press, 1969.

Casdorph, Paul D. *Republicans, Negroes, and Progressives in the South, 1912–1916.* Tuscaloosa: University of Alabama Press, 1981.

Cash, William T. *History of the Democratic Party in Florida.* Tallahassee: Democratic Historical Foundation, 1936.

Cassanello, Robert. "The Great Migration, Migrants and Identity in the Making of New South Jacksonville, Florida, 1865–1920." Ph.D. dissertation, Florida State University, 2000.

Cecelski, David S., and Timothy B. Tyson, eds. *Democracy Betrayed: The Wilmington Race Riot of 1898 and Its Legacy.* Foreword by John Hope Franklin. Chapel Hill: University of North Carolina Press, 1998.

Cell, John W. *The Highest State of White Supremacy: The Origins of Segregation in South Africa and the American South.* Cambridge: Cambridge University Press, 1982.

Chafe, William. *Civilities and Civil Rights: Greensboro, North Carolina, and the Black Struggle for Freedom.* New York: Oxford University Press, 1980.

Chafe, William, Raymond Gavins, Robert Korstad, Paul Ortiz, Robert Parrish, Jennifer Ritterhouse, Keisha Roberts, and Nicole Waligora-Davis, eds. *Remembering Jim Crow: African Americans Tell about Life in the Segregated South.* New York: New Press, 2001.

Chandler, Billy Jaynes. "Harmon Murray: Black Desperado in Late Nineteenth-Century Florida." *Florida Historical Quarterly* 73 (October 1994), 184–199.

Chandler, David Leon. *Henry Flagler: The Astonishing Life and Times of the Visionary Robber Baron Who Founded Florida.* New York: Macmillan, 1986.

Chaterjee, Partha. "Claims on the Past: The Geneology of Modern Historiography in Bengal." *Subaltern Studies: Essays in Honour of Ranajit Guha,* 8, Bombay: Oxford University Press, 1994.

Clark Hine, Darlene. *Black Women in White: Racial Conflict in the Nursing Profession, 1890–1950*. Bloomington: Indiana University Press, 1989.

———. "Rape and the Inner Lives of Black Women in the Middle West: Preliminary Thoughts on the Culture of Dissemblance." *Signs* 14 (summer 1989), 912–920.

Cohen, William. *At Freedom's Edge: Black Mobility and the Southern White Quest for Racial Control, 1861–1915*. Baton Rouge: Louisiana State University Press, 1991.

Colburn, David R. *Racial Change and Community Crisis: St. Augustine, Florida, 1877–1980*. 1985; reprint, Gainesville: University of Florida Press, 1991.

Colburn, David R., and Jane L. Landers, eds. *The African American Heritage of Florida*. Gainesville: University Press of Florida, 1995.

Colored Knights of Pythias. *History and Manual of the Colored Knights of Pythias*. Nashville: National Baptist Publishing Board, 1917.

Cooper, Frederick. *Decolonization and African Society: The Labor Question in French and British Africa*. Cambridge: Cambridge University Press, 1996.

———. *From Slaves to Squatters: Plantation Labor and Agriculture in Zanzibar and Coastal Kenya, 1890–1925*. New Haven: Yale University Press, 1980.

Cornish, Dudley, T. *The Sable Arm: Negro Troops in the Union Army, 1861–1865*. New York: W. W. Norton, 1966.

Cox, LaWanda. "The Promise of Land for the Freedmen." *Mississippi Valley Historical Review* 45 (December 1958), 413–440.

Cox, Oliver C. *Capitalism and American Leadership*. New York: Philosophical Library, 1962.

———. *Caste, Class, and Race: A Study in Social Dynamics*. New York: Doubleday, 1948; reprint, London: Modern Reader Paperbacks, 1970.

Crooks, James B. *Jacksonville after the Fire, 1901–1919: A New South City*. Jacksonville: University of North Florida Press, 1991.

Crosby, Oliver Martin. *Florida Facts Both Bright and Blue: A Guidebook*. New York, 1887.

Dabbs, Lester J. "A Report of the Circumstances and Events of the Race Riot on November 2, 1920 in Ocoee, Florida." M.A. thesis, Stetson University, 1969.

Dailey, Jane. *Before Jim Crow: The Politics of Race in Postemancipation Virginia*. Chapel Hill: University of North Carolina Press, 2000.

Dailey, Jane, Glenda Gilmore, and Bryant Simon, eds. *Jumpin' Jim Crow: Southern Politics from Civil War to Civil Rights*. Princeton: Princeton University Press, 2000.

Daniel, Pete. *Breaking the Land: The Transformation of Cotton, Tobacco, and Rice Culturessince 1880.* Chicago: University of Illinois Press, 1985.

———. *The Shadow of Slavery: Peonage in the South, 1901–1969.* Oxford: Oxford University Press, 1972.

Daniels, Jonathan. *Prince of Carpetbaggers.* New York: J. B. Lippincott, 1958.

Davidson, James Woods. *The Florida of Today: A Guide For Tourists and Settlers.* New York: D. Appleton, 1889.

de Jong, Greta. *A Different Day: African American Struggles for Justice in Rural Louisiana, 1900–1970.* Chapel Hill: University of North Carolina Press, 2002.

Denby, Charles. *Indignant Heart: A Black Worker's Journal.* Boston: South End Press, 1978.

Dittmer, John. *Local People: The Struggle for Civil Rights in Mississippi.* Urbana: University of Illinois Press, 1994.

Dollard, John. *Caste and Class in a Southern Town.* New Haven: Yale University Press, 1937.

D'Orso, Michael. *Like Judgment Day: The Ruin and Redemption of a Town Called Rosewood.* New York: Boulevard Books, 1996.

Drobney, Jeffrey A. "Where Palm and Pine Are Blowing: Convict Labor in the North Florida Turpentine Industry, 1877–1923." *Florida Historical Quarterly* 72 (April 1994), 411–434.

Du Bois, W. E. B. *Black Folk Then and Now; An Essay in the History and Sociology of the Negro Race.* New York: Octagon Books, 1939.

———. *Black Reconstruction in America: An Essay toward a History of the Part Which Black Folk Played in the Attempt to Reconstruct Democracy in America, 1860–1880.* 1935; reprint, New York: Meridian Books, 1965.

Due, Tananarive, and Patricia Stephens Due. *Freedom in the Family: A Mother-Daughter Memoir of the Fight for Civil Rights.* New York: Ballantine Books, 2003.

Eagan, Dennis. *Sixth Annual Report of the Commissioner of Lands and Immigration of the State of Florida for the Year Ending December 31, 1874.* Tallahassee: Charles H. Walton, 1874.

Edwards, Laura. *Gendered Strife and Confusion: The Politics of Reconstruction.* Urbana: University of Illinois Press, 1997.

Egerton, Douglas R. *Gabriel's Rebellion: The Virginia Slave Conspiracies of 1800 and 1802.* Chapel Hill: University of North Carolina Press, 1993.

Ergood, Bruce. "The Female Protection and the Sun Light: Two Contemporary Negro Mutual Aid Societies," *Florida Historical Quarterly* 50 (July 1971), 25–38.

Fairclough, Adam. *Race and Democracy: The Civil Rights Struggle in Louisiana, 1915–1972*. Athens: University of Georgia Press, 1995.

Fanon, Frantz. *Black Skin, White Masks.* Trans. Charles Lam Markmann. 1952; reprint, New York: Grove Press, 1967.

———. *The Wretched of the Earth.* Translated by Constance Farrington. Preface by Jean-Paul Sartre. New York: Grove Press, 1963.

Field, Henry M. *Bright Skies and Dark Shadows.* New York: Charles Scribner's Sons, 1890.

Fields, Barbara. "Ideology and Race in American History." In J. Morgan Kousser and James M. McPherson, eds., *Region, Race, and Reconstruction: Essays in Honor of C. Vann Woodward.* New York: Oxford University Press, 1982, 143–177.

Fields, Mamie Garvin. *Lemon Swamp and Other Places: A Carolina Metaphor.* New York: Free Press, 1983.

Fink, Leon. *Workingman's Democracy: The Knights of Labor and American Politics.* Urbana: University of Illinois Press, 1983.

Fitch, Franklin Y. *The Life, Travels and Adventures of an American Wanderer.* New York: John W. Lovell Company, 1883.

Fitzgerald, Michael. " 'To Give Our Votes to the Party': Black Political Agitation and Agricultural Change in Alabama, 1865–1870." *Journal of American History* 76 (September 1989), 489–505.

Fluker, Walter E., and Catherine Tumber, eds. *A Strange Freedom: The Best of Howard Thurman on Religious Experience and Public Life.* Foreword by Martin E. Marty. Boston: Beacon Press, 1998.

Flynt, Wayne. *Cracker Messiah: Governor Sidney J. Catts of Florida.* Baton Rouge: Louisiana State University Press, 1977.

———. *Duncan Upshaw Fletcher: Dixie's Reluctant Progressive.* Tallahassee: Florida State University Press, 1971.

———. "Religion at the Polls: A Case Study of Twentieth-Century Politics and Religion in Florida." *Florida Historical Quarterly* 72 (April 1994), 469–483.

Foner, Eric. *Free Soil, Free Labor, Free Men: The Ideology of the Republican Party before the Civil War.* New York: Oxford, 1970, 1995.

———. *Reconstruction: America's Unfinished Revolution, 1863–1877.* New York: Harper and Row, 1988.

———. *The Story of American Freedom.* New York: W. W. Norton, 1999.

Foner, Philip, ed. *Paul Robeson Speaks: Writings, Speeches, Interviews, 1918–1974.* New York: Citadel Press, 1978.

Foner, Philip, and Ronald Lewis, eds. *Black Workers: A Documentary History from Colonial Times to the Present.* Philadelphia: Temple University Press, 1989.

Fortune, T. Thomas. *Black and White: Land, Labor, and Politics in the South.* New York: Fords, Howard and Hulbert, 1884.

Foss, James H. *Florida: Its Climate, Soil, Productions, and Agricultural Capabilities.* Washington, DC: Government Printing Office, 1882.

Franklin, John Hope. *The Emancipation Proclamation.* Garden City, NY: Doubleday, 1963.

Franklin, John Hope, and Alfred A. Moss, Jr. *From Slavery to Freedom: A History of Negro Americans.* 6th ed. New York: McGraw-Hill, 1988.

Franklin, John Hope, and Loren Schweninger. *Runaway Slaves: Rebels on the Plantation.* New York: Oxford University Press, 1999.

Frazier, E. Franklin. *Black Bourgeoisie.* New York: Free Press, 1957, 1997.

Fredrickson, George. *Black Liberation: A Comparative History of Black Ideologies in the United States and South Africa.* New York: Oxford University Press, 1995.

Freire, Paulo. *Pedagogy of the Oppressed.* New York: Seabury Press, 1970.

Frey, Sylvia. *Water from the Rock: Black Resistance in a Revolutionary Age.* Princeton: Princeton University Press, 1991.

Fry, Joseph A. *Henry S. Sanford: Diplomacy and Business in Nineteenth-Century America.* Reno: University of Nevada Press, 1982.

Fuller, Linda. *Where Was the Working Class? Revolution in Eastern Germany.* Chicago: University of Illinois Press, 1999.

Gaines, Kevin K. *Uplifting the Race: Black Leadership, Politics, and Culture in the Twentieth Century.* Chapel Hill: University of North Carolina Press, 1996.

Gaston, Paul. *The New South Creed: A Study in Southern Mythmaking.* Baton Rouge: Louisiana State University Press, 1970.

Gatewood, Willard B., Jr. "Negro Troops in Florida, 1898." *Florida Historical Quarterly* 49 (July 1970), 1–15.

———. *"Smoked Yankees" and the Struggle for Empire: Letters from Negro Soldiers.* Urbana: University of Illinois Press, 1971.

Gavins, Raymond. "North Carolina Black Folklore and Song in the Age of Segregation: Toward Another Meaning of Survival." *North Carolina Historical Review* 66 (October 1989), 412–442.

———. *The Perils and Prospects of Southern Black Leadership: Gordon Blaine Hancock, 1884–1970.* Durham: Duke University Press, 1977.

Gerster, Patrick, and Nicholas Cords. "The Northern Origins of Southern Mythology." *Journal of Southern History* 43 (November 1977), 567–582.

Giddings, Paula. *When and Where I Enter: The Impact of Black Women on Race and Sex in America*. New York: Bantam Books, 1988.

Gilmore, Glenda. *Gender and Jim Crow: Women and the Politics of White Supremacy in North Carolina, 1896–1920*. Chapel Hill: University of North Carolina Press, 1996.

Gilroy, Paul. *The Black Atlantic: Modernity and Double Consciousness*. Cambridge: Harvard University Press, 1993.

Goodwyn, Lawrence. *Breaking the Barrier: The Rise of Solidarity in Poland*. New York: Oxford University Press, 1991.

———. *Democratic Promise: The Populist Movement in America*. New York: Oxford University Press, 1976.

———. "Populist Dreams and Negro Rights: East Texas as a Case Study." *American Historical Review* 76 (December 1971), 1435–1456.

Gottlieb, Peter. *Making Their Own Way: Southern Blacks' Migration to Pittsburgh, 1916–1930*. Urbana: University of Illinois Press, 1987.

Gould, Jeffrey. *To Lead as Equals: Rural Protest and Political Consciousness in Chinandega, Nicaragua, 1912–1979*. Chapel Hill: University of North Carolina Press, 1990.

Graff, Mary B. *Mandarin on the St. Johns*. Gainesville: University of Florida Press, 1963.

Gramsci, Antonio. *Selections from the Prison Notebooks*. Edited and translated by Quintin Hoare and Geoffrey Nowell Smith. 1971; reprint, New York: International Publishers, 1995.

Green, Ben. *Before His Time: The Untold Story of Harry T. Moore, America's First Civil Rights Martyr*. New York: Free Press, 1999.

Green, G. N. "Republicans, Bull Moose, and Negroes in Florida, 1912." *Florida Historical Quarterly* 43 (October 1964), 153–164.

Greenberg, Mark I., William Warren Rogers, and Canter Brown, Jr. *Florida's Heritage of Diversity: Essays in Honor of Samuel Proctor*. Tallahassee: Sentry Press, 1997.

Greider, William. *Who Will Tell the People: The Betrayal of American Democracy*. New York: Simon and Schuster, 1992.

Griggs, Sutton E. *The Hindered Hand, Or, The Reign of the Repressionist*. Nashville: Orion, 1905.

———. *Unfettered*. Nashville: Orion, 1902.

Grossman, James R. *Land of Hope: Chicago, Black Southerners, and the Great Migration*. Chicago: University of Chicago Press, 1989.

Guha, Ranajit. "Dominance without Hegemony and Its Historiography." *Subaltern Studies* 6 (Delhi, 1989), 210–309.

Gutman, Herbert. *The Black Family in Slavery and Freedom, 1750–1925.* New York: Pantheon Books, 1976.

———. *Work, Culture and Society in Industrializing America.* New York: Vintage Books, 1977.

Hahamovitch, Cindy. *The Fruits of Their Labor: Atlantic Coast Farmworkers and the Making of Migrant Poverty, 1870–1945.* Chapel Hill: University of North Carolina Press, 1997.

Hahn, Steven. *A Nation under Our Feet: Black Political Struggles in the Rural South from Slavery to the Great Migration.* Cambridge: The Belknap Press of Harvard University Press, 2003.

Haimowitz, Morris L. "Population Trends in Florida." M.A. thesis, University of Florida, 1942.

Hale, Grace Elizabeth. *Making Whiteness: The Culture of Segregation in the South, 1890–1940.* New York: Pantheon Books, 1998; reprint, Vintage Books, 1999.

Hall, Jacqueline Dowd. *Revolt against Chivalry: Jessie Daniel Ames and the Women's Campaign against Lynching.* New York: Columbia University Press, 1979, 1993.

Hanson, Joyce A. *Mary McLeod Bethune and Black Women's Political Activism.* Columbia: University of Missouri Press, 2003.

Harcourt, Helen. *Home Life in Florida.* Louisville: John P. Morton and Company, 1889.

Harding, Vincent. *There Is a River: The Black Struggle for Freedom in America.* New York: Harcourt Brace Jovanovich, 1981.

Hardy, Lady Duffus. *Down South.* London: Chapman and Hall, 1883.

Hardy, Iza Duffus. *Oranges and Alligators: Sketches of South Florida Life.* London: Ward and Downey, 1886.

Harris, William. *The Harder We Run: Black Workers since the Civil War.* New York: Oxford University Press, 1982.

Hawk, Emory. *Economic History of the South.* New York: Prentice-Hall, 1934.

Henry, Paget. *Caliban's Reason: Introducing Afro-Caribbean Philosophy.* New York: Routledge, 2000.

Henshall, James A. *Camping and Cruising in Florida.* Cincinnati: Rovert Clarke, 1884.

Herbert, Hilary A., et al., *Why the Solid South? Or, Reconstruction and Its Results.* Baltimore: R. H. Woodward, 1890.

Hewitt, Nancy A. *Southern Discomfort: Women's Activism in Tampa, Florida, 1880s–1920s.* Urbana: University of Illinois Press, 2001.

Higginbotham, A. Leon, Jr. *In the Matter of Color: Race and the American Legal Process: The Colonial Period.* New York: Oxford University Press, 1978.

Higginbotham, Evelyn Brooks. *Righteous Discontent: The Women's Movement in the Black Baptist Church, 1880.* Cambridge: Harvard University Press, 1993.

Holt, Rackham. *Mary McLeod Bethune: A Biography.* Garden City, NY: Doubleday, 1964.

Holt, Thomas. *Black over White: Negro Political Leadership in South Carolina during Reconstruction.* Urbana: University of Illinois Press, 1977.

———. *The Problem of Freedom: Race, Labor, and Politics in Jamaica and Britain, 1832–1938.* Baltimore: Johns Hopkins University Press, 1992.

Honey, Michael K. *Black Workers Remember: An Oral History of Segregation, Unionism, and Freedom Struggle.* Berkeley and Los Angeles: University of California Press, 1999.

———. *Southern Labor and Black Civil Rights: Organizing Memphis Workers.* Chicago: University of Illinois Press, 1993.

Hopley, Catherine C. [Sarah E. Jones, pseud.]. *Life in the South; From the Commencement of the War, By a Blockaded British Subject.* London: Chapman and Hall, 1863.

Hudson, Larry E., Jr. *Working toward Freedom: Slave Society and Domestic Economy in the American South.* Rochester: University of Rochester Press, 1994.

Huggins, Nathan Irvin. *Black Odyssey: The African-American Ordeal in Slavery.* New York: Vintage Books, 1990.

———. *Harlem Renaissance.* New York: Oxford University Press, 1971.

Hunter, Tera W. *To 'Joy My Freedom: Southern Black Women's Lives and Labors after the Civil War.* Cambridge: Harvard University Press, 1997.

Hurston, Zora Neale. *Dust Tracks on a Road.* 1942; reprint, New York: Harper Collins, 1996.

———. *Mules and Men.* 1935; reprint, New York: Harper and Row, 1990.

Jackson, David H., Jr. "Booker T. Washington's Tour of the Sunshine State, March 1912." *Florida Historical Quarterly* 81 (winter 2003), 254–278.

Jackson, Jesse Jefferson. "Republicans and Florida Elections and Election Cases, 1877–1891." Ph.D. dissertation, Florida State University, 1974.

James, C. L. R. *Black Jacobins: Toussaint L'Ouverture and the San Domingo Revolution.* 1938; reprint, New York: Vintage Books, 1962.

———. *The Future in the Present.* Westport, CT: Lawrence Hill, 1977.

———. *History of Negro Revolt.* London: *Fact* Monograph No. 18, 1938.

———. *Nkrumah and the Ghana Revolution.* Westport, CT: Lawrence Hill, 1977.

————. *Party Politics in the West Indies.* Port of Spain: privately published, 1962.

James, Winston. *Holding Aloft the Banner of Ethiopia: Caribbean Radicalism in Early Twentieth-Century America.* London: Verso, 1998.

Jaynes, Gerald. *Branches without Roots: Genesis of the Black Working Class in the American South, 1862–1882.* New York: Oxford University Press, 1986.

Jeffries, Hasan Kwame. "Freedom Politics: Transcending Civil Rights in Lowndes County, Alabama, 1965–2000." Ph.D. dissertation, Duke University, 2002.

Johnson, Charles S. *Statistical Atlas of Southern Counties: Listing and Analysis of Socio-Economic Indices of 1104 Southern Counties.* Chapel Hill: University of North Carolina Press, 1941.

Johnson, Clifton. *Highways and Byways of the South.* New York: Macmillan, 1904.

Johnson, James Weldon. *Along This Way: The Autobiography of James Weldon Johnson.* New York: Viking, 1933.

————, ed. *The Book of American Negro Spirituals.* New York: Viking Press, 1925.

Johnston, C. W. *The Sunny South and Its People.* Chicago: Rand McNally, 1918.

Jones, Jacqueline. *American Work: Four Centuries of Black and White Labor.* New York: W. W. Norton, 1998.

Jones, Norrece T., Jr. *Born a Child of Freedom, Yet a Slave: Mechanisms of Control and Strategies of Resistance in Antebellum South Carolina.* Hanover, NH: University Press of New England, 1990.

Kachun, Mitch. *Festivals of Freedom: Memory and Meaning in African American Emancipation Celebrations, 1808–1915.* Boston: University of Massachusetts Press, 2003.

Kantrowitz, Stephen. *Ben Tillman and the Reconstruction of White Supremacy.* Chapel Hill: University of North Carolina Press, 2000.

Kelley, Blair Murphy. "Right to Ride: African American Citizenship, Identity, and the Protest over Jim Crow Transportation." Ph.D. dissertation, Duke University, 2003.

Kelley, Robin D. G. *Hammer and Hoe: Alabama Communists during the Great Depression.* Chapel Hill: University of North Carolina Press, 1990.

————. *Race Rebels: Culture, Politics, and the Black Working Class.* New York: Free Press, 1994.

Kelly, Brian. *Race, Class, and Power in the Alabama Coalfields, 1908–1921.* Urbana: University of Illinois Press, 2001.

Key, V. O., Jr. *Southern Politics in Race and Nation.* 1949; reprint, Knoxville: University of Tennessee Press, 1984.

Keyssar, Alexander. *The Right to Vote: The Contested History of Democracy in the United States.* New York: Basic Books, 2000.

Kharif, Wali Rashash. "Refinement of Racial Segregation in Florida." Ph.D. dissertation, Florida State University, 1983.

King, Edward. *The Great South: A Record of Journeys.* Hartford, CT: American Publishing Co., 1875.

Klingman, Peter D. *Josiah Walls, Florida's Black Congressman of Reconstruction.* Gainesville: University of Florida Press, 1976.

———. *Neither Dies nor Surrenders: A History of the Republican Party in Florida, 1867–1970.* Foreword by Samuel Proctor. Gainesville: University Presses of Florida, 1984.

Kluger, Richard. *Simple Justice: The History of Brown v. Board of Education and Black America's Struggle for Equality.* New York: Vintage Books, 1977.

Korstad, Robert, and Nelson Lichtenstein. "Opportunities Found and Lost: Labor, Radicals, and the Early Civil Rights Movement." *Journal of American History* 75 (1988), 786–811.

Kousser, J. Morgan. *Colorblind Injustice: Minority Voting Rights and the Undoing of the Second Reconstruction.* Chapel Hill: University of North Carolina Press, 1999.

———. *The Shaping of Southern Politics: Suffrage Restriction and the Establishment of the One-Party South, 1880–1910.* New Haven: Yale University Press, 1974.

Kousser, J. Morgan, and James M. McPherson, eds. *Region, Race, and Reconstruction: Essays in Honor of C. Vann Woodward.* New York: Oxford University Press, 1982.

Kropotkin, Peter. *Mutual Aid: A Factor of Evolution.* Edited with an introduction by Paul Aurich. New York: New York University Press, 1972.

Landers, Jane. *Black Society in Spanish Florida.* Foreword by Peter H. Wood. Urbana: University of Illinois Press, 1999.

Lanza, Michael L. *Agrarianism and Reconstruction Politics: The Southern Homestead Act.* Baton Rouge: Louisiana State University Press, 1990.

Lawson, Steven. "Freedom Then, Freedom Now: The Historiography of the Civil Rights Movement." *American Historical Review* 96 (April 1992), 456–471.

Lempel, Leonard R. "The Mayor's 'Henchmen and Henchwomen, Both White and Colored': Edward H. Armstrong and the Politics of Race in Daytona Beach, 1900–1940." *Florida Historical Quarterly* 79 (winter 2001), 267–296.

Levenson-Estrada, Deborah. *Trade Unionists against Terror: Guatemala City, 1954–1985.* Chapel Hill: University of North Carolina Press, 1994.

Levine, Lawrence W. *Black Culture and Black Consciousness: Afro-American Folk Thought from Slavery to Freedom.* Oxford: Oxford University Press, 1977.

Lewinson, Paul. *Race, Class, and Party: A History of Negro Suffrage and White Politics in the South.* New York: Oxford University Press, 1932.

Lewis, David Levering. *W. E. B. Du Bois: Biography of a Race, 1868–1919.* New York: Henry Holt, 1993.

———. *W. E. B. Du Bois: The Fight for Equality and the American Century, 1919–1963.* New York: Henry Holt, 2000.

Lewis, Earl. *In Their Own Interests: Race, Class, and Power in Twentieth-Century Norfolk, Virginia.* Berkeley and Los Angeles: University of California Press, 1990.

Lichtenstein, Alex. *Twice the Work of Free Labor: The Political Economy of Convict Labor in the New South.* London: Verso, 1996.

Lincoln, C. Eric, and Lawrence H. Mamiya. *The Black Church in the African-American Experience.* Durham: Duke University Press, 1990.

Litwack, Leon. *Been in the Storm So Long: The Aftermath of Slavery.* New York: Alfred A. Knopf, 1979.

———. *Trouble in Mind: Black Southerners in the Age of Jim Crow.* New York: Alfred A. Knopf, 1998.

Litwack, Leon, and August Meier, eds. *Black Leaders of the Nineteenth Century.* Urbana: University of Illinois Press, 1988.

Lloyd, Henry Demarest. *Wealth against Commonwealth.* New York: Harper and Brothers, 1894.

Logan, Rayford. *The Betrayal of the Negro: From Rutherford B. Hayes to Woodrow Wilson.* Introduction by Eric Foner. 1965; reprint, New York: Da Capo Press, 1997.

Loring, F. W., and C. F. Atkinson. *Cotton Culture and the South: Considered with Reference to Emigration.* Boston: Office of Loring and Atkinson, 1869.

Mancini, Matthew J. *One Dies, Get Another: Convict Leasing in the American South, 1866–1928.* Columbia University of South Carolina Press, 1996.

Marable, Manning, and Leith Mullings, eds. *Let Nobody Turn Us Around: Voices of Resistance, Reform, and Renewal.* New York: Rowman and Littlefield, 2000.

McCall, George A. *Letters from the Frontiers: Written During a Period of Thirty Years' Service in the Army of the United States.* Philadelphia: J. B. Lippincott, 1868.

McCluskey, Audrey Thomas, "Ringing Up a School: Mary McLeod Bethune's Impact on Daytona." *Florida Historical Quarterly* 73 (October 1994), 200–217.

McDonogh, Gary. *The Florida Negro: A Federal Writers' Legacy.* Jackson: University Press of Mississippi, 1993.

McGovern, James R. *The Emergence of a City in the Modern South: Pensacola 1900–1945.* DeLeon Springs, FL: E. O. Painter Printing Company, 1976.

McKinnon, John. *History of Walton County.* Atlanta: Byrd Printing Co., 1911.

McLaurin, Melton. *The Knights of Labor in the South.* Westport, CT: Greenwood Press, 1984.

McLemee, Scott, ed. *C. L. R. James on the "Negro Question."* Jackson: University Press of Mississippi, 1996.

McMillen, Neil. *Dark Journey: Black Mississippians in the Age of Jim Crow.* Chicago: University of Illinois Press, 1990.

McQuade, James. *The Cruise of the Montauk: To Bermuda, The West Indies and Florida.* New York: Thomas R. Knox, 1885.

Meier, August, and Elliot Rudwick. "The Boycott Movement against Jim Crow Streetcars in the South, 1900–1906." *Journal of American History* 55 (March 1969), 756–775.

———. *CORE: A Study in the Civil Rights Movement, 1942–1968.* New York: Oxford University Press, 1973.

Melton, Faye Perry. *Memories of Fort McCoy.* Ocala, FL: Typeworld Printing and Typesetting, 1987.

Menard, John Willis. *Lays in Summer Lands.* Larry Eugene Rivers, Richard Mathews, and Canter Brown, Jr., eds. Tampa: University of Tampa Press, 2002.

Michaels, Brian E. *The River Flows North: A History of Putnam County, Florida.* Palatka: The Putnam County Archives and History Commission, 1976.

Miller, J. L. *An Guide into the South: An Open Gate to the Laborer, Large Returns to the Investor, An Index for the Traveler, A Great Welcome to the Deserving.* Atlanta: Index Printing Co., 1910.

Mizell, William, Jr. *The Vanished Town of Kings Ferry Located on the South Banks of the St. Mary's River Nassau County, Florida.* 1965.

Mohl, Raymond A. "The Settlement of Blacks in South Florida." In Thomas D. Boswell, ed., *South Florida: The Winds of Change.* Miami, 1991.

Mohlman, Geoffrey. "Lincolnville: An Anthropological History of St. Augustine." Senior B.A. thesis, University of South Florida, 1991.

Montgomery, David. *Beyond Equality: Labor and the Radical Republicans, 1862–1872.* New York: Alfred A. Knopf, 1967.

———. *Citizen Worker: The Experience of Workers in the United States with Democracy and the Free Market during the Nineteenth Century.* Cambridge: Cambridge University Press, 1993.

Morris, Aldon D. *The Origins of the Civil Rights Movement: Black Communities Organizing for Change.* New York: Free Press, 1984.

Moses, Wilson Jeremiah. *Afrotopia: The Roots of African American Popular History.* Cambridge: Cambridge University Press, 1998.

Murray, Pauli. *Proud Shoes: The Story of an American Family.* New York: Harper and Row, 1956.

———. *States' Laws on Race and Color and Appendices.* Cincinnati: Woman's Division of Christian Service, 1951.

National Association of Colored Women. *Minutes of the Twelfth Biennial Convention.* Published by the Association, 1920.

Nelson, Bruce. *Divided We Stand: American Workers and the Struggle for Black Equality.* Princeton: Princeton University Press, 2001.

Newton, Michael. *The Invisible Empire: The Ku Klux Klan in Florida.* Foreword by Raymond Arsenault and Gary R. Mormino. Gainesville: University of Florida Press, 2001.

O'Rell, Max [pseud.]. *Jonathan and His Continent: Rambles Through American Society.* Trans. Paul Blouet. New York: Cassell, 1889.

Ortiz, Paul. " 'Eat Your Bread without Butter, but Pay Your Poll Tax!': Roots of the Florida Voter Registration Movement, 1919–1920." In Charles Payne and Adam Green, eds., *Time Longer than Rope: A Century of African American Activism.* New York: NYU Press, 2003, 196–229.

———. "Farm Worker Organizing in America: From Slavery to Cesar Chavez and Beyond." In Charles D. Thompson and Melinda Wiggins, eds., *The Human Cost of Food: Farmworker Lives, Labor, and Advocacy.* Austin: University of Texas Press, 2002, 249–275.

———. " 'Like Water Covered the Sea': The African American Freedom Struggle in Florida, 1877–1920." Ph.D. dissertation, Duke University, 2000.

Oshinsky, David M. *"Worse than Slavery": Parchman Farm and the Ordeal of Jim Crow Justice.* New York: Free Press, 1996.

Painter, Nell Irvin. *Exodusters: Black Migration to Kansas after Reconstruction.* New York: Alfred A. Knopf, 1976.

Palmer, Colin A. *Passageways: An Interpretive History of Black America.* Vol. 2, *1863–1965.* New York: Harcourt Brace, 1998.

Parker, Paige Alan. "Political Mobilization in the Rural South: A Case Study of Gadsden County, Florida." Ph.D. dissertation, University of Florida, 1980.

Payne, Charles M. *I've Got the Light of Freedom: The Organizing Tradition and the Mississippi Freedom Struggle.* Berkeley and Los Angeles: University of California Press, 1995.

Pearce, George F., *Pensacola during the Civil War: A Thorn in the Side of the Confederacy*. Gainesville: University Press of Florida, 2000.

Peek, Ralph L. "Aftermath of Military Reconstruction, 1868–1869." *Florida Historical Quarterly* 43 (October 1964), 123–141.

———. "Lawlessness in Florida, 1868–1871." *Florida Historical Quarterly* 40 (October 1961), 164–185.

Peeples, Harry A. *Twenty-Four Years: In the Woods, On the Waters and In the Cities of Florida*. Tampa: Tribune Printing Company, 1906.

Perry, Jeffrey B., ed. *A Hubert Harrison Reader*. Middletown, CT: Wesleyan University Press, 2001.

Piven, Frances Fox, and Richard A. Cloward. *Poor People's Movements: Why They Succeed, How They Fail*. New York: Vintage Books, 1979.

Powell, J. C. *The American Siberia*. Chicago: Donohue, Henneberry, 1892.

Powell, Lawrence N. *New Masters: Northern Planters during the Civil War and Reconstruction*. New Haven: Yale University Press, 1980.

Proctor, Samuel. *Napoleon Bonaparte Broward: Florida's Fighting Democrat*. Gainesville: University of Florida Press, 1950.

Quarles, Benjamin. *The Negro in the American Revolution*. Foreword by Thad W. Tate and introduction by Gary Nash. Chapel Hill: University of North Carolina Press, 1961, 1996.

Rabinowitz, Howard. *Race Relations in the Urban South: 1865–1890*. Urbana: University of Illinois Press, 1978.

Rachleff, Peter. *Black Labor in Richmond, 1865–1890*. Chicago: University of Illinois Press, 1984.

Raper, Arthur. *Preface to Peasantry: A Tale of Two Black Belt Counties*. Chapel Hill: University of North Carolina Press, 1936.

———. *The Tragedy of Lynching*. 1933; reprint, New York: Dover, 1970.

Rawick, George P., ed. *The American Slave: A Composite Autobiography*. Vol. 17, *Florida Narratives*. Westport, CT: Greenwood, 1972.

Reed, Adolph, Jr. *Class Notes: Posing as Politics and Other Thoughts on the American Scene*. New York: New Press, 2000.

———. *Stirrings in the Jug: Black Politics in the Post-Segregation Era*. Minneapolis: University of Minnesota Press, 1999.

———. *W. E. B. Du Bois and American Political Thought: Fabianism and the Color Line*. New York: Oxford University Press, 1997.

Reich, Steven A. "Soldiers of Democracy: Black Texans and the Fight for Citizenship, 1917–1921." *Journal of American History* 92 (March 1996), 1478–1504.

Reid, Whitelaw. *After the War: A Southern Tour.* New York: Moore, Wilstach and Baldwin, 1866; reprint, New York: Harper Torchbooks, 1965.

Rerick, Rowland H. *Memoirs of Florida.* Edited by Francis P. Fleming. Atlanta: Southern Historical Association, 1902.

Revels, Tracy J. "Grander in Her Daughters: Florida's Women during the Civil War." *Florida Historical Quarterly* 77 (winter 1999), 261–282.

Reynolds, Charles Bingham. *Old Saint Augustine: A Story of Three Centuries.* St. Augustine: E. H. Reynolds, 1888.

Richardson, Joe M. *The Negro in the Reconstruction of Florida, 1865–1877.* Tallahassee: Florida State University, 1965.

Rivers, Larry Eugene. *Slavery in Florida: Territorial Days to Emancipation.* Gainesville: University Press of Florida, 2000.

Rivers, Larry Eugene, and Canter Brown, Jr. *Laborers in the Vineyard of the Lord: The Beginnings of the AME Church in Florida, 1865.* Gainesville: University Press of Florida, 2001.

Robeson Burr, Anna. *Alice James: Her Brothers, Her Journal.* New York: Cornwall Press, 1934.

Robinson, A. A. *Florida: A Pamphlet Descriptive of its History, Topography, Climate, Soil, Resources and Natural Advantages.* Tallahassee: Floridian Book and Job Office, 1882.

Robinson, Cedric J. *Black Movements in America.* New York: Routledge, 1997.

Rodney, Walter. *How Europe Underdeveloped Africa.* Foreword by Vincent Harding. Washington, DC: Howard University Press, 1982.

Roediger, David. *The Wages of Whiteness: Race and the Making of the American Working Class.* New York: Verso, 1991.

Rose, Willie Lee. *Rehearsal for Reconstruction: The Port Royal Experiment.* London: Oxford University Press, 1964.

Rosenberg, Daniel. *New Orleans Dockworkers: Race, Labor, and Unionism, 1892–1923.* Albany: State University of New York Press, 1988.

Rosengarten, Theodore. *All God's Dangers: The Life of Nate Shaw.* New York: Avon Books, 1975.

Royster, Jacqueline Jones, ed. *Southern Horrors and Other Writings: The Anti-Lynching Campaign of Ida B. Wells, 1892–1900.* Boston: Bedford Books, 1997.

Rymer, Russ. *American Beach: A Saga of Race, Wealth, and Memory.* New York: Harper Collins, 1998.

Salvatore, Nick. *We All Got History: The Memory Books of Amos Webber.* New York: Random Books, 1996.

Sapp, Richard Wayne. "Suwannee River Town, Suwannee River Country: Political Moieties in a Southern County Community." Ph.D. dissertation, University of Florida, 1976.

Saville, Julie. *The Work of Reconstruction: From Slave to Wage Laborer in South Carolina, 1860–1870.* New York: Cambridge University Press, 1994.

Scott, Emmett J., comp. "Letters of Negro Migrants of 1916–1918." *Journal of Negro History* 4 (July 1919), 290–334.

———. *Scott's Official History of the American Negro in the World War.* Chicago: Homeward Press, 1919.

Scott, James. *Domination and the Arts of Resistance: Hidden Transcripts.* New Haven: Yale University Press, 1990.

———. *Weapons of the Weak: Everyday Forms of Peasant Resistance.* New Haven: Yale University Press, 1985.

Sherman, Richard B. *The Republican Party and Black America: From McKinley to Hoover, 1896–1933.* Charlottesville: University Press of Virginia, 1973.

Shoemaker, W. B. *Florida As It Is: It Tells All About the Industries of the State, Its Climate and Resources.* Newville, PA: Times Steam Print, 1887.

Shofner, Jerrell H. *History of Jefferson County.* Tallahassee: Sentry Press, 1976.

———. *Jackson County, Florida—A History.* Marianna: Jackson County Heritage Association, 1985.

———. "The Labor League of Jacksonville: A Negro Union and White Strikebreakers." *Florida Historical Quarterly* 50 (January 1972), 278–282.

———. "The Legacy of Racial Slavery: Free Enterprise and Forced Labor in Florida in the 1940s." *Journal of Southern History* 47 (August 1981), 411–426.

———. "Mary Grace Quackenbos, a Visitor Florida Did Not Want." *Florida Historical Quarterly* 58 (January 1980), 273–290.

———. "Militant Negro Laborers in Reconstruction Florida." *Journal of Southern History* 13 (November 1972), 388–400.

———. *Nor Is It Over Yet: Florida in the Era of Reconstruction, 1863–1877.* Gainesville: University Presses of Florida, 1974.

Singletary, Otis A. *Negro Militia and Reconstruction.* New York: McGraw-Hill, 1963.

Smith, J. Douglas. *Managing White Supremacy: Race, Politics, and Citizenship in Jim Crow Virginia.* Chapel Hill: University of North Carolina Press, 2002.

Smith, John David. *An Old Creed for the New South: Proslavery Ideology and Historiography, 1865–1918.* Westport, CT: Greenwood Press, 1985.

Smith, Lillian. *Killers of the Dream.* 1949; reprint, New York: W. W. Norton, 1961.

Solomon, Irvin D., and Grace Erhart. "Race and Civil War in South Florida." *Florida Historical Quarterly* 67 (winter 1999), 320–341.

Spero, Sterling D., and Abram L. Harris. *The Black Worker: The Negro and the Labor Movement.* Preface by Herbert G. Gutman. New York: Atheneum, 1969.

Stampp, Kenneth M. *The Era of Reconstruction.* New York: Knopf, 1966.

Stanley, J. Randall. *History of Gadsden County.* Quincy: Gadsden County Historical Commission, 1948.

———. *History of Jackson County.* Marianna: Jackson County Historical Society, 1950.

Stowe, Charles Edward. *Life of Harriet Beecher Stowe, Compiled from Her Letters and Journals.* Boston: Houghton Mifflin, 1891.

Stowe, Harriet Beecher. *Palmetto Leaves.* Boston: J. R. Osgood, 1873.

Straker, D. Augustus. *The New South Investigated.* Detroit: Ferguson Printing Company, 1888.

Stuckey, Sterling. *Slave Culture: Nationalist Theory and the Foundations of Black America.* New York: Oxford University Press, 1987.

Tallahassee Geneological Society, Inc. *Florida Voter Registration Lists, 1867–68.* Tallahassee, 1992.

Tebeau, Charlton. *A History of Florida.* Coral Gables: University of Miami Press, 1972.

Thompson, E. P. *Customs in Common: Studies in Traditional Popular Culture.* New York: New Press, 1993.

Thurman, Howard. *Jesus and the Disinherited.* Foreword by Vincent Harding. 1949; reprint, Boston: Beacon Press, 1996.

———. *The Luminous Darkness: A Personal Interpretation of the Anatomy of Segregation and the Ground of Hope.* New York: Harper and Row, 1965.

Tindall, George B. *The Emergence of the New South, 1913–1945.* Baton Rouge: Louisiana State University Press, 1967.

Tolnay, Stewart E., and E. M. Beck. *A Festival of Violence: An Analysis of Southern Lynchings, 1882–1930.* Chicago: University of Illinois Press, 1995.

Tomlins, Christopher. *Law, Labor, and Ideology in the Early American Republic.* Cambridge: Cambridge University Press, 1993.

Trotter, Joe. *Black Milwaukee: The Making of an Industrial Proletariat, 1915–45.* Urbana: University of Illinois Press, 1985.

———. *Coal, Class, and Color: Blacks in Southern West Virginia, 1915–32.* Urbana: University of Illinois Press, 1990.

————, ed. *The Great Migration in Historical Perspective: New Dimensions of Race, Class, and Gender.* Bloomington: Indiana University Press, 1991.

Tucker, Susan. *Telling Memories among Southern Women: Domestic Workers and Their Employers in the Segregated South.* Baton Rouge: Louisiana State University Press, 1988.

Twain, Mark, and Charles Dudley Warner. *The Gilded Age: A Tale of Today.* 1873; reprint, with an introduction and notes by Louis J. Budd, New York: Penguin Books, 2001.

Tyson, Timothy. *Radio Free Dixie: Robert F. Williams and the Roots of Black Power.* Chapel Hill: University of North Carolina Press, 1999.

Umoja, Akinyele K. "Eye for an Eye: The Role of Armed Resistance in the Mississippi Freedom Movement." Ph.D. dissertation, Emory University, 1996.

Walker, Jonathan. *Trial and Imprisonment of Jonathan Walker at Pensacola, Florida.* Boston: Anti-Slavery Office, 1850.

Wallace, John. *Carpetbag Rule in Florida: The Inside Workings of the Reconstruction of Civil Government in Florida After the Close of the Civil War.* Jacksonville: Da. Costa Printing and Publishing House, 1888.

Walsh, Lorena S. *From Calabar to Carter's Grove: The History of a Virginia Slave Community.* Charlottesville: University Press of Virginia, 1997.

Weiss, Nancy J. *Farewell to the Party of Lincoln: Black Politics in the Age of FDR.* Princeton: Princeton University Press, 1983.

Wetherell, Ellen. *Facts from Florida.* Lynn, MA, 1897.

Wheeler, Marjorie Spruill. *New Women of the New South: The Leaders of the Woman Suffrage Movement in the Southern States.* New York: Oxford University Press, 1993.

White, Deborah Gray. *Too Heavy a Load: Black Women in Defense of Themselves, 1894–1994.* New York: W. W. Norton, 1999.

White, Walter. *The Rope and the Faggot: A Biography of Judge Lynch.* New York: Knopf, 1929.

Wiener, Jonathan M. *Social Origins of the New South: Alabama, 1860–1885.* Baton Rouge: Louisiana State University Press, 1978.

Wiggins, Kenneth Porter. *The Black Seminoles: History of a Freedom-Seeking People.* Revised and edited by Alcione M. Amos and Thomas P. Senter. Gainesville: University Press of Florida, 1996.

Williamson, Edward C. "Black-Belt Political Crisis: The Savage-James Lynching, 1882." *Florida Historical Quarterly* 45 (April 1967), 402–409.

————. *Florida Politics in the Gilded Age, 1877–1893.* Gainesville: University Presses of Florida, 1976.

Wilson, Forrest. *Crusader in Crinoline: The Life of Harriet Beecher Stowe.* London: J. B. Lippincott, 1941.

Womack, John. *Zapata and the Mexican Revolution.* 1968; reprint, New York: Vintage Books, 1970.

Wood, Peter H. *Black Majority: Negroes in Colonial South Carolina from 1670 through the Stono Rebellion.* New York: Alfred A. Knopf, 1974.

Woodruff, Nan Elizabeth. *American Congo: The African American Freedom Struggle in the Delta.* Cambridge: Harvard University Press, 2003.

Woodson, Carter G. *A Century of Negro Migration.* Washington, DC, 1918; reprint, New York: AMS Press, 1970.

———. *The Miseducation of the Negro.* 1933; reprint, Nashville: Winston-Derek, 1990.

Woodward, C. Vann. *Origins of the New South, 1877–1913.* Baton Rouge: Louisiana State University Press, 1951.

———. *Reunion and Reaction: The Compromise of 1877 and the End of Reconstruction.* 1951; reprint, New York: Oxford University Press, 1991.

———. *The Strange Career of Jim Crow.* 3rd ed. New York: Oxford University Press, 1974.

Wright, George. *Racial Violence in Kentucky, 1865–1940: Lynchings, Mob Rule, and "Legal Lynchings."* Baton Rouge: Louisiana State University Press, 1990.

Wright, Thomas A. *Courage in Persona: An Autobiography.* Ocala: Special Publications Inc., 1993.

INDEX

African American politics, post-emancipation content of, 9–10, 17–22
African American religious practices: in
slavery, 1–2; ring shouts, 95–97;
controversies over worship styles,
95–98; biblical verses mentioned, 1,
20, 157; and critique of white religion, 95; anti-Jim Crow beliefs in,
120; and prayer services against Jim
Crow, 186. *See also* churches; *names
of individual churches*
African American soldiers: in First Battle
of Gainesville, 5; in Civil War battles,
5–6; liberation of Tallahassee by, 6; in
World War I, 144–145, 154–161; in
Spanish-American War, 206
African American women: and dignity in
the workplace, 13–14, 34–35; as
political actors in Reconstruction, 23;
anti-lynching activism of, 38; and
getting out the vote, 50; and Emancipation Day events, 91; and organized
mutual aid, 106–107; and streetcar
boycott movements, 120–121; and
resistance against streetcar segregation, 124–125; and Great Migration,
132; and fight for better pay during
WWI, 151; as activists in the Negro
Uplift Association (NUA), 167; and
Florida voter registration movement,
172–173, 175–176, 182–183,
187–192; social activism of, 231
African American workers, xx; and resistance against employers, 13–14,
34–35, 36–37, 125; in Key West
politics, 39–40; strikes of, 46–50,
110, 162–165; in Jacksonville unemployed protests, 50–51; visions of

democracy of, 52–53; in timber,
turpentine, and phosphate industries,
69–71; anti-lynching struggles and
armed self-defense by, 77, 80–81; and
dangerous occupations, 103–105;
and mutual aid, 103–110; and
streetcar boycott discipline, 120–123;
violence against, 69–71, 129; and the
Great Migration, 128–135; and
federal intervention, 151–153; and
union organization, 151–153; and
railroad unions, 152; barred from
skilled trades, 163; wartime service
of, 152; postwar strikes of, 162–165;
as base of the Florida movement,
181, 183, 195. *See also names of individual unions and occupations;
African-American women*
African Methodist Episcopal Church
(AME), 96, 155; and landownership, 17–19, 20; and educational
projects, 22
African Methodist Episcopal Zion Church,
175
Afro-American (Baltimore), 133, 201, 202
Afro-American League: proposed by T.
Thomas Fortune, 55, 72; T. V. Gibbs
opposes, 55–56
Afro-American Life Insurance Company,
149, 198
agricultural employers, 64, 130; disapprove
of black political activism, 15; seek to
crush black workers' vote, 25, 26, 33,
44; and complaints about black labor,
36, 162–163; seek immigrant labor,
153; interfere with U.S. war needs,
154; combine to combat strikes,
162–164

agricultural workers, 13, 16; viewed as enemies, 23, 24, 25; targeted for disfranchisement, 26, 44; and Great Migration, 129–132; State Department increases supply of, 153; unionization of, 162–164

Akerman, Alexander, 222

Alachua County, 57–58, 71; political violence in, 40–41; vagrancy statutes in, 53; mutual aid in, 106; economic oppression, 130; racial terrorism, 130–131; election-day turnout in, 218

Alexander, L. A., 160–161

Allen, Richard, 112

Ambrose, Nancy, 1–2

American Federation of Labor, 173

American Federation of State, County, and Municipal Employees (AFSCME), xvi

American Italy, Florida conceived as, 10, 15–16

American Revolution, 3

American Sumatra Tobacco Corporation, 129

Anderson, S. W., 87

Andrews, Malachia, xiii, 2, 88, 130

Andrews, W. W., 146

anti-labor laws: vagrancy, "after dark," and anti-enticement laws, 53, 54, 164, 175, 202; labor recruitment laws, 136; debt peonage, 56; "work or fight" laws, 151

Apalachicola, 5; general strike in, 49–50

Arendt, Hannah, 67–68

armed self-defense: to protect schools, 22; to preserve voting rights, 33, 38, 40; ideology of, 62–63, 72, 74; debates over, 72, 78; to prevent lynching, 73–74, 76–81, 83–84; Ida B. Wells lauds, 78–79; and anti-lynching movement, 83–84; Miami bombing wave, 200–201; in Florida movement, 203, 215, 216, 222

Artrell, William, 78, 96

Aswell, James, 224–225

Attucks, Crispus, 112

Austin, James, 73–74

Bahamian immigrants: attitudes towards Jim Crow of, xxii, 22, 39; resistance to white supremacy, 201–202; in the Florida movement, 206

Bailey, H. C., 38

Baker, S. G., 154

Baker County, 70

Ballou, J. H., 137

Banner, B. B., 108

Bartow (Polk County), 62, 70

Bartow *Courier-Informant,* 62, 71

Bay County, 62, 135

Beard, John, 83

Bee, Carlos, 225

Beecher, Charles, 12

Beecher, Harriet Stowe: plans to uplift black Floridians of, 12–13; and philosophy of black rights, 13, 29; conflict with domestic workers, 13–14; as Florida booster, 15; defends state after 1876 election, 29–30

Beecher, Henry Ward, 12

Bell, William, 193

Berry, Frank, 97

Bethel Baptist Church (Tallahassee), 38, 159

Bethel Baptist Institutional Church (Jacksonville): Emancipation Day events of, 120, 145; and streetcar boycotts, 120. *See also* J. Milton Waldron

Bethune, Mary McCleod, xiv, 87, 167, 169; and Daytona Educational and Industrial Training School for Negro Girls, 87; and WWI, 146–147; on equal citizenship and historical memory, 155–156; as lead activist in Florida movement, 188–189, 194; rallies community on election day, 217

Betts, S. H., 166; and leadership in the Florida movement, 196–197; post-Florida movement activism, 234

Birth of a Nation, African Americans protest against, 126–127

Blanton, Kelsey, 185–186, 202

Blodgettt, J. H., 149–150

Bloxham, William, 66, 76, 79

Bordner, Sadie Ash, 176–177

159, 180; whites' memory of the
Civil War, 43; whites' memory of
racial violence, 68; of the Civil War,
74, 93–95, 156–157; and politics,
85–88, 155; enhancing black pride,
86–87; and testimonial culture,
87–88, 100; of emancipation, 88; of
Reconstruction, 97–98; William
Lloyd Garrison Centenary, 98;
Crispus Attucks Suffrage Club, 99;
names of lodges reflect, 112; after
WWI, 155–156; and demand for
equal citizenship after the Armistice,
156–158; informs Florida voter
registration movement, 173, 180,
206–207, 231. *See also* Decoration
Day; Emancipation Day; oral
traditions
Holly, A. P., 217
Holmes County, 65; turpentine workers
driven out of, 66
Homestead (Dade County), 218
Hooper, C. M., 68–69
Hopley, Catherine, 6
Household of Ruth, 111
Humphreys, F. G., 69
Hurlbut, Samuel, 27
Hurst, John, 151, 167, 171
Hurston, Zora Neale, xxi, 96; analyzes oral
traditions in Florida, 2; on limits of
community, 115; account of Ocoee
election day terror, 220–221

Independent Afro-American Relief Union,
112
Independent Party, 41–45; platform of,
42; conservative critique of, 43
Indianapolis Freeman, 121
Interdenominational Ministerial Alliance
(Jacksonville), 113
intergenerational organizing, 100,
140–141, 154–161, 173, 178, 192,
193, 231
Interlachen (Putnam County), 193
"Interracial Conference" of 1916,
136–139, 169
interracial organizing: in Key West, 39–40;
Independent Party and, 41–45; in

1887 Pensacola dock and warehouse
strike, 46; in Jacksonville, 50–51; in
St. Augustine, 140
International Union of Mine, Mill and
Smelter Workers, 164

Jack Johnson and Jim Jeffries fight of
1910, 126
Jackson, Mary, 124
Jackson, S. D., 63
Jackson County, 18, 115; Klan violence
in, 24; during 1876 election, 27;
post-Reconstruction violence in,
29, 68–69; slaves' burial practices
in, 108
Jacksonville: unemployed protests in,
50–51; city charter of revoked,
51–52; Theodore Roosevelt's visit to,
58–59; organized armed self-defense,
76–79; residents of seek to reunite
with relatives lost during slavery, 89;
Emancipation Day celebration, 91;
Decoration Day in, 93–94; Great Fire
in, 112; 1901 streetcar segregation
ordinance of, 119; Great Migration
in, 132–133; "Interracial Conference," in, 136–137; NAACP chapter
founded in, 140; Florida voter registration movement in, xiv; and voter
registration, 154–155; Florida move-
ment in, 179–181, 189–190; KKK
of marches on eve of 1920 election,
215; election officials of stall voters'
lines, 217, 219
James, Allen, 109
James, C. L. R., 204, 233
James, Garth, 24
James, P. R., 104
Jasper News, 161
Jefferson, Harriet, 98
Jefferson, S. W., 139
Jefferson County, 26
Jenkins, H. R., 166
Jennings, William, 69
Jessup, Thomas, 4
Johnson, Andrew, 10
Johnson, Eliza, 125
Johnson, Hattie, 111

Johnson, James Weldon, xiv, xxii, 75, 99–100; sees hope in Great Migration, 140; coordinates new NAACP membership drive in Florida, 140; and "rise" of black resistance during WWI, 142–143; and Jacksonville Encouragement Meeting, 148–150; and the Florida movement, 205, 208; testifies before U.S. House Census Committee, 224–226; on racism and democracy, 235

Johnson, Sylvanus, 79

Johnson, Wilhelmina W., 146

Jones, Alonzo R., 77

Jones, B. J., 167, 198, 213

Jones, D. J., 167, 198, 213

Kershaw, A. J., 99, 203

Key, V. O., xxii

Key West, 39–40, 109; charter of revoked, 52; and armed defense of Sylvanus Johnson, 79; Emancipation Day ceremonies in, 90–91; religious practices in, 96–97; fraternal lodges in, 114; Civil War veterans' commemoration service in, 157

kinship, 89, 198–199

Kissimmee, 65

Knights of Labor, 39, 46, 50; organizer A. W. Johnson assassinated, 64; burial ceremonies for members of, 104–105

Knights of Pythias, 77, 103, 106, 112, 158; as practitioners of mutual aid, democracy, and reciprocity, 116–118; and resistance to white supremacy, 118; political activism of, xvii; WWI service activities of, 145–146; and voter registration, 165; and poll taxes, 177; and the Florida movement, 183, 186

Knights of Roslyn Castle, 115

Ku Klux Klan: (KKK) violence of during Reconstruction, 23–24, 25; in post-Reconstruction, 69; anti-voter activities of in Miami, 204; reorganizes to combat Florida movement, 206–207; controls mail in parts of the state, 211; in Gadsden County, 211; in Columbia County, 213; in Ocoee,

214; in Orlando, 214; marches of in Orlando, Jacksonville, and Daytona, 215–216

labor control, duel for, 10–21, 23–24, 27–28, 153–154, 195–196. *See also* strikes; unions

Lafayette County, 71; 1876 election violence in, 27; lynchings in, 65–66

Lake City, 21

Lakeland (Polk County), 104, 108–109, 114, 151; Florida movement in, 186

Lakeland Star, 186

land ownership: struggles for, 17–20, 197–198; white employers oppose, 21

LaRoche, J. S., 166

Larsen, William W., 225

Latson, E. W., 158

Laura Street Presbyterian Church (Jacksonville), 156

Lawtey (Bradford County), 76

League for Democracy, 161

Lee, Joseph E., 94, 136; armed defense of, 38; and labor manifesto on unemployment, 51; and "Black and Tan" politics, 57; as Emancipation Day speaker, 91; on Great Migration, 137; and African American trade unionists, 138; and Jacksonville Welcome Home parade, 158; as activist in the Florida movement, 178–182; death of, 181; summary of life's work, 182

Leesburg (Lake County), 164

Leon County, 17–18, 75, 98, 131; and labor, 53–54; Great Migration in, 131–132; welcome-home ceremony for troops in, 155

Levy County, 27

Lewey, Matthew, 34, 75; stricken from Republican ticket, 58; at Decoration Day ceremonies in Jacksonville, 94; at troops' welcome home ceremonies after Armistice, 156; as activist in the Florida movement, 180

Lewis, A. L., 149

Lewis, W. I., 75, 146, 148, 171, 177; and Jacksonville Welcome Home Parade, 158; in Florida movement, 179

public education: as critical demand of black politics, 21, 22, 32, 127; and segregation, 130

Putnam County, Florida movement in, 193

Putnam County Republican Club, 192

Purcell, I. L., in 1905 streetcar boycott movement, 123; voter registration activities of, 180

Quarterman, R. S., 73

Quincy (Gadsden County), Emancipation Day ceremony in, 92; WWI resolution of, 144; election day terror in, 218

Quincy Herald, 45

racial terrorism, 61–84; one-party rule and, 67–68; and segregation, 63, 65; threatened, 24, 44; rape, violence against black women, 62; against workers, 64; for employing whites, 64; for "talking back," 64; tradition of collective punishment, 65, 66; teenager murdered by sheriff's posse in Tallahassee, 75; Manatee County Race War, 81–82; violence against black patrons, 125, 172; against black farmers, 130; Fort Meade Terror, 171–172; 1920 election violence in Ocoee, 220–223; post-1920 election wave of violence, 227. *See also* lynching; *violence in individual counties*

railroads, 30–31; and segregation, 55–56, 60, 63, 118; and economic oppression, 69–71; workplace accidents, fatalities on, 103–104; and Great Migration, 132

railroad workers, 104, 132; and unions; link wartime service with citizenship, 152

Railway Men's International Benevolent Industrial Association, 151–152

Randolph, A. Philip, xxii, 87

Ransome, R. C., 155

Readjuster Party, Virginia, 41–42

Reconstruction, 9–31; and Black Codes, 14–15; election of 1876, 25–27; and

coercion against black voters, 26–27; end of, 27–32; "Great Compromise" between Democrats and Republicans finishes, 27; Gov. Drews' inauguration and, 28

Reed, Harrison, 11, 57

Reese, James D., 135

registering to vote, 172–199

Reid, Whitelaw, 7

Remley, Jacob A., 9–10

Republican Party, 50–51; African Americans accuse of betrayals, 42; in Key West, 39–40; Lily White faction of, 57–59; "Black and Tan" patronage politics of, 180; activities of, 187; black Floridians reinvent, 199; Harding refuses to investigate, 227; African Americans turn away from, 234

resistance to segregation, 55, 120–125, 171–172, 192

ring shout, 96–97

River Junction: anti-black violence in, 64; Florida movement in, 184; Harding-Coolidge Club in, 184–185; post-1920 election violence in, 227

Robinson, Allen, 109

Rockefeller, John, 56

Rodgers, Allan, 54

Roosevelt, Theodore, 58–59

Rose of Sharon lodge, 110

Rosewood, 232

rules-based solidarity, 106, 115

Sanford, electoral fraud in, 57; Emancipation Day ceremony in, 92; Great Migration in, 135; League of Women Voters of, 210; 1920 election terrorism in, 213

Sanford, Henry, 36, 57

Santa Rosa County, 118

Saunders, W. B., 69

Scott, John R., 19, 27

Scott, R. A., 156

secret societies, 103. *See also names of individual societies*

segregation, 54, 63; on juries, 55; on railroads and public facilities, 55–56, 118; on streetcars, 119–125 self-confidence, organizing and, 119, 199, 207, 216

Seminole County, 164

Seminole Indians, 1; alliance with African American slaves, 3–4

Seminole Wars: memory of, 2; Second Seminole War (1835–1842), 4–5

Shaw, J. L., 112–113

sick visits, 106, 111; and the Florida movement, 177. *See also* mutual aid

Siegel, Isaac, 224

Simmons, C. B., 109

slavery: African Americans' memories of, 1–2, 7–8, 85, 87–93, 98–100, 108, 109, 155–156, 157; resistance to, 3–6; in Florida, 1–5. *See also* Seminole War

slavery reparations: black Floridians' belief in justice of, 42, 89–90

slave revolts, 2–4; Stono Uprising, 3. *See also* Seminole Wars

Smith, Hattie, 221

Smith, J. T.: as Gadsden NAACP leader, 184, 203; and political terrorism in Gadsden, 212, 219; takes Gadsden NAACP underground, 234; driven out of Gadsden by white violence in the 1960s, 235

Smith, Sallie B., 189

Socialist Party, 59

social movements: how formed, xv–xvi; xvii, xviii, xix, xx; self-confidence, trust necessary to build, 119, 127, 174, 178; streetcar boycott movement as model of organizing, 119–124; intergenerational components of, 140–141, 173, 178, 192, 193, 231; and Florida movement, 172–208, 230–232, 234–236; mutuality vs. militancy in, 231; working-class in, 232. *See also* African American women; African American workers; Florida voter registration movement; organizing; streetcar boycott movements

social spaces, necessity of for organizing, xx, 120, 174, 178, 181, 206–207

Spain, colonial regime of in Florida, 2–4

Spanish-American War, 66; black Floridians volunteer to fight for *Cuba Libre,* 82

Standard Oil Company, 69

Stanton Public School (Jacksonville), 159

Starke (Bradford County), 183

State Conference of the Colored Men of Florida (1884), 41–42; advocate interracial political alliance and the Independent Party, 42; support slavery reparations, 89–90

State Federation of Colored Women's Clubs, and the Florida movement, 167, 176, 179, 188

state legislature: and Black Codes, 14–15; revokes city charters to facilitate disfranchisment, 51–52; and anti-labor statutes, 53–54; considers nullifying Fourteenth and Fifteenth Amendments to the U.S. Constitution, 83; rejects petition from Negro Uplift Association (NUA), 168

state militia: white militia used to break strikes, 47, 49; black militia, 74–75; clashes with blacks in St. Augustine, 75

St. Augustine, 75, 140; Florida movement in, 192

Stevens, W. S., reads resolution on black war service, 144; activism in the Quincy movement, 183–184; prevented from voting, 218

Stevens-Jones, Inez, 184, 211

St. John's Church (Miami), 90

St. Joseph's Church (Jacksonville), 99

St. Lucie County, 166

St. Paul's AME (Jacksonville), 121

St. Petersburg, 166; Emancipation Day in, 155; Florida movement in, 177, 182–183

streetcar boycott movements, 120–124; black women spearhead, 120–121; sabotage of cars, 121; class tensions in, 121, 123. *See also* hack drivers

strikes, 46–50, 110, 162–165. *See also* African American workers

Sumter County, 68

Sutton, William, 223

Compositor: International Typesetting & Composition
Cartographer: William L. Nelson
Text: 11.25/13.5 Garamond
Display: Belizio and Gotham Book
Printer and binder: Sheridan Books, Inc.

Lightning Source UK Ltd.
Milton Keynes UK
UKOW03f1928290117
293147UK00001B/25/P